Edito

L ....al in
....respects. By virtue of its privileged position
.... at the crossroads of the major valleys which cross
France from north to south (from Paris to Marseille) and from
west to east (looking towards the neighbouring Alps), Lyon is a
thoroughfare for millions of holiday-makers who seldom take
the time to discover the exceptional wealth of a city in which
several districts are nevertheless classified as Human Heritage
Sites.

*A temporal capital (Lyon was the Capital of the Gauls and is
still a politically influential city), a spiritual capital (the
Colline de Fournière and its cathedral testify to the Canuts
Revolts and to the independent spirit for which the Lyonnais
are famous) and an industrial capital (Lyon combines the
traditional textile industry with modern industries such as the
petrochemical industry), Lyon is, above all, the world capital of
gastronomy and boasts some of the very finest restaurants in
the country.*

*To help you discover Lyon, Le Petit Futé has prepared a
guidebook which will prove indispensable during any stay. So,
the next time you happen to be driving past, leave the
motorway and come and visit a city which is full of surprises.
Who knows, you may even make Lyon your capital !*

Merry Weather Ladder
- 1923 -

LE PETIT FUTÉ LYON 2001 ■ *Editor* **Nouvelles Editions de l'Université**
18, rue des Volontaires 75015 Paris ℗ 01 53 69 70 00 - Fax 01 42 73 15 24 - Internet : www.petitfute.com
Authors/Translators Dominique Auzias, Marie-France Ballandras, Roger Huggins, Jean-Paul
Labourdette, Audrey Lamarque, Julie Nicolas, Alban Razia, Jacques Roybin, Jacques Rouzet, Anthony
Serex, Hélène Villata *Advertising salesmen* Coralie Deleage, Michel Granseigne, Paul-André Rascle,
Marc Thoral. *Distribution in France* Nouveau Quartier Latin *Distribution in Great Britain* Windsor Books
(Oxford) *Printing* Corlet, France *Page-setting* Manhattan AWS, Sandrine Mecking *Photo credit* © JLG/CDT
Rhône, OT Lyon, Ville de Lyon, UIVB, pays du Beaujolais, P. Perche, M. Troncy, P. Cottin, D. Brandelet
Copyright 2nd trimester 2001 *Editing department* Jean-François Pissard, Romain David, Myriam Kuhn. ■

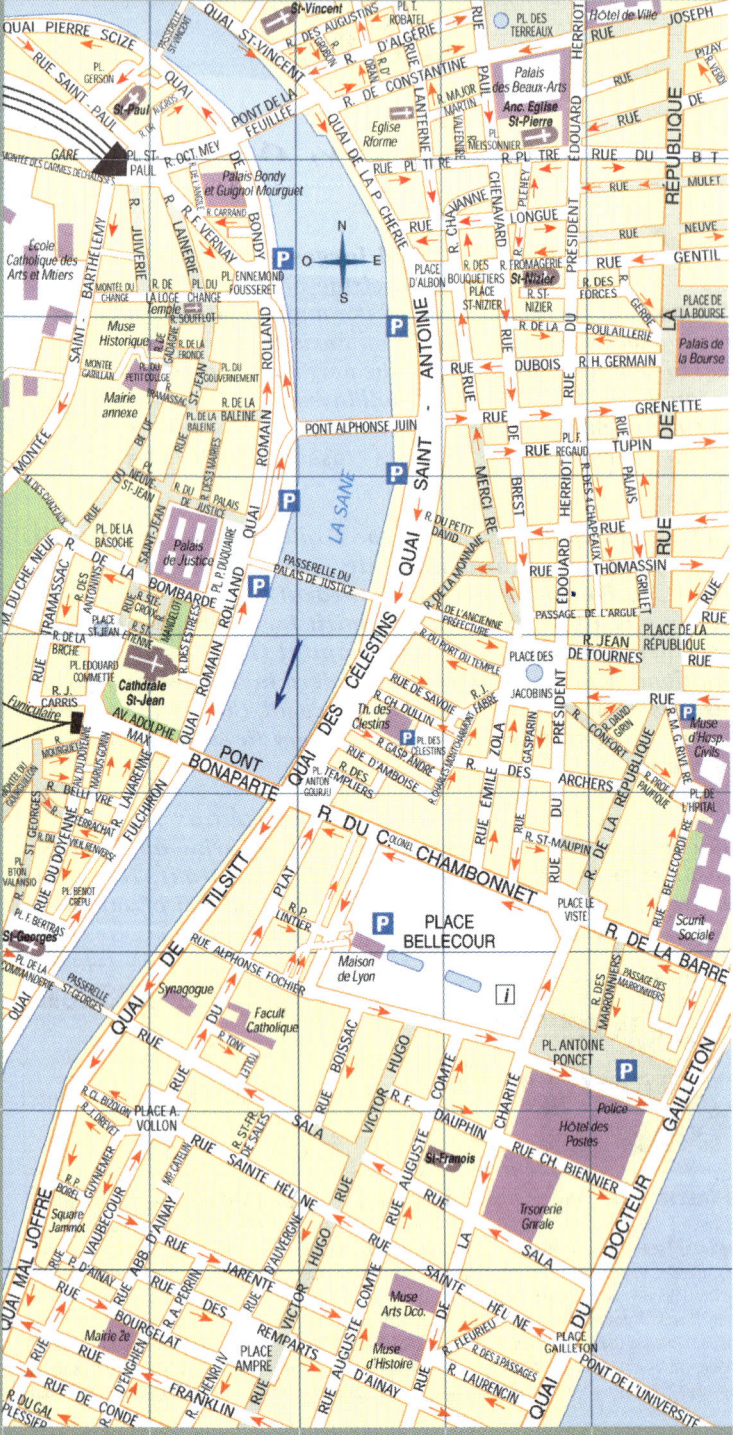

LYON

0   100 m

LE RHNE

Streets and places:

SERLIN
L'ARBRE SEC
D'ARGENT
MOULIN
Lycée Ampère
BOURSE
PASSAGE MENESTRIER
R. GENTIL
R. ANTOINE SALLES
R. CLAUDIA
QUAI JEAN
RUE DE
PL. DES CORDELIERS
St-Bonaventure
CHAMBR
R. PL ST-BONAVENTURE
R. GROLÉE
CARNOT
FERRANDI RE
R. THOMASSIN
PETIT COURMONT
JUSSIEU
GROLÉE
STELLA
CHILDEBERT
Hôtel-Dieu
QUAI JULES
PONT DE LA GUILLOTIÈRE
PL. ANTOINE JUTARD
COURS
BERNARD
R. BASSE COMBALOT
CAVENNE
D'AGUESSEAU
RUE
PASTEUR
PASSET
MARSEILLE
R. DES 3 ROIS
GRANDE
Piscine
CLAUDE
RUE
BONALD
R. SALOMON REINACH
St-André
MONTESQUIEU
PL. CLAUDE BULARD
PL. OLLIER
QUAI

PASSERELLE DU COLL GE
QUAI DU GENERAL SARRAIL
RUE
BUGEAUD
PIERRE
IMP MOLI RE
MOLI RE
VAUBAN
CORNEILLE
PASSAGE COSTE
RUE
AVENUE DU MAL DE SAXE
CUVIER
BOSSUET
RUE
PLACE ED. QUINET
St-Pothin
BUGEAUD
R. AMÉDÉE BONNET
Lycée Ed. Herriot
VAUBAN
FÉNELON
VEND ME
R-LOUIS
CRÉQUI
BLANC
ROBERT
DUGUESCLIN
PONT LA FAYETTE
COURS
LA FAYETTE
COURS AUGAGNEUR
Square Jussieu
IMP. RABELAIS
Pompiers
RABELAIS
RUE
SAXE
RABELAIS
ROYER
MOLI RE
BONNEL
RUE DE
Église Rforme
RUE DE
RUE DE BONNEL
Jardin Gal Delestraint
Préfecture
R. PRAVAZ
PIERRE
AVENUE
VEND ME
CRÉQUI
DUNOIR
PONT WILSON
R. CDT DUBOIS
RUE DE
Immaculée Conception
DIEU DU
SERVIENT
RUE DE LA PART DIEU
Bourse du Travail
VOLTAIRE
VICTOR
RUE DE LA PART
SCHÉNNE
CORNEILLE
MAZENOD
Lycée
LA
LIBERTÉ
LARRIVE
R. MAR ADIN
MAZENOD
CHAPONNAY
DUPHOT
R. PEYBORDIN
DDE
MARÉCHAL
CHAPONNAY
QUAI
JEAN
R. A.
R. DE LA VICTOIRE
R. DU MONTEBELLO
COLLOMB
R. GUTENBERG
RUE EPÉE
MARIGNAN
R. DE TURENNE
MONCEY
R. ST-JACQUES
RUE CORNEILLE
RUE VAUDREY
EDISON
PLACE VOLTAIRE
COURS
PL. GABRIEL PÉRI
RUE
R. BONNEFOI
R. AUGST LACROIX
R. HUMILITÉ
R. DU CDT FUZIER
PAUL
BERT
DE
VILLEROY
R. DES RANCY
GAMBETTA
VEND ME
SAXE
R. D'ARMÉNIE
CRÉQUI
R. BECHEVIN
R. G. DRU
RUE ST-MICHEL
RUE ST-MICHEL
RUE DE LA GUILLOTI RE
RUE SÉBASTIEN GRYPHE
AV. JEAN JAURÈS
R. J.M CHAVENT
PLACE VICTOR BASCH
R. TRESSOUDER
R. L'AMBRE
R. L. DANSARD

4

5

Summary
Lyon

6

Summary
Lyon

Summary
Lyon

Facts
about France

MONEY

Currency

The French monetary unit is the French franc (F), which divides into 100 centimes. The 5, 10, and 20 centimes coins are yellow ; the 50 centimes, 1 F, 2 F, and 5 F coins are white ; and the 10 F and 20 F coins are a combination, yellow with a white centre. The size of each coin (within each specific colour) is proportionate to the coin's monetary value. The French paper money consists of a 500 F bill (green, with a representation of Pierre and Marie Curie), a 200 F bill (pink, with a representation of Gustave Eiffel), 100 F (orange, with a representation of Paul Cézanne), and 50 F (blue, with a representation of Antoine de Saint-Exupéry). Careful : the 100 F and 200 F bills are easily confused in poor light. Payment in Euro (cards or cheques) is already accepted in some establishments (Euro cash payments as of January 1st, 2002).

Banks-Change-Credit cards

Banks are generally open from 9:00 to 17:00, from Monday to Saturday. However, outside large city-centres, banks often close between 12:00 and 14:00, and are altogether closed on Mondays. Also, banks close early the day before a holiday.

Official identification is necessary for the exchange of Traveller's cheques. When changing your money, the commission taken varies according to the establishment (avoid changing your money in hotels).

Dispersed throughout France are numerous automatic distributors (bank machines). Where the logo CB is indicated, you may withdraw French francs from your personal bank account. After inserting your card, type your password (code), then the amount desired in French francs and whether you would like a receipt for your transaction. Retrieve your card in order to obtain the currency. Visa, Eurocard/MasterCard, American Express and Diners Club credit cards are accepted in most stores, hotels, restaurants and petrol stations. In the event of theft, contact the closest commissariat de police (police station) and immediately telephone your credit card 24 hour service : Visa : 01 42 77 11 90 - Eurocard/MasterCard : 01 45 67 84 84 - American Express : 01 47 77 72 00 - Diners Club : 01 47 62 75 50.

Facts about France

DRIVING

Certain basic rules are essential for driving in France.

In France, as in most countries, cars drive on the right-hand side of the road and overtaking is on the left. The speed limit is 90 km/h on normal roads, 130 km/h on the motorway, and 50 km/h in the city, unless otherwise indicated. Speed must be reduced in hazardous weather such as in rain or fog. Seat belts must be worn (by law) by all passengers in the car, both in the front and the back of the vehicle. Children must be equipped with proper security devices which vary according to age and weight (baby car-seats, car-seats for children age 9 months to 3-4 years, and booster car-seat for children age 4-10 years). Helmets are required for both driver and passenger on motorcycles, mopeds, and scooters. Low beams are required day and night while driving a motorcycle. The required driving age is 18 years, however, in order to rent a vehicle, a minimum of age 21 is often required. European cars are usually manual, but automatic cars are available upon request (reserve an automatic car in advance).

The legal driving alcohol limit (in the blood) is 0.5g/l (over 0.8g/l is considered an offence).

Parking is not usually free in the city. It is recommended to lock all the doors of your vehicle and not to leave any valuables inside.

TELEPHONE COMMUNICATION

From home to France

France's country code is 33. French telephone numbers have ten figures, but do not dial the initial 0 when calling from another country. For example, if you are calling 04 ******** from outside France, you must dial +33+4********. Warning : numbers beginning with 08, indicate a specific rate, and are not always accessible outside of France.

International calls from France

For international calls from France, after the tone, dial :00 + the country code+the telephone number (with operator assistance : 00 33 + country code except for Canada or the United States in which case dial 11 instead of 1). For information on rates for international calls, consult the yellow pages or call 0 800 202 202 (toll free). You may also contact an operator (for free) who will connect your call either reverse charges, or with a telephone card (or another acceptable mode of payment) : United Kingdom ✆ 0 800 99 00 44 or 02 44 or 60 44 (BT) ; 0 800 99 09 44 (Mercury) - Ireland ✆ 0 800 99 0353 - Canada ✆ 0 800 99 0016 - United States ✆ 0 800 99 0087 (US Sprint) ; 0 800 99 0013 (IDB Worldcom). For other countries consult the yellow pages.

Welcome to   the new Bird Park

PARC DES OISEAUX
01/VILLARS-LES-DOMBES

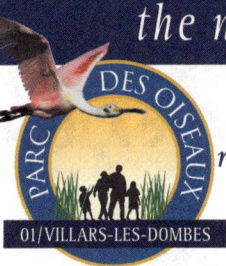

Birds from   round the world

At the heart of the Dombes region,
30 minutes north of Lyon,

discover the international Bird Park: 30 hectares of protected Nature including 10 étangs. More than 2000 birds and 400 species from round the world, including some very rare species. Among the novelties: the Pantanel Aviary and the Perroquet City which you enter to discover the most beautiful birds from South America, Africa and the Far East. You will also enjoy the walk round the étangs, the large pontoon where you can discover local fauna and flora, the Intranet network with interactive terminals and large screens
to follow the birds' secret lives.
An unforgettable day!

3 restaurants, 350 equipped picnic places. Small train. Boutique.
Open till nightfall, 21.30 in summer.
RN 83. 01330 Villars-les-Dombes.
Tel. 04 74 98 05 54 - Fax 04 74 98 27 74

Facts about France

In France

The national telecommunications company in France is France Telecom. The country is divided into 5 separate tariff zones. Price varies according to length of communication (time), distance, and the time at which the call was placed (consult the yellow pages).

Phone boxes

It is important to note that in most French hotels, fees for telephone calls are increased by 10%. Thus, in order to avoid any unpleasant surprises, request specific information on the telephone calls rates at your hotel reception desk and locate the nearest public telephone booth (phone booths are often placed in hotel entrances or lounges). Most public telephones in France require a telephone card which may be purchased in France Telecom outlets, in post offices, tobacco stores (tabacs), in Relais H stores, and in all other certified establishments (where it is posted "Télécartes en vente ici"). Some public phone booths allow the use of a bankcard. For cheaper overseas calling rates, private operators offer cards of differing rates (sold in tobacco stores or KERTEL inside Monoprix/Prisunic stores).

Cellular phones

Telephone numbers for cellular phones in France always start with 06. Operators (France Telecom's Itinéris network, Cégétel's SFR, and Bouyges Telecom) sell prepaid cards, without subscription, which are inserted into your cellular phone if it is compatible with the French network (GSM 900 and 1800 Mhz). There is also the possibility of renting a cellular phone : Ellinas Phone Rental ✆ 01 47 20 70 00 - Euro Exaphone ✆ 01 44 09 77 78 - Rent a Cell Express ✆ 01 53 93 78 00.

IN THE EVENT OF ILLNESS

Pharmacies

Pharmacies are indicated by a green cross and are generally open from 9:00 to 20:00. Certain pharmacies "de garde" are open at later hours. The list of these "nocturnal pharmacies" is posted in the front window of every pharmacy. This list also indicates the names, addresses, and telephone numbers of doctors "de garde" who offer services outside regular hours, at night, and on weekends. Also, doctors often make house calls in France.

Hospitals

Hospitals are public establishments, clinics are private. The service in public health establishments is generally high quality. For emergencies, dial 15, 18 (fire department), or 112 (European number).

Medical charges

Citizens of the European Union (Community) may be reimbursed for French medical fees (official form E111, make inquiries before your departure or once in France, at the Caisse Primaire d'Assurance Maladie). It is important, however, to contact your insurance company before your departure.

HOLIDAYS, VACATIONS

Public holidays

Apart from certain establishments such as bars, restaurants, and souvenir shops, it is relatively difficult to find businesses or services open on official holidays in France since these are official non-working days. An official day off work is a good reason to celebrate, isn't it ?

- January 1st : New Years Day
- April 16th, 2001 : Easter Monday
- May 1st : Labour Day
- May 8th : 1945 Victory Celebration
- May 24th, 2001 : Ascension Day
- June 4th, 2001 : Whit Monday

- July 14th : Fête Nationale (French National Celebration)
- August 15th : Assumption
- November 1st : All Saints' Day
- November 11th : 1918 Armistice
- December 25th : Christmas

School hoildays

Dates of official school vacation periods vary according to academic zones. France is divided into three academic zones. Thus, school holidays are spread out during specific time periods, often with one week difference between zones. Specific dates of school holidays vary annually yet are always within five specific periods : between Christmas and New Years, winter holidays (end of February to beginning of March), Easter holidays, summer vacation (July and August), and All Saints' Day (in November). It is important to note that with warm weather, Provence is a popular vacation spot, especially for Parisians and Lyonnais.

The French generally take their work holidays in August (often during the first half of the month). As a result, during this time period, it is quite common to find certain business establishments closed for holidays, especially those outside of tourist areas. As for the other areas, you will definitely not be the only vacationers…

STORES

Department stores, as well as most stores in larger cities within France, are open every day, except Sundays, from 10:00 to 19:00. Smaller stores generally close for lunch between 13:00 and 15:00, as well as on Sundays and Mondays.

Facts about France

RESTAURANTS

Hours

Apart from food stands and certain brasseries, restaurants do not serve food uninterrupted throughout the day. In most restaurants, meals are served from 11:45 to 14:30 and 19:00 to 23:00. Restaurants are often closed on Sundays. During tourist season (from May to October), most restaurants will serve food after 23:00, and are often open every day of the week. As oppose to Anglo-Saxon counties, the French eat large amounts late in the evening. Do not be surprised to find yourself surrounded by tourists if you decide to eat at 19:00 !

Tips, Gratuity

Service (or gratuity) is always included in France, and must be indicated on the bill. Tipping is left to the customer's discretion according to general satisfaction and the size of the bill. Aside from waiters in bars and restaurants (the restaurant service industry), most service industries traditionally receive tips, such as gas tenants, hotel porters, and taxi drivers.

Smoking

It is forbidden to smoke in public areas (however, do not be surprised if this rule is not followed in certain areas such as in train stations). Restaurants and bars have designated smoking and non-smoking areas, but even in this case, the laws are not always fully respected, especially in smaller establishments where smokers usually have the advantage.

TAXES

VAT tax (value-added tax) varies according to product marks and allowances (from 5.5% to 19.6%). The tax is always included in the price indicated (it is not added to the indicated price). Non-citizens of the European Community may buy certain products tax free (however not general consumer products).

Meanings of the metric symbols used
Centimetre : cm • Hour : h • Centilitre : cl • Gramme g • Metre : m • Minute : mn • Litre l • Kilogramme : kg • Kilometre : km • Second : s • Hectare : ha

929 cm • 1 cubic yard : 0.7646 m³ • 1 square yard : 0.836 m • 1 square mile : 259 ha • 1 inch : 2.54 cm • 1 acre : 0.4047 ha • 1 foot ; 30.48 cm • 1 yard : 0.9144 m • 1 mile : 1.609 km

Liquid, mesures, poids 1 fluid once : 2.5 cl • 1 ounce : 28.35 g • 1 pint : 0.568 l • 1 pound : 0.4536 kg • 1 gallon (Commonwealth) : 4.546 • l gallon (U.S.A) : 3.785 l

Températures Temperature in degrees Celsius (°C) 20 °C = Temperature in degrees Fahrenheit 59 °F = 5/9 (F-32) and F = 9/5 °C + 32

Volumes, surfaces and distances 1 cubic inch : 16.387 cm³ • 1 square inch : 6.45 cm • 1 cubic foot : 28.317 dm³ • 1 square foot :

Electricity. The electrical current in France is 220 volts and plugs have two or three round-ended prongs.

Ville de Saint-Etienne

Saint-Etienne !
There are places that no traveller can forget,
even if their attachment is only a brief memory
recalled years later.
Decidedly, Saint-Etienne is not just another
city.
Because here, when you're from Saint-Etienne,
be it by birth or adoption, you cannot help but
take on this heritage as your own.
Here, one is inevitably stimulated by the force
of the builders, inventors and creators that
have provided France with arms for its
defence, with steel for construction, with
energy to live and with solidarity to surpass
themselves.
Today, Saint-Etienne is facing the challenges of
the third millenium with this same drive and
courage. With the power of repeated success,
with a passion for ambitious projects and the
determination and confidence built on past
achievements, Saint-Etienne is and will remain
a reference for years to come.
Be sure its continued expansion will surprise no one.

185 000 inhabitants
10 parks (190 ha) + a 100 ha public
golf course
1st place in french urban development,
1999
2nd city in the Rhône-Alpes region
14th city of France by population
2nd modern art collection in France
170 000 jobs
11 500 companies, including 4 000 in
industrial firms
2 400 retail stores
20 000 students

www.mairie-st-etienne.fr

BEFORE LEAVING

MAISON DE FRANCE

The *"Maison de la France"* can give you information about Lyon and the surrounding region (brochures, maps, etc.) and can help you plan your journey.

Internet

http://www.maison-de-la-france.com

Canada

30, St Patrick's Street - TORONTO   ✆   (416) 593 4723

1981, avenue McGill College - MONTREAL   ✆   (514)288 4264

Eire

35, Lower Abbey Street - DUBLIN   ✆   (1) 703 40 46

United Kingdom

178, Piccadilly - LONDON   ✆   (0891) 244 123

United States

444, Madison Avenue - NEW-YORK   ✆   (212) 838 7800

676, North Michigan Avenue - CHICAGO   ✆   (312) 751 7800

9454 Wiltshire Boulevard - LOS ANGELES   ✆   (310) 271 2693

IN LYON

TOURIST OFFICE > Place Bellecour ✆   **04 72 77 69 69.** *Http://www.lyon-france.com.* Naturally, the Tourist Office can provide you with maps and tourist information which makes your life easier, but you can also contact it before leaving in order to choose an hotel or to find out what the weather's like so as to avoid packing too many things in your suitcase...

Internet sites

Before leaving, you can also get a foretaste of what's waiting for you on the different Internet sites devoted to Lyon which provide an English version.

www.lyon-france.com. This site, set up by the Tourist Office, gives practical information on your journey to Lyon, on your stay (list of hotels) and on latest news in the city. The site particularly targets companies and business tourism (presentation of conference infrastructures). However, there's plenty of information for the public at large.

Facts about France

www.mairie-lyon.fr. This site, run by the Lyon Town Hall, invites you to discover the city (or to get to know it better) by means of a series of texts and pictures : history, economy, culture, events, etc. There's also practical information for planning your stay in the Capital of the Gauls. In July 2001, an English version of the micro-site devoted to the area classified by UNESCO as a World Heritage Site should also be available on this site.

www.rhone-alpes-passions.com. Are you coming to the region for the food and wine ? In that case, this site gives you information to avoid your scratching your head when you look at a regional wine list. It also gives recipes of excellent dishes to accompany the wine and enables you to plan your excursions in and around Lyon.

www.petitfute.com. OK, the site doesn't yet exist in English, but there's nothing wrong with advertising your own product. Here, you'll find 22 French City Guides, 14 Departmental Guides, 43 destinations throughout the world and some very interesting thematic guides (shows, wine, 'Saucy France', etc). All that, on-line and just for you.

Lodging

Lyon has more than 10 000 hotel rooms, of which 1 500 are in 4 and 5-star establishments, 3 000 in 3-star hotels, 4 500 in 2-star hotels and nearly 500 rooms in 1-star hotels.

For places recommended by Le Petit Futé, consult the chapter "Where to sleep".

HAVE A GOOD WEEKEND !

Approximately 50 hotels in the city (from 1-star to 4-stars) participate in this national promotional offer which consists of offering two nights for the price of one ! Interesting, no ? The reservation has to be made a week bfore the date of arrival (which has to be a Friday or a Saturday). For a list of participants, all you have to do is contact the Tourist Office (see above).

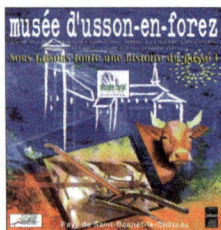

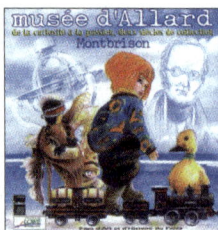

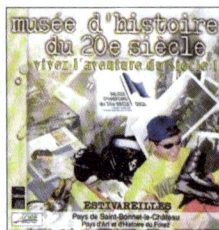

Welcome
to Lyon

HOW TO GET THERE ?

BY CAR

On the road to Lyon

French drivers haven't necessarily visited the Capital of the Gauls, but all know by reputation the Fourvière Tunnel or, more precisely, the miles of traffic jams leading into Lyon during the busiest hours at long weekends or during school holidays. Indeed, for many Frenchmen and foreigners, the roads leading to the *Côte d'Azur* and to ski resorts in the Alps go through the tunnel. So, watch out !

"*Bison Futé*" (the "Street-wise Bison" is the National Traffic Information Service's 'mascot') has nothing to do with *Le Petit Futé,* but, if you want to avoid virtually-inevitable traffic jams on the A6 Motorway at rush hours and peak-traffic periods, you would do best to follow his advice, which you can hear on TV and on the radio (stick to "B Itineraries"). And, even then... ! It has to be clearly stressed that, even if it's taken you an hour to cover 10 miles bumper-to-bumper with the car in front, motorways are not free. France has one of the densest road networks in the world, so that you shouldn't hesitate to leave major roads to take minor ones. The latter are, on th whole, well-maintained and they're certainly more attractive from a touristic and gastronomic point of view. On the road, you can listen to Motorway Radio FM (107.7 Mhz in the South) or local radio stations which often give bulletins in English during the tourist season.

If you're coming from Paris, the A6 isn't the only road going to Lyon, so why not try a more adventurous route by heading towards Clermond-Ferrand (follow the A10, and then take the A71, the A72 and the A47). It's true that the journey's roughly 150 kms longer, but you have the advantage of continuous motorway and, what's more, of motorways where the traffic's normally fluid. In addition, when you cross the Auvergne you've got some beautiful panoramic views... If you're coming from elsewhere, Lyon is also served by the A6, A7, A42, A43, A47 and A48 Motorways.

Whatever your choice, don't forget to check on traffic conditions before you leave :

TRAFFIC INFORMATION 24H/24
✆ **08 36 68 20 00**
REGIONAL CENTRE
✆ **04 78 54 33 33 (Lyon)**

Drive...

Warning to drivers : Lyon's full of surprises... First of all, it has to be said that Lyonnais don't enjoy a good reputation at the steering-wheel (like a lot of Frenchmen, moreover). Local driving's rapid and brutal. Pedestrian right of way's rarely respected, the amber traffic light's often mistaken for the green, and the car horn's a frequent punishment for the driver who's slow to accelerate from the lights.

Next, road signs. Even though tourist curiosities are relatively well signposted, you're well advised to buy a map showing the direction of traffic-flow because there are a lot of one-way streets ! In addition, forks on major roads sometimes appear very suddenly to drivers who don't know local streets. In short, keep your eyes peeled !

Parking

If you want to park on the Presqu'île or in the Saint-Jean quarter, you should also keep your eyes open, especially on Saturdays. Car parks are often full and parking spaces are rare. We advise you to park your car on the quays or on the left bank of the Rhône and cross over by foot. However, be careful : the quays along the Rhône are reserved for pedestrians, bicycles and other non-motorized vehicles every Sunday from Spring to Autumn (see below), and parked vehicles are ruthlessly towed away to the pound !

You should also be aware of a curious, local custom when it comes to parking in the evening on the busy quays along the Saône. Because of the lack of available spaces, and because the Lyonnais is manifestly not a fan of walking, you'll note a line of cars on the pavement and, on the left (in the direction of the traffic flow), a second line of parking which is more or less organized by end-of-the-week 'parkers'. If you decide to stop for dinner or for a drink, the rule to follow is simple : don't put on the handbrake (which would allow cars parked near the pavement to get out, having pushed a line of cars...). Of course, this parking method is illegal, but it's a sort of local tradition and, in France, tradition is tradition !

MUNICIPAL CAR POUND >
2, place Bir-Hakeim (3rd)

℗**04 72 60 26 00.** *Open everyday except Sundays from 08.00 to 22.00.* Your car has disappeared ? The best thing's to go to the nearest police station where a check will be made with the municipal authorities before a complaint for theft is lodged. The car that brought you here may not, infact, have been the object of covetous desire by an unknown third party, but may, quite simply, have been badly parked. There are days when we count ourselves lucky to pay the fine and go and recover our car at the pound (nevertheless, count roughly 800 FF, although that's better than going home by foot, isn't it ?).

Domaine de Champos

SAINT-DONAT-SUR-L'HERBASSE

In the heart of the Drôme des Collines, on a woody estate of more than 40 hectres, Champos welcomes you from the beginning of May to the end of September.

- **Supervised swimming**
- **Sailing**
- **Windsurfing**
- **Pedal craft**
- **Water slides**
- **Diving pontoons**
- **Beach–volley**
- **Mountain bikes**
- **Games for children**
- **Tennis**
- **Pétanque**
- **Picnic areas**
- **Rapid food**
- **Walks and rambles, montain biking and horseriding**

grand BLEU

rouge PLAISIRS

vert DÉTENTE

toutes les couleurs de vos loisirs !

LA DROME
Drôme des Collines

Quality of water systematically controlled

Fax 04 75 45 03 63

Camping-caravaning
04 75 45 17 81

E-mail : pays-herbasse@cg26.fr

Sleeping room for 4 to 6 people

Welcome to Lyon *How to get there*

Breakdowns and other little problems

In theory, we never need to have the names and addresses of a breakdown specialist because we all have motor insurance, and all insurance policies include assistance in the event of breakdown. But, you never know, situations may arise in which even the most prudent tourist needs a breakdown specialist. So, here are a few for you :

CENTRE TECHNIQUE DE DEPANNAGE > 3, rue Ollier (Villeurbanne) **04 78 84 55 56** • **DEPANNAGE AUTO** > 47, rue Maurice Flandin (Vénissieux) **0 800 209 289** • **DEPANN'VITE** > 231, avenue Jean Jaurès (7th) **04 78 75 61 62** • **PICOT DEPANNAGE** > 37, avenue Sidoine Apollinaire (9th) **04 78 47 76 76**

Maintenance

EUROMASTER > 22bis, rue A Lumière (8th) ✆ **04 78 77 01 61.** Euromaster's a huge network, and no Euromaster shop hesitates to contact the others to find the spare part which is missing from its stock. Using good-quality, Sachs spare parts often allows them to reduce the bill compared with other outfits and, when it comes to tyres, you'll have difficulty in finding better elsewhere. The reception's very friendly, even warm. **Other addresses : 190, avenue Berthelot (7th) 04 78 72 41 76 • 55, boulevard des Brotteaux (6th) 04 72 75 00 18 • 234, cours Lafayette (3rd) 04 72 68 87 40.**

EXPRESS OIL > **Shopping Centre Ecully Grand Ouest.** An oil-change in 15 minutes, without an appointment – it's been seen. An oil-change in 15 minutes, without an appointment, at a low price and with a cup of coffee while you wait has also been seen. But an oil-change in 15 minutes, without an appointment, at a low price, with a cup of coffee while you wait and with so much friendliness, so many explanations, so many little adjustments and controls, with two people looking after your car in a practical spot and with a 20% reduction if you intoduce a friend – well, no, my friend, that has never been seen. And when you learn that you can come and top up on oil between two oil-changes if your engine eats a lot, well, you quite simply go for it.

FEU VERT > 345, rue Garibaldi (7th) ✆ **04 78 58 96 06.** This Car Centre in the Rue Garibaldi is difficult to get to. If ever there's a car already parked in front of the entrance, you may as well simply drive on ! Mind you, further on there's a Midas shop but you have the same problem there. So, if you want to stop at *Feu Vert*, it's usually best to have an appointment for work on your car. The customer's never pushed to consume more because the advice given is always honest – and we all like that. It's worth noting that, right at the beginning and at the end of the season, good deals are available on open roofs.

METIFIOT PNEU > 71, avenue Jean Mermoz (8th) ✆ **04 78 78 82 82.** As its name suggests, Métifiot Pneu is a tyre specialist. So, you can ask for anything – even the rare tyre, like the 175.65.R13 (some Volkswagen, even recent ones). There's a lot of choice when it comes to brands, and the prices are amazing. As its name does not suggest, *Métifiot Pneu* also works in general maintenance : brake pads (no special guarantee), disks, exhaust pipes, oil-changes, suspension – in short, a classic range with an excellent reception. **Other addresses : 210, rue Garibaldi (3rd) 04 72 84 60 70 • 5, place Tabareau (4th) 04 78 39 16 54.**

LE HAMEAU EN BEAUJOLAIS
THE WINE HAMLET IN BEAUJOLAIS
DAS WEINDORF IM BEAUJOLAIS

La Gare - 71570 ROMANECHE-THORINS
Between LYON and MACON (RN 6)

Welcome to Lyon *How to get there*

MIDAS > 382, rue Garibaldi (7th) ✆ **04 78 72 52 52.** Maintenance without an appointment, provided the spare parts are in stock ! And, above all, come early in the morning. If not, you'd do better to go somewhere where they give appointments. The prices offered for a general revision are sometimes interesting, sometimes not. Everything depends on the price of spare parts for your car (oil filter, gas-oil filter or sparking plugs...). Brake pads guaranteed two years or 30.000 kms. **Other addresses : 272, boulevard Pinel (8th) 04 78 78 00 88 • 65, rue Marietton (9th) 04 78 83 05 34 • 46 bis av Jean Jaurès (7th) 04 78 61 08 26 • 57, rue Challemel Lacour (7th) 04 72 76 94 43**

NORAUTO > 72, avenue Tony Garnier (7th) ✆ **04 72 76 51 31.** At Norauto, you always make an appointment. The rates are sometimes very competitive, so that you understand why, for example, the brake pads aren't guaranteed ! On the other hand, a good point is that, while they're working on your car, you can have a stroll through the shop. Norauto's become a specialist for roof-racks but you can also find good things for decorating your car (steering-wheels, pedals...), spare parts or oil for DIY-men, everything to do with music and car radios plus, of course, the usual accessories (carpets, thermometers...). **Other address : "Porte des Alpes" Shopping Centre 04 72 37 04 30.**

POINT S > 43, cours Albert Thomas (3rd) ✆ **04 78 53 25 73.** You don't always find the spare part you're after at Point S but, when you do, you're always satisfied. With or without an appointment, they always do their best to take care of your car as quickly as possible. When you come across the boss, you can even negotiate the price of an oil-change or of an oil filter and, sometimes, it's very interesting. **Other address : 200, avenue J Jaurès (7th) 04 72 73 00 98.**

SPEEDY > 108, avenue Berthelot (7th) ✆ **04 78 58 09 13.** As at Midas, the lack of a shop makes waiting very long. But at least that allows you the time to watch what the mechanic's doing to your car. In this way, you can ask for explanations and have a look under the car. Brake pads guaranteed 2 years, without mileage limit.
Other addresses : 131, cours A.Thomas (3rd) 04 72 33 74 95 • 80, rue Marietton (9th) 04 78 43 45 99.

VULCO > 161, boulevard Stalingrad (6th) ✆ **04 72 44 00 66.** A tyre specialist who always has what you want : all models, all makes, always. A push of the computer key and you see the price you're going to have to pay, so no unpleasant surprises. The same for maintenance and smaller repairs. No worries !

Hire

Ready to adventure into the city or the surroundings ? You can get information on the spot or before leaving from Reservation Centres of all principal French companies (agencies located outside the city or without a branch at the airport aren't mentioned below) :

ADA ✆ **08 36 68 40 02.** *Lyon-Saint-Exupéry Airport, Lyon 2nd (Quai Gailleton).*

ALL ON THE TRACK !

Every Sunday from mid-April to mid-October, "Operation Lyon on the Track" allows pedestrians, bikes and rollerblades calmly to use the quays along the left bank of the Rhône. Indeed, between 09.00 and 18.30, all motorized vehicles are strictly banished from some 5 kilometres between the *Pont Churchill* (Churchill Bridge) and the *Pont Pasteur*. The keener among you can continue as far as *Miribel-Jonage* (along the canal) to the north, and as far as Solaize to the south. Rollerbladers can safely enjoy outings in the city on Friday evenings (ask for the circuit when you hire your blades). The madder you are, the more fun you have !

AVIS ✆ **0 802 05 05 05.** *(http://www.avis.com) Lyon-Saint-Exupéry Airport, Perrache and Part Dieu Stations, Lyon 7th (corner of Garibaldi and Route de Vienne).*

BUDGET ✆ **0 800 10 00 01.** *Lyon-Saint-Exupéry Airport, Part Dieu Station, Lyon 7th (Avenue Berthelot).*

EUROPCAR   ✆   **0 803 352 352.** *(http://www.europcar.com) Lyon-Saint-Exupéry Airport, Perrache and Part Dieu Stations, Lyon 3rd (Avenue Félix Faure).*

HERTZ   ✆   **01 39 38 38 38.** *(http://www.hertz.com) Lyon-Saint-Exupéry Airport, Perrache and Part Dieu Stations, Lyon 3rd (Cours Albert Thomas), Lyon 7th (Avenue Jean Jaurès) and Lyon 9th (Rue de Bourgogne).*

RENT A CAR   ✆   **08 36 694 695.** *(http://www.rentacar.fr) Lyon 3rd (Rue de Bonnel).*

OPTION WITHOUT A CAR

Lyon's a pleasant city to walk around in because it has a lot of pedestrian streets and relatively wide pavements and quays. It's true that the ritual climb up the Colline de Fourvière (Fourvière Hill) or the slopes of the Croix Rousse is reserved for those in good shape but, for the others, there's always public transport.

Public Transport

LYONNAIS PUBLIC TRANSPORT   ✆   **04 78 71 70 00.** Four métro lines, one hundred bus routes and two, more recent, tram routes (opened in December 2000) allow you to get about in Lyon and the near suburbs. Tickets are on sale in *TCL* (Lyonnais Public Transport) boutiques (*Bellecour* and *Perrache* Stations, *Parvis de la Gare Part-Dieu* and 43, rue de la République) as well as in automatic distributors and at other points indicated by posters. Don't forget to punch your ticket in the bus and métro (punching machines at station entrances). A ticket's valid for an hour for the single journey. It costs 8 FF a ticket and 68 FF for a book of 10 tickets (in buses, only individual tickets are sold). There are formulae for a day's travel, which can be interesting if you foresee a number of journeys. These formulae include the *Ticket Liberté* which allows you to travel as often as you like during the day for 24 FF. The last métro's at around 0.15 (for buses, check, because it varies depending on the route).

Taxis

The taxi you hail in the street is now a rare animal in the city. It's best to head for a taxi rank (the main ones are located on the *Place Terreaux*, the *Place des Cordeliers*, the *Place des Jacobins*, the *Place Bellecour* and at train stations). Taxis also come to pick you up with a simple phone call.

ALLO TAXI   ✆   **04 78 28 23 23**
LYON INTERNATIONAL TAXI   ✆   **04 78 88 16 16**
TAXIS LYONNAIS   ✆   **04 78 26 81 81**

Bicycles

For bicycle fans, Lyon's a jungle in which it's best to be highly vigilant. Whilst the bike paths on the quays along the Rhône, and which connect Gerland to the Parc Miribel, appear to be safe, the painted lines on the roads along the quays of the Saône and in the city centre are extremely precarious because drivers simply fail to respect the lines intended to indicate a reserved area for cyclists between the buses and cars. If you're still brave enough to try it, here are a few addresses where you can hire a bike or mountain-bike (between 80 FF and 100 FF a day) :

HOLIDAY BIKES > 8, quai Lassagne (1st)   ✆   **04 72 07 06 77**
L'ESPACE GITANE > 139, avenue de Saxe (3rd)   ✆   **04 78 60 46 40**

Rollerblades

(between 40 FF and 50 FF a day) :

LE CRI DU KANGOUROU > 21-23, rue d'Algérie (1st)   ✆   **04 72 00 99 10**
NOMADES > 14, rue d'Auvergne (2nd)   ✆   **04 72 40 07 92**

BY TRAIN

Lyon has two train stations in the city centre. *Lyon-Perrache* is situated on the *Presqu'île* in the 2nd arrondissement, whilst *Lyon-Part-Dieu* is opposite the shopping centre of the same

25

Welcome to Lyon *How to get there*

name in the 3rd arrondissement, on the Left Bank of the Rhône. A third station wsa recently opened at Saint-Exupéry Airport.

The **SNCF** (*Société Nationale des Chemins de Fer* or the equivalent of British Rail) proposes a number of reduced tariffs ('Discovery', 'Stay', 12-25 years old, senior citizens, etc.). Leaving Paris-Gare-de-Lyon, TGV's (High Speed Trains) serve the stations of *Perrache* and *Part-Dieu* in two hours (every 30 minutes in rush hours) from 06.00 to 22.00. Most trains stop at both stations in the city centre.

Be careful : reservation is obligatory in the TGV. In 2nd Class, the price of a ticket (single, full rate) varies from 318 FF in normal periods to 398 FF at peak periods. This line is used by a lot of businessmen, so that it's wise to reserve in advance for trains leaving between 06.00 and 09.00 and between 17.00 and 19.00. You can change reservations up to the last moment without charge (except on certain special tariffs, check when you reserve).

We remind you that Eurostar goes from London-Waterloo to *Paris-Gare-du-Nord* in 3 hours, and it's worth knowing that, if you don't want to change in Paris, you can go via the station *Lille-Europe*, which is 2 hours from London by Eurostar and 3h30 from Lyon by TGV (some ten connections a day, check).

Some trains go directly from these stations to *Paris-Charles-de-Gaulle* or *Lyon-Saint-Exupéry* Airports.

If you've missed the last TGV, you can always take a night-train. In this event, count on a 5-hour journey (last departure from paris at midnight).

The *Train Express Régional* (TER) has nothing "express" about it except the name, since it stops more often than not at all stations along the line. Nevertheless, it allows you to get to other towns in the region and to enjoy the countryside.

SNCF > Information and reservations ✆ **08 36 35 35 35 (39 for the Eurostar).** *Http://www.sncf.fr*
RAIL EUROPE IN THE UK ✆ **0990 848 848**
TRAVEL CENTRE > 179, Picadilly - LONDON ✆ **0891 515 477**

BY BUS

EUROLINES UK > 52, Grosvenor Gardens - VICTORIA ✆ **0171 730 8235**

PERRACHE INTERNATIONAL BUS STATION - LYON ✆ **04 72 56 95 30.** Ready to spend part of the evening, an entire night and a morning between bus, ferry and bus ? It may not be the quickest solution, but it's undoubtedly the most economical (count 700 FF for a return). Eurolines proposes three departures a week from London (Monday, Wednesday and Friday) or from Lyon (Wednesday, Friday and Sunday).

In France

It's not the fastest way of travelling, but it's one of the most practical means of discovering the the villages and countryside around the city. The bus networks belonging to the SNCF and to regional companies allow you to criss-cross the French countryside by programming stop-overs. You decide if you want to take the next bus or to stay. You'll find the timetables and the routes in bus stations (Perrache Station in Lyon) and practical fold-outs in Town Halls, Tourist Offices and Tourist Reception Centres.

BY PLANE
Airport

Lyon-Satolas Airport was re-named *Lyon-Saint-Exupéry* Airport on 29th June 2000 during the centenary celebrations of the famous aviator's birth in the city. Situated 25 kms from the city centre, you can get to the centre by taxi (count 250 FF) or by shuttle service (see below).

France's second largest airport after *Paris Charles de Gaulle*, the airport handles 5 million passengers a year. On 14th April 2000, *Lyon-Saint-Exupéry* inaugurated its 38th daily international flight which connected the city with New York (Delta Airlines) in 7 hours. There are nearly 40 weekly flights to London (1h35), and numerous daily flights leave for other European capitals.

It should also be noted that Air France proposes a dozen daily flights between Lyon and Paris' two airports (1 hour roughly).

AIRPORT INFORMATION ✆ **04 72 22 72 21**

AIRPORT SHUTTLE > Perrache Bus Station ✆ **04 72 68 72 17.** *Tarif : 45.50 FF.* Departures every 20 minutes from *Perrache* (from 05.00 to 21.00) and from *Saint-Exupéry* (from 06.00 to 23.00). The shuttle terminal is located in the Central Hall, Level 1 of Perrache Bus Station in the 2nd arrondissement. The shuttle stops at *Mermoz, Grange-Blanche, Gare de la Part-Dieu and Jean-Macé.*

SO AS NOT TO GET LOST IN THE CITY

TOURIST OFFICE > Place Bellecour ✆ **04 78 42 04 32.** *Open everyday except 25th December, 1st January and 1st May till 19.00.* The City of Lyon recently launched a publicity campaign designed to attract foreign tourists. So, a number of English-speaking hostesses are waiting for your visit. They'll advise you about the different formulae for entrance to museums (Lyon City Cards), guided visits (some are in English, some are audio tours) and excursions into the surrounding region. You can also buy (5 FF) a city map containing all principal tourist information (a bit thin, but it's a start).

TO READ

In the Tourist Office boutique and in certain bookshops (Espace Tourisme), you'll find guides and photo-filled books which recount the city's history in English. Here's a non-exhaustive list :

Discover the city and its history

COLOURS OF LYON, L. Jacquemin, La Taillanderie, Châtillon-sur-Chalaronne, September 1998 (127 pages).

DISCOVER LYON, L. Jacquemin, La Taillanderie, Châtillon-sur-Chalaronne, 1998 (48 pages).

DISCOVER LYON AND ITS WORLD HERITAGE, S. Griffe, La Taillanderie, Châtillon-sur-Chalaronne, August 2000 (63 pages).

HISTORICAL GUIDE OF LYON, R. Neyret, Le Tricorne Editions, Lyon, 1998 (107 pages, small format).

LE VIEUX LYON ET SES TRABOULES (OLD LYON AND ITS ALLEYWAYS), M.A. Nicolas, translation M. Fryer, Editions Lyonnaises d'Art et d'Histoire, Lyon, 1999 (127 pages). Five circuits in English (p. 84 to 127).

LYON AU BORD DE L'EAU (LYON BESIDE THE WATER), L.F. Lacroux, Bilingual Edition, Xavier Lejeunes Ed., Bron, October 1999 (112 pages).

LYON ET LE RHONE, Collective Work, translation L.Stephan, Trilingual Edition (French, English, Italian), COMCO, Lyon, April 2000 (145 pages).

LYON, PATRIMOINE DE L'HUMANITE, Y. Neyrolles and JL. Chavent, translation C.Hadley, Bilingual Edition, Editions les Points Cardinaux, Grenoble, 1999 (192 pages).

VISITING THE TRABOULES OF LYON, L. Jacquemin, La Taillanderie, Bourg-en-Bresse, 1992 (32 pages).

Gastronomy

LYONNAISE GASTRONOMY, Jean Etévenaux, La Taillanderie, Bourg-en-Bresse, 1996 (64 pages).

LYON RESTAURANTS, JF. Mesplede, Bilingual Edition, Editions Traboules, Brignais, 1999 (128 pages).

Practical Guides

BREAKING THE ICE LYON, I.Corbett, No Man's Land, Grenoble, 1999 (193 pages, small format).

Welcome to Lyon *Useful*

ENJOY ! GUIDE TO LYON, managed by P. Jones, Lyon Capitale, Lyon, June 2000 (50 pages, small format)

Where to buy them

DECITRE > 6, place Bellecour (Saône entrance)   ✆   04 72 40 54 71
FLAMMARION > 19, place Bellecour   ✆   04 72 56 21 21
FNAC > 85, rue de la République   ✆   04 72 40 49 49
VIRGIN MEGASTORE > 43, rue du Président Edouard Herriot (2nd)   ✆   04 78 92 61 61

USEFUL

EMERGENCIES

EUROPEAN EMERGENCY LINE   ✆   112
POLICE   ✆   17
FIRE BRIGADE   ✆   18
MEDICAL EMERGENCIES   ✆   15 or 04 72 68 93 00

IN THE EVENT OF SICKNESS

DOCTORS AND CHEMIST'S/PHAMACIES > Chemist's can de identified by the green cross outside the shop and are generally open from 09.00 to 20.00. They can give the names and addresses of general practitioners or specialists in the area where you happen to be. Outside normal opening hours, there's always a chemist's "on call" and open in every town. The list of these is to be found in the shop window of all chemist's. On the same list, you'll find the names and addresses of doctors "on call" at night and at the weekend (doctors can come to you).

SOS MEDECINS   ✆   04 78 83 51 51

Chemist's open all night

BLANCHET > 5, place des Cordeliers (2nd)   ✆   04 78 42 12 42
DEFAUX > 26, rue Victor Hugo (2nd)   ✆   04 78 37 81 31
PERRET > 30, rue Duquesne (6th)   ✆   04 78 93 70 96

Hospitals

The standard of the public health service is, generally, very high.

EDOUARD HERRIOT HOSPITAL EMERGENCIES > 5, place d'Arsonval (3rd)   ✆   04 72 11 60 80 / 04 72 11 78 90

HOSPITAL DEBROUSSE PEDIATRIC EMERGENCIES > 29, rue des Sœurs Bouvier (5th)   ✆   04 72 38 57 45

Medical Expenses

European Community members can generally be reimbursed medical expenses incurred in France (Form E111, enquire before leaving or at the *Caisse Primaire d'Assurance Maladie* in France). In any event, don't forget to contact your insurance company before leaving.

IN THE EVENT OF PROBLEMS

In the event of the loss or theft of your identity papers, your wallet or your car, you have to make a declaration or lodge a complaint at the police station. In the event of a major problem, don't hesitate to contact your Consulate. However, don't abuse it – your consul's not there to take care of minor administrative problems...

Canada

EMBASSY > 35, avenue Montaigne - PARIS   ✆   01 44 43 29 00

CONSULATE > 21, rue Bourgelat (2nd)   ✆   04 72 77 64 07. *Open from Monday to Friday from 09.00 to 12.00.*

Eire

EMBASSY > 4, rue Rude - PARIS ℭ 01 44 17 67 00

United States

EMBASSY > 2, avenue Gabriel - PARIS ℭ 01 43 12 22 22

CONSULAT > 16, rue de la République (2nd) ℭ 04 78 38 36 88. *By appointment.*

Great Britain

EMBASSY > 35, rue du Faubourg-St-Honoré - PARIS ℭ 01 42 66 91 42

CONSULATE > 24, rue Childebert (2nd) ℭ 04 72 77 81 70. *Open from Monday to Friday from 09.00 to 12.30 and from 14.00 to 17.30.*

EVERYDAY LIFE

Useful numbers

TELEPHONE ENQUIRIES ℭ 12

TALKING CLOCK ℭ 36 99

SNCF (Rail information) ℭ 08 36 35 35 35

MÉTÉO FRANCE (Weather) ℭ 08 36 68 08 08/08 36 68 02+n°department (69 : Rhône-Alpes)

TRAFFIC INFORMATION ℭ 04 78 54 33 33 (Lyon)

LOST OBJECTS > 65, rue du Bourdonnais (9th) ℭ 04 78 47 72 89

CENTRAL POST OFFICE > 10, place Antonin Poncet ℭ 04 72 40 60 50

ASSOCIATION LYON INTERNATIONAL (Reception for long stays) > 7, rue Major Martin (1st) ℭ 04 78 30 59 37

MONEY

Exchange

An identity card is required to change Traveller's Cheques. The commission varies from one establishment to another (avoid changing money in hotels). Some bank agencies also change money (generally indicated outside). In Lyon, you'll find Currency Exchanges at the following addresses :

AOC > 20, rue Gasparin (2nd) ℭ 04 78 38 12 00 • 3, rue de la République (1st) 04 78 27 35 45 • Lyon-Saint-Exupéry Airport 04 72 22 76 95

AMERICAN EXPRESS > 6, rue Childebert (2nd) ℭ 04 72 77 74 50

GOLDCHANGE > 81, rue de la République ℭ 04 72 40 06 00

KANUMIS > 16, rue Mail (4th) ℭ 04 72 07 70 72

THOMAS COOK > Part-Dieu Station(3rd) ℭ 04 72 33 48 55 • Perrache Station (2nd) 04 78 38 38 84

Bank Cards

You'll find many automatic distributors indicated by the logo " CB " (Carte Bleue), where you can directly withdraw money in Francs (having inserted your card, tap your confidential code and indicate the amount required and whether or not you want a receipt. Withdraw your card to get the money). VISA and EUROCARD/MASTERCARD function in all distributors. For other cards, check the instructions on the distributor.

VISA, EUROCARD/MASTERCARD, AMERICAN EXPRESS and DINERS CLUB cards are accepted in most shops, hotels, restaurants and service stations. In the event of loss or theft, make a declaration at the police station and contact 24h/24h :

AMERICAN EXPRESS 01 47 77 72 00 • DINERS CLUB 01 47 62 75 50 • EUROCARD/MASTERCARD 01 45 67 84 84 • VISA 01 42 77 11 90

Welcome to Lyon *Useful*

HOW TO TELEPHONE

In France

The national operator is *France Télécom*. The country's divided into 5 zones with a tariff which depends on the duration of the call, the distance and the hour you call at (consult the Yellow Pages). Lyon is in Zone 4 (south-east), so that all numbers begin with 04. The numbers consist of 10 figures, including numbers within the same zone (except emergency numbers).

There are special rates for numbers beginning with 08 : 0 800 (green) : free • 0 801 (blue) : price of a local call regardless of where you're calling from. • 0 802 and 0 803 (indigo) : 0.79 and 0.99 FF/mn • 08 36 65 or 66 : 3.71 FF/call • 08 36 64 or 67, 68 or 69 : between 0.74 and 2.23 FF/mn • 08 36 70 : 8.91FF/call + 2.23 FF/mn.

INTERNET

A bit homesick ? Fancy giving some news or consulting your messages and, at the same time, keeping up-to-date with novelties on the Web ? here are a few connection points :

ESPACE FRANCE TELECOM > 4, rue du Président Carnot (2nd) ℂ **0 800 69 20 01 (free call).** *Open everyday except Sundays from 10.00 to 19.00. 40 FF for an hour.*

MONDWEST MULTIMEDIA > 7, rue de Marseille (7th) ℂ **04 72 71 05 05.** *Open everyday except Sundays and on Monday mornings. 40 FF for an hour.*

Cyber-Cafés

CONNECTIK CAFE > 19, quai Saint-Antoine (2nd) ℂ **04 72 77 98 85.** *Open everyday except Sundays from 11.00 to 19.00. 60 FF for an hour.*

RACONTE-MOI LA TERRE > 38, rue Thomassin (2nd) ℂ **04 78 92 60 23.** *Open everyday except Sundays from 10.00 to 19.30. 50 FF for an hour.*

READING

You've forgotten your bedside reading material ? You'll find novels and other books in English at the following bookshops :

ETON > 1, rue du Plat (2nd) ℂ **04 78 92 92 36.** Lyon's bookshop for English-speaking people closed its doors in the Autumn of 2000. At the time of writing, we are, regrettably, unable to say if this is a temporary or a permanent closing. However, you've got nothing to lose by having a quick look. You never know !

FNAC > 85, rue de la République (2nd) ℂ **04 72 40 49 49.** This famous national shop has a well-stocked Novels section, including classics and the latest bestsellers. You'll find this section on the 1st floor, in the section called *Romans en anglais* ('Novels in English' - which is written in French, obviously !)

VIRGIN MEGASTORE > 43, rue du Président Edouard Herriot (2nd) ℂ **04 78 92 61 61.** On the 1st floor, next to the section *Littérature étrangère* (Foreign Literature), you'll find a choice of English novels, dominated by all the big names on the Bestsellers List.

The International Press

The International Press is available in most hotels as well as at *Saint-Exupéry* Airport and in *Perrache* and *Part-Dieu* Stations. It can also be found in kiosks in and around tourist sites.

SHOPPING

Opening hours

Most shops in Lyon are open everyday, except on Sundays, from 10.00 to 19.00. Small shops are generally closed between 13.00 and 15.00 and on Sundays and Mondays.

You should note that certain shops (principally in the Rue Herriot, where you'll find the luxury boutiques) are equipped with alarms at the entrance. Unless you look suspicious, they'll open the door rapidly for you.

The reception isn't always of the warmest in the shops ? If it's any consolation, shopkeepers are scarcely politer with their compatriots !

Clothing Sizes

Clothes are normally marked in French sizes and, sometimes, in European sizes (EUR) which are one size below. Here are a few examples of equivalent sizes to help you. However, don't hesitate to ask the sales staff, who can very often tell your size by just looking at you.

MEN

Suits, Trousers, Overcoats, Sweaters :

French	• 44	• 46	• 48	• 50	• 52	• 54	• 56
UK	• 34	• 36	• 38	• 40	• 42	• 44	• 48
American	• 34	• 36	• 38	• 40	• 42	• 44	• 46

Shoes :

French	• 40	• 41	• 42	• 43	• 44	• 45	• 46
UK	• 7	• 8	• 9	• 10	• 11	• 12	• 13
American	• 71/2	• 81/2	• 91/2	• 101/2	• 111/2	• 121/2	• 131/2

WOMEN

Dresses, Coats, Suits, Skirts, Trousers :

French	• 36	• 38	• 40	• 42	• 44	• 46	• 48
UK	• 6	• 8	• 10	• 12	• 14	• 16	• 18
American	• 4	• 6	• 8	• 10	• 12	• 14	• 16

Shoes :

French	• 36	• 37	• 38	• 381/2	• 39	• 40	• 41
UK	• 31/2	• 41/2	• 51/2	• 6	• 61/2	• 71/2	• 81/2
American	• 5	• 6	• 7	• 71/2	• 8	• 9	• 10

AT THE RESTAURANT

Lyon is the capital of French gastronomy, but you risk being disappointed by certain establishments in the Rue Mercière (2nd) or in the Saint-Jean Quarter (5th) which are real "tourist traps", to say the least. A piece of advice : if you don't have time to try all the restaurants in the city, follow our chapter on the subject. Another word of advice : make sure you're really hungry if you order the full menu, which often includes both cheese and dessert on top of a main dish which is often copious and nourishing.

Tips

Service charge is always included and specified on the bill. Tipping is, consequently, left to the customer's discretion, and the amount of any tip depends on the size of the bill and how satisfied he is with the meal and service. As a rough guide, it's normal to tip 2 F to 5 F for bills under 100 F and to add 5 F to 10 F for every 100 F of bill thereafter. Outside bars and restaurants, people providing a service traditionally receive a tip (service station, porters, taxis, etc.).

SMOKING

Cigarettes (20 to 25 FF for a packet of 20) are on sale in tobacconists identified by a red lozenge. In Lyon, rare are the tobacconists open after 20.00 or on Sundays (you'll find one on the quays of the Saône, beside the old Law Courts and opposite the footbridge). However, most bars and restaurants sell cigarettes at a price which is inflated by a couple of Francs).

A LITTLE LEXICON OF TYPICALLY-LYONNAIS WORDS AND EXPRESSIONS

Bouchon

In France, this word normally means 'cork' or traffic-jam', depending on the context. In Lyon, it often signifies a typical Lyonnais restaurant serving a popular cuisine in a friendly atmosphere (watch out for imitations !)

31

Welcome to Lyon *Useful*

Canuts
The name for Lyonnais silkworkers.

Fromage frais or fromage sec ?
Restaurants propose a *fromage frais*, which is a sort of cheese served with thick or liquid cream, or a *fromage sec*, which is a cheese with a hard or soft rind and a great French speciality.

Gône
In Old French, a child.

J'y mets où ?
If you have a good notion of French, don't be surprised in Lyon to hear an "y" replacing the pronouns le, la or les. The Lyonnais won't ask of an object "*où je le mets* ?" (where shall I put it ?) but, rather, "*où j'y mets* ?".

La Tour Eiffel
The nickname for the transmitter, located on the *Colline de Fourvière* (Fourvière Hill), which can be seen from afar and which vaguely resembles the famous Prisian monument.

La vogue aux marrons
The name given to the fair which is held in Autumn on the Boulevard de la Croix-Rousse (4th).

Les pentes et la colline
Les Pentes (The Slopes) are, of course, the slopes of *La Croix-Rousse* and *La Colline* (The Hill) refers to the Colline de Fourvière.

Pot
Here, quite naturally, the pot (jug) is often a jug - that is to say, 46 centilitres (roughly) - of Côtes du Rhône wine, often served in the restaurant or brasserie (less expensive than a bottle).

Presqu'île
Normally, a 'peninsula', it designates the city's shopping centre, located between the Rhône and the Saône.

Rue de la Ré
Rue de la République.

Saône et le Rhône
The city's two rivers, the Rhône being THE river for the Lyonnais. Pronounce 'Rone' and 'Sone'.

Traboules
Whether they be in Old Lyon or on the slopes of La Croix-Rousse, these passageways allow silkworkers to transport their goods from street to street through the house courtyards without getting wet (information a t the Tourist Office).

Vieux Lyon
Old Lyon, it designates the historic quarters of *Saint-Georges*, *Saint-Jean* and a small section of *Saint-Paul*.

FIND US ON THE NET
www.petitfute.com

THE CITY IN ALL LETTERS OF THE ALPHABET

AMPERE

Here's a family which illumintaes Lyon ! Why ? Simple. Electricity or, more precisely, the theory of electromagnetism, the galvanometer (the machine allowing the measurement of the intensity of electrical currents), the first electrical telegraph and its friend called "Arago", the magnet – all these were invented by Monsieur André Marie Ampère, born in Lyon in 1775. But that's not all, because the same Monsieur Ampère also left his mark on the development of mathematics, chemistry and philosophy. And so as not to stop at the age of 25 (he had plenty of time, how frustrating…) the same Dédé Ampère had a son, Jean-Jacques, who was also born between the Rhône and the Saône in 1800, and who became an historian and was elected to the French Academy. Today, Lyon commemorates them both by naming a métro station after them…

BATEAU MOUCHE

Everyone has dreamt of, or has lived, an evening under a full moon with his sweetheart, and with his camera and camescope under his arm… Yes, that's it – a cruise on the Seine in a in *bateau mouche* : the ultimate in Parisian tourism. To start at the foot of the Eiffel Tower and to finish at Notre Dame with, along the way, tourists or Parisians on every bridge waving "Hello" - beautiful vision, isn't it ? "But", you're saying to yourself, "that's got nothing to do with Lyon. There must be an error at the start of the guidebook". Not at all ! The *bateaux mouches* which , today, are very Parisian, were actually born in Lyon. So there ! And those who thought that this strange name was due to the fact that they're "flying" boats, a sort of hydroplane, are in for a surprise because the name comes quite simply from the place they were born… the Lyonnais *Mouche* district, situated at the tip of the Presqu'île.

CONFLUENCE

In the past, the place where the Rhône and the Saône meet (the Confluence) was simply a site devoured by the car and dominated by the railbridge. The extreme southern tip of the *Presqu'île* subsequently assumed the position it deserves in the city, and even gave its name to the entire *Presqu'île* area, starting at *Perrache*. The current "Confluence Project" is highly ambitious and will mark the city every bit as much as the "Paris se réveille à l'est (Paris wakes up in the East) Project" marked Paris or the "Dockland Project" marked London. The project concerns 150 hectares of land, of which 50 hectares are green spaces. The project figures are impressive : in all, nearly 13 billion Francs will be necessary over a 30-year period ; the population of the area will increase from 7 000 to 25 000 and the number of local jobs from 2 000 to 16 000 ! Enormous building sites will be opened. In 2007, the Perrache Exchange Centre (an architectural wart which cuts the Presqu'île into two) will be demolished and the *Saint Paul* and *Saint Joseph* Prisons will be moved. In 2004, a pleasure port will be created and, in 2003, traffic in the west of Lyon will be directed round a new ring road, thereby alleviating current traffic on the banks of the Rhône along the motorway to the south. In addition, the station market at *Corbas* will be moved. These are but a few examples of the changes foreseen by the project and, before then, other changes will take place : a large strolling area will be built along the Rhône in 2000, and a Confluence Museum, devoted to Science and Techniques, will be opened. The métro or the tramway should be extended as far as this – an indispensable measure to encourage Lyonnais to return to a quarter which has been cut off from the rest of the city ! Rendez-vous in *Le Petit Futé*'s 2031 edition !

DANCE (MAISON DE LA DANSE)

The Maison de la Danse celebrated its 20th birthday in 2000, and remains the only major site in Europe entirely devoted to choreographic art. It was born on 17th June 1980 on the *Croix Rousse* plateau. Twelve years later, and with more than 600 000 spectators in a decade, it had become too small for the quality of the choreographic representations it produced, and it moved to the theatre in the 8th *arrondissement*. The theatre had been built in 1968 by the architect, Pierre Bourdeix, and had been run by some of the most prestigious directors-producers, notably Marcel Maréchal, Jacques Weber and Jérôme Savary. Nevertheless, in September 1992, the theatre became the *Maison de la Danse*. This has 1100 places, a stage

33

THE CITY IN ALL LETTERS OF THE ALPHABET

measuring 14x30 metres and a rehearsal studio of 300 m² – enough to keep dancers, choreographers and spectators happy. Before celebrating its birthday, the *Maison de la Danse* offered itself a face-lift : 6 months of works and 22 million Francs of investment allowed a total refit, greater comfort (including the replacement of all the seats) and security which conforms to modern norms. For the 2000 Season, subscriptions increased by 30% and a total of 170 000 spectators came here. The 2000/2001 Season promises to be equally successful, with 181 performances, 400 dancers, musicians and actors, 38 companies and 13 countries represented. Since 1980, the theatre's seen 500 choreographers and has welcomed 1.5 million spectators. What's the secret of its success ? Doubtless, the man who's been Director since the very start, the man who fought so that a *Maison de la Danse* could exist – the Lyonnais, Guy Darmet, to whom Lyon also owes the creation of the *Biennale de la Danse*. In 16 years, the *Biennale de la Danse* has become a world event in this domain. Its large procession through the streets of the *Presqu'île* is prepared months in advance in all districts and has become a really popular spectacle. Guy Darmet's work has been rewarded by different Ministers of Culture, both Right-wing and Left-wing. That's proof, if ever there was one, that he's a good man !

ELEGANCE

Paris has its Golden Triangle, formed by three avenues : the Avenue des Champs-Elysées, the Avenue George V and the Avenue Montaigne. The latter houses numerous fashion houses. Well, Lyon has nothing to be ashamed of, with its Golden Rectangle, located on the *Presqu'île* and enclosed by the prestigious *Rue Edouard Herrio*t, the *Rue d'Emile Zola*, the *Place Bellecour* and the *Place Jacobins*. This 'City within a City' includes a good number of famous establishments : *Louis Vuitton, Cartier, Hermès, Gucci* and Baccarat. Elegance in Lyon isn't a meaningless word ! All these famous labels and others, located principally on the *Presqu'île* and in the 6th *arrondissement,* have created a club, the *Lyon Labels*, whose purpose is "to contribute to the development and the promotion of high-quality trade in Lyon". The internal regulations lay down draconian criteria for getting into, and staying in, the club : the quality of the facade and the interior comfort, selective credit cards : American Express, Diners, information in foreign languages. The Silk Capital has clearly lost none of its prestige !

FOURVIERE

From below, from above, from within and from the top – *Fourvière* is the place in Lyon. For its hill, its tunnel which is famous for its traffic-jams, its Basilica, its Roman theatre or its superb view – *Fourvière* is a place you simply have to visit. From the esplanade, the view's superb. Those who are always finding fault might tell you that the view is, indeed, superb over the *Feyzin* refineries on the right, the dirty *Part-Dieu* in the centre and, on the left, the TGV viaduct or the smoke from the *Bugey* Power Station. But *Fourvière* also, and above all, offers a view of the rows of roofs in the Saint Jean Quarter and of its cathedral at the foot of the hill, of the entire *Presqu'île* from *Bellecour* to *Terreaux,* of the Town Hall and the superb dome on the Operahouse and of the left bank of the Rhône, with the 'green lung' which is the *Tête d'Or* on the left. From here, you get a real idea of the size of France's third largest city. The Basilica, built after 1870, can be visited, as can its roof. A bit lower down, the Roman theatre's open all year and, in June and July, is home to the Nuits de Fourvière, a series of dance shows, cinema projections, Rock and Variety concerts.

GUIGNOL

Guignol was born in Lyon thanks to Laurent Mourguet. In 1789, at the age of 21, he was cast (along with many others) by the hazard of the French Revolution onto the streets of Lyon. To feed his family, he became a peddlar and then a tooth-puller. For his clients' amusement, he installed a small puppet theatre next to his tooth-puller's armchair and, in this way, a vocation was born, and he made puppeteering his profession. An avant-garde caricaturist, he created created his characters by taking notably as a model a certain *Guignol*, who had a jovial face. At the end of the 19th century, there were more than 80 puppet-theatres in the city, all inspired by Mourguet's model, using folkloric language and expressing contentious ideas. But, over the years, *Guignol* became denatured and sweetened to such an extent that he became essentially an amusement for children. Since 1966, the Lyon *Guignol* (Puppet House) has been installed in the *Palais Bondy* (5th) at the heart of the World Heritage Site. However, a new and young company, set up in 1994, has been fighting to promote the image of the original *Guignol*, with all his insolence and with his original purpose as a conveyor of ideas and information. The City of Lyon has just granted it the right to run the palace and, on 15th June last, the *Zonzons*

THE CITY IN ALL LETTERS OF THE ALPHABET

received the Lyonnais Tourist Trophy for its work in enhancing cultural heritage. Encouraged by this success, the company's launching the April Harvest Festival in 2001, with the intention of giving the puppet theatre a new dimension by proposing to its spectators the completest possible panorama of its creation and history.

HERRIOT (EDOUARD)

A street, the most beautiful in the city, a hospital, a school and a port... The four corners of Lyon pay tribute to the man who was mayor of the city for more than half-a-century, from 1905 to 1957. But this Left-winger (President of the Radical Party for more than 30 years) also enjoyed a career at a national level as *Président du Conseil* (the equivalent of Prime Minister) with the portfolio for Foreign Affairs. Having failed in his fereign policy, the man with the pipe and the moustache became President of the Chamber of Deputies in 1936 and, later, of the National Assembly from 1947 to 1955. This historic character, born in Troyes in 1872, had found his peaceful haven and had retired to a stone house, his little stronghold, which was built at the top of an impressive cliff in the *Val d'Amby*, near Crémieu (Isère). Edouard Herriot was a member of the French Academy and died in 1957.

INTERNATIONAL

Lyon wants to be an international city and a European pole. It's true that its geographical location is an asset – it's a virtually unavoidable passageway between Southern and Northern Europe. That Lyon should be an international city is one of Raymond Barre's dearest wishes. Once, during his single mandate as mayor of the city, the occasion arose to reveal Lyon to the eyes of the world. To create this occasion, Barre opened his Prime Minister's address book and succeeded in bringing to the Capital of the Gauls several major events, including a number of international conferences and gatherings. The highlight was the G7 meeting in 1996, when the 22nd Summit of the seven most industrialized nations in the world, along with its 5000 participants, met in the city. Naturally, the Lyonnais were subjected to the inevitable traffic-jams caused by the draconian security measures, and the *Tête d'Or* Park was closed so that Bill Clinton could jog undisturbed. There were other inconveniences, too, but, for three days, all the world's cameras were focused on Lyon... The *Cité Internationale* is a reflection of this wish. It was built on the site of the late *Palais de la Foire* which was, itself, a site destined for major events since the Universal Exhibition was held there in 1894. The *Cité Internationale*'s characterized by the "light and transparent" architecture of Renzo Piano. It houses the *Palais des Congrès* (Conference Centre), which will be enlarged in the next few years, a luxury hotel and casino (see the chapter "Games"), a multiplex cinema, a Contemporary Art Museum (in the only building which was kept) and, very shortly, flats. But the *Cité Internationale* has its weaknesses : it's poorly served by public transport, and many call it a "luxurious ghetto" because the originally-intended social mix was so little respected. It's not exactly a dormitory for the rich, but, nevertheless, the plebs are kindly requested to go and sleep elsewhere... neither the prices practised in the hotel, nor those required to buy the flats, are for them !

JEUX (GAMES)

On the 1st April last, the Hilton Hotel's casino opened its doors between the *Tête d'Or* Park and the banks of the Rhône... and it wasn't an April Fool joke ! After months of negotiations and a series of decisions and counter-decisions, Lyon became the first non-thermal town in France to have a casino. Its name is "Pharaoh", and its entire decoration is inspired by Ancient Egypt. For the time being, the casino's operating at half-throttle – a sort of breaking-in period. Only the traditional games tables are authorized and it's not, perhaps, for everyone – no pumps allowed, identity card requested, 70 F admission fee, and it's advisable to know the customs and rules of English roulette and Black Jack, for example. But, after a year of operation and "if everybody behaves", the Partouche Group will be authorizd to install 400 one-arm-bandits ! These machines attract a much more 'popular' clientèle – there's no doubt about it, and that's what they're made for ! Opponents of the casino are worried that the attraction of "easy money" risks seducing an economically and socially fragile population, particularly the young. Some don't hesitate to call Lyon "The Las Vegas of the Rhône".

KILOMETRES

Watch out, if you like figures, you're going to get your money's worth ! Here goes : Lyon has 523 kilometres of streets, 8 kilometres of banks along the Rhône and 18 along the Saône, 98 bus routes covering 1 173 kilometres of road, 29.7 kilometres of métro split between 4 lines, 2

THE CITY IN ALL LETTERS OF THE ALPHABET

trams covering 1.2 kilometres (and shortly 19 kilometres) of tram-track. The city and surroundings have no less than 2 100 of road for 2 500 kilometres of sewers. The figures haven't sent you to sleep yet ? OK, let's continue. The inner city covers an area of 4 787 and its population is 445 452, whilst the population of Greater Lyon is 1 167 532, split over 50 000 hectares. Consequently, Lyon has ceased its eternal rivalry with Marseille and has ceded the coveted title of "2nd largest city in France". Anyway, nobody gives a damn since the Lyon Football Club had a better season than OM – and, straightaway, the war starts all over again ! Now for a percentage. According to a public opinion poll carried out in 2000, 34% of the population believe that the best thing would be to ban cars from the city centre (also see "Lumieres" below if you like opinion polls). A few more figures : Lyon has 594 hairdressers, 20 400 trees and 10 municipal swimming-pools. You may be interested to know that most of these figures were given to us free of charge after a simple phone call to the new Municipal Telephone Information Service called "Lyon en direct" on 08 25 08 15 15 (0.98 F per minute all the same) from Monday to Friday from 08.00 to 19.00 and on Saturdays from 08.00 to 12.00. They're friendly and give a rapid and efficient reply to administrative and practical questions to do with the city. Hats off to the "Lyon en direct" team !

LUMIERE (LIGHT)

There are *Lumière* and *lumières.* The former are the Lumière brothers, inventors of the cinema and of photography. Born in Besançon, in 1862 for Auguste and in 1864 for Louis, they worked on their inventions in the *Montplaisir* district (8th *arrondissement*). Today, the Lumière Institute and the *Château Lumière* perpetuate their memory and organize a large number of events. Other traces of this past are to be found in the *Montplaisir* district, and the first street to appear in a film and the first film hangar, now converted into a projection room, bear witness to this flourishing period. But, *Lumières* in Lyon also means 8th December. On that date, in order to commemorate the installation of the gold Statue of the Virgin on the *Chapelle de Fourvière* bell-tower in 1852 (a statue erected to thank Mary for ridding the city of the plague in 1643), Lyonnais put little candles in their windows. The sight of millions of flickering lights is absolutely superb ! Today, this event has largely lost its religious dimension but has gained in popularity. A Festival of Lights has just been created and, in years to come, it could become what the cinema is to Cannes and the cartoon strip to Angoulême : the event will make people talk about Lyon ! In 1999, the lighting-up of the Town Hall facade or the *Théâtre des Célestins* may presage better things to come. Finally, *Lumière* in Lyon is the "Lumière Plan", launched in the 90's by the then mayor, Michel Noir. Today, the city's buildings and bridges are lit up every evening. Paris is in the process of copying the plan – which is an indication of how successful it is ! In an opinion poll carried out for the daily paper, *Le Progrès* (Progress), Lyonnais voted the "Lumière Plan" the initiative which has most enhanced the image of the city over the last decade.

MURS PEINTS (PAINTED WALLS)

It has always been said that walls have ears... In Lyon, walls have more than that – they have a soul ! For more than 20 years, the city's mural frescoes have been a major attraction, and both tourists and Lyonnais stop and disover, or rediscover, this part of the city's heritage. These works are produced by different artists, like the *Mur'art* Group and, of course, the *Cité de la Création* Group. The latter painted more than 40 frescoes throughout the city and the surroundings – many of which are a tribute to the cinema (*Cours Gambetta*, 7th. 1996), to books (*Quai de la Pêcherie,* 1st. 1998), to famous Lyonnais (*Quai Saint Vincent,* 1st. 1997) and to the theatre (*Rue Gabriel Péri* in Villeurbanne. 1998). The urban Tony Garnier Museum in the *Quartier des Etats-Unis* (8th. 1988-1998) has the merit of having transformed blocks of flats into a site which is visited for its 24 frescoes ! Other painted walls (once again, the work of the *Cité de la Création* Group, can be found in the city's historical areas, and include the frescoe in *Montluc* (*Rue du Dauphiné,* 3rd, 1999), where Jean Moulin bursts out in filigree. Avenue Lacassagne (3rd, 1989) retraces a century of public transport in Lyon, but the most famous fresco remains, undoubtedly, the *Mur des Canuts* in the *Croix Rousse* (*Boulevard des Canuts* 4th. 1987 and 1997). The largest frescoe in Europe (1 200 m²), it's superb and the trompe l'œil is really successful (rumour pretends that a pigeon even tried to perch on the roof, and that a tramp tried to sit down on the bench). The 12 artists who painted it even tried, 10 years later, to develop the work in order to make it resemble the surrounding district. Most of these frescoes are lit up in the evening. A tour of them is a 'must'. There are also frescoes in the surroundings, and the Genas commune has superb mural frescoes, and the most recent (2000) are to be found in Trept in the Isère. Entitled *"Au Fil du Temps"* (As Time Passes), they depict stonemasons at work.

THE CITY IN ALL LETTERS OF THE ALPHABET

NOUVELLES HALLES TONY GARNIER (THE NEW TONY GARNIER HALL)

The Hall in the *Gerland* Quarter has just begun a third life. Having been, since the beginning of the century, a slaughter-house, and then, more recently, a pseudo-music hall, it has just been modified a third time. One year of works and 110 million Francs were necessary, so great was the task of creating a real centre for cultural and sporting events. The building built by Tony Garnier – an iron and glass construction, which is now classed as an historic monument – has become entirely modulable. An impressive series of jacks and other mechanical equipment were installed in the underground galleries in order to raise four slabs (200 tons) off the ground so as to put in seats for 3 000 and create room for 17 000 places. The hall was made soundproof and had to be protected against the heat of light 800 spotlights. This summer, the Tony Harnier Hall re-opened its doors for the biennial Contemporary Art Exhibition.

TETE D'OR

An institution ! The *Tête d'Or* park, nicknamed the 'Green Lung', occupies a special place in the hearts of Lyonnais. This urban park has the reputation of being the most beautiful in France – a subjective point of view, and, hence impossible to confirm although though it's certainly very beautiful ! Its 105 hectares contain very different 'countryside' : the lake, the rose garden, the island, the lawns, the botanical garden and, of course, the zoological garden (see " Zoo " section below). At sunrise, the view onto the lake is striking – it quite simply makes you feel like getting up before dawn every morning ! Every year, more than 2 million visitors walk by the parks 8 000 trees and, certain Sundays, the number of visitors exceeds 40 000. The park's open longer every day than any other park in France (06.00 to 21.00 from 15th October to 14th April and from 06.00 to 23.00 the rest of the year. It was nearly closed for financial reasons and also because, at nighfall, things happen in the bushes which risk shocking certain visitors... During the day, it's a place for practising sports : bicycles and rollerblades are authorized, and, up to 13.00 and after 19.00, boats and tricycles can be hired. The park's also the ideal site for a family stroll. In an opinion poll last May, Lyonnais declared the *Pavillon du Parc* building to be "mediocre and badly integrated", and it may be pulled down. Unfortunately, over recent years the lake has become polluted and may be emptied for several months so that it can be cleaned : watch this space. Rumours regularly circulate round the city that an admission fee to the park may be introduced, but what mayor would dare take such an unpopular decision ? The *Tête d'Or* Park's untouchable, like the legend of the same name (the park's called the "Golden Head" because a treasure, consisting of gold coins arranged in the shape of a head, is supposed to be buried here. No digging allowed !

PART-DIEU

When you see so many cars and so much concrete and glass, you wonder what God has to do with all this ! But you mustn't forget that P*art Dieu* wasn't born with the opening of the shopping centre in 1975 and that it didn't arrive with the first *TGV* (High Speed Train) in 1982. Another story for you : in the 18th century, it was nothing but a small, partially-flooded estate of 140 hectares, which was given by Catherine de Mazenod to Lyon's *Hôtel Dieu* (Hospital). 90 hectares consisted of wild shrubland, dotted with small parcels of land called "la part de Dieu" (God's share). That's the little story ! Corn-growing and the raising of dairy cows, which provided food for the hospital patients, gave way to a military barracks. But, in December 1960, this military site was ceded to the City of Lyon. The mayor at the time decided to construct eight blocks of flats. Fortunately for humanity and for its heritage, only two actually saw the light of day and these are still a mar on the surrounding area. Since then, *Part Dieu* has become Lyon's second 'city', and the shopping mall (with its 260 shops) welcomes 80 000 people everyday and enjoys a turnover which is greater than that of the *Presqu'île*. But, *Part Dieu's* also a major administrative centre, with an urban community, a new Law Court and a business centre which includes the Head Offices of many companies and banks, employing some 30 000 people. The district has never found its soul, which has, doubtless, been suffocated by so much concrete and trafic (typical of the 1970's). So, after a quarter of a century, *Part Dieu's* undergoing more than a face-lift – more a major surgical operation. The station interior's being renovated to welcome the Mediterranean *TGV*. Footbridges have been destroyed so that pedestrians can find their rightful place, and the arrival of the tram has allowed the creation of a real esplanade linking the station to the shopping centre. The latter will be renovated in the next 18 months, and a second tower, 140 metres-high, will be built (work will begin in the summer of 2001, with delivery scheduled for

THE CITY IN ALL LETTERS OF THE ALPHABET

2003 : shops, offices, 3-star hotel with 200 rooms and a car park). By the way, do you know where you can get the best view of Lyon ? From the *Part Dieu* Tower, which is also called the 'Crayon' or the '*Crédit Lyonnais* Tower'. Why ? Because it's the only place you can't see it from ! All right, Parisians tell the same joke about the *Tour Montparnasse*, but it's quite amusing, all the same !

QUADRETTE

The sport of *boule* is to Lyon what *choucroute* is to Alsace, or the Eiffel Tower to Paris - anchored, rooted. Nevertheless, it was only in 1980 that the Ministry of Youth and Sport recognized this game as a sport. Life hasn't been a long, tranquil river for *boules*. People have been throwing *boules* since Antiquity, six centuries before Jesus Christ, but, at that time, was then similar to throwing the discus. The Greeks, the Romans – everybody adopted the game. But why is the game of *boule* so popular in the South of France ? Quite simply because it was imported into France by Phoenecian sailors, so that the Rhône Valley constituted a sort of entrance corridor ! Charles IV and Charles V banned the game in the 14th century because they considered that it was preventing the people from pursuing more profitable activities ! Then, in the 16th century, doctors came up with a contrary theory and maintained that the game was good for the health. In 1894, the first official rules were drawn up in Lyon during the first major tournament, which was held on the *Cours du Midi*, the old site of the present *Cours de Verdun*. The following year, the Pentecost Tournament was created, and this is still held every year. The Pentecost Tournament is the oldest and the most important tournament in the world ! In 1924, the very first French *Boules* Championship was held in Lyon. So, as you may have guessed, Lyon is the real *Boules* Capital : National and International Boules Federations (34 countries) have their Headquarters in the city. Several variations of the sport exist : *pétanque, jeu provençal*, Breton wooden *boules* and, of course, *Boule Lyonnaise*. It's played on beaten earth, in an area sufficiently large to allow the boule to be thrown fast. Its played in singles, doubles, in triples or in Q*uadrette* : four against four, each team being split into 'pointers' and 'shooters', with two *boules* per player.

RAYMOND BARRE

Does Raymond Barre play *Boules à la Lyonnaise* ? Born on the Island of Réunion in 1924, Prime Minister from 1976 to 1981, Deputy of Lyon's 4th constituency since 1978 and Mayor since 1995, Raymond Barre occupies a vey particular place in the hearts and minds of Lyonnais : a sort of mutual "I don't love you either" ! Very early during his mandate, he publicly decalred that he wouldn't stand for re-election, so only History will tell if he leaves his mark on the city. Raymond Barre indisputably woke Lyon up at an International level by making his old Prime Minister's 'address book' available to the city. As a result, several International Events have taken place in recent years, including the G7 Summit in June 1996, whilst other ambitious projects (the "Confluent Project", for example) may materialize one day. Vicious tongues pretend that Raymond Barre comes to 'his' city only one day a week, although the publication of his work-schedule by the mayor's Press Service demonstrated that this criticism was unfounded. An expression regularly comes to the Mayor of Lyon's lips – "Lyonnais Microcosm", thereby showing a certain detachment, or even disdain, for the 'little world' of the Rhonalpine Capital. As for his successor, Raymond Barre hasn't named his Dauphin to date. Will he ? The Majority can't get its act together, and the Left, encouraged by the results of recent opinion polls, is preparing to retake the Town Hall.

SAINT EXUPERY

The aviator-writer, Antoine de Saint Exupéry, was born in Lyon exactly 100 years ago and, until recently, this fact had passed unnoticed, in spite of a plaque outside the house he was born in, near the P*lace Bellecour*. But, the centenary of the birth of the author of "The Little Prince" and of "Fly by Night" was the opportunity to make amends for this silence. Since 29th June last, Lyon has been paying tribute to its 'hero'. The *Lyon Satolas* Airport was re-named *Lyon Saint-Exupéry* (for international baggage-labelling, this presented relatively few problems because the initials are identical !).The street the aviator was born in (*Rue Alphonse Fochier* in the 2nd *arrondissement*) now also bears the name of the little Lyonnais who became great, and the Post Office has issued a stamp with his face on it. But the work which most marked this centenary was created by the Lyonnaise artist, Christiane Guillaubey. Nearly 7 metres-high, and on a white column in Carrara marble, the sculpture of the aviator thrones over the P*lace Bellecour*, a few steps (or wings !) away from the house he lived in. On Saint-Ex's (as he is called, here) shoulder, you'll see the Little Prince's hand. The sculpture's a superb success. It was unveiled during the week of tribute, when a number of

THE CITY IN ALL LETTERS OF THE ALPHABET

aircraft, as well as an exhibition on the aviator-writer-philosopher's life, drew tens of thousands of visitors. Saint Ex is now more than ever Lyonnais, and the festival was very popular. Ironically, as Fate would have it, one of the planes exhibited at *Bellecour* – a hydroplane which was about to set off on a round-the-world flight - crashed as it was leaving Lyon… The ghost of Saint Ex, yet again !

TRAMWAY

In Greater Lyon, which counts more than one million inhabitants and four million daily journeys (of which 75% are made by car), the tramway is the major project which has most marked, and will continue to mark, Lyonnais. Launched in 1997 with a budget of more than 2 billion Francs, the tramway should become operational on 8th December 2000. It has been a Titanic operation which has thrown local life into confusion. For ages, the entire city was nothing but a vast construction site, and the traffic-jams, which were already legendary (indeed, the tramway was prinicpally built to eliminate them), got even longer. Consequently, the tramway has been unpopular. But, was it the tramway or the construction work Lyonnais were complaining about ? Answer in a few weeks' time, when the two lines (N°1 *Perrache-La Station* via *Part Dieu*, 19 stops along 8.7 km, and N°2 *Perrache- Campus de Bron*, 20 stops along10 km ; later, a tram will start running to *Saint-Priest*). But certain critics question the tramway's rationale : Why multiply means of transport rather than continuing to develop the métro network ? Injudicious routes or badly-thought out trams : why didn't they build lawn between the rails along the length of the track, like in Rouen, so as to make the city gayer and greener ? Rendez-vous on 8th December !

UNESCO (WORLD HERITAGE)

The 5th December 1988 will be engraved in Lyon's history, as its past is in the stones of the Capital of the Gauls. On that day, Lyon was inscribed as a World Heritage Site – an honour it shares with the pyramids, the *Château de Versailles,* Prague or the *Mont Saint-Michel*. If Lyon was chosen for this honour by UNESCO, it's because of its particularity : 2000 years of architectural history are to be found on a single 500-hectare site. From *Lugdunum* in 43 B.C to the Present Day, the city's different quarters have been, and remain, inhabited. From the Roman Theatre in *Fourvière* or the *Trois Gaules* on the slopes of the *Croix-Rousse* to the Opera House, which was renovated at the end of this 20th century by Jean Nouvel, or the *Place des Terreaux* (owed to Buren), and including the Renaissance quarters of *Saint Georges, Saint Jean* and *Saint Paul*, the Middle Ages passageways and the Romanesque *Saint Martin d'Ainay,* the streets of Lyon are a veritable history book. Included in the heritage site (and this is slightly more surprising) is the *Célestins* car park and its *Tour Creuse* (another work by Buren) ! To be classed as a World Heritage Site is a huge asset for Lyon and for its tourism. There can be no doubt that such recognition attracts a public. The publicity campaign launched last spring seeks to take advantage of the fact. But there's a danger that Lyon becomes a 'Museum City', and, to avoid this, the city must continue to live and evolve as it has done for more than 2000 years. This exemplary architectural continuity must go on !

VIEUX LYON (OLD LYON)

The historic quarter of Lyon ! The *Cathédrale Saint Jean* marks the separation between the two quarters of *Saint Georges,* to the south, and of *Saint Jean. Saint Paul* closes this ensemble in the north. Each quarter is the extension of the others, and yet, all three are very different, some would say, almost antithetical. *Saint Jean* is known for its restaurants, its nightlife, its tourist-packed streets, its quays and its double - or triple parking, whilst *Saint Georges* has succeeded in keeping all its 'authenticity'. Litle known, it still has its old calm, its houses (which have aged less well than in Saint Jean), its little squares and its district-life. Every spring, *Saint Georges* becomes lively during its carnival, which gives a glimpse of this district spirit. *Saint Georges* must absolutely be (re)discovered, but don't tell everyone this, so that it doesn't lose its fantastic tranquillity. The trio, composed of Georges, Jean and Paul constitutes France's largest Renaissance ensemble : 25 hectares. From the 4th century onwards, the inhabitants of the Gallo-Roman town left the *Colline de Fourvière* and came to live in the lower town on the right bank of the Saône. In the 15th century, Lyon was home to large international fairs and became France's principal exchange centre. But the 18th century saw the decline of the area : it got poorer, overpopulated and, later on, the arrival of the motorcar in its narrow streets proved fatal. It wasn't until André Malraux's Law for the Protection of the Heritage that Old Lyon became France's first protected area in 1964. Today, mullion windows, towers, spiral staircases, galleries and vaulted alleyways have been restored. So, as you leave the bars or restaurants, take the time to look around you ! (see also World Heritage Site).

THE CITY IN ALL LETTERS OF THE ALPHABET

WOW ! NEW *GERLAND*

A new quarter is in the process of being born in the south of the city - *Gerland*, the municipality's second major development project. There's a difference of scale, all the same, with the "Confluence Project" (see above) on the *Presqu'île* : the project has already begun, work started this summer, and the major part will be completed in the next two years. Since this last September, Line B has connected gerland to the football stadium and the *Palais des Sports*. This new service puts the quarter within a few minutes of *Bellecour* or *Part-Dieu*, and the stops along the way have been designed to be real public areas, decorated on themes like "Invitation to Travel" or "The Fantastic Universe of the Forest". An immense, 80-hectare park, Lyon's second 'green lung' is being built. It's resolutely modern in concept, and is designed not to be looked at but to be lived in : it's the countryside in the city. The ensemble will be split into several open areas, with wide walk-gardens and a huge 10-hectare lawn. Is this paradise ? Not exactly ! The skate-park, which characterizes the 'young' philosophy prevailing in the park's design, already seems to have lead in its wings ! It was inaugurated on 13th July, after more than 20 million Francs of works and endless delays, and, already, the opinion of the young is : "*Gerland*'s useless, it's far away and you have to pay to get in... They don't understand, skateboarding means freedom, it's in the streets and on the stairways". New *Gerland*'s also a pole where grey matter is very concentrated : the university, numerous major schools and scientific laboratories, including *Mérieux*, the *CNRS* and the *INRA*. But Gerland's also the Tony Garnier Hall. Its renovation lasted a year, and it has now become a real site for shows, with accoustic, thermal and visual comfort for artists and public alike - finally worthy of a major city. It will also house exhibitions and sporting events. Finally, *Gerland*'s a real quarter for its 20 000 inhabitants : small shops, markets and numerous gardens, and nobody wants this to disappear as the result of a whirlwind of public and private investment !

CHIRAC CAME BY

From one presidency to another... In Lyon, you can make a real presidential pilgrimage. In spite of the fact that we're miles from Corrézian territory, everywhere Jacques Chirac has visited is marked and inscribed, sometimes on shiny plates. He came to eat at *Chez Léon de Lyon*, in the *Rue Pleney,* with his office colleagues : Bill, Helmut, John and the rest. That was in June 1996, during the G7 Summit. Still on the *Presqu'île*, between *"Jac... obins"* and *République*, in the shopwindow of the chocolate-maker, *La Potinière*, in the *Rue Jean de Tournes*, there's a letter from Jacques Chirac, thanking them for the delicious little chocolates. Finally, south of the *Place Bellecour* in the *Rue Sala*, Chirac's visit to the restaurant, *La Cuvée,* is immortalized by a photo. J.C. Superstar in the Capital of the Gauls.

ZOO

An institution in the institution. If the park occupies a special place, the zoo occupies two special places in the hearts of all Lyonnais. They all remember having stood as a youngster with wide-open eyes and mouth in front of the "hefalumps", the monkeys, the lions or the wolf. Obviously, once they've grown up, they begin to say, "these poor creatures would be better off at liberty". But they still return with their own kids and start to dream again. Today, more than 750 animals live here, and every internal event assumes the dimensions of Affairs of State : the death of an elephant nearly brought the flags to half-mast, and the most recent birth of a giraffe gave rise to a Christian Name Competition in the columns of a daily regional newspaper, *Le Progrès*, and replies came from well outside the department. But the fact is that the zoo is a rather sad and out-of-date spot, which is the reason why it's at the heart of a vast modernization project. The number of species represented will diminish as and when animals die, and only endangered species will be kept. Consequently, the way the zoo's set out will be completely re-thought, and attempts will be made to create a natural habitat. So, Goodbye cages and Hello African plains ! Compatible species (giraffes and zebra, for example) will be regrouped in enormous enclosures, and the animals will be able to run around – something they haven't done for a very long time ! As in the rest of the park, admission to the zoo is free.

Lyon

FOOD

◆FOOD STORES / CHOCOLATE MAKERS / CONFECTIONERS / ICE CREAM MAKERS

Chocolate makers / Confectioners

BERNACHON > 42, cours Franklin Roosevelt (6th) ℂ **04 78 24 37 98.** A 'must' in Lyon for nearly half-a-century, B*ernachon*'s a symbol of quality. Here, there's little innovation but a lot of respect for quality and taste, authenticity and selection. The cocao beans, which are roasted in the shop, come exclusively from Central America. The truffles and the *palets d'or*, which are bestsellers and as simple as they appear to be, are living proof that chocolate on its own is more than enough. No eccentricities, a touch of cinnamon and of tea in certain concoctions, and only the very best chocolate.

CHOCOLYON > 14-22, avenue Thimonier - CALUIRE ℂ **04 72 27 13 96.** This chocolate maker is hidden in the Industrial Zone. *Chocolyon* offers those who go out of their way the possibility of leaving with their arms full of all sorts of chocolates which come direct from the manufacturing workshop, having paid a price slightly lower than those charged in the city centre.

DRAGEES BENIER > 24, rue Laporte (9th) ℂ **04 78 83 27 28.** Since 1828, this family firm's been producing chocolates using nothing but traditional methods. Consequently, *Bénier*'s sugared almonds have been enjoyed at all festive occasions. It's difficult to choose between the sugared almonds (almonds from Sicily and Spain, if you please !), the chocolates (even in heart shapes and with a high cocoa content) and the pralines. In addition, you'll find *dragées aux noisettes*, fruit jellies, anis grains and, of course, sweets.

DRAGEES BLANC > 29, rue de la Thibaudière (7th) ℂ **04 78 72 31 04.** Oval and smooth, *dragées* (sugared almonds) are associated with the happy events of our life : christenings, bar-mitzvahs, weddings. *Blanc's dragées* offer a wide range of tastes and colours (chocolate, fruit nougatine) allied with considerable experience. Did you know that it takes at least 10 days to make a *dragée* ?

LEONIDAS > 40, rue du Président Edouard Herriot (1st) ℂ **04 78 30 04 70.** The famous Belgian pralines, sold in their white paper containers (from 250g to 2kg). For around 160 F a kilo, you can make your selection of Manon coffee, Manon white (with butter cream), *Lingot, Mystère, Orangette, Tutti-frutti, Napolitain, Moka, Gianduja, Princesse moulée, Princesse enrobée…* watch the weight if you eat too many. **Other addresses : 96, cours du Docteur Long (3rd) 04 78 54 65 65 • 5, place de la Croix Rousse (4th) 04 78 28 81 86 • 35, cours Franklin Roosevelt (6th) 04 78 89 00 21.**

LE PALAIS DU CHOCOLAT > 117, avenue Pierre Dumont – CRAPONNE. To work chocolate, what better than butter and fresh cream ? In this palace of chocolatey marvels, which has recnetly been completely renovated, they've understood this, so that their chocolates are softer, smoother and delicious. Since chocolate's an anti-depressant, there's no reason to deprive yourself.

RICHART DESIGN ET CHOCOLAT > 1, rue du Plat (2nd) ℂ **04 78 37 38 55.** Creative and whimsical, Michel *Richart* creates collections of chocolates like collections of designer clothes. Soft on the outside, crunchy inside, his works have wild and unexpected tastes. Astonishing designs give them colour, thanks to cocoa butter which is used like paint. Sugar's used like a spice – sparingly, so as not to destroy the taste of the cocoa.

TOURTILLER > 4, cours Franklin Roosevelt (6th) ℂ **04 78 52 20 69.** Guy *Tourtiller* has left his place to his daughter and son-in-law, so that the guard has changed in this great Lyonnais chocolate shop. For purists, the chocolate here is bitter, very bitter (up to 70% cocoa) and it's made according to the best rules. The prices are right for a relatively limited range.

VOISIN > 14, place de la Croix Rousse (4th) ℂ **04 78 27 34 32.** With shops throughout the city, gourmets can't ignore Voisin, and they may even have a shop nextdoor to them where they can go in an emergency. If they do, they'll find refined chocolates and specialities which have made the establishment's reputation : Duc de Praslin, Palets d'Or, Coussins de Lyon, crystallized fruit, packets of jellied fruit, sarments au vieux marc, pralines, chocolated filled with alcohol, truffles and confectionery. **Other addresses : 36, Grande Rue de Vaise (9th)** 04 78 83 22 50 • **24, place des Terreaux (1st)** 04 78 28 28 46 • **11, place Bellecour (2nd)** 04 78 37 79 41 • **132, boulevard de la Croix Rousse (4th)** 04 78 27 33 72 • **32, rue Grenette (2nd)** 04 78 37 55 61 • **3, cours Lafayette (6th)** 04 78 24 27 96 • **60, cours de la Liberté (3rd)** 04 78 60 60 74 • **La Part Dieu Shopping Centre (3rd)** 04 78 60 10 56 • **28, rue de la République (2nd)** 04 78 42 46 24 • **38, rue Victor Hugo (2nd)** 04 78 37 42 40 • **10, cours Vitton (6th)** 04 78 24 29 25.

WEISS > 50, rue de Brest (2nd) ℂ **04 78 38 08 88.** Weiss makes and sells delicious chocolate in discs, bars or grains. All are presented in superb brightly-coloured cardboard boxes – pink, orange, blue – which add a classy touch. Weiss promises to use in his chocolates nothing but the butter extracted from the coffee beans without the addition of other vegetable fats, and guarantees that his production contains no trace of genetically modified organisms.

XAVIER GORREL CHOCOLATIER > 7, place Xavier Ricard – SAINTE FOY LES LYON. The Gorrel family is a long history of passion, experience, gourmandise and love of the profession. Quality products in a pretty shopwindow are the expression of work well done. The chocolates are crunchy, made with milk or pure cocoa, and prepared using traditional methods, thereby ensuring a taste which will satisfy all chocolate-lovers.

Ice cream makers

ICE CREAM PARLOURS > *Open every day of the year.* This place is a 'must' for all those who like American ice cream : rich, unctuous, creamy, with chocolate nuggets, fruit sauces, bits of caramel, pecan nut… the choice is as vast as America. Others can try the alcohol-free cocktails, the waffles and the American pastries (Brownies, Cookies and Co.).

L'ARLEQUIN > 1, quai des Célestins (2nd) ℂ **04 78 37 41 80.** On the quays of the Saône, the Arlequin brasserie is also an excellent ice cream parlour. The 100 m^2 terrace, with its multi-coloured chairs and false mosaic tables, is to be found opposite the market on the Quai Saint-Antoine. The striped Italian-style awnings and the olive trees planted in terracotta pots give a Mediterranean feel. Inside, the choice of colours (yellow, orange, red, blue) create a Latin ambiance, reminding you of the Harlequin. The list of ices is long bearing in mind the low prices : between 35 F and 41 F for a superb classic, exotic or digestive bowl. For a milk shake (choice of 25 flavours), count 28 F only.

NARDONE > 3, place Ennemond Fousseret (5th) ℂ **04 78 28 29 09.** *Open everyday from March to December.* The two boutiques' terraces are both very pleasant. Aluminium chairs and tables, and sorbets and ice creams to make your mouth water. **Other address : 9, place Tobie Robatel (1st)** 04 78 27 90 28.

REGAL GLACE > 43, rue Mercière (2nd) ℂ **04 72 77 91 39.** *Open everyday from 1st April to 30th September.* Here, you feast on Italian ice creams and sorbets. Children drag their parents here by the hand, even if the parents don't need to be dragged because ice creams as good as this are good for the health – everybody knows that. **Other address : 42, cours Aristide Briand – CALUIRE** 04 78 23 09 05.

◆FOOD STORES / FINE GROCERIES

French specialities

BOCUSE ET BERNACHON > 46, cours Franklin Roosevelt (6th) ℂ **04 72 74 46 19.** Bocuse, culinary Lyonnais superstar, needs no introduction. Bernachon's his son-in-law and the two of them got together to open this superb little boutique, where salmon, foie gras, caviar and other fine produce take pride of place. To drink it down, there's a section with fine wines, rare alcohols and other little marvels.

MALLEVAL > 11, rue Emile Zola (2nd) ℰ **04 78 42 02 07.** The shop's prestigious, and the products are famous : honies of all sorts, champagne, wines and spirits from throughout France, loose tea and tea in teabags, spices, oils and vinegars – your shopping basket's quickly filled. If it's got too heavy during the visit, *Malleval* offers to deliver it to your home.

MARECHAL CENTRE – LE VILLAGE DES SAVEURS > 9, rue de la Platière (1st) ℰ **04 72 98 24 00.** *http://www.marechal-online.com.* In the city centre, 1 000 m² of fine groceries and an equally impressive range of services (open till 20.30, order by telephone, home delivery and throughout France, Wedding Lists). Incredibly fresh fruit and vegetables, the entire *Fauchon* range of products, more than 200 different sorts of beer, teas, honies, superb and aromatic cheeses…Many products can be bought in amazingly practical doses, like the little pot of fresh cream containing little more than two spoonfuls.

Foreign specialities

BAHADOURIAN SUPERMARCHE > 20, rue Villeroy (3rd) ℰ **04 78 60 32 10.** In the centre of Lyon, offer yourself a trip to the East. You're served by an army of staff, all and always smiling. The multitude of spices, olives and dried fruit are a delight for the eye and the the nose. In the catering section, there are some delicious specialities (beurek, keufté, pastilla). You'll find fresh and dried produce as well as cooking utensils from round the world which you'll never find elsewhere.

MARKS AND SPENCER > "La Part Dieu" Shopping Centre- Level 3 (3rd) ℰ **04 72 84 42 60.** Great Britain and its gastronomy, which are often unjustly misunderstood, hide some priceless treasures : Salt and Vinegar Crisps which sting the tongue deliciously, crumpets, muffins, scones, small and very English rolls to be eaten toated with fresh butter, teas in teabags or loose in pretty tin boxes, Lemon Curd jam, Christmas puddings which weigh at least 10 kilos and which keep for months, and psychedelically-coloured sweets which stick to the teeth. In the Fresh Food section, you'll find the famous triangular sandwiches, made with fresh bread delivered everyday direct from England, ready-cooked Indian dishes, coleslaw, fresh fruit juice and everything you need to prepare a quick snack between midday and two.

SAVEURS ET CONTINENTS > 6, rue Petit David (2nd) ℰ **04 72 41 83 05.** A pretty boutique proposing a culinary trip round the world without obliging you to empty your bank account. Some 20 countries are represented. A quasi-exclusivity in Lyon - the bagels Americans adore, and small, soft rolls to eat as brunch or with your aperitif : natural, with sesame seeds, with onion, with blueberry, cinnamon or banana.

◆ FOOD / CHEESEMONGERS

ALAIN MARTINET > 102, cours Lafayette (3rd) ℰ **04 78 95 44 20.** Cheese-lovers rush to Alain Martinet who, like all good cheesemongers, knows that, from January to March, it's *Tomme de Savoie, Vacherin, Beaufort, Comté* and blue cheeses, whilst goat's cheeses are at their best till October. In summer, don't forget to order a *Reblochon*. Alain Martinet knows a lot about the cheeses he delivers to his customers, and he's both courteous and highly professional. Pity that these succulent cheeses are so expensive.

CELLERIER HALLE > 102, cours Lafayette (3rd) ℰ **04 78 62 37 75.** A quality cheesemonger's in the market in the 3rd arrondissement. It offers cheeses from throughout the region, the department and, indeed, from throughout France. Céllerier prepares beautiful cheese platters, which he carefully arranges and decorates so that they're as beautiful as they are delicious.

RENEE & RENEE RICHARD > 102, cours Lafayette (3rd) ℰ **04 78 62 30 78.** If you come to Lyon, you have to visit the two Renées. Their *Saint Marcellin* has become a real star, and you'll find it, quite rightly, in all fine restaurants, both in the region and well outside. Rich, creamy, unctuous, tasty – when you taste it, you understand why it's so popular.

◆FOOD / FISHMONGERS

BOZZO > 1, rue d'Austerlitz (4th) ✆ **04 78 28 22 02.** Salmon, cod, tuna, sole, ray, mussels, oysters, trout... they're all to be found at Bozzo's. This fishmonger's real name is Georges Maury and what he offers is fresh and tasty.

CARREFOUR > "Le Pérollier" Shopping Centre - ECULLY ✆ **04 72 86 19 00.** Here, you'll find fish stalls selling fish on shiny chrome tables, generally next to fresh fruit and veg stalls. The fish is washed down with fresh water throughout the day and is sold as rapidly as in the best shellfish markets. There's fish, shellfish and, just opposite, a shop selling bread, butter, lemons and tarama for a 'marine starter'. **Other address : Shopping Centre "la Part-Dieu" (3rd) 04 72 60 61 62.**

GOGUILLOT > 102, cours Lafayette (3rd) ✆ **04 78 62 35 71.** When you visit Les Halles (the covered market), it's best to come with no fixed dish in mind. This fish stall, which has tons of mussels, turbots, sea bream and shellfish, is a real inspiration for a cook who's run out of ideas. The fishmonger gives advice about recipes, cooking times and things to eat and drink with the fish.

MERLE > 102, cours Lafayette (3rd) ✆ **04 78 62 30 29.** To be found in the Lyon Halles (covered market), Merle does everything possible to satisfy his clients. The love of the profession and of shellfish – that's Alain Merle's creed, and he looks for the best produce from oyster farmers, pampers his customers, gives long explanations about his produce and concocts fabulous, fresh seafood platters.

◆FOOD / PATISSERIES AND TEA ROOMS

BERNACHON PASSION > 46, cours Franklin Roosevelt (6th) ✆ **04 72 74 46 19.** Bernachon has a passion for chocolate, cakes, confectionery and other delicacies which are high in calories but really delicious.

VITAL ET JEAN PAUL PIGNOL > 17, rue Emile Zola (2nd) ✆ **04 78 37 39 61.** This patisserie, which is as chic as they come, is also a tea room and is ideal for an endless chat among friends or for inviting the grandmother to nibble a few tarts or cakes made with chocolate, crunchy nougatine, fruit or almond paste.

◆FOOD / WINES AND SPIRITS

Home delivery

MARECHAL – LE VILLAGE DES SAVEURS > 9 rue de la Platière (1st) ✆ **04 72 98 24 00.** Maréchal offers wine-lovers the best wines from all countries (Argentina, the United States, Hungary, Portugal), as well as everything France has to offer by way of wine, and God knows there's a lot of it. Burgundy, Bordeaux, Alsace - more than 200 sorts of beers and 160 champagnes from 65 F. Wine-lovers get advice from the sommelier (wine steward) on how long to lay down their precious bottles, whilst cooks will be interested in knowing the best wines to serve with their recipes. You get excellent advice and service as well as an enormous range of wines, tools and accessories for optimum conservation and tasting : identification collars to recognize your best wines, cellar books for those with large cellars, corkscrews, appropriate carafes for different wines depending on their age, and glasses from all regions so that each wine has the glass it deserves. **Other addresses : 17, rue de la Charité (2nd) 04 78 42 26 05 • 98, rue Duguesclin (3rd) 04 78 93 45 60 • Halles de Lyon (1st), 102, cours Lafayette (3rd) 04 78 62 33 28 • 17, Grande Rue de la Croix-Rousse (4th) 04 78 28 64 79.**

NICOLAS > 1, rue du Président Edouard Herriot (2nd) ✆ **04 78 29 85 87.** *Internet : http://www.nicolas.tm.fr.* Nicolas is easily recognizable, with its yellow and bordeaux awning and its low-priced bottles with colourful labels. The dynamic sales team knows how to suggest the wine which is the best adapted to such and such a dish, and the services offered are multiple : delivery, gift wrapping, bottle-personalization, chilled champagne for an intimate evening, business presents...Spend the the pretty sum of 1300 F and the bottles can be

delivered to your home. **Other addresses : 7, place de la Croix Rousse (4th) 04 78 39 80 60 •
17, cours Vitton (6th) 04 78 89 92 45 • 12, rue de l'ancienne Préfecture (2nd) 04 78 42 28 85
• 9, rue Victor Hugo (2nd) 04 78 37 27 77 • 102, cours Lafayette (3rd) 04 78 62 32 73.**

In the shops

LA VIEILLE RESERVE > 1, place Tobie Robatel (1st) ℭ **04 78 28 69 98.** Since 1929, L*a Vieille
Réserve* has been working with wines and alcohols of all sorts. These lovely boutiques,
decorated in shiny wood and selling all sorts of wines beautifully set out by section, are run by
the pleasant Morel Father and Son, Alain and Fabrice, who are only too happy to let you
discover their best selection of fine wines, champagnes and rare alcohols. **Other address :
59, avenue Foch (6th) 04 78 89 15 17.**

MALLEVAL > 11, rue Emile Zola (2nd) ℭ **04 78 42 02 07.** The boutique's superb and looks
like the cellars you find on winemaking estates. Here, they sell wines from all over France at
all prices, but there's also a large selection of champagnes and spirits, classic or unusual
liqueurs, whiskies which are as old as Herod, rare armagnacs, and even cakes and sweet and
savoury delicacies to accompany all this alcohol : Breton butter *galettes*, macaroons with
vanilla or coffee, cheese cigarettes.

A LITTLE TOUR OF *LES HALLES* (THE COVERED MARKET)

At N° 102, *Cours Lafayette*, there's a large building which is, admittedly, rather ugly but
which hides a thousand and one marvels for lovers of good food, fresh produce and
friendly conversation. Here, more than 600 tradesmen supply Lyon's restaurateurs and
others on the look-out for fresh produce. At the entrance, a map of the market points
out all the stalls. The atmosphere's relaxed, jovial and amazingly young. Shopowners
hail passers-by, proposing a warm loaf, an excellent dried sausage or fresh and juicy
fruit. The key words are quality and professionalism. Housewives ask advice and
religiously listen to ideas about what to eat with what ; they know that, here, they can't
go wrong. It's simple – in *Les Halles*, you find everything because the whole of
gastronomic Europe's represented. *Roberto* makes fresh, Italian pasta ; *La Caféone* sells
coffee which is roasted on the spot, jams and fine chocolate from round the world ;
Bahadourian, Ciao-Ciao, Marinette and a few others have shelves full of all the exotic
produce you can dream of. Each shop's specialized, but that doesn't prevent it from
selling other things : a *charcutier* - caterer proposes Ninkasi beer, olive oil sits
alongside cheeses, and hams and pork produce are hung above dressed salads. At Chez
Georges, people line the bar to taste whelks, shellfish and oysters which have just been
opened, accompanied by a glass of wine, a good slice of bread and a thick layer of
butter. Having filled your shopping basket with ultra-fresh fruit and vegetables, a
bouquet of flowers, beautiful, smelly cheese and some good bottles of wine, go to the
"Fer à cheval" and stand at the bar for a coffee, a small glass of white wine and prolong
your stroll in this incredibly lively place.

◆ THE MARKETS

Food markets

THE QUAI SAINT-ANTOINE MARKET > Quai Célestin/Quai St Antoine (2nd). *From Tuesday to
Friday from 07.30 to 12.30, on Saturdays and Sundays from 07.30 to 12.00.* In this large and lively
market, you'll sometimes bang into famous restaurateurs who've come to choose their
vegetables themselves. Between two purchases, shoppers stop at a bar for a coffee or a glass
of dry white wine accompanied by a piece of cheese bought at the stand opposite..

HALLES DE LYON > 102, cours Lafayette (3rd). *From Tuesday to Thursday from 07.00 to 12.30
and from 15.00 to 19.00. On Fridays from 07.00 to 19.00. On Sundays from 07.00 to 14.00.
Tastings and restaurants from Monday to Saturday from 08.00 to 22.30, on Sundays from 08.00 to
14.00.* High-quality and various produce in a friendly and family atmosphere, with an
impressive number of stands. If you spend 100 F or more, stallowners contribute to the cost of
your car park ticket – all you have to do is ask them.

THE QUAI AUGAGNEUR MARKET > **Quai Victor Augagneur (3rd).** *Every Wednesday and Saturday morning.* A lively and colourful market, where young 'Sloane' mothers from the 6th arrondissement, loaded up with children and baskets, mix with Lyonnaise grandmas and veiled women from the 7th arrondissement. On Sunday mornings, the market has additional stalls selling manufactured products.

THE CROIX-ROUSSE MARKET > **Boulevard de la Croix-Rousse (4th).** *From Tuesday to Sunday from 08.00 to 12.00. Tuesday mornings : Itinerant Market. Saturday mornings : Bio market.* The market stretches along the boulevard, and then turns into the little Place de la Croix-Rousse (Croix-Rousse Square). Local inhabitants adore their market and find no need "to go down into town". We perfectly understand them – it's really pleasant to stroll between stalls and to bang into the personalities in the Croix-Rousse.

BEAUTY

◆ BEAUTY / HAIRDRESSERS

VERT TENDRE > **166, avenue des Frères Lumières (8th)** ✆ **04 78 01 75 45.** A terrified child, screaming and struggling as the hairdresser's scissors approach – this is a scene you put away into a cupboard, thanks to this clever hairdresser's which is rather like a colourful games room. For the last 13 years, and since *Vert Tendre* has existed, the haidresser's work is made easier by the cartoon books and video games in the salon. Kids are hypnotized by them and make not a sound as their hair is cut.

For men

LES INCORRUPTIBLES > **1, rue Montcharmont (2nd)** ✆ **04 78 42 76 18.** The tariffs are worthy of an Al Capone racket, but the old-fashioned setting's magnificent, the service is rapid and professional, and the hair cuts are well done. So, why not once in a while ?

LINECOL BARBER > **63, rue Mercière (2nd)** ✆ **04 78 37 51 45.** The old-fashioned décor of an American barber (English high chairs, bought in antique stalls by Evelyne) where the man who takes care of his appearance and who likes his comfort puts himself into the expert hands of a team devoted to doing everything for him : an excellent haircut, a shave in the purest of traditions (cut-throat razor and hot towel), a facial massage and a manicure.

For all

AFRO'STYL > **8, rue d'Algérie (1st)** ✆ **04 78 27 20 69.** Ladies and Gentlemen, if you come here with short hair (3 to 6 cm minimum, we didn't say scalped !), you can leave a while later with 20 to 80 cm more of *real* hair - and the result looks absolutely genuine. Here, everything's possible, whether you want colour, volume, straight or curly hair, small or large curls.

JACQUES DESSANGE > **25, rue Jarente (2nd)** ✆ **04 78 42 99 11.** One of France's most famous hairdressers and a specialist in blondes (but all others are welcome) proposes cuts which are always inventive, a superior-quality service, varied treatment including manicures, face treatment and make-up, and prices which are higher than average but fully justified. **Other addresses : 1, rue Grenette (2nd) 04 78 42 96 08 • Place du Maréchal Lyautey (6th) 04 78 24 47 13.**

JEAN MARIE GAVET > **21, place de la Croix-Rousse (4th)** ✆ **04 78 28 06 58.** In a resolutely modern salon, which is both warm and inviting, Jean-Marie and his team wield the scissors with incredible dexterity and give their clients a style and look which are always a success. Their success probably resides in the fact that they really listen to what their clients want as well as in the judicious advice they give about styles and colourings. The prices are a hair-width higher than in the salons which are part of hairdressing chains, but they're justified by the very personalized service. **Other address : 50, avenue du Point du Jour (9th) 04 72 42 04 14.**

PIERRE CHAMBORD > 9, rue du Bât d'argent (1st) ☏ **04 78 28 32 12.** In an attractive and bright salon, Pierre *Chambord* and his team welcome you with a smile and chat about everything and anything. They listen, find out what their clients want, and carry out their wishes with dexterity. Everyone leaves delighted with the service and with so much friendly courtesy.

◆ BEAUTY / INSTITUTES AND SHOPS

CAPITAL BEAUTE > 13ter, place Jules Ferry (6th) ☏ **04 72 74 07 07.** An institute-flat of 100 m², with 7 treatment rooms for men and women : traditional and laser hair removal, permanent make-up, treatment for the face and body, manicure and foot care, false nails… and we've saved the best for the end – Shiatsu, Japanese massage. Natural products are used and treatment's personalized in function of personality, skin-type, age and the season. You feel listened to, advised and understood for everything to do with little skin problems. We bet that, after a Shiatsu session, many will discover a passion for this ancestral method which increases vitality and physical and psychological balance. **Other address :10, rue d'Austerlitz (4th) 04 78 30 04 00.**

CHRISTIAN DRILLEN > 8, cours Lafayette (3rd) ☏ **04 78 71 07 12.** For all panther-women or Cruella who dream of steel claws for an evening, a day or forever, Christian Drillen fulfills their wish by putting on false nails which are as real as life, as tough as diamonds, and which stay in place thanks to an ultra-efficient hardening gel. The answer to bitten or boken nails is a manicure performed by a professional. While you're here, you can also have your feet looked after. **Other address : 13, cours Franklin Roosevelt (6th) 04 78 93 60 66.**

INSTITUT DERMO-ESTHETIQUE REINE > 106, rue du Président Edouard Herriot (2nd) ☏ **04 78 37 77 53.** The woman (or man) who pushes open the door of this institute immediately feels royally welcomed by a very professional team. For the last 40 years, Reine has offered every imaginable beauty care for the skin, the body and the face, so you know you're in expert hands. The speciality's 'fundamental everlashing' – a permanent make-up to retrace the eyebrows and the shape of the lips, so that every face is harmonious. Among the other treatments on offer – whole-body peeling, treatment for heavy legs, breast-firming, manicure, pedicure, make-up, look-counselling and acne treatment. Let yourself go in a dream décor ! **Other addresses : 8, rue de la Barre (2nd) 04 78 37 06 83 • 44, rue Villon (8th) 04 78 00 86 47.**

MAC > 89, rue Edouard Herriot (2nd) ☏ **04 72 41 71 56.** The in-crowd's favourite make-up establishment has just opened a large boutique in Lyon, where you can listen to techno music as you're looked after. The salesgirls/make-up specialists help you to choose among all the lipstick colours, blushes, powders and shades, and make you up very gently. You'll leave made up like a real pin-up and not like a stolen car.

◆ BEAUTY / PERFUMERIES

BAISER SAUVAGE (WILD KISS) > 37, rue de la République (2nd) ☏ **04 78 37 01 72.** An immense perfumery with a décor which is, indeed, wild because of the presence of a number of tropical trees. The perfumes are at the shop entrance, set out by brand and type, men's on one side, women's on the other – watched over by attentive and impressive doormen. At the bottom of the shop, you'll find beauty products for the face, the body and the hair, as well as all the best-known brands of makeup. In the middle, there's a section for cheaper products, like Bourjois, L'Oréal or Nivea. Salesgirls with white gloves advise the clintèle and answer all questions you may have to ask as politely as can be. There's an impressive section of stockings, socks tights and suspender-belts. **Other addresses : 17, rue du Docteur Bouchut (3rd) 04 72 84 90 65 • 4, place des Jacobins (2nd) 04 78 37 45 73.**

LES HUILES ESSENTIELLES > 10, rue d'Austerlitz (4th) ☏ **04 78 87 04 75.** With years of experience in the Drôme Provençale region, these professionals decided to open a boutique in Lyon. You'll find incense sticks for the garden (ideal for repelling insects without suffocating yourself – lavender, geranium, citronella) sold by the unit, Merlin lamps (shaped like a pointed cone – hence their name, perhaps ?) in which you burn a natural and delicately-perfumed Cade powder (which brings the smell of the garrigues into your house and, legend has it, chases away the witches), paper from Armenia whose effectiveness has been proved and the famous 100% pure and natural oils which are used in aromatherapy and are marvellous for the health and the well-being. Another style of living ? It's a bit that, or, at least another way of looking at life. What's more, here, they take their time to listen, explain and politely inform with simplicity, calm and serenity – and that's, perhaps, the essential thing.

Piercing Tatoo

MARQUIS > 22, rue Terme (1st) ℂ **04 78 39 72 38.** The Marquis (de Sade ?) pierces the skin or colours it - depending on what you want, and always with your agreement. We're talking about piercing and tattooing – in perfect security, of course, since all instruments are carefully cleaned and disinfected following the rules of the art. The operation remains painful (you wanted it !), but the result's worth it because the Marquis is a dexterous artist with unlimited imagination. You'll also find rare and astonishing books and videos on subjects as various as sculpture, photography and French Cinema.

PRESENTS

◆PRESENTS / JEWELLERY

Jewellers

AUGIS > 32, rue de la République (2nd) ℂ **04 72 41 18 30.** Since 1830, this highly-reputed (and justifiably so) jeweller has been making the hearts of jewel-lovers beat rapidly. It's one of Lyon's oldest institutions and, at the age of 170, continues to produce marvellous creations (rings from 2000 F), and also sells jewellery made by famous brands, like Gucci, Poiray, Cartier, Chanel, Chaumet and Rolex. The reception's incredible and the advice, informed and professional.

BIJOUTERIE KORLOFF > 12, rue de la République (1st) ℂ **04 72 68 05 25.** A little anecdote – this jeweller's name comes from a famous 88 carat diamond, the *"Black Korloff"*, which was named as a tribute to a noble Russian family. A creator and jewellery-maker, Korloff is distinguishable by its inimitable style, which is very classy, pure and inventive at the same time, and which harmoniously combines diamonds and other precious stones with coloured laquers. It puts its signature on a range of high-quality products, including watches and jewellery, but also pens, glasses and perfumes. **Other address : 32, avenue Foch (6th) 04 78 17 39 55.**

CARTIER > 101, rue du Président Edouard Herriot (2nd) ℂ **04 78 38 11 08.** *Internet : www.cartier.com.* A jeweller and watchmaker since 1847, Cartier has largely deserved its reputation as an international reference. Its *"Must"* range and its three bands (rings and bracelets) have become classics. Purity and beauty – aren't these the very essence of a jewel ?

HENRI GAREL JOAILLIER > 15, rue Emile Zola (2nd) ℂ **04 78 42 41 10.** The Henri Garel boutiques can help you, dear husbands, to find the right inspiration for your darling wives' next birthday. They adore the madly modern creations exhibited here – beautifully-matched stones and gold, brilliant rings, silver items, too... and if you hesitate too long, the sales staff will be delighted to guide you in your choice. **Other addresses : Le Pérollier Shopping Centre - ECULLY 04 78 33 52 85 • "Saint-Genis II" Shopping Centre- SAINT-GENIS-LAVAL 04 78 56 45 04.**

When you're the jeweller

KAHOKIA CREATIONS > 7, rue Juiverie (5th) ℂ **04 78 28 52 07.** In this warm and intimate boutique-workshop, Elsa Somano works pearls and wire in front of you. With so little, she creates jewels, lamps, lightshades and mobile sculptures which are as ravishing as they are original. Tell her what you want by way of a jewel and she'll make it.

LA DROGUERIE > 12, rue de la Monnaie (2nd) ℂ **04 78 42 37 71.** Hundreds of pearls, pastes and trinkets…a load of ideas you can pinch in this shop to transform an old-fashioned bag, an old scarf or a spangled, flowery or feathered marvel. Be patient as you wait till a salesgirl is (finally) available and counts the pearls, cuts the ribbons and dispenses her precious advice.

Lyon *Presents - Jewellery*

Watch specialists

J. L. MAIER HAUTE HORLOGERIE > 91, rue du Président Edouard Herriot (2nd)
℗ **04 78 42 08 81.** When Time and luxury are united, that gives, among other things, perfect, bevelled watches decorated with diamonds, like the *Diamond Watch* by *Boucheron.* You'll also find *Rolex, Jaeger Lecoutre, Piaget, Tag Heuer, Breitling, Cartier, Beaumet Mercier* and many others.

SWATCH STORE > 105, rue du Président Edouard Herriot, Lyon (2nd)
℗ **04 72 40 96 03.** The shp alone is worth a look : a small, very blue and ultra-modern boutique, with a play of mirrors on the ceiling, TV screens and the now famous Swiss watches, from 160 F to 550 F. You'll find the "*Classic*" range, but also the "*Irony*", "*Scuba*" and "*Skin*" (so thin, you can hardly feel them on your skin) models.

Fantasy

AGATHA > 4, rue Emile Zola (2e)
℗ **04 78 92 90 26.** This brand isn't just to be seen on grandmothers. A lot, an enormous amount of jewellery is on display in the shpwindow, on the walls, on the salesgirls. Large silver or gold chain bracelets, discreet or monumental necklaces, earrings for Stars… The famous dog, which is the brand's mascot, is never very far away… attached to a bracelet, on a watch face or hanging from the ears. If you don't like the animal, walk on by.

BICHE DE BERE > 38, rue Edouard Herriot (1st)
℗ **04 72 00 09 00.** Nelly *Biche de Bère* learnt industrial design before creating jewels, bags and even futurist dresses. In a large, beautiful and very 'design' boutique, where pride of place is given to her own creations, pearl or pewter necklaces and multi-stone bracelets are distinguishable from a thousand and one others by their modernity.

REMINISCENCE > 33, rue du président Edouard Herriot (2nd)
℗ **04 72 77 58 64.** In this pretty little shop, there's all sorts of jewellery : from the simplest (silver ring, paste earrings) to the most sophisticated (necklace sets worthy of Scheherezade, large rings, Baroque bracelets). Every year there are collections, all of which are faithful to the brand's image without, for as much, resembling one another. Réminiscence is also prefume : "*Rem*", which reminds you of the holidays, the famous "*Patchouli*", or sweet and tender musk which has been lovingly worn by women for 2000 years.

Old jewellery

BIJOUTERIE GEMME > 4, cours Lafayette (3rd)
℗ **04 78 60 55 33.** A specialist in second-hand jewellery, the jeweller, Gemme, is a real goldmine. For example, the plain ring in white gold set with a diamond is sold for 13 000 F instead of the 35 000 F it costs new. Ideal for those who need to save or who, quite simply, feel like a change. Prestigious watches - *Cartier, Rolex, Hermès* - are also sold at around half-price.

CRESUS > 1, rue Emile Zola (2nd)
℗ **04 78 42 72 15.** Purchase and sales of chronometers, prestigious watches, ancient jewellery, diamonds, precious stones, from 30% to 60% less expensive than on the new market. More than 100 watches in stock (*Rolex, Cartier, Jaeger Lecoutre, Hermès, Breitling*) ans jewellery signed by the most famous jewellers.

JOHN NATHAN > 10, rue de la République (1st)
℗ **04 78 28 17 49.** New and second-hand jewellery, between 30% and 50% less expensive – that's enough to give ideas to fathers for Mother's Day or to those paralyzed with love. Lovers can offer their future wives a second-hand watch in excellent condition, like the brands Ebel or Breitling.. John Nathan repairs and re-works gold, silver and precious metal and pays cash (and the best prices) for gold ingots or coins, diamonds and precious stones. **Other address : 58, cours Vitton (6th) 04 78 52 85 52.**

◆ PRESENTS / FLOWERS

AU NOM DE LA ROSE > 4, rue Childebert (2nd)
℗ **04 72 41 86 66.** Who would have believed that there are so many different varieties of rose ? Madame Hazot and her team will give you the demonstration. Here, roses are roses, of course, but they're also red, white, yellow, orange, multi-coloured… Among the sweetest-smelling are roses from Provence, whilst roses from Ecuador can be kept for an incredibly long time. For those unforgettable events, this charming team prepares decorations for birthdays, weddings, receptions, cocktail parties and anniversaries.

JACQUES HAFFNER > 12, quai Saint Antoine (2nd) ℭ **04 72 77 64 05.** The most famous florist in Lyon, the one who composes dozens of wedding bouquets every year, the one who decorates hundreds of official soirées and cocktail parties, the one, too, who prepares prepares pretty bouquets and floral compositions, some simple and spring-like, others much more sophisticated, in his beautiful green shop on the *Quai Saint-Antoine.*

LA VILLA BORGHESE > 6, place Saint Nizier (2nd) ℭ **04 78 42 76 27.** La Villa Borghèse offers a charming mixture of floral compositions and leaves to create superb decorations which change with the seasons, or even to decorate a hat. As little presents - loads of little characters, angels or fairies and perfumes for ambiance.

◆ PRESENTS / GADGETS

LA BOUTIQUE DE L'HOMME MODERNE > 15, rue de la République (1st) ℭ **04 72 00 05 05.** Modern Man loves his car as much as his wife and wants both to shine with a thousand and one lights (*Nenette* cream for the machine, brooch for *madame*). He's also an overgrown child who plays with the "space-mask to talk like a robot" and the electronic flipper. A DIY man (tool box), an adventurer (knife, compass) or a man who likes a scrap (Napoleonic pistol) – they'll all find useful gadgets here.

LA SOURIS PAPIVORE > 21, rue Chavanne (1st) ℭ **04 78 28 59 18.** This pretty boutique will make you forget the time when exercise books were for library bookworms. Here, you'll find lovely notebooks, cardboard boxes, paper napkins, albums, and an entire collection of candles.

LE DOMAINE DES AROMES > 3,rue Emile Zola (1st) ℭ **04 78 38 23 11.** Candles, incense, pots-pourris and lamps will make you forget that, yesterday, you had a raclette party in your flat. This is the domain of aromas, allowing you to get rid of nasty, lingering, little smells and replace them forever with the smell of roses, pine or nutmeg. Pamper your body (and your soul) with aromatherapy by rubbing yourself down with essential plant oils. There are also soaps, lotions, creams and 100% natural flower-scented water.

LYON STYLO > 26, rue Victor Hugo (2nd) ℭ **04 78 37 68 42.** *Internet : www.lyonstylo.com.* For yourself or as a gift, superb, ball-point pens which are as precious as jewels and which you'll keep all your life. Amusing pens in modern materials, but also ink pens, felt-tips and pencils as well as attractive diaries, notebooks and, of course, all sorts of ink bottles and re-fills.

MASCULIN COMPOSE > 2, rue Grenette (2nd) ℭ **04 78 37 47 59.** In an amusing cartoon-book décor, you'll find your favourite characters : Tintin, Milou and their red rocket, the entire Simpson family, Gaston Lagaffe and Lucky Luke, Mickey and Minnie Mouse and the rest of the Disney band... all as real as life.

PLANET O. L. > Rue Grolée (2nd) ℭ **04 78 37 49 49.** Before going to the football stadium to support his favourite team, no self-respecting supporter forgets to come to buy his ticket in this enormous boutique. It's devoted exclusively to *Olympique Lyonnais* scarves, tee-shirts, caps, sweat-shirts, but also photos, cards, lighters and banners.

◆ PRESENTS / FABRICS AND MATERIALS

LA BOUTIQUE DES SOYEUX LYONNAIS > 33, rue Romarin (1st) ℭ **04 78 39 96 67.** The mannequins in the shopwindow are draped in magnificent fabrics which are worthy of the Lyonnais silk tradition. Materials are sold by the metre or the portion, and the silk is shot, refined, colourful or in more classic hues. Those who know how to wield scissors will find everything they want to make an evening- or a wedding dress.

LA MAISON DES CANUTS > 12, rue d'Ivry (4th) ℭ **04 78 28 62 04.** Whilst you're in Lyon, why not buy for your favourite great-aunt Dorothy a scarf with a hand-painted picture of the horse in the *Place Bellecour* or of the buildings in the city ? Here, there's a wide choice of hand-painted articles in pure silk. Scarves, stoles, shawls, ties, bowties – there's something for every taste, for all ages and in all styles.

CULTURE

◆ART AND TRIAL CINEMAS

CNP TERREAUX > 40, rue président Herriot (1st) ℭ **08 36 68 69 33.** Films in the original version only with, in the entrance hall, criticisms taken from reference daily papers and reviews. Seats 45 F or 34 F for reduced rate. **Other addresses : Bellecour - 12, rue de la Barre (2nd) • Odéon - 6, rue Grolée (2nd)   Unique number : 08 36 68 69 33.**

L'INSTITUT LUMIERE > 25, rue du Premier Film (8th) ℭ **04 78 78 18 95.** Before, the cinema wasn't bad although it was small. Today, the new cinema, built on the site of the Lumière Brothers Factory, is worthy of so-called 'commercial cinemas'. Large screen, hyper-comfortable seats, digital sound… It's the only cinema of its type which was paid for out of public funds. Prices are reasonable, and the programme allows you to see (or see again) the old classics, and even follow cycles based on such and such an author. In addition, every entrance and exit is an emotion in itself, since you're going to a place where the first films in history were made. At that time, the cinema used to be the exit from the film studios which was reserved for the factory workers, so it's almost the hangar where the first films were shot.

◆CULTURE / READING

General bookshops

DECITRE > 6, place Bellecour (2e) ℭ **04 72 40 54 54.** A large bookshop, with an intimate atmosphere and organized into several 'universes', thereby allowing you to find what you want more easily. Everything's clearly visible, shelves are easy to get to, and sections are clearly marked and well-stocked, so that you can save time. In the 'Nature' section, gardening books are to be found next to books on sport and dietetic food. In the 'Cartoon' section, all the cartoon books are well within children's reach. There's also a 'Psychology' section, with family-style works as well as more specialized manuals for teachers and students. **Other addresses : 29, place Bellecour (2nd) 04 72 40 54 54 • "Le Pérollier" Shopping Centre – ECULLY 04 72 18 75 40 • 43, boulevard du 11 Novembre 1918 – VILLEURBANNE 04 72 44 93 92.**

FLAMMARION > 19, place Bellecour (2nd) ℭ **04 72 56 21 21.** The *Flammarion* shop is at the corner of the *Place Bellecour* and is split over several floors. At the entrance, you'll find latest publications, novels and political works. Upstairs, the pocketbook section is pleasant and if, in spite of the excellent lay-out, you can't find what you're looking for, a smiling salesman will come to your rescue. Specialized books are grouped according to theme and set out in different alleys. There's a large section for stationery, pens and cards, with excellent ideas for presents at low prices. The shop's pleasant, bright, relatively quiet and encourages you to dawdle.

FNAC > 85, rue de la République (2nd) ℭ **04 72 40 49 49.** *Internet : www.fnac.fr - Minitel : 3615 FNAC.* The *Fnac* in the *Place Bellecour* had a face-lift last year. Those who grumbled during the works in their favourite shop haven't been disappointed by the result. The shop's superb, large, bright and spacious, now that it's pinched a few dozen square metres from the neighbouring building. You find everything, absolutely everything – books, records, DVD's, CD Roms, hi-fi material, video and computer equipment, cameras and even tickets for the next Madonna concert in the concert-ticket section. Books and discs are classified by type, and current bestsellers are clearly visible so that you have no problem finding them. If what you're looking for isn't on the shelves, they'll be delighted to order it for you and will inform you by letter as soon as it arrives in the shop. The *Fnac* regularly organizes photo exhibitions in its shops, and numerous musicians come to play in front of their public and to promote their latest album. **Other address : "La Part Dieu" Shopping Centre –Level 2 (3rd) 04 78 71 87 00.**

VIRGIN MEGASTORE > 43, rue du Président Edouard-Herriot ℭ **04 78 92 61 61.** Virgin has opened a second store in Lyon, after the store in *Part-Dieu*. The one in the city centre's large and airy, enjoys an exceptional location in a building which has been carefully decorated in Virgin's colours (red and black) and was inaugurated by the eccentric Richard Branson himself. 2 000 m² of sales space is open to the public, with, on the groundfloor, DVD's and videos ; on the 1st floor, books and, on the 2nd floor, an immense collection of the product which made the store's reputation – records. There are good promotions and special offers throughout the year. For example, you can pay for your records with Virgin Cola bottle-tops, and, during the Music Festival, no VAT is charged.

Specialised bookshops

RACONTE MOI LA TERRE > Corner of rue Thomassin and rue Grolée (2nd) ℰ **04 78 92 60 20.** *Internet : www.raconte-moi.com - E-mail : bienvenue@raconte-moi.com.* At the heart of the 'Travel Agents Quarter', this multi-media bookshop invites you to leave on a discovery trip of the world. Tourist guides, maps for your next trip, foreign recipes, photo and rambling books, novels, CD Rom's, videos, CD's – whatever you're looking for to go on holiday or to get away from your settee is to be found on this attractive bookshop's shelves. The bookshop's also a cyber-bar, and the Mundo Café proposes Dishes of the Day, snacks and all sorts of international food and drink and allows you to surf on the Internet by proposing a selection of the best sites devoted to travel. Evey month, there are slide-conferences, meetings with writers or explorers, concerts of music from round the world and art and photography exhibitions. Just to make everything perfect, the reception is both efficient and friendly.

◆ CULTURE / MUSEUMS

CATHEDRALE SAINT JEAN > Place Saint-Jean (5th) ℰ **04 78 92 82 29.** *Open everyday except on Sundays and Mondays, from 10.00 to 12.00 and from 14.00 to 18.00, on Saturdays from 10.00 to 12.00 and from 14.00 to 19.00.* The commented visit of Saint John's Cathedral allows you to discover the treasures within its walls. Assembled in the 19th century by Cardinals Fesch and Bonald, the cathedral collection includes a multitude of splendid objects from the Byzantine period to the 19th century : liturgical garments and tapestries, silverwork, enamelwork and stained glass make you realize to what extent art and ecclesiastical objects were intimately related.

FONDATION FOURVIERE > 8, place de Fourvière (5th) ℰ **04 78 25 13 01.** *Visits everyday at 14.30 and 16.00. Normal rate : 25 F. reduced rate 15 F. Groups limited to 20 people.* This foundation, whose principal role is to exhibit our beautiful city's known or hidden treasures, received the Tourist Trophy in 2000 and lets everyone discover the historical site of Lyon from the roofs of the *Fourvière* Basilica. It's an unusual and instructive visit. Everyday at 14.30 and 16.00, rendez-vous is given at the top of the stairs leading from the square to the cathedral for 1h15 of visit. Visits begin with with the *Grande Tribune* and continue to the *Atelier des Architectes* (Architects' Workshop), the Angels' Gallery, the attics, the basilica's battlements and the *Terrasse Saint-Michel,* which is normally closed to the public, and finish in beauty in the Observatory Tower from where the view of Lyon is splendid.

L'ATELIER DE SOIERIE > 33, rue Romarin (1st) ℰ **04 72 07 97 83.** Lyon, a silk city since the 16th century, houses in the heart of the 1st *arrondissement* this superb silk workshop which is still operational. During the visit, all stages of silk printing are minutely explained with the help of demonstrations.

Lyon *Culture - Museums*

Techniques have remained unchanged since the 'grand era', and printing is made using craft techniques which could be called artistic because the result is astonishingly fine, delicate and tasteful. At the end of the visit, it's difficult not to crack in the boutique and offer yourself scarves, stoles, shawls or ties.

L'INSTITUT LUMIERE POUR LE CINEMA ET L'AUDIOVISUEL > 25, rue du Premier Film (8th) © **04 78 78 18 95.** *Open from Monday to Friday from 09.00 to 13.00 and from 14.00 to 18.30. On Saturdays, Sundays and Public Holidays from 14.00 to 18.30. Normal rate : 25 F. rate for students, the unemployed and senior citizens : 20 F. Cinema hall, shows at 18.00, 20.00 and 22.00. Normal rate : 35 F. reduced rate : 29 F.* Since 1982, the Lumière Institute, presided over by the film producer, Bertrand Tavernier, has been located in the sumptuous *Villa Lumière.* This enormous town house is typical of turn-of-the-century architecture and has a fine Winter Garden and multi-coloured windows. At the bottom of the garden, the hangar which served as the décor for the first film in the history of the cinema, *"La Sortie des Usines Lumière"* (Leaving the Lumière Studios) in 1895, has been saved and recreated. The institute's, first of all, a magnificent conservatory of cinematographic and photographic heritage and strives to promote this artistic medium. In an absolutely fascinating exhibition, it retraces the birth and history of the cinema and of its techniques – from the Lumière Brothers' "Magic Lantern" to current techniques. It has a media-library and a pedagogical centre and regularly organizes meetings between actors, directors and cinema fans. In summer, open-air screenings are held in the nearby P*lace des Frères Lumière.*

LA MAISON DES CANUTS (THE HOUSE OF THE SILK WORKERS) > 10-12, rue d'Ivry (4th) © **04 78 28 62 04.** *Open from Monday to Friday and on Public Holidays from 08.30 to 12.00 and from 14.00 to 18.30. On Saturdays from 09.00 to 12.00 and from 14.00 to 18.00. Normal rate : 20 F. Reduced rate : 10 F.* Silk artisans are responsible for commented visits of this pleasant and instructive little museum. In honour of inventors of the various silk professions, they lovingly explain the techniques and gestures necessary for weaving these precious fabrics as they did in the old days. The museum retraces not just the history of the canuts, but the history of the *Croix-Rousse* Quarter and of Lyon in general.

LA MAISON DES TUPINIERS > 2, chemin Neuf (5th) © **04 72 77 92 42.** The Maison des Tupiniers organizes the large, annual pottery market, which takes place on the 2nd weekend of September and, throughout the year, holds a number of amusing exhibitions. The objects on display are various : soup tureens, plates, basins, earth and glass jewellery designed by contemporary creators, sculptures and ceramics and incredibly realistic fruit and figurines in faience.

LE CENTRE D'HISTOIRE DE LA RESISTANCE ET DE LA DEPORTATION > 14, avenue Berthelot (7th) © **04 78 72 23 11.** *Open from Wednesday to Sunday from 09.00 to 17.30. Normal rate : 25 F. reduced rate for students and the unemployed : 13 F. Free for the under-18's.* This museum's located in the old Military School of Health, a highly symbolic site which was occupied by the Gestapo (headed up by the infamous Klaus Barbie) between 1943 and 1944. This is a way of paying tribute to the men, women and children who were imprisoned here, and the museum tells how Lyon became the centre of the French Resistance Movement. It's a place for memories, but not only memories because regular temporary exhibitions deal with wars everywhere, using photos and witness-reports as supporting documentation.

LE MUSEE D'ART CONTEMPORAIN > Cité Internationale - 81, quai Charles de Gaulle (6th) © **04 72 69 17 18.** *Open from Wednesday to Sunday from 12.00 to 19.00. Normal rate : 25 F. Free for the under-18's.* Opposite the *Tête d'Or* Park, and on the exceptional site of the *Cité Internationale* designed by Renzo Piano, this museum, which was installed here in 1995 on a surface area of 2 500 m², offers an ever-changing display of astonishing, bizarre, hilarious or sad works by both famous and unknown artists. It gives an original presentation of Art from the 60's to the Present Day, and includes paintings, sculptures, photography and video-films. Most of the works exhibited have never been seen before. They're created specifically for the museum and often have a thematic connection with the city of Lyon. Artists are allowed to work using unusual material, shapes and sizes, producing works which are often monumental and which are exhibited in a space which is entirely modulable. Each exhibition provides the visitor with the chance of exploring unknown paths, of being amazed, of asking himself questions and of discovering conceptual art. The museum also contains a conference room, an ultra-specialized museum, a bookshop selling books, posters, photos, postcards and other objects, as well as a café-restaurant offering a view over the park. The museum was at the origin of the Contemporary Art Biennial and of the *FIAC* (International Contemporary Art Fair) which attracts more and more exhibitors and visitors every year.

LE MUSEE D'ART SACRE > 8, place de Fourvière (5e) ℂ **04 78 25 13 01.** *Open from Monday to Sunday from 10.00 to 12.00 and from 14.00 to 18.00. Normal rate : 30 F. Free for the under-18's.* The Fourvière Museum exhibits many art objects to do with religion : silverwork by Armand Calliat, sculptures, liturgical clothes, statues of the Virgin, Gallo-Roman fragments and ornaments. Two permanent exhibitions are on offer to visitors, covering the themes of Architecture and Symbols and concerning the history of the basilica and the chapel as well as the reconstruction of the Temple of Cybele. The old *Chapelle de Fourvière* can also be visited. It houses moving ex-voto illustrating the extraordinay piety of 19th century Lyonnais.

LE MUSEE LA RENAISSANCE DES AUTOMATES > 100, rue Saint Georges (5th) ℂ **04 72 77 75 28.** *Open everyday. Rates : 25 F for the under-10's, 30 F for students, 40 F for adults. Group rates from 30 people.* The show's live, like at the theatre. The museum has more than 250 mechanical automatons which are presented in 20 living tableaux paying tribute to arts and letters, music, cultural heritage and tradition. It's a great success and a marvel for those of all ages, particularly for the very young who simply gape at these life-like automatons (from 60 cms to 1 metre high). Famous painting scenes are recreated, like Vermeer's "Young Woman with a Water Jug", Cézanne's "Cardplayers" or Dégas' gracious "Dancers". There are scenes based on literature, including Provençal scenes taken from Marcel Pagnol and Quasimodo and Esmeralda from Victor Hugo. For lovers of melodrama, there are musical scenes inspired by Mozart and by the leg-throwing Moulin Rouge dancers. Since we're in Lyon, you'll also find the puppet Guignol at the theatre or playing cards and drinking Beaujolais with other famous puppet characters.

LE MUSEE DES BEAUX-ARTS PALAIS SAINT PIERRE > 20, place des Terreaux (1st) ℂ **04 72 10 17 40.** *Open everyday except Tuesdays from 10.30 to 18.00. Normal rate : 25 F. Reduced rate for students : 13 F. Free for the under-18's and the unemployed.* This is one of France's most beautiful Fine Arts Museums, after the Louvre. Indeed, some call it "The Little Louvre". Everything starts with the quiet little garden belonging to the *Palais Saint Pierre* - a real haven of peace at the city centre which, from the *Place des Terreaux,* you wouldn't believe existed, and where you can hear birds chirping not far from the city traffic. On permanent exhibition, and set out on 7 000 m², the collections are a real Museum of Civilisation. There are many works of art from Antiquity, covering the Egyptian, Greek and Roman civilisations, including many sculptures, everyday objects and pieces of pottery. As far as paintings are concerned, you'll find works by Picasso, Chagall, Bonnard, Veronese, Le Perugin, Delacroix, Monet, Manet... A major donation by a private collector, Jacqueline Delubac, allowed the museum to enlarge its collection to cover Degas, Bacon and the Impressionists. Upstairs, there's a charming restaurant-bar-tea room, which is as quiet as the garden outside. The museum boutique's worth a look because you'll always find an original gift-idea.

LE MUSEE DE LA CIVILISATION GALLO-ROMAINE > 17, rue Cléberg (5th) ℂ **04 72 38 81 90.** *Open everyday except Mondays, Tuesdays and Public Holidays, from 09.30 to 12.00 and from 14.00 to 18.00. Normal rate : 20 F. reduced rate for students and groups : 10 F. Free for the unemployed and for the under-18's. Visits and animations on 04 78 25 74 44.* A voyage through the first four centuries of our era, from the time when the well-named City of the Gauls was called "*Lugdunum*" in Latin. The museum's located right next to the well-conserved Antique Theatre where open-air shows are regularly organized. Everything is recounted here - from prehistory to the city's foundation – and there are supporting expanations and maps. There's a lot of historical information on our ancestors' everyday life, as well as on military activity, the Cult of the Dead, political life and architecture. The many objects exhibited make the ensemble more 'alive' : dishes, ceramics, glasswork, jewellery, tools, work instruments. The collection's very rich and the visit, fascinating.

Lyon *Culture - Museums*

LE MUSEE DE L'OURS EN PELUCHE ET DU JOUET ANCIEN (THE TEDDY BEAR AND OLD TOYS MUSEUM)
> 28, rue Lanterne (1st) ℭ **06 15 63 78 07.** *Open everyday from 09.00 to 18.00.* The cutest, the most adorable, the most moving of museums has opened its doors in Lyon. With more than 6000 teddy bears and as many old toys, this museum's unique in France and even in Europe. Its founder, Serge Toutant, having built up an incredible personal collection, decided to share it with the public. He personally renovated this 220 m^2 site. Saved from oblivion and from attic dust, his protégés finally have their museum. As soon as you go in, you'd think you were in a vast child's room in which the bears play out their everyday life : King bears, teacher bears, mason bears, Mother Bear at the oven, sports-playing and film-making bears... Serge Toutant wants to renew these little scenes twice a year, and he enthusiastically replies to vistors' questions and knows a host of moving and amusing anecdotes – like the story of the old lady who came face to face with her childhood teddy bear during her visit and who recognized it by the dress she had made for it when she was small. Serge Toutant has bought it in an antique shop and, today, it's still there, surrounded by its cousins.

LE MUSEE GADAGNE > Place du Petit Collège (5th) ℭ **04 78 42 03 61.** *Open everyday except Tuesdays and Public Holidays, from 10.45 to 18.00. Normal rate : 25 F. Reduced rate for students, large families and groups of 10 or more : 13 F. Free for the under-18's and the unemployed.* On the right bank of the Sâone, the *Hôtel Gadagne* is one of the most beautiful Renaissance houses in Old Lyon, and its pink and orange colours have been softened by time. The museum tells the history of the city and allows you to 'visit' Lyon by looking at archeology, ethnography and history. The building, which was erected between 1511 and 1527 for the sons of a rich spice-trader, was bought in 1545 by the Gadagnes, who were wealthy Florentine bankers and famous for the sumptuous parties they used to throw between these very walls. Even Rabelais, himself famous for enjoying the good life, wrote about the Gadagnes in his Quarto. Opened in 1921, this museum takes you through Lyon and through time, from the Middle Ages to the 19th century, by exhibiting archeological remains (pre-Roman and Romanesque stones from religious monuments which have now disappeared), sculptures, furniture, faïence, pewter and paintings. Maps, plans and engravings describe the rise of the city and of its monuments. The Rosaz Collection, containing more than 9000 objects, tells the history of Modern Lyon. Two rooms also recount the History of the *Compagnonnage* (an Association, formed between workers of the same profession for purposes of professional instruction and mutual aid). The *Hôtel Gadagne* also houses the International Puppet Museum.

LE MUSEE D'HISTOIRE NATURELLE > 28, boulevard des Belges (6th) ℭ **04 72 69 05 00.** *Open from Wednesday to Sunday from 13.00 to 18.00. Normal rate : 20 F. Reduced rate for students : 10 F. Free the under-11's. Guided visit : 10 F.* The Guimet Museum covers the History of the World and of Man in a captivating way. The collections are vast, and you have to spend hours and hours, and come back time and time again, if you want to exhaust the wealth to be found here. Because life first appeared and began to develop in the oceans and on the continents 4 billion years ago, there's a long story to tell. The museum reveals the world's diversity, be it extant or extinct, and the permanent exhibition is divided into 8 sections. Land and sea mammals enjoy a privileged position : fossilized horses, stags with enormous horns, skeletons of bison, bears, koala, African gazelles, Siberian tigers, American possums and kangaroos. The star of the museum is the famous Giant Mammoth of Lyon whose skeleton was discovered in 1859 during construction work. In the regional gallery, you'll find geography and fauna from the surrounding area, particularly the heron, the ermine and the wild cat. A collecion of minerals allows you to observe animals and insects which are incredibly fossilized within the rock. "Man's Evolution" allows you to travel through Time from Australopethicus to Homo sapiens, whilst the insect and bird world is particularly well represented. The section on "Peoples of the World" tells you about different ways of life, about art and religion, and there's, notably, a great deal of information on Japan. This is a superb museum for a family visit – the kids love it.

LE MUSEE DES HOSPICES CIVILS DE LYON HOTEL DIEU > 1, place de l'Hôpital (2nd)
ℭ **04 72 41 30 42.** *Open from Mondayfrom 13.30 to 17.30. Entrance fee 10 F for adults, 5 F for students. Commented visits by appointment : 35 F.* Situated in the historical, 17th century part of the *Hôtel-Dieu*, this museum gives a concrete and evocative vision of the hospital of yesterday in all its aspects : astonishing (and terrifying, for many) 18th century surgical

instruments can be seen alongside doctors' uniforms, sickbeds and medicinal plants. Three rooms from the old *Hôpital de la Charité* (destroyed in 1934) have been reconstructed and are listed as Historic Monuments. They include the Consultation Room, the Archives Room and the Apothecary. Flanders and Aubusson tapestries, faïences, furniture and precious objects testify to the wealth and artistic diversity which was to be found in many hospitals of the past.

LE MUSEE DE L'IMPRIMERIE ET DE LA BANQUE (THE PRINTING AND BANK MUSEUM) > 1, place de l'Hôpital (2nd) - 13, rue de la Poulaillerie (2e) ℰ **04 78 37 65 98.** *Open from Wednesday to Sunday from 14.00 to 18.00. Normal rate : 25 F. Reduced rate for students and groups of more than 10 people : 13 F.* In a beautiful and typically Lyonnais interior courtyard, this museum has existed since 1964, when, on the initiative of the master printer Maurice Audin, it opened in the old *Hôtel de la Couronne*. After the museums in Mayence and Anvers, this is one of the biggest Printing Museums in Europe. The collections are exhibited so as to provide as much information as possible, and, during each stage of the visit, clearly-visible panels explain the history of printing, of books and of printing methods. The visitor learns what the back-up to writing was before the invention of printing and how paper first appeared in Europe, and he discovers the first engravings on wood and metal, the birth of typography, the first books printed in France and in Lyon, the distribution of books and the apogee of the book in Lyon. The documents exhibited are rare and precious and include, for example, the 42-line Gutemburg Bible and the first photocomposed works. In the field of illustrtation, many original printing dice can be found. The development of techniques is very well illustrated, as are the extension of printing to posters, to musical notation and to paper money. The *Salle des Bois Gravé* (The Engraved Wood Room) exhibits an impressive collection of 600 wooden blocks of Biblical illustrations which were engraved in Lyon from the 16th to the 18th centuries. Finally, the vistor finds a collection of presses – hand presses, metallic presses, amateur presses, etc. – and paper-cutters used in the manufacture of books and bank notes.

LE MUSEE INTERNATIONAL DE LA MARIONNETTE DE LYON > Hôtel de Gadagne - Place du Petit Collège (5th) ℰ **04 78 42 03 61.** *Open everyday except Tuesdays from 10.45 to 18.00. Normal rate : 25 F. Half-rate for students. Free for the under-18.* This Museum of Specialized Arts and Popular Traditions has been in the *Hôtel Gadagne since* 1950. We're in Lyon, and this is where, around 1808, Laurent Mourguet created his famous marionettes - Guignol, Gnafron and Madelon. The museum pays tribute both to them and to their creator. Next to them, you'll find all sorts of puppets, which can be made to move by a variety of techniques using sleeves, wires or rods. The puppets come from round the world – England, Belgium, Italy, Russia, Cambodia and Japan. The Léopold Dor Collection contains some 600 items, including a very beautiful series of Javanese profiles and wooden jumping-jacks.

LE MUSEE DES TELECOMMUNICATIONS > 12bis, rue Burdeau (1er) ℰ **04 78 39 88 89.** *By appointment only. Free for private individuals (telephone beforehand to see if it's open). Commented visits for groups of 15 or more : from 25 F per head to 500 F for the group.* This museum groups in a single and vast room all the types of telephone and means of long-range communication which have been used in the last two centuries. Visitors can try the old phones, which are still in perfect working order : they can scoff at the first Minitel which now seems obsolete ; they can remember the dial-phones and laugh at the very 'design' models used in the 70's. The size of the oldest machines makes you realize how much technological development there has been with circuit miniaturizalion. Some explanations are highly technical, so that it's interesting to be part of a explanatory, guided visit.

LE MUSEE DE L'AUTOMOBILE HENRI MALARTRE > Rochetaillée-sur-Saône ℰ **04 78 22 18 80.** *Open everyday except Mondays and the last week of January from 09.00 to 18.00, in July-August from 09.00 to 17.00. Normal rate : 35 F. Reduced rate for group and students : 15 F. Free for the under-18's and the unemployed.* Henri Malatre, who created this museum, was a car demolitions expert who became a collectioner by remorse, and the museum owes many fine pieces to him. The museum's located high up in a very beautiful, 3-hectare park, from where you can see the banks of the Sâone and villages surrounded by greenery. It's in the old Counts of Lyon's château – a magnificently-renovated 15th century architectural ensemble - that you'll find this collection of old cars from 1890 to the present day. In all, there are 120 cars, but also 50 motorbikes from 1904 to 1964, bicycles, Lyonnais public transport vehicles, including a

Lyon *Culture - Museums*

very old tram, old publicity posters, essential accessories for driving (like leather hemelts and goggles !) and many precious miniatures. All the vehicles are in working order, and some are taken out for a spin during exhibitions and special events. Some models are unique in the world, and all the major manufacturers with evocative names are represented : De Dion Bouton, Peugeot, Renault, Ford, Fiat, Mercedes and also the manufacturers of sports cars, like Lotus, Gordini, Talbot and Mac Laren. Astonishing and amusing discoveries include the 1926 Monotrace, which was designed to go at 80 km/h on two wheels and to stop on four.

LE MUSEE DES SAPEURS-POMPIERS DU GRAND LYON (THE GREATER LYON FIREMEN'S MUSEUM)
358, avenue de Champagne (9e) ℂ **04 72 17 54 54.** *Open from Monday to Friday from 09.00 to 12.00 and from 14.00 to 17.00.* Unique of its type, this museum, paying tribute to fire-fighters, is one of the largest in France and, probably, in Europe. Set out over two floors, it's divided into four parts. In the Pump Room, you'll find hand-pumps, steam-pumps, engine-pumps, force-pump and suction-pumps. Explanations are technical but clear and accessible to everyone. What development there's been since the 18th century ! The Memory Room traces the history of firemen and recounts their exploits with the support of photos and texts. In the section devoted to Equipment and Clothes, there are the famous shiny helmets (more than 1800 of them), boots, raincoats and leather parkas. Finally, the section covering Moveable Equipment contains more than 100 vehicles and red lorries. The restoration work that was carried out here is exhibited in the Renovation Workshop. **Annex at 39, avenue Debourg (7th) 04 78 72 84 81.**

LE MUSEE HISTORIQUE DES TISSUS ET DES ARTS DECORATIFS > 30/34, rue de la Charité (2nd)
ℂ **04 78 38 42 00.** *Open from Tuesday to Sunday from 10.00 to 12.00 and from 14.00 to 17.30.* This museum's particularity is to bring together collections of fabrics in general, as well as those used specifically in the decorative arts. Created in 1864 to back up the Support Movement for the Applied Arts in Industry, in 1890 the museum devoted itself entirelyto fabrics on the initiative of its founder, Edouard Aynard – politician, banker, collector and President of the Chamber of Commerce and Industry. An extraordinary testimony to the history and evolution of fabric, the museum attacks two themes : the East and the West. Coptic tapestries, Persian and Byzantine fabrics and carpets, along with Moorish weaving trace several millennia of Eastern tradition in fabrics. As far as the West is concerned, there are works from Sicily and Italy, whilst a special place is reserved for Lyonnais weaving as well for religious embroideries and French costumes. The Decorative Arts Museum, which was designed as an addition to the Fabrics Museum, has been here since 1925 – in this private residence, built in 1739 by Jacques Germain Soufflot for Jean de Lacroix Laval, adviser to the Currency Exchange. This is an 'atmosphere' museum, where the visitor can enjoy the ambiance which prevailed in an 18th century French house. Moreover, the arts in that century are also well-represented here, so as to be in perfect harmony with the building. The wealth of the collections is largely due to private donations. Many objects are Baroque and very precious : chairs by the Lyonnais, Nogaret and Cannot, desks by some of the great Parisian cabinet-makers, like Oeben and Riesner, clocks, chests of drawers, tapestries, porcelain and faïence, as well as magnificent pieces in silver and gold. The collections are completed by an ensemble of majolica. Since 1997, the museum has begun to assemble a collection of contemporary gold - and silverwork, thereby opening the museum to more recent creations (works by Daraspe, de Maurin) and to design (Botta, Gagnère).

MUSEE DE LA POUPEE (THE DOLL MUSEUM) > Domaine de Lacroix-Laval – MARCY-L'ETOILE
ℂ **04 78 87 87 00.** *Open from Tuesday to Sunday from 10.00 to 17.00. Full rate : 20 F. Reduced rate : 10 F. Free for schoolchildren and children up to 12 years old.* Children adore them, even little boys, and, moreover, the museum's right in organizing regular pedagogical animations to initiate little ones to the museum, to tell them about dolls by means of stories and tales, and to get them to understand their own relationship with their dolls. Located just 12 kilometres from Lyon at the heart of the vast Lacroix-Laval estate and in a superb 18th century house, this museum contains one of Europe's largest and most complete collection of dolls – from old porcelain dolls with white faces and made-up eyes to the modern Barbie we all know. The dolls are exhibited in the middle of inventions and 'scenes' relating to their own period.

MUSEE URBAIN TONY GARNIER > 4, rue des Serpollières (8th) ℰ **04 78 75 16 75.** *Open from Tuesday to Saturday from 14.00 to 18.00. Guided visits every Saturday and Sunday at 14.00 and 16.00 and for groups by appointment.* For those who detest traditional museums, this one offers an original formula because it's in the open air, so that you admire the works on display whilst strolling through the streets. These works are, in fact, immense graffiti – but, beautiful, clean and structured graffiti. The 22 painted walls trace the history of the project thought up by Tony Garnier who, at the beginning of the century, imagined an ideal city he hadn't, unfortunately, been able to realize. A visionary and humanist, the architect dreamt of workers living in a vast architectural ensemble, harmoniously combining industrial constraints with airy, monumental spaces of greenery. Buildings are at the service of Man, who doesn't feel crushed by low, 'friendly' structures which let light through. A walk here allows you to discover Tony Garnier's architectural style – simple, elegant and contemporary. The visit ends with a visit to a flat, reconstructed in a style typical of the 1930's. The museum regularly invites foreign artists to express their own vision of the ideal city – on the walls, of course !

LE PALAIS DE LA MINIATURE > 2, rue Juiverie (5th) ℰ **04 72 00 24 77.** *Open everyday from 10.00 to 12.00 and from 14.00 to 19.00, on Sundays without interruption from 10.00 to 19.00. Normal rate : 25 F. Students, the under-12's and schoolchildren. Free for the under-4's. Groups of 10 people : 20 F for adults and 15 F for children.* Mini-maniacs go mad in this marvellous palace where houses, street scenes, interior scenes and scenes from everyday life are reproduced in miniature and in the minutest detail. The result of this meticulous work is impressive, and it's easy to imagine, as you go from one work to another, the hours of patience, toil and dexterity required to achieve a result you could put into your top pocket. There are also works by the famous miniaturist, Dan Ohlman. In addition to these permanent collections, the *Palais de la Miniature* regularly organizes exhibitions based round a variety of themes, but always on a reduced scale

PLANETARIUM DE VAULX-EN-VELIN > Place de la Nation ℰ **04 78 79 50 13.** This place's motto is that the sky's a show. So, come and dream under the stars ! From the age of 5, everyone can learn about the sky and participate in astronomy shows, learn the history of the Universe and of distant galaxies and understand the role of the seasons and the sun's power - enough to make you feel very small indeed in the immensity of the sky. The planetarium organizes scientific meetings, workshops and exhibitions.

SOIERIE VIVANTE > 21, rue Richan (4th) ℰ **04 78 27 17 13.** *Open on Tuesdays from 14.00 to 18.30 and from Wednesday to Saturday from 09.00 to 12.00 and from 14.00 to 18.30. Normal rate : 15 F. Schoolchildren : from 8 to 10 F. Groups by appointment : 13 F.* Thanks to living 'silk circuits', everyone can discover the knowledge and the life of silk-weavers by visiting authentic family workshops. It was in the 19th century that Lyon became the silk capital and, during this period, many lodgings-workshops were built outside the city's ramparts, and these were entirely equipped with Jacquard looms. In 1852, the *Croix-Rousse* commune on the plateau became the city's 4th arrondissement and extended outwards to the slopes. At the end of the 19th century, more than 40 000 workshops were working at full speed, and this is what these circuits allow you to discover. Visitors are accompanied by a guide, who tells the history of the quarter and recounts the life and work of silkworkers at that time, most of whom lived and worked in family units in the same flat. You'll visit the Municipal Passementeric, Handloom Weaving and Gimping Workshop, as well as the Municipal Hand Decoration Workshop.

Merry Weather Ladder
- 1923 -

Lyon *Culture - Concert halls & theatres*

◆CULTURE / CONCERT HALLS AND THEATRES

Concert halls

AUDITORIUM MAURICE RAVEL > 149, rue Garibaldi (3rd) ℂ **04 78 95 95 95.** Inaugurated in 1975, and named after Maurice Ravel, the Auditorium was intended to be the largest concert hall of its day. Unfortunately, the honeycomb ceiling and the installation of comfortable seats and carpeting didn't lead to the very best accoustics. The scallop-shaped concert room was the subject of many criticisms and arguments, which didn't prevent the public from flocking here. Following recent renovations and stage alterations, designed to improve accoustics, the Auditorium can now welcome the very best musical formations without embarrassment. Moreover, it's the permanent residence of the Lyon National Orchestra, directed by David Robertson, who succeeded Emmanuel Krivine. Equipped with a monumental organ, which is unique in France, the concert hall's used for all sorts of music, including jazz and different international musical styles, so as to interest as many people as possible. It has 2090 seats, and receives more than 150 000 annual visitors. Its tariffs and interior lay-out are such that it's accessible to all : the young, the elderly and the handicapped included. In summer, the Auditorium participates in the *"Fourvière Nights"* in the magical setting of the *Colline de Fourvière*.

LA BOURSE DU TRAVAIL > 205, place Guichard (3rd) ℂ **04 78 60 88 56.** With a new facade, the *Bourse du Travail* was entirely re-done, so that it would be as beautiful outside as inside – ready to be inaugurated by Axelle Red. Axelle The Red – the choice was, perhaps, not a coincidence ! As soon as you go in, immense frescoes come into action. The hall's entirely pearl-grey, but this conservative colour isn't sufficient to calm excited spectators. The ceiling's covered with lights, which shine like stars and which remind you that, in the absence of demonstrations, this is Show Biz Land.

HALLE TONY GARNIER > 20, place Antonin Perrin (7th) ℂ **04 72 76 85 85.** Seen from a distance or from above, the Tony Garnier Hall looks like a modern pyramid covered with stairways. This building, which was designed and constructed by the architect, achieved the exploit of covering a surface area of 18 000 m² and of attaining a height of 24 metres without any interior supports. The recently-renovated building reflects its author's very particular style : the flat, tiered roof, a strong use of glass for maximumum luminosity. Initially, the hall housed the cattle market, then served as a munitions factory during the war. It's now the venue for numerous shows, concerts, professional fairs and various other events. Its 5000 seats allow it to welcome performers as varied as Lara Fabian, André Rieu, NTM, Lionel Richie, Liz Mac Comb, Jean-Jacques Goldman, Elton John or Alpha Blondy. The hall can be visited free, provided that you make an appointment in advance with Mme Massin.

LE GUIGNOL DE LYON > 2, rue Louis Garrand (5th) ℂ **04 78 28 92 57.** The ZonZons Company, directed by Filip Auchère, offers shows which are highly popular, 100% Lyonnais, amusing, moving or instructive – it just depends on the show. Their favourites are called The Toupan Arts and The Canuts' Secret. Both children and adults adore them, and there are also Cabaret Evenings from time to time.

LE HOT CLUB DE LYON > 26, rue Lanterne (1st) ℂ **04 78 39 54 74.** Behind the *Hot Club de Lyon*'s red facade, there's been a jazz club since 1948. Most of the time, Gérard Vidon and his Band choose regional groups and organize 5 concerts a week at 21.30. On Saturdays, there's a jam session between 16.00 and 19.00. The *Hot Club*'s favourite styles ? All styles – from modern jazz to hard bop, and including be-bop, swing and New Orleans. The basement room can take 50 people and (a nice little touch, this) the public's not obliged to buy drinks during the concert. So that everyone can enjoy the place, prices vary between 35 F and 80 F, and there's a good reduced rates system.

MAISON DE LA DANSE > 8, avenue Jean Mermoz (8th) ℂ **04 72 78 18 18.** *Internet :* *www.maisondeladanse.com.* Guy Darmet, who has directed the *Maison de la Danse* since its creation in 1980, fervently defends dance in France. Based in the theatre in the 8th arrondissement, the hall's a real theatre, with boxes, an open stage and a hall which slopes gently down so as to maximize visibility for a capacity audience of 1200. The public can also go to rehearsals free of charge and talk with the dancers and choreographers. The programme's varied, so as to please a wide public, and is entirely devoted to the choreographic art. You'll find all sorts of dance : modern, traditional, classical, jazz, flamenco, martial arts, Asian and Arab dance, hip-hop... In its 20 years of existence, the *Maison de la Danse* has put on more than 500 French and foreign creations and has given a chance to more than 100 young choreographers. Concerts and video-meetings are regularly organized.

OPERA NATIONAL DE LYON > Place de la Comédie (1st) © **04 72 00 45 45.** *3615 OPÉRA DE LYON* • *http://opéra.lyon.org.* The Opera, which some Lyonnais call "the cheese grater" because of their vague resemblance, is, above all, remarkable for its architectural design, which was the work of the very innovative Jean Nouvel. The ensemble is resolutely modern, consisting largely of glass and of iron and black marble beams. The interior's astonishingly black (without being suffocating) from floor to ceiling, from the reception area to the upper floors, from where you have a picturesque view over the roofs of Lyon. Guided visits are regularly organized. At the very heart of the hall, red takes over from black and really explodes as soon as you go through the doors of the show room. For all the season's shows (opera, dance, concerts, amphitheatre, young public) there are a number of subscription formulae at all prices, depending on the number of shows included. Tickets left over are sold at 50 F 1/4 hour before the curtain. The 2000/2001 Season is, mainly, light, humorous and gay, if you exclude The Rape of Lucretius and Romeo and Juliet for the dance, with Mozart : Cosi fan tutte and The Magic Flute, Giuseppe Verdi and La Traviata, Rossini and The Barber of Seville. Separate from the principal hall, the amphitheatre's a small semi-circle with 200 places, which puts on short and various shows : the world's music, jazz, choreographies, chamber music, et. And the admission fee varies between 20 and 65 F.

Théâtres

THEATRE DES CELESTINS > 4, rue Charles Dullin (2nd) © **04 72 77 40 00.** A little more than 200 years old, the *Théâtre des Célestins* welcomes its numerous public in the magnificent setting of an Italian-style theatre : Baroque, classic red and gold theatre colours, superb decorative paintings, impressive trompe l'œil curtains and superb lighting. Along with Paris' *Comédie Française* and *Théâtre de l'Odéon*, it's the only theatre in France whish has celebrated more then 200 years od dramatic art. It puts on a wide variey of quality plays – both classics and contemporary pieces : Ondine, Andromaque, Faust, The Three Musketeers, Barnum... The public owes it the discovery of authors like Jean Cocteau and Bertold Brecht. It can proudly claim to hold the European record for the number of subscription holders.

THEATRE DE LA CROIX-ROUSSE > **Place Joannès Ambre (4th)** ℂ **04 78 29 05 49.** Directed by Philippe Faure, the *Théâtre de la Croix-Rousse* is a favourite spot for local inhabitants who flock to its performances. The bar's open both before and after the show. At the end of the peformance on Wednesdays, a debate is opened between the public and the artistic team. A bookshop sells works based round the evening's theme. Finally, all subscription holders can return – at no additional charge and subject to seat availability – to see a show they particularly enjoyed. During the 2000/2001 Season, there will be 12 shows, 12 plays, 12 different universes, 4 'house creations' and 4 directors. On the programme – "Galileo's Life" and "Fatzer" by Bertolt Brecht, *"Depuis hier"* ("Since Yesterday") by Michel Laubu, one of the most original artists in the Lyonnais scene, "The Glass Menagerie" by Tennessee Williams, "The Tempest" by Shakespeare, "Honeymoon of Blood" by Frederico Garcia Lorca, "Electra" by Sophocles, "Oh ! Wonderful Days" by Samuel Beckett and *"Les Etreintes"* ("The Embraces") and *"Les Papillons Blancs"* ("The White Butterflies") by Philippe Faure.

THEATRE NATIONAL POPULAIRE > **Villeurbanne.** For 26 years, this theatre's been co-directed by Roger Planchon and Patrice Chéreau (then, by Georges Laurondant), and, over this period, has put on 81 creations, invited more than 100 directors and put on 250 shows – to the delight of Lyonnais and the inhabitants of Villeurbanne, who are crazy about their theatre. It's one of the principal crossroads for theatrical creation, and, every year, it goes on tour. Subscription systems. Full rate for a show is 178 F, whilst the reduced rate (the unemployed, students, schoolchildren) costs 90 F.

LARGE SHOPS AND DEPARTMENT STORES

◆SHOPPING CENTRES

ECULLY GRAND OUEST > **Pérollier (Ecully).** This is quite simply one of Europe's largest shopping centres. It's also one of the most pleasant. Spacious and rarely crowded, it has an incredible number of shops and, of course, several restaurants. Tied in with the *Carrefour* Hypermarket, which is also very large and pleasant, *Ecully Grand Ouest* is a lively and interesting spot.

LA PART DIEU > **17, rue du Docteur Bouchut (3rd)** ℂ **04 72 60 60 60.** For the last 25 years, the *Part-Dieu* Shopping Centre has been one of the pillars of Lyonnais shopping. Having been enlarged two years ago (notably, with the arrival of Go Sport on two floors), this famous shopping centre is to undergo a face-lift in the course of the year. In the meantime, you can stroll around on three floors with no risk of getting bored. With 260 shops and an enormous turnover in terms of the shops represented, you're bound to find what you're after. For a complete visit, you should count at least half-a-day, take off your sweater and jacket, and add another half-a-day for a rest. Don't forget to bring a bottle of water or the money necessary to buy yourself a beer, and try to avoid the place during the year-end festivities !

LA PORTE DES ALPES > **Saint Priest.** The *Auchan* Shopping Gallery's rather oppressive, but it has the advantage of containing a very complete selection of shops, including *Ikea, BHV, Boulanger, Norauto, Kiabi*, the excellent Amarine restaurant... Curiously, although the gallery's car park must be one of the biggest, it's often impossible to find a parking space. Obviously, the whole of East Lyon does its shopping here, and many clients come from miles around to spend some time at *Ikea.*

◆DEPARTMENT STORES

FNAC > **85, rue de la République (2nd)** ℂ **04 72 40 49 49.** The *Bellecour* Fnac lost a few years for the 1999 Season, and the shop's now much more pleasant, with a larger number of cash counters to reduce waiting time. You can even have a drink here. This French giant sells prticularly well equipped when it comes to multi-media and home cinema products. It sells excellent technical copy-books and has a very well-stocked photography section. **Another shop in the Part-Dieu Shopping Centre.**

PLANETE SATURN > 6, place des Cordeliers (2nd) ℰ **04 72 40 80 00.** *Planète Saturn* arrived in the old *Galeries Lafayette* building in 1999, and has proved a popular success. This shop, which is originally German, is very pleasant and well-stocked. You'll find all you could possibly want, including (something extremely rare for a shop in the city centre) electrical household appliances. On the other hand, there's no bookshop. The shop has an excellent After Sales Service for immediate repairs (including the repair of articles bought elsewhere).

VIRGIN MEGASTORE > 43, rue Edouard Herriot (2nd) ℰ **04 78 92 61 61.** *Virgin* is the most recent newcomer to the *Presqu'île*'s department stores. Smaller than its rivals, it's not limited to hi-fi, computer, photo and phone equipment... because Virgin's particularly well-known for its bookshop, where you can find a host of books at very cheap prices (some cost only 20 F) and even sit down for 5 minutes on the seats provided – something which is very pleasant when you've decided to visit all the sections. On the groundfloor, Virgin has a huge selection of records, video games and DVD's, all set out by zone.

◆GENERAL HYPERMARKETS

CARREFOUR > Ecully Grand Ouest Shopping Centre ℰ **04 72 86 19 00.** *Carrefour*'s a sort of high-quality hypermarket with normal, hypermarket prices. For *Carrefour*-brand products, it offers excellent value for money, but also has a surprising bakery, a ticket office, employees on speedy rollerblades to find out the price which isn't marked on the article you want to pay for, and sections for hi-fi, electrical household appliances, sport... It's very modern and, like in many specialist stores, has 'seller-advisers'. The place is clean, bright and spacious. What's more, you can make a mistake and get reimbursed on an article you've bought but haven't used (unwrapped or not). **Other addresses : 145, rue Anatole France (Villeurbanne) 04 72 65 52 52 • 136, boulevard Joliot Curie (Vénissieux) 04 78 78 46 46 • Part Dieu Shopping Centre 04 72 60 61 62.**

JUNIORS

◆TOYS

DISNEY STORE > Part Dieu Shopping Centre ℰ **04 78 60 60 69.** No speech is necessary, because you already know that Disney's got the heavy artillery out. Here, you'll find Disney in all its shapes and forms : teddy bears, statues, glasses, pendants... everything that could ever be devised in marketing based on the Little Mermaid, the Lion King, Tarzan. The bonus is... that someone's paid to stand at the entrance to do nothing except say "Good morning" and "Goodbye". This is America, folks.

◆FASHION

Shoes

MINI SHOES > 41, rue de Brest (2nd) ℰ **04 78 38 04 92.** When you like something, the price doesn't matter. Parents who worship their offspring aren't afraid of paying through the nose so that their kids are beautifully-shod in brands like Mod 8 and Péché d'Amour. Baby boots, rain boots, shiny slippers – you'll find everything to shoe your children elegantly.

Ready-to-wear

AU REVE BLEU > 155, boulevard de la Croix-Rousse (4th) ℰ **04 78 28 06 08.** Two large floors devoted to child-raising, with toys and other items for babies, and, for their mothers, room to park nearby.

BABY CITY > 9, rue du professeur Tavernier (8th) ℰ **04 78 74 09 50.** Over the years, or decades, rather, *Baby City* has become known as the shop for children in the entire south-east of Lyon. Today, Madame Zolémian's only here on Fridays, but you can come throughout the week to this American shop which tries to do the impossible – combine quality reception and advice with low prices.

CAMAIEU ENFANT > 12, rue de Brest (2nd) ✆ **04 78 38 30 30.** *Camaïeu Enfant* is, first and foremost, a Camaïeu. Which means that, here, you'll find – and mothers know this well already – a host of fashionable and, often, good-quality articles at very reasonable prices. Women who like *Camaïeu* for their own clothes will like this shop for their children up to 16 years old. **Other address : Part Dieu Shopping Centre 04 78 60 43 23.**

CATIMINI > 51, rue du président Herriot (2nd) ✆ **04 78 38 16 43.** Choice, quality, good advice, clear lay-out – *Catamini* dresses babies and the young up to 16 years old. A shop which cultivates excellence. **Other address : 30, cours Franklin Roosevelt (6th) 04 78 24 33 16.**

DIPAKI > 29, grande rue de la Croix-Rousse (4th) ✆ **04 78 28 19 23.** A polo-neck at 49 F, that's pretty good ! You'll find it at *Dipaki*, which is a clothes shop for babies and children. A wide selection of clothes and very fair prices. The little plus at *Dipaki* is the décor, which the children adore. It's important that, when mothers come with their children, their children enjoy themselves. If they don't, they're a pain after just two minutes ! **Other address : 3, rue Victor Hugo (2e) 04 78 42 04 83.**

JAC'GIL > 58, grande rue de la Croix-Rousse (4th) ✆ **04 78 29 23 84.** OK, it's not large, but it's well stocked. Many articles and brands for babies and for children up to 16 years old. **Other address : 6-8, avenue Maréchal de Saxe (6th) 04 78 24 75 77/04 78 24 49 92.**

LA COMPAGNIE DES PETITS > 20, rue Victor Hugo (2nd) ✆ **04 78 42 53 86.** Very colourful clothes (nicely presented, too) for babies and children. You're given clear advice if you ask for it (you're not jumped on as soon as you arrive) and, in this shop, which is neither too large nor too small, prices are very reasonable.

LECONS COULEURS > 59, grande rue de la Croix-Rousse (4th) ✆ **04 78 27 06 06.** The 0-8 years old occupy a place of honour at *Leçons Couleurs*. An original shopwindow and a very beautiful boutique designed by an architect. Inside, the clothes are very beautiful and top quality.

NATALYS > 22, grande rue de la Croix-Rousse (4th) ✆ **04 78 29 53 99.** This is a large, very pleasant, rather classy shop, which is full of attractive clothes for the little ones (up to 6 years old). It also sells clothes for pregnant mothers, as well as a few toys and a bit of furniture. **Other address : 88, rue Edouard Herriot (2nd) 04 78 42 01 91.**

SERGENT MAJOR > 25, grande rue de la Croix-Rousse (4th) ✆ **04 78 28 12 29.** A very small shop with very low prices : 59 F for a top, that's good ! Other articles are a bit more expensive, but are more than reasonable thoughout the year. **Other addresses : 7, avenue de Saxe (6th) 04 78 52 59 09 • 6, place des Jacobins (2nd) 04 78 37 32 33.**

Z > 12, grande rue de la Croix-Rousse (4th) ✆ **04 78 27 92 78.** Z must be the only clothes shop for children to look like a really large clothes shop. You don't find yourself nose to nose with the salesgirl and having to explain what you're doing here. What's more, you can buy babies' tee-shirts for 19.90 F. So, people happily push Z's doors open. **Other address : 99, avenue des frères Lumière (8th) 04 78 76 99 83.**

◆ATTRACTION AND LEISURE PARKS

AERO CITY > Route de l'Aérodrome (Aubenas) ✆ **04 75 35 00 00**

AQUA CENTRE > Route de Grand Champ (Saint Bel) ✆ **04 74 01 55 00.** *Open from mid-June to the beginning of September, everyday from 10.00 to 20.00. Rates : 25 F for adults, 18 F for children. Extra charge of 47 F for the sauna, the hammam, the jet bath. Route to take : On the N7, heading towards L'Arbresle. At the roundabout, head for Saint Bel on the N89.* You'll have guessed that Aqua Centre's into water, which is popular recipe in summer. Swimming-pool, giant waterslide, 'against the current' swimming basin, jet baths, hammam, sauna, paddling pool – in short, everything to do with water ! Plus a weights room for those masochistic enough to pump iron, especially when it's hot.

Welcome to   the new Bird Park

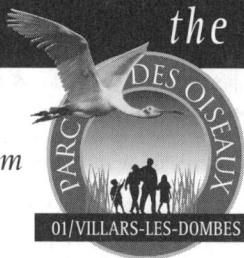

Birds from   *round the world*

PARC DES OISEAUX

01/VILLARS-LES-DOMBES

At the heart of the Dombes region, 30 minutes north of Lyon,

discover the international Bird Park: 30 hectares of protected Nature including 10 étangs. More than 2000 birds and 400 species from round the world, including some very rare species. Among the novelties: the Pantanel Aviary and the Perroquet City which you enter to discover the most beautiful birds from South America, Africa and the Far East. You will also enjoy the walk round the étangs, the large pontoon where you can discover local fauna and flora, the Intranet network with interactive terminals and large screens to follow the birds' secret lives.
An unforgettable day!

3 restaurants, 350 equipped picnic places. Small train. Boutique.
Open till nightfall, 21.30 in summer.
RN 83. 01330 Villars-les-Dombes.
Tel. 04 74 98 05 54 - Fax 04 74 98 27 74

CONSEIL GÉNÉRAL
l'ain
PERFORMANCE & QUALITÉ

ADHÉRENT
Maison de la FRANCE

Lyon *Juniors - Attraction & leisure parks*

CAPTIVA > Avenue Andreï Sakharov (9th) ✆ **04 78 35 70 71.** *Open everyday except Mondays by appointment. From 09.30 to 11.30 and from 13.00 to 17.00 from Tuesday to Friday or from 14.00 to 18.00 on Saturdays and Sundays. Tariffs : 25 F for the under-6's, 30 F for the rest. To get here : Bus n°36, 44 or 66, get off at La Duchère-Piscine bus stop.* Captiva's a concept which should be developed because it offers all sorts of things for the holidays. It's been put together by the *Cité des Sciences de La Villette,* and provides an exploratory tour of the sciences, of industry, of Nature and of biology by means of little demonstrations. In short, an intelligent and amusing place to visit.

ISLAND PLAGE > Ile Roy (Collonges au Mont d'Or) ✆ **04 72 27 88 95.** *Open from 1st may to the beginning of October. In May, June and September : on Wednesdays, Saturdays, Sundays and Public Holidays from 11.00 to 18.00. In July and August : everyday from 11.00 to 18.00. Tariffs : 60 F for adults and 40 F for children up to 13 years old. Free for the under-3's. Route : on the banks of the Saône (right bank), heading towards Collonges.* You feel good in the beautiful setting of the Saône Valley. On the *Ile Roy,* you feel even better. Firstly, you get here by boat, which is always pleasant. Then, you see nothing but greenery and hills as you watch the children amuse themselves on one of the mini-attractions. Swimming-pool with waterslide, swings, trampoline, table tennis, pony riding, mini-motorbikes, mini-golf, roundabout, archery... you can unwind, just 15 minutes from Lyon.

LA PLAINE TONIQUE > Open-air base – MONTREVEL EN BRESSE ✆ **04 74 30 80 52.** For many years, Montrevel-en-Bresse has been carving out a solid reputation in the world of leisure activities with its 'tonic plain'. Its aquatic centre, which was built using gravel from the region's various motorway construction sites, rapidly had a camping site installed on it. Today, the camping site has 4 stars and serves as the central point for a large number of activities, including sailing, tennis, waterskiing, go-karting, mountain-biking and horseriding (at Malafretaz). But the Star of these leisure activities is the *Aquatonic Centre* (04 74 30 80 52), which opened last year over a warm-water spring. 1 000 m^2 of supervised water-basin allow you to practise diverse water activities, and you'll find, among other things, a giant water-slide and wave basins.

LA VALLEE BLEUE > Montalieu Vercieu ✆ **04 74 88 49 23.** *Open all year from 14.00 to 19.45. In summer, Aqua park from 10.30. Entrance fee : 30 F for the 12 and over and 20 F for those between 4 and 12 years old. Route map : Motorway A4 heading towards Geneva, Meximieux and Pérouges exit, then, head towards Lagnieu.* A leisure complex in a very beautiful setting. You'll find tennis, minigolf, pony riding and, above all, all imaginable water activities on the Rhône (boats, pedal-boats, windsurfing, waterskiing…), including jet-skiing (it's expensive, but fun, and worth doing at least once in your life).

LE JARDIN FERROVIAIRE > 2, route de Lyon (Chatte) ✆ **04 76 38 54 55.** *Open from 15th March to 15th November, everyday from 09.30 to 18.30. Lasts about an hour. Tariffs : 41 F for adults and 28 F for children from 4 to 14 years old. Ticket for two with The Giant Mushroom Forest (7 kms away) : 70 F for adults and 50 F for children. Route map : Motorway A7, Vienne exit, head towards La Côte Saint-André and Roybon on the D27, then, Saint-Antoine de l'Abbaye.* Those who like trains and miniature trains will love this place. In reconstructed villages and countryside, 30 trains and 250 carriages wind their way around a 13 000 m^2 circuit.

LE PAL > Saint-Pourçain-sur-Besbre (Dompierre sur Besbre) ✆ **04 70 42 68 10.** *Open in June, everyday from 10.00 to 18.00. On Sundays in June and everyday in July and August, from 10.00 to 19.00. Tariffs ; 90 F for adults and 75 F for children from 3 to 9 years old. Route map : Motorway A6, head towards Paris, Mâcon exit, then, towards Charolles, Moulins, Dompierre-sur-Besbre and Saint-Pourçain-sur-Besbre. Le Pal* is both an Animal Park and an Attraction Park. One of the Attraction Park's stars is King-Kong. His cry may terrify the little ones even before they've even seen him, but, once they've seen the beast, they love him. The most recent addition is the 'dynamic cinema', which has become very fashionable since the success enjoyed by Futuroscope. This is aa park which has something to please everybody.

LE PARC DES OISEAUX > Villars les Dombes Ⓒ **04 74 98 05 54.** *Open all year everyday from 10.00 to 21.00 (17.30 in winter). Tariffs : 39 F for adults, 29 F for children (4 to 11 years old) until 23rd June, and then 45 F for adults and 35 F for children until 31st August. How to get here : head towards Bourg-en-Bresse on the N83.* Here, you'll find 23 hectares in the middle of the Dombes, with *étangs* (water pans/basins) and more than 400 species of bird to discover on foot or aboard a little train. All this, just half-an-hour from Lyon.

SAFARI DE PEAUGRES > RN82 (Peaugres) Ⓒ **04 75 33 00 32.** *Open all year, from 09.30 to nightfall. Tariffs : 90 F for adults and 57 F for children from 3 to 12 years old. Included : foot circuit, car circuit and animations. Possibility of taking the foot circuit or the car circuit only. How to get here : Motorway A7 towards Marseille, Chanas exit, then towards Sernières and Peaugres on the N82.* This is, without doubt, the most complete and the most impressive of Animal Parks. Down one side of it, there's a circuit you take by car to discover lions, monkeys, bears…wandering around freely (the bear's always attracted by the car, but it's forbidden to open the car windows). Then, there's an immense zoo, which is more classic but equally astonishing, with a series of 'shows' using birds of prey. The park's vast and very green, and, since the animals enjoy themselves here, so should you.

TOURO PARC EN BEAUJOLAIS > RN6 (Romanèche Thorins) Ⓒ **03 85 35 51 53.** *Open all year. From May to October : everyday from 09.00 to 19.00. Aquatic base : from 10.00 to 18.30. From the end of October to the end of February : from 10.00 to 12.00 and from 13.30 to 17.30. Tariffs : 85 F in summer and 75 F in winter. Free for the under-4's. How to get here : Motorway A6 heading for Paris, Belleville exit.* Touro Parc is one of the best compromises between an Animal Park and an Attractions Park. There are more than 800 species of animal to see – in the shade most of the time – and dozens of aerial, terrestrial and aquatic attractions.

WALIBI RHONE-ALPES > Les Avenières (38) Ⓒ **04 74 33 71 80.** *Open everyday from the end of May to the beginning of September from 10.00 to 18.00, and till 19.00 or 21.00 between the beginning of July and 20th Augus. From the end of April to the end of May and from the beginning of September to the beginning of October, open only at the weekend and on Public Holidays. Tariffs : 139 F for adults, 120 F for the elderly, 67 F for children between 1 metre and 1.4 metres tall or up to 9 years old, free for children less than 1 metre tall.* Walibi has been, without question, the most popular Attractions Park in the region for a number of years. You'll find some 30 different attractions set out on 35 hectares, as well as 2 shows. The biggest successes are, of course, the water games (a novelty in 2000 : the water-shoot) and the "Infernal Totem" which rises vertically and brutally, thereby subjecting volunteers' bodies to a gravity of 4.5 G.

ZOO DE SAINT-MARTIN-LA-PLAINE > Saint Martin La Plaine Ⓒ **04 77 75 18 68.** *Open everyday of the year. In summer, from 09.00 to nightfall. Tariffs : 50 F for the over-10's and 30 F for children between 3 and 10 years old. How to get here : Motorway A47 heading for Saint-Etienne, take the Rive-de-Gier and Saint-Martin-la-Plaine exit and, then,follow the signs.* Between Lyon and Saint-Etienne, the Saint Martin La Plaine Zoo is a classic for school outings. First of all, you wind your way between the animal cages (more than 350) before you get to the Star's cage : Plato, the gorilla, is mighty impressive when he bangs his fists against the plexi-glass which separates him from the public.

LEISURE ACTIVITIES

◆ PHOTO AND VIDEO

Equipment

CAMARA > 55, place de la République (2nd) Ⓒ **04 78 42 15 55.** When it comes to photography, this shop's as complete as you could possibly hope for. At *Camara,* you'll find everything that exists – the *Canon, Pentax, Nikon* ranges, hundreds of lenses, flashes, measuring equipment... For most people, this would be more than enough, but Camara's speciality's digital equipment. Hence, you'll also find all the ranges of digital camera, all the memory systems, all the scanners, all the printers... Add to this the films, the bags, the tripods, the frames, the camescopes, TV's, walkmen, radiocassettes, CD's, video tape-recorders, DVD's... and you've got a real Ali Baba's cave, only better.

Lyon *Leisure activities - Photo & video*

FNAC > 85, rue de la République (2nd) ℂ **04 72 40 49 49.** In photography, as in many fields, the FNAC excels. There's choice, advice and, very often, impeccable prices.

PASSION PHOTO > 83, grande rue de la Croix-Rousse (4th) ℂ **04 72 07 02 30.** Photo development, obviously, but also frames and some equipment : camera cases, lenses, filters… both new and second-hand. Equipment's bought and sold here. It's checked by specialists and and guaranteed six months. Pity that there's not enough second-hand equipment.

STUDIO JOSE > 24, place de la Croix-Rousse (4th) ℂ **04 72 10 61 80.** Christine Balastéguy, who's from *Studio José*, is a portrait photographer (she also covers weddings) who sells frames, films and cameras. You'll find some of the most sophisticated equipment from the *Minolta* range, *Vivitar* lenses, *EOS Canon*, but also, and above all, small pocket-cameras at very reasonable prices.

Development

PHOTO HERWEY KODAK EXPRESS > 53, place de la République (2nd) ℂ **04 72 77 11 20 • 7, rue de la République (1st) 04 72 07 97 65 • 4, rue Victor Fort (4th) 04 78 27 98 58**

PHOTO STATION > 45, rue de la République (2nd) ℂ **04 78 37 92 76 • 47, rue Victor Hugo (2nd) 04 78 37 92 67 • 13, cours Gambetta (3rd) 04 72 61 10 65 • Part-Dieu Shopping Centre 04 72 61 13 33**

SYG PHOTO > 23, rue Edouard Herriot (1st) ℂ **04 78 28 32 38.** Photo development in one hour, digital ID photos, photo retouches, the transfer of old 8mm spools onto VHS – bags of different services, but no cameras. Strange. **Other addresses : 6, rue du Bât d'Argent (1st) 04 78 27 04 05 • 5, place Jules Guesde (7th) 04 78 69 23 24.**

THE HOME

◆FURNISHINGS

AFFAIRE DE FAMILLE ℂ **04 78 57 49 05.** This business is run by two cousins, Philippe Batifoulier, the architect, and Sylvie Fonlupt, a Fine Arts graduate. The story's simple : solid pine furniture, which is made by craftsmen and painted and weathered in four natural colours – white, ivory havana and grey. Each collection allows you to redecorate your house entirely. The dining room tables, low tables, bookcases, sideboards, chairs, consoles and sofa-arms all blend together artistically. The patina's applied by hand to give a classic or an old look.

ARRIVETZ > 24, rue Jarente (2nd) ℂ **04 72 41 17 77.** Here, the client walks through a world of design, in an enormous 800 m² shop with white walls and a large window to let the light filter through. Arrivetz is a French precursor in the field of 20th century design and decoration. Three interior architects/designers are employed to create furniture which is very comfortable and perfectly adapted to the needs of modern men and women. The furniture's extraordinary, and it's the sort of furniture you invest in for life ; it's timeless, artistic and defies fashion trends. There are more than 60 brands represented, most of them great classics in contemporary decoration : Le Corbusier, Cassina, Desalto, Starck, Knoll, Giorgetti... A few amusing examples : the waste-paper basket's tilted so that you can throw paper into it from a distance, and the chairs have names, as if they were works of art – coffee chairs called Marly and Costes.

CERFOGLI > 26, avenue de Saxe (6th) ℂ **04 78 24 70 44.** In a superb showroom, *Cerfogli* displays sofas and matching low tables in rattan. But you can also choose to decorate your salon in wooden or in wrought iron furniture, with all the accessories which go with it, like lamps, carpets, vases and small decorative objects at all prices.

CINNA > 28, cours Lafayette (3rd) ℂ **04 78 62 71 88.** The Cinna shop in the Cours Lafayette has been entirely renovated this year and has got a new lease of life. Since 1984, this boutique's been selling a quality, contemporary collection of furniture, which is signed by the big names : Pascal Mourgue, Peter Maly, Didier Gomez, D'Urbino Lomazzi, Thibault

Desombres and Pagnon Pelhaîtres, as well as many young creators showing promising style. In a 300 m² shop, split over three floors, you'll find a collection of sofas and furniture for the sitting-room and bedroom, along with carpets, lamps and decorative objects. **Other addresses : 4, cours de la Liberté (3rd) 04 78 62 89 10 • 94, route de Grenoble - SAINT-PRIEST 04 78 90 90 82.**

DU VENT DANS LES VOILES > 32, rue Cuvier (6th)   ℂ   **04 78 52 98 10.** So that your home is decorated with harmony and good taste, and not with a disordered collection of bric-à-brac, Du *Vent dans les Voiles* offers to match bedspreads, sofa cushions, lampshades and curtains in the same material. There are roughly a dozen models to choose from.

GENTIL HOME > 24, rue de la Charité (2nd)   ℂ   **04 78 42 40 21.** Ultra-chic and contemporary, this beautiful boutique has a collection of modern, prestigious furniture which (provided you can afford it) will make your flat a comfortable and pleasant place to live in. An interior decoration team will help you to choose the leather sofa and glass-paned bookcase which are the best suited for the size of your flat, to design the most practical chest of drawers (made-to-measure), or to choose lamps, tables, chairs and king-size mattresses. Everything's beautiful and luxurious, the design's perfect and the advice given, informed and judicious.

GEROMINO > 6, place Fernand-Rey (1st) ℂ **06 60 13 63 66.** *Géromino*, or *"Little Jeremy"* in Spanish, is a young creator/artist/designer... who's not short of ideas and resources for the creation of contemporary furniture. An ace when it comes to retrieving old articles, he makes his creations from old furniture, bits of wood, aluminium and steel, plastic salad bowls or lamps, mirrors or chairs. The wood's natural, painted or varnished - depending on how he feels and on what you want, because he also also takes orders to create made-to-measure furniture and objects.

GRANGE > 1, rue du Colonel-Chambonnet (2nd)   ℂ   **04 78 38 23 77.** This uperb shop is 1 000 m² large and is built into the old *Hôtel de l'Europe*, which was renovate for the purposes. It sells beautiful family furniture which you can easily picture in a home filled with friends and laughing children. There's alot of wood, but also rattan, wrought iron, terracotta... and other noble materials. The *Meubles Mémoire* Collection reconstructs the offices of famous people like Napoleon or Saint-Exupéry. The boutique's spacious, and everyone just strolls around as he likes, from the little salon to the dining room where the table's laid, or from the reading corner to the material room.

KAOLIN > 1, place Bellecour (2nd)   ℂ   **04 78 37 53 56.** Lamps, fittings, carpets... Kaolin offers a wide choice of articles, including those made by the big names in furniture, and some made by very modern creators. The new sofa collections are nearly all covered with material which can be removed and machine-washed, and the furniture's sober and modern or round and comfortable, just inviting you to sit on it. **Other address : 4, rue Colonel-Chambonnet (2nd) 04 78 42 80 70.**

L'ARBRE A CHAISES > 47, avenue Jean-Jaurès (7th)   ℂ   **04 78 58 20 88.** Whetever little space is looking for its chair will find it here : modern loft, Swiss chalet, student's one-room flat, bourgeois flat, caravan, château, family house... all styles, all chairs, all prices.

L'OBJET DU DESIR > 4, rue Grenette (2nd)   ℂ   **04 78 92 81 87.** Feminine curves applied to furniture and to objects in the spirit of a modern boudoir : voluptuous sofas, rounded lamps, gracious dressing tables, delicately sculpted mirrors, Venus-like vases. Girls will be more at home here than professional rugbymen.

LA GALERIE DU CONVERTIBLE > 1, quai de la Pêcherie (1st)   ℂ   **04 78 28 13 42.** All the sofas on display in this vast boutique with pretty walls are convertible into beds, but are, nevertheless, comfortable to sit in. The materials covering them are only there to give you an idea of possibilities, and you can change them at your leisure once you've looked at an enormous choice of sample materials. Prices vary between 4 000 F and 16 000 F. To complete the ensemble, there are cushions matching each model, as well as little decorative objects (trays, jars, shelves) in wickerwork.

Lyon *The Home - Furnishings*

LA MAISON DE FELIX > 11, rue de la Charité (2nd) ℰ **04 72 40 07 32.** Both in the shop and in the catalogue, *La Maison de Félix* is a Lyonnais manufacturer of wrought-iron furniture, offering more than 250 models in its creation-collection. Canopy beds, matching tables and chairs, consoles, shelves... you'll find everything to furnish your house, from the attic to the cellar. A novelty in the shop is the marriage of wood and iron for Provençal-style furniture, including cupboards and 'jam-closets'. You'll also find furniture in painted teak, which resists the very worst weather conditions, and Indonesian cupboards.

LA MAISON COURTIEU > 64, cours Vitton (6th) ℰ **04 78 52 14 68.** *E-mail :* *raoul.courtieu@hol.fr* • This prestigious establishment, which was created in 1853, is specialized in household accessories. It sells carpets, curtains, bed- and table linen, wallpaper and lamps, made by brands such as Christian Dior or Yves Saint Laurent. The Courtieu workshop produces very beautiful, made-to-measure creations. **Other addresses : 24bis, place Bellecour (2nd) 04 78 37 26 38 • 50, Grande-Rue-de-la-Croix-Rousse (4th) 04 78 29 54 36.**

LA MAISON DU FAUTEUIL > 59, quai Saint-Vincent (1st) ℰ **04 78 27 13 99.** For more than 30 years, this large shop has been selling armchairs, chairs and sofas, but also lovely wooden furniture made by cabinet-makers, tapestry work and decorative objects – all of it very beautiful quality. **Other address : 1, place Henri-Barbusse (9th) 04 78 83 91 26.**

LE VISTEMBOIR > 33, rue Sala (2nd) ℰ **04 78 37 61 67.** *Le Vistemboir* is a showroom which is a model of refinement, of good taste and of attention to the smallest detail. The furniture and decorative objects necessary for personalizing your flat are presented harmoniously and in soft, diffused lighting. The sofas are enormous and comfortable (in red velvet, for example), the mirrors are Baroque and gilded, whilst the low tables are made in dark, polished wood. You need to have room in your flat to house this superb furniture, as well as a very thick wallet.

LES MAISONS DU SOLEIL > 88, Grande-Rue-de-la-Guillotière (7th) ℰ **04 72 71 91 22.** This old warehouse was entirely converted and decorated with warm, bright colours on the walls (sun-yellow, orange, blood-red), and now sells a superb selection of Mediterranean-inspired furniture, made in wood and wrought-iron. The sofas are shaped like an arabesque and are padded with large, natural-coloured cushions ; the lamps have feet which are heavily 'worked' in the shape of garlands and leaves ; the lampshades and rugs are the same colour as the walls, and the tables and pedestal tables are gracious and would blend into any décor. Finally, there's a light note to all this because, even if the models are, in the main, exclusive, they're often sold at very competitive prices because they're sold direct.

LITERIE GAMBLIN > 50, boulevard des Belges (6th) ℰ **04 78 17 41 18.** This manufacturer sells directly to the public, and, because intermediaries are eliminated, the bill's considerably lighter. Payment facilities are proposed, and you can pay in four instalments without interest being charged. *Gamblin* will tailor-make the bed of your dreams for the price of a simple, standard bed. That's life in a château for you !

LITERIE PRODUCTION > 83, boulevard de la Croix-Rousse (4th) ℰ **04 78 30 40 27.** The shop has more than 300 models, and you can spend hours trying them all. There are bed-frames and mattresses of every imaginable type, for all tastes and for all backs. The sales staff aren't mean with their advice and explanations, and will remind you that you keep a bed for at least 10 years.

MAISON DE FAMILLE > 65, rue Edouard-Herriot (2nd) ℰ **04 72 56 00 00.** A house of good family, half a colonial residence, half a country house, where you wander from one room to the next, dreaming that this superb (and very expensive) wooden furniture could be in your home. You'll also find tableware, beautiful dishcloths for the kitchen, accessories, pyjamas, an astonishing linen scent for the linen cupboard and a wide range of classic and chic sportswear.

MERVEILLES D'ASIE > 71, cours Lafayette (6th) ℰ **04 37 24 17 70.** This shop sells the most refined craftwork made in Asia and the Far East. The porcelain and knick-knacks are precious ; the silk embroidery from Vietnam is entirely hand-made and can be personalized at your request ; the silk or cotton kimonos are equally beautiful. Lovely cedar opium-tables serve as sitting-room tables since opium smoking's no longer authorized in France. Ancient Chinese furniture in solid elm testify to the refinement of the Chinese civilization, and connoisseurs will particularly appreciate the laquered furniture, some of it incrusted with jade or mother of pearl, and some of it decorated with copper and with hand-painted flowers or birds.

NOUVEAU > 9, boulevard des Brotteaux (6th) ✆ **06 80 16 64 65.** The pin-up on the shopsign can only attract attention. This boutique-house, spread over two floors and opening onto a garden, is a classic antique shop, where you can find Art Deco tableware, old advertising posters, table linen and furniture. The shop also displays and sells creations made by the boss, David Spanu, who dropped his job as a window-dresser to dabble, design, paint and sandpaper. He humorously turns objects away from their original function : shells and wire netting become amusing, luminous garlands, a tennis raquet serves as a mirror-support, a bike lamp becomes a bedside lamp. Long live fantasy in the home !

PATRICK CLERTANT > 45, rue de Fontanières - VILLEURBANNE ✆ **04 78 84 18 97.** This "furniture couturier", who sells directly from his manufacturing workshops, offers to make the tailor-made furniture we all need or want. He's as much at ease with the Louis XIV style as with the Regency, Louis-Philippe or Louis XVI styles. If you prefer more modern furniture, that's no problem because he knows how to make that, too. His workshop makes kitchens, bathrooms, dining-rooms, chairs and dressers in walnut, oak or cherrywood, and the wood itself can be laquered or stratified. The price : from 1 500 F for the chairs to 19 000 F for a superb book-case with bevelled panes on a low dresser.

PRAHO > 36, avenue de Saxe (7th) ✆ **04 78 52 21 66.** The furniture and decorative objects at *Praho*'s come directly from Asian craft stalls. The entire range of polished furniture, in beige and white colours and in walnut or teak, blend perfectly with all interiors, be they classic or modern. The style's Asian, sober and refined, and you can buy Baroque consoles or dressers in solid walnut at low prices. There are a few typically-Moroccan models, including mosaic tables in bright colours.

SOGOLY > 12, place du Maréchal-Lyautey (6th) ✆ **04 78 52 13 12.** Sogoly's the King of the Carpet, and his shop's a veritable Ali Baba's cave, worthy of the Grand Bazaar in Istanbul, with carpets in all materials, all colours and all motifs warming the floor and the walls. You'll find a wide choice of rugs, including the famous Persian rugs, at interesting prices. You can also sell, exchange or have items valued.

TOSCANE > 2, rue Gaspard-André (2nd) ✆ **04 72 40 23 92.** A complete and matching range of contemporary furniture by the great Italian creators who you can't escape when it comes to design. The shop has the the the exclusive right in Lyon to sell tables, chairs, sofas, low tables and armchairs in the *Casa Milano* line. The style's pure, sober and zen, and gives a warm look, thanks to super-comfortable materials which are easy to keep clean. But, if that's what you want, you have to be willing to pay the price.

TOULEMONDE BOCHART > 29, rue de la Ferrandière (2nd) ✆ **04 72 56 97 77.** Here, there's a ground floor, a basement and another room devoted to little objects. You'll find wooden furniture in different styles, as well as a wide choice of modern carpets signed by Hilton Mac Conico : no need to unfold them to admire them – they're displayed on struts. The shop has the entire Italian collection of *Alessi* objects and accessories in coloured plastic, in flashy colours and with amusing shapes : spice jars, biscuit boxes, containers and hilarious figurines. **Other address : 48, avenue Foch (6th) 04 78 94 18 18.**

East Lyon

IKEA > ZAC du Champ du Pont - SAINT-PRIEST ✆ **04 72 15 28 28.** Even if you're just accompanying a friend who's come to furnish her flat, you're bound to crack for some item or another : 19 F for a lamp, 9 F for a teddy bear… difficult to resist. Everything to furnish or give another look to Home Sweet Home : floors, kitchens, bathrooms, sofas (890 F for a basic convertible sofa, 15 900 F for the same in leather), and even light bulbs and green plants. You'll find modern or warm materials (wood, steel, plastic, cardboard), creative items (very Andy Warhol carpet), clever ideas (furniture on wheels, inflatable sofas), a large dose of freedom (modular shelves) and good service (advisers, sale by phone). For such low prices, you have to mount the furniture yourself (the instructions sometimes leave you perplexed), and you won't keep it all your life. If you want to be original, avoid the basic *Ikea* items because everybody's got them !

Lyon *The Home - Tableware*

◆TABLEWARE

BENOIT UTILE > 14, rue Emile Zola (2nd) ✆ **04 78 56 50 99.** Yes, kitchen objects **and** utensils can sometimes be useful (like at Benoit's) and beautiful. The proof : the ultra-design shopping caddy in coloured plastic, the washing-up brush which stands on its feet… at prices which allow you to crack without stress.

INTERIO BOUTIQUE > 5, place Saint Nizier/2, rue de Brest (2nd) ✆ **04 78 42 85 61.** After Switzerland and Germany, *Interio*'s come to Lyon, where it's set up shop in the city centre. This shopping chain, which is better-known in the East, offers a wide choice of objects, utensils and decorative gadgets for the home and, above all, for the kichen. It sells lots of aluminium, inox, white porcelain, wood and glass - sober, useful, decorative items at more than reasonable prices.

REYNAUD > 18, rue de Brest (2nd) ✆ **04 78 37 33 43.** Reynaud sells a magnificent cocktail of big names in tableware, glass, porcelain and pewter, as well as decorative objects. The shop's a favourite of engaged couples who come here to leave the traditional list of wedding presents.

XAVIER PIVARD > 60, rue Auguste Comte (2nd). For connoisseurs of divine nectars, it's a sacrilege to drink a fine wine in a beer glass or a delicious champagne in a mustard glass, because it's well known that the shape of the glass has an influence on the taste. A crystal glass seen through a microscope reveals a surface which is covered in relief and is not at all smooth, and it is this rugged surface which allows the aroma molecules to release themselves. Xavier Pivard, who's Bordelais by origin, knows the subject well : he's a connoisseur of fine wines and a glass engraver. In his shop, you'll find the Sommelier series, which is also sold in New York's Modern Art Museum, as well as the collection prepared by a famous line of Austrian crystal makers.

◆ANTIQUE SHOPS AND ARTWORK SHOPS

Rue Auguste Comte

ACHEROFF	✆	**04 78 42 15 76.** Persian carpets.
B. VERNAY ET G. CHANTREL	✆	**04 78 42 87 55**
GALERIE MICHEL DESCOURS	✆	**04 78 37 34 54.** 17th and 18th century furniture. Objects of Art. Gilded wood.
PIERRE BOURGEOIS	✆	**04 78 42 61 23**
THIERRY MORIN	✆	**04 78 37 31 08.** 18th century objects. Furniture
TEMPLIER	✆	**04 78 37 74 27.** Silverwork. Ancient jewellery. Precious stones.
GERARDIN	✆	**04 78 37 61 49.** 18th century furniture. Sculpted wood.
GALERIE SAMANI	✆	**04 78 37 63 34**
GALERIE GIRARD	✆	**04 78 38 21 54.** Carpets. Tapestries.
LES CLASSIQUES D'AUGUSTE COMTE	✆	**04 72 77 69 97.** Decoration.
GALERIE L'EAU FORTE	✆	**04 78 37 89 14.** Drawings. Ancient engravings.
CHARLES BALAY	✆	**04 78 37 05 90**
JEAN REY	✆	**04 78 37 09 09.** Furniture. 18th century paintings.
GALERIE GILBERT MOLLE	✆	**04 78 37 04 56.** Antique paintings.

ARCHAIA	✆	**04 78 92 93 91**. Archaeology. Primitive Art. Religious Art.
L'AIR DU TEMPS	✆	**04 72 40 00 53.** Quimper faïence. Jewellery.
VICOMTE	✆	**04 78 42 25 42.** Exotic Art.
GALERIE LAURENCIN	✆	**04 78 37 86 19**
GALERIE DE L'ESTAMPE	✆	**04 78 37 88 26.** Prints. Ancient drawings and engravings.
MARIE JO PERRIN	✆	**04 78 37 31 27**
HERVE DEVAUX	✆	**04 78 37 77 11.** Antiques.
POUR LA GALERIE	✆	**04 72 40 06 43.** Curiosities.
GALERIE YVES CHALVIN	✆	**04 78 38 21 46.** 18th and 19th century paintings. Lyonnais School.
THIERRY ROCHE	✆	**04 78 37 13 21.** Art Nouveau. Art Deco.
LIBRAIRIE CHAMINADE	✆	**04 78 92 87 40**
CLAGAHE	✆	**04 78 37 21 35**
L'ENCRE ALDINE	✆	**04 78 42 07 60**
LE VERSEAU	✆	**04 78 37 45 24.** Old books.
AU BATELEUR	✆	**04 78 42 36 32.** Esoteric bookshop.
JACQUES MONIN	✆	**04 72 40 90 50**
PIERRE RICHARD	✆	**04 78 37 01 19**
PASCAL GUILLEMIN	✆	**04 78 37 91 51.** 18th and 19th century furniture and objects.
FREDERIC CHARLES DUCOTE	✆	**04 78 37 31 29.** Scientific and maritime objects.
GALERIE FRED	✆	**04 78 38 19 90.** 20th century decorative art.
GALERIE ALAIN GEORGES	✆	**04 78 42 07 31.** Old and contemporary paintings.
LONDON MARKET	✆	**04 78 37 30 73.** 19th century English furniture.
MARCOU ANTIQUAIRE	✆	**04 78 38 38 25.** Furniture. 19th and 20th century objects.
LAZ'ART DECO	✆	**04 72 41 97 74.** Antiques from 1900, 1930 and 1940.
GALERIE ARTIS	✆	**04 78 38 28 01.** Figurative sculptures.
MARYLIN ANTIQUITES	✆	**04 72 41 88 12**
DOLL TOYS	✆	**04 78 42 91 51.** Dolls, silverwork and knickknacks. Ancient toys.
GALERIE MANSIET	✆	**04 78 37 99 39.** Ancient art from China and Japan.
LA BOURSE AUX TIMBRES	✆	**04 78 37 47 47.** Philately. Coins.

Lyon *The Home - Antique shops & artwork shops*

La Cité des Antiquaires

In Villeurbanne, at the edge of the *Parc de la Tête d'Or and* near the *Cité Internationale,* the *Cité des Antiquaires* groups 150 professionals in a superb building with an ultra-modern architecture. It's the perfect place for discovering (or buying) 18th and 19th century furniture, Art Deco, Popular Art, jewellery, paintings, bronzes, carpets, porcelain pieces or lace. You can leave your Wedding List here, and there's always an expert available on the first Saturday of every month.

◆DECORATION

ABC DECO > 7,rue Marietton (9th) ℂ **04 78 43 44 24.** In this workshop boutique, with yellow walls and crammed with catalogues filled with samples of material, you'll find all sorts of styles for re-covering old seats and sofas. The work is well done by hand, and you'd have to be very difficult not to find a motif you like because the choice is vast : you'll find watered silk and flowery, striped, pastel, bright, romantic or resolutely modern designs.

A MAREE HAUTE > 24, avenue du Maréchal de Saxe (6th) ℂ **04 78 24 33 22.** In a decor inspired by a fisherman's cabin, you'll find a load of ideas for presents or decoration to add some warmth to the bathroom or bedroom. There are colourful sponge towels by Kenzo, furniture, linen baskets and beautiful-smelling toiletry products.

AMARYLICE COTE DECO > 47, rue de Sala (2nd). The flower version of *Amarylice* already existed in the same gallery in the *Hotel Sofitel.* Now, an indispensable complement – a decoration shop – has opened. The flowers can be kept for life, because they're dry-frozen or made with material, and, for false flowers, they're incredibly real. To give a more refined touch to your decoration, you'll find candles, photo frames, interior scents, pots, vases and festive table accessories, including chic and original little objects at affordable prices – the first starts at 100 F. A good address for nice little presents without ruining yourself.

CHARLOTTE DECO > 23, rue du président Edouard Herriot (2nd) ℂ **04 72 98 38 03.** Have you ever thought about how much a house needs attractive material ? If not, Charlotte has thought about it for you. The shop sells table cloths and matching napkins, bath towels and gloves, ready-made or made-to-measure curtains and material to cover sofa, armchairs and walls. You can realize all your decoration plans without spending a fortune.

DECOR DISCOUNT > 19, rue Tissot (9th) ℂ **04 78 83 66 55.** This shop promises its customers incredible prices. It achieves that in a simple way – it buys factory batches, ends of series and 'second-choice' items which the clever know how to turn into 'first-choice' items, and offers promotions throughout the year. You can buy painted paper from 19.9 F a roll, lino and carpet for 7.9 F a m², parquet flooring you can easily lay down yourself, carpets at rock-bottom prices and litres and litres of paint. **Other address : RN6 route de Grenoble – SAINT BONNET DE MURE** ℂ **04 78 90 98 27.**

DORGA DESIGN > 1, rue Tronchet (6th) ℂ **04 78 94 02 56.** *Dorga's* more than an interior decoration shop. It's a design office which listens to its clients' needs, so as to prepare made-to-measure bookcases, kitchens and multi-media areas, or to design or renovate flats, houses, villas and offices. The in-house team takes care of everything – from design to completion – and uses tried and tested craftsmen. Hence, you can make even your wildest decoration-dream come true without having to worry about or supervise the works.

D'UN SOLEIL A L'AUTRE > 34, rue des Remparts d'Ainay (2nd) ℂ **04 78 38 77 40.** Here, you'll find all the bright Mediterranean decoration under the sun. This charming boutique offers Moroccan authenticity and know-how in matters of wrought-iron, traditional pottery, jewellery, carpets and citron-wood furniture. To brighten the interior of your flat, you can also order made-to-measure furniture.

FUTUR ANTERIEUR > 9, rue Ferrandière (2nd) ℂ **04 72 40 00 86.** An angel passed by and, in a beat of wings, left a few feathers and turned everything white. So, everything here's white – from the dishes to the small furniture, from the tablecloths to the candles, and from the frames to the lamps. Here and there, white or off-white items are enlivened by a few feathers, glints of gold, trinkets and leaf-work. A very pleasant address for wedding lists and little presents.

GEOLOGICA SHOP > 99, avenue du Maréchal de Saxe (3rd) ℂ **04 72 84 63 95.** The Italian *Granitifiandre* Group opened its Lyonnais boutique in January 2000. The shop's spacious, luxurious and 'technological', and sells in a thousand shapes and forms an innovative material consisting of a mixture of minerals, granite and natural stone and which, according to the salesman, is "as beautiful as marble, but more adaptable". The collection's enormous, so there's something for every taste. You're given patient advice, and computers help to draft a decoration scheme which is both unique and adapted to your needs.

HAPPY DAYS > 33, rue Baraban (3rd) ℂ **04 78 54 82 38.** "Sunday, Monday, *Happy Days*… Tuesday, Wednesday, what a day !" – does this remind you of something ? Yes, as you go into this very American boutique, you can be sure that The Fonz, Ralph and the others aren't far away – probably near the jukebox or sipping a milkshake as they play on the flipper, unless, of course, they happen to be buying one of the numerous Statues of Liberty, a pin-up poster or a typically Yank decorative object. For a party or a theme evening, *Happy Days* even offers certain items you can hire.

JARDINS DE MEDITERRANNEE > 22, avenue de Saxe (6th) ℂ **04 37 24 11 22.** All the colours, tastes and smells of the South in a refined boutique, decorated with warm colours (sun yellow and 'setting-sun' orange) and Provençal material. Along the walls, you'll find pots and bottles lined up on blue shelves, like in a fine grocery store. The dishes and plates are gay and colourful, the bedspreads and linen are lovely, and the flasks and bottles contain the thousand and one odours of the *garrigue*, of lavender and of rosemary.

L'ART ET CREATIONS > 3, rue Juiverie (5th) ℂ **04 78 30 91 81.** The artist-creator who runs this little boutique has unbounded imagination, and has created hilarious objects, somewhere between The Arabian Nights and the Cartoon World. Mirrors, lamps, candles and furniture are made even more beautiful with bold colours, trinkets and jewellery paste. You can't miss the rounded or extravagant and distorted shapes – they're evrything but classical. Lots of unique items. If you've got a particular idea in mind, the artist can create made-to-measure objects for all purses.

L'HOMME D'OSIER > 22, rue Paul Chenavard (2nd) ℂ **04 78 28 35 33.** This boutique, which is divided into two parts (one on each side of the street), is entirely devoted to a material which was so dear to the hippies of the 60's. The shop sells wickerwork, which has been updated for modern tastes - an excellent thing because it's both attractive and solid. So, you'll find wickerwork, wickerwork and wickerwork – made into lampshades, small shelves, baskets, trunks and toys, as well as a host of chairs and armchairs.

LA DAME DU CABANON > 34, rue Franklin (2nd) ℂ **04 78 38 05 82.** This is a place to stroll around in, taking care at the same time not to knock a pile of plates or a leopard lamp over. There's a mixture of antique objects and of the most recent trends in matters of decoration. You'll find all colours and all materials – from wood and wickerwork to wrought-iron, lace, porcelain and ivory. You can pretend to be a seasoned traveller and buy objects from round the world. At the end of your visit, they may offer you a tea or a coffee in front of the fireplace. It's a place you'll come back to.

LES ARMOIRES DE BERYL > 2, rue Grenette (2nd) ℂ **04 72 41 05 50.** This shop is brimming over with old-style tableware, perfumed candles, silk and cotton articles and dishcloths which are as beautiful as scarves. Decoration material has its own little room, and, for those who are useless at sewing, there's a service which can tailor-make your curtains, blinds, bedcovers and cushions. Even the prices make you feel like changing everything : material from 55 F a metre, making-up service from 105 F a width. At the top of the staircase and at the end of the corridor, there are clothes for chic women in all the classic colours – beige, black, grey and red.

N COMME NANCY > 36, rue Cuvier (6th) ℂ **04 37 24 02 03.** Nancy likes weddings, anniversaries, births and flat-warming parties to be the occasion for offering small or large presents. All budgets will find what they're looking for (from 10 to 2000 F), and all tastes are catered for (consoles, frames, pots, table linen, scents). A nice touch – the paintings brought here by amateur painters.

PAUL Ô BANN > 4, rue du colonel Chambonnet (2nd) ✆ **04 72 40 24 01.** A newcomer to the world of design, *Paul ô Bann* offers objects made in craft workshops, one of them in Lyon and the other in Thailand. There are also works by Lyonnais creators. More than a brand, it's a 'concept', which seeks to discover tomorrow's talents by freeing them from commercial restraints, so that they can develop their potential. The material worked includes hand-cast pottery, terracotta, polished inox, a resin which loses its plastic look and is worked like pottery or glass, and hand-painted ceramics with resin. The objects are beautiful and useful, the purpose being to integrate art into everyday life : vases, plates, cups, bowls...

STEFF > 89, Grande Rue – OULLINS. You can still find bargains at *Steff*'s, even if the shop's changed activity and has dropped women's ready-to-wear in favour of a new concept – the consignment of a host of different goods at ultra-competitive prices. You have to drop in regularly in order to find that little marvel for your flat which will make all your friends jealous – from tableware to kitchen utensils, and including household linen, decorative objects and DIY products.

TEMPS PRESENT > 29, cours Lafayette (6th) ✆ **04 78 52 34 47.** Like all interior decoration shops today, *Temps Présent* offers little furniture and rather Zen decorative objects, made with noble and natural materials like wood, osier, glass, and organza. Colonial chairs invite relaxation, tableware and silverwork remind you of family dinners, whilst frames are just waiting for the photos of the children. All these objects make you feel like creating a quiet, intimate and warm atmosphere at home.

THIVEL ET BEREZIAT > 108, avenue Jean Jaurès (7th) ✆ **04 72 76 80 40.** The doorknobs and buttons on display come straight from the workshop and they're little short of works of art. There are very original handles for the kitchen cupboard in the shape of knives, forks and spoons, and you'll find attractive material (resin, Murano glass, wrought-iron, aluminium) made into different shapes (flowers, shells, animals).

◆ MOVING HOUSE

ACCESS SELF STOCKAGE > 17, rue des Rosiéristes – CHAMPAGNE AUX MONT D'OR ✆ **04 72 52 44 44.** This furniture warehouse stores bulky and other objects during your house-move. Their containers (2.25 m² to 30 m²) are neither humid nor dirty. They're under permanent surveillance and can be hired for a minimum of one month. *Access Stockage* takes care of everything, so you can leave with no worries. Parking areas, boxes and trolleys are available to clients for all types of handling and it's not expensive, either.

ADEL > 34, rue Cazeneuve (8th) ✆ **04 78 00 85 54.** *Allo Déménagement Economique Location* (*ADEL* or Hello, Economical Moving and Hire) : a whole programme ! Two solutions are proposed. If you have a light vehicle driving licence, you can hire vans of 9.18 m³ or 21 m³, which are as easy to drive as a car and which you fill with cardboard boxes for your precious things. Alternatively, *ADEL* provides the whole team : a large truck and beefy movers who will empty your flat in a blink.

AGS > 131/141, rue Bataille (8th) ✆ **04 78 77 54 33.** Right, I've decided, we're dropping everything and moving to Papua New Guinea. For all long-distance moves, there's no problem. AGS is the specialist for distant and exotic countries.

DEMECO > 38, avenue des Frères Lumière (8th) ✆ **04 78 00 36 18.** The black stallion with the mane blowing in the wind, that's them. They take care of all moves for private individuals, office or factory moves, throughout France and abroad. They also offer a furniture storage service. **Other addresses : 207, avenue Charles de Gaulle – TASSIN LA DEMI LUNE 04 78 34 14 18 • 99, rue Claude Bernard – VILLEFRANCHE SUR SAONE 04 74 60 60 08.**

LES DEMENAGEURS BRETONS > 42, rue Chevreul (7th) ✆ **04 78 69 45 58.** Beefy Bretons, but without the round hats, and specialists in moving both heavy grand pianos and small items of great sentimental value. For those who are broke, the *Dém'Junior* formula provides you with an upholstered van and two strong-armed assistants. Others can opt for the *Dém'Aménagemen* formula : there's nothing to do, even the reinstallation's taken care of. **76** **Other address : 78, rue du Marais – VILLEURBANNE 04 72 71 49 66.**

MICHEL HOLL > 17, avenue du 24 aout 1944 – CORBAS   ℂ   **04 72 23 04 04.** After a free estimate, *Michel Holl*, who has 30 years of experience in the business, moves all your furniture and objects of art in France or abroad. He'll take care of your foreign posting, and installs the furniture at the other end.

FASHION

◆ACCESSORIES

CHAPELLERIE WEISS > 74, passage de l'Argue (2nd)   ℂ   **04 78 37 80 38.** The hat has come back into fashion. And that's a news, because a hat beautifully rounds off an elegant outfit, keeps you warm in winter and protects you from the sun in summer... In this attractive shop with an old-fashioned, wood décor, men, women and children won't know where to start because the choice is so vast : shapes, colours, materials, the classic, the extravagant – there's a hat for every head.

FLORIMODE > 9, rue de Belfort (4th)   ℂ   **04 78 29 44 56.** At the heart of the large village which is *Croix Rousse*, you'll find a shop for those who have the right head for a hat, as well as for those who don't, because there's an enormous choice, with something for everyone. And if you don't find what you want, *Florimode* also tailor-makes hats. All models, for all occasions, in all mateials and at all prices – from 70 F to 1 300 F.

LOUISE TOSSIVAR > 10, rue du Plat (2nd)   ℂ   **04 72 77 58 76.** A fashion designer by training, *Louise Tossivar* has no equal for helping her customers find the right hat, the one that goes with their outfit and best suits their face. The models are chic or extravagant, colourful or natural, simple or with feathers, ribbons and hair pins to keep them in place or to make them more attractive. For special occasions, like weddings and receptions, you can even hire a hat.

◆SHOES

Ladies

CORDOAN > 21, rue Victor-Hugo (2nd)   ℂ   **04 78 37 80 39.** A reference in the city in matters of shoes. The shop offers chic and, generally, classic models, which are always of the best quality and sold at reasonable prices. The reception's traditional, there's a good choice of city or sports models, and there are regular deliveries of new items. **Other addresses : 11, rue Childebert (2nd) 04 78 37 49 15 • 10, avenue du Maréchal-de-Saxe (6th) 04 78 52 96 49.**

GALIX > 31, rue Grenette (2nd)   ℂ   **04 72 41 04 26.** Come on, girls, put on your best shoes and we'll go dancing. Your cupboard's empty, apart from that old pair of trainers ? Come and look round *Galix* to find shoes, boots, ankle-boots, high- or low heels, in rose pink or crow black. There you go, now you're perfectly equipped to go and swing.

J. B. MARTIN > 15, rue Victor-Hugo (2nd)   ℂ   **04 78 37 97 36.** *J.B Martin* sells (at fairly expensive prices, it has to be said) superb shoes for sophisticated young ladies and their very chic mothers. The models, which are invaraibly black, are perfect for evening wear, but can be worn during the day – preferably with a dress or an elegant outfit, and with a handsome man on your arm to go with the shoes.

LOLITA > 25, rue Paul-Chenavard (1st)   ℂ   **04 72 07 67 67.** The reception's charming, the choice is varied and the models are modern – three good reasons for coming often. The prices are low for the quality on offer, so what more can the people want ?

NICOLE CROIBIER > 27, rue Cuvier (6th)   ℂ   **04 37 24 14 61.** For extremely chic and elegant shoes, this is the address. You'll find prestigious labels (*Christian Lacroix, Pollini, Thierry Mugler, Rossetti, Yves Saint Laurent*) and irreproachable quality, so that ladies can go off to the most elegant of soirées dressed like queens. Obviously, it's expensive, but you have to pay for luxury.

PARALLELE > 42, rue Mercière (2nd) ℂ **04 78 37 25 61.** There's not an enormous choice of models in this boutique, but they're renewed regularly, and the woman who wears them feels much more feminine, dressed in shoes with magnificent heels, which make the legs more elegant, and pointed caps, which give a divine shape – all at around 800 F a pair. It may not be a give-away price, but don't they say that in any outfit it's the shoes that make all the difference ?

Men

BEXLEY > 20, rue Lanterne (1st) ℂ **04 72 07 99 51.** Beautiful shoes in a boutique which is decorated in wood, that's Bexley. The shoes are dressy, casual, country or boat, but always top class. The shop's specialized in hand-stitched Goodyears and Norwegian shoes, and connoisseurs know that that's a guarantee of quality. The sales staff aren't mean with their advice about how best to take care of the shoes, they're generous with their technical explanations, and they show off their knowledge on the subject extremely seriously.

JEAN BOOTS CAFE > 45, passage de l'Argue (2nd) ℂ **04 78 42 04 78.** The legendary cowboy with the fag in his mouth had better behave. His official supplier was hiding in the *Passage de l'Argue*, and he's been found out ! Here, there's a festival of Texan and Mexican boots and half-boots in classic leathers (black, brown) or in more extravagant colours (red, turquoise, green). Their quality and price vary. City men, once you've got the boots on your feet, don't forget to buy the hat and the string tie which go with them. The boys are waiting for you in front of the saloon door.

Mixed

ADRIEN > 42, rue Edouard-Herriot (2nd) ℂ **04 78 28 15 51.** At *Adrien's*, you'll find shoes in colours to match the occasion, the season and your outfit. In both summer and winter, you wear red, pink or white shoes for the big or small events – not to mention the black shoes which you wear every day. The shoes are fashionable, and there are so many models available that you'll have to go inside to check on the shoes which aren't on display in the shopwindow.

ARTHUR > 68, rue de la République (1st) ℂ **04 78 37 75 64.** In the shopwindow, you'll find all sorts of shoes for both sexes, and they're right up to fashion. The boys swear by the *Campers*, with round or square toes and a thick sole, in black, beige or brown. The girls always go for the feminine styles, and crack for the boots with incredibly - high heels, the casual shoes in fake leather or zebra, the sandals with thongs you wrap round your legs like a Spartan or the trainers with heavily-built up soles by *No Name*. You'll leave the shop happy to have such attractive shoes.

BALLY > 26, rue de la République (2nd) ℂ **04 72 41 11 30.** *Bally* offers very chic and very classy shoes. They're in leather and suède, they're comfortable and they're in excellent taste. In addition to all the shoes, boots and ankle boots carrying the *Bally* label, you'll also find famous names like *Timberland*, for example. To crown it all, the shop's bright, spacious and airy. **Other address : 44, rue de la République (2nd) 04 72 41 11 00.**

BATA > "La Part Dieu" Shopping Centre - Level 2 (3rd) ℂ **04 78 62 31 72.** The soles aren't always leather, and nor are the shoes, for that matter. But, at *Bata*, the choice is sufficiently large for all the family (kids, teenagers, parents and grandparents alike) to find something for their feet without carving a hole in the family budget. **Other addresses : 9, Grande-Rue-de-la-Croix-Rousse (4th) 04 78 27 08 92 • 16, rue Victor-Hugo (2nd) 04 78 37 18 22.**

CHARLES JOURDAN > 13, rue Emile-Zola (2nd) ℂ **04 78 37 38 41.** Magnificent leather, superb lines and models which are both beautiful, comfortable and worth the price you pay for them. Since 1921, the year in which it opened its first workshop, the Jourdan label has acquired in France and throughout the world the reputation we all know about and which it isn't about to lose. Beautiful, very beautiful shoes. **Other address : 31, cours Vitton (6th) 04 78 89 40 33.**

DELPOL > 4, cours Vitton (6th) ℂ **04 37 24 31 09.** Delpol offers a Gargantuan choice for an orgy of shoes in all styles, all sizes and covering dozens of labels : *Converse, Doc Martens, Clarks, Arthur, Triver Fligh*t for the men and *Elizabeth Stuart, No Name, Free Lance, Lolita Bis, Georges Rech Sport, Frida* and *Esprit* for the ladies. **Other addresses : 28bis, route de Saint-Cyr (9th) 04 78 83 71 75 • 30, cours Emile-Zola - VILLEURBANNE 04 78 24 58 27.**

JEAN-PAUL DEBOURG > 16, cours Tolstoï - **VILLEURBANNE** ℂ **04 78 84 66 12.** With boxes nicely- piled up as high as the ceiling, and with a host of labels (*Salamander, Church's, Timberland, Bocage, Caterpilar...*) displayed on 100 m², *Dubourg* is a goldmine for those looking for a large choice of comfortable and solid shoes.

LA SANDALE DU PELERIN (THE PILGRIM'S SANDAL) > 1, rue du Vieil-Renversé (5th) ℂ **04 78 42 00 23.** You don't have to be planning a pilgrimage to Lourdes or to Santiago de Compostella to wear these sandals. In fact, that would be a bad idea since a pair of trainers would be more appropriate. On the other hand, those with a touch of the hippy in them, and all those who like to feel the air around their toes when summer comes, will find what they're after among the sandals in all colours and sizes you'll find here.

LE PALAIS DE LA CHAUSSURE > 18, rue Pizay (2nd) ℂ **04 78 28 11 14.** Little feet are cute – everyone loves them, and those who have them can easily find shoes. So, what about big feet ? Anyone interested ? Top models (with big feet) and basketball players will find what they need in this shop to avoid walking around barefooted – up to Size 45 for ladies (yes, it exists) and up to Size 50 for men.

MEPHISTO SHOP > 14, rue Grenette (2nd) ℂ **04 78 42 83 27.** *Mephisto* sells shoes to those who, like the Germans, are more interested in having comfortable arches than the trendiest of shoes. Here, you'll find ultra-light sandals, moccasins and boots, which you can twist and bend in all directions without deforming them, which don't heat up the feet (goodbye, foot odour), and which don't give you back-ache.

PALLIO > 65, rue de la République (2nd) ℂ **04 78 42 36 88.** Here, you'll find labels like *Ted Lapidus* or *René Derhy* and very interesting prices for classic or slightly more (but not a lot more) fashionable models which you can wear at the office, in the country or to soirées at the Embassy.

ROBERT CLERGERIE > 17, rue Emile-Zola (2nd) ℂ **04 78 37 28 44.** The boutique's small, but it doesn't have to be any bigger to present the models proposed by this label every year. The style's avant-garde, innovative and highly fashionable, so that the prices are high but justified. The leather's beautiful, the models are hyper-comfortable and, for snobs, the *Clergerie* style has been distinguishable from a thousand others for more than the century that the label has existed. Count around 1 000 F for a pair of shoes.

STEPHANE KELIAN > 11, rue Emile-Zola (2nd) ℂ **04 78 42 19 07.** Born in the provinces, then manufactured at Romans, shoes made by the *Kélian* family are often in plaited leather, in sober and classic lines with the occasional fantasy. A sure sign of success – you no longer ask your friends, "Have you seen my new shoes ?", but, "Do you like my new *Kélians* ?". From 800 F.

YEARLING > 14, rue des Archers (2nd) ℂ **04 72 41 08 55.** Here, you'll find chic, sports lines in an attractive Italian décor, with rounded furniture and red-ochre colours. As you sit in club armchairs, you can try on tennis shoes, laced-up Derbies by *Geox* and *Triverflight*, trainers by *Andrea Tokio* and shoes in multi-coloured canvas by *Bensimon.* There are also more dressy shoes by *Myma* in pink, beige, sky-blue or black calf's leather.

◆ LEATHER AND FUR

ANAF > 36, rue de Brest (2nd) ℂ **04 78 42 05 31.** During the 80 years of its existence, *Anaf* has forged a solid reputation for the quality of its leathers, skins and furs. The shop doesn't go unnoticed in the *Rue de Brest* becuase, in the shopwindow, there's an enormous and ferocious-looking polar bear standing on two legs. The choice isn't enormous, because Albert Anaf rigorously selects his products among the biggest names in the the *haute-couture* world. He can also bring a damaged fur back to life, mend a torn jacket or even update a jacket which has become a bit old-fashioned.

CANADIENNE GRIFFES > 19bis, quai Augagneur (3rd) ℂ **04 78 71 79 49.** Wild men and women like the labels on sale here. They include the many models made by *Guy Laroche, Révillon* or *Cerruti :* long coats, short jackets, parkas, blazers, Canadians, reversible coats and jackets in leather, fur and suède.

Lyon *Fashion - Leather and fur*

JEAN FOUGEROUSE FOURREUR > 20, quai Gailleton (2nd) ✆ **04 78 37 88 00.** Animal skins, leathers, furs and fleeces – they're coming back into fashion. Jean Fougerouse, whose shop is located at the foot of the Sofitel Hotel, offers a vast choice of his own creations as well as the big labels - particularly the spectacular fur collections by Gianfranco Ferré, Yves Saint Laurent and Christian Lacroix. The prices, too, are spectacular, but the reception's as soft as the furs on sale.

LA CANADIENNE > 19, quai Augagneur (3rd) ✆ **04 78 60 00 56.** Big sister to *Canadienne Griffes*, *La Canadienne* knows what it's talking about when it's a question of braving the polar cold and the glacial kiss of winter. Its clients put on their mittens, and warm themselves in all sorts of soft, animal or synthetic furs, lined leather or skin coats, airmen's jackets or sheepskins. Thus protected, they welcome the arrival of the snow.

LUCIEN GOMBERT > 28, cours Franklin-Roosevelt (6th) ✆ **04 78 52 35 88.** The boutique's existed since 1967, so that it's seen a host of styles, trends and fashions come and go. Lucien Gombert has always stayed up-to-date, and knows how to share his love of fur with his faithful clients. Faithful, because Lucien Gombert and his wife reserve for all their clients that type of friendly welcome which makes you want to come back. In addition to superb furs, you'll find leather and skin models signed by *Christian Dior* or *Jean-Louis Scherrer*, bags by *Christian Lacroix* and *Kenzo* and little chain pullovers by *Nina Ricci* (because you still have to wear something under the fur).

MAC DOUGLAS > 8, rue Gasparin (2nd) ✆ **04 78 37 80 79.** For a modern, elegant and relaxed look, modern men and women opt for clothes signed by *Mac Douglas* which cross time and fashions without ever showing a wrinkle. The choice is vast and pleases all generations : soft and comfortable sheepskins, jackets, coats, trousers, shirts, accessories and bags. All articles are guaranteed, and the after sales service is excellent : alterations, maintenance and repairs. **Other addresses : 13, avenue du Maréchal-de-Saxe (6th) 04 78 24 98 55 • "La Part Dieu" Shopping Centre (3rd) - Level 3 04 78 60 93 96.**

RIZAL > 9, rue du Président-Edouard-Herriot (2nd) ✆ **04 72 10 91 10.** The shop's deliberately white and stylized, using the play of mirrors and screens to enhance the beauty of the magnificent skins, lamb furs, minks and jackets made by the biggest names in fashion : *Jean-Paul Gaultier, Yves Saint Laurent, Louis Féraud*. When it's warmer, the skins get lighter, and you'll find trousers and tops, lined with python or with leopard printing.

VENT COUVERT > Rue du Président Edouard-Herriot (2nd). The collection targets a fairly young and trendy clintèle, and offers mixed models in beautiful quality skins offering good value for money. The lamb's leather's smooth and models are short, tapered at the waist or with zips. The boutique's very small, but the choice is large and you're well received.

◆SECOND-HAND CLOTHES SHOPS

FEMININ TOUJOURS > 112, rue de Sèze (6th) ✆ **04 78 24 76 07.** This place looks like anything but a second-hand clothes shop. Everything's nicely laid out by colours, neatly folded and attractively presented, with the labels at the top. You choose the new outfits, and leave those which have been worn too much (or not at all). You'll find good labels, like *Kenzo, Marithé* and *François Girbaud, Irié, Issey Miyaké, Indies...* it all depends on the day and on the arrivals. You can also find shoes by *Kélian* and *Clergerie,* and accessories by *Vuitton* and *Gucci.*

GRIFFES ET DEGRIFFES > 40-42, rue Tête-d'Or (6th) ✆ **04 78 89 91 31.** Every ten days, new arrivals of prestigious labels attract those who know the shop and who like wearing *Versace, Cerruti* and *Iceberg*, because these major labels are sold here at very reasonable prices.

MARIE CLAIRE TROC > 10, rue Palais-Grillet (2nd) ✆ **04 78 37 32 14.** It's impossible to head to Megève or Saint-Tropez without first doing a tour at *Marie-Claire* in order to dress from head to foot in designer labels. The labels on offer are all highly fashionable, and are deposited here by fashion victims who've grown tired of them - *Chanel, Vuitton, Hermès, Yves Saint Laurent, Armani, Versace, Sonia Rykiel, Valentino...* Nothing but luxurious names, and a few new items, which are sold at a reduced price.

TROC'CINELLE > 330, rue André-Philip (3rd) ℰ **04 78 62 84 39.** Here, Mums are happy to deposit the clothes of their darling kids who grow far too quickly, and to buy new models which have been won by other kids who are slightly older and bigger. Because, even when you're small, the look counts. You'll find all styles – from the classic, blue dufflecoat to the pink miniskirt all girls dream of, not forgetting the classic jeans, dungarees and shirts.

TROC GONES > 74, Grande-Rue-de-la-Croix-Rousse (4e) ℰ **04 78 29 62 76.** At *Troc*'s, the principle is simple – clothes for women, pregnant women and children are deposited here for a maximum of two months. If they're not sold at the end of that time, you leave the shop with your clothes in your arms. Otherwise, you share the sale price with the shop. Sometimes it's worth it, sometimes it's less so, particularly if you only have a few articles to sell. When you've got nothing to sell, obviously you can look for something to buy and make a good deal.

◆LINGERIE

Women

AMARYLLIS > 64, rue de Trion (5th) ℰ **04 78 25 61 40.** Behind the shopwindow of an attractive draper's shop, buttons, thread and needles are sold alongside tights and lingerie. You'll find *Lejaby* and *Playtex* for classic, attractive underwear, and *Wonderbra* for a spectacular low-cut look. In addition, the reception's pleasant, and you'll get as much advice as there are models.

BAISER SAUVAGE LINGERIE > 4, place des Jacobins (2nd) ℰ **04 72 37 45 73.** If the woman who (un)dresses her is wild, the boutique's far from being the jungle. Everything's well set out and lined up according to types and creators : for glamorous or comfortable lingerie, there's *Chantal Thomass* or *Calvin Klein*, and all sorts of styles are to be found. To make trying-on more pleasant, the cabins are vast and draped with superb curtains in bordeaux velvet.

CUPIDON > 26, cours Vitton (6th) ℰ **04 78 24 26 13.** The shop's been renovated thereby making shopping even more pleasant. Ladies will choose their 'outfits' among the numerous labels on offer : *Aubade, Lise Charmel, Christian Dior, Simone Pérèle, Ravage*, as well as *Wacoal* which enhances all busts and pulls up the buttocks thanks to its magic pants. All these names are a guarantee of quality and of the power of seduction.

ETAM > 45, rue de la République (2nd) ℰ **04 78 92 90 76.** In cotton or unstitched, in lace or colourful stretch, the little pants at low prices match the bras. *Etam* follows the fashions, regularly receives new models, and offers an attractice choice of pyjamas, bathrobes and silk or cotton nightshirts which you can match with slippers and toilet bag. You can really crack without ruining yourself, and build up points on your fidelity card. **Other addresses : 32, Grande-Rue-de-la-Croix-Rousse (4th) 04 78 39 45 84 • "La Part Dieu" Shopping Centre - Level 1 (3rd) 04 78 62 87 27.**

DARJEELING > "La Part Dieu" Shopping Centre - Level 1 (3rd) ℰ **04 78 95 20 18.** The name of one of the great teas for some devilish female underwear. The nightshirts and pyjamas are very tempting and few men will let a woman go to sleep when she's dressed in this sort of silk, lace or satin. There's a section selling swimming costumes all year round in black, white, and lively colours – choice, bags of choice.

LAURIANE > 22, avenue du Maréchal-de-Saxe (6th) ℰ **04 78 52 46 83.** Very trendy colours ! There's a good idea – the section for the more developed (up to D and F and 115 around the bust). You'll find a large number of labels on sale, some well known, some less so : *Lou, Boléro*, the great *Christian Dior, Lejaby* and even *Le Chat*. For the night, you can sleep either cool and relaxed or super-sexy - it just depends who with. More sophisticated women will go for the 'relaxed wear' to stroll around the house or beside the pool.

MARIE CAROLINE > 81, rue du Président-Edouard-Herriot (2nd) ℰ **04 78 42 10 31.** On the attractive *Place des Célestins*, opposite the fountain, this ultra-feminine lingerie boutique offers the most refined women (and those who want to be) elegant and sophisticated undergarments by the best French and Italian creators : wasp-waisters, suspender belts, nightshirts, body-stockings, bathrobes and matching pyjamas – lovely outfits and, throughout the year, a large selection of swimming costumes.

Lyon *Fashion - Lingerie*

ORCANTA > "La Part Dieu" Shopping Centre- Level 1 (3rd) ℂ **04 78 95 17 48.** A beautiful and feminine selection of tempting underwear for all women and all shapes. The models make you look thinner or add rounded forms (depending on what you're after), and guarantee comfort whatever your activity.

PAIN DE SUCRE > 4, rue de l'Ancienne-Préfecture (2nd) ℂ **04 78 38 30 87.** Women always need a nice swimming suit for the holidays on the coast or for a trip to the Seychelles in winter. From 36 to 44, the *Pain de Sucre* collection is very beautiful and adapts to all shapes : boxer's shorts, one piece, strings and mini-pants and an entire selection of beach wear (tunics, skirts and sandals) because you need to be chic even at the beach.

PETIT BATEAU > 9, rue Gasparin (2nd) ℂ **04 78 37 30 40.** Since grown-ups have been buying their clothes in children's shops, the famous tee-shirt in white cotton can be seen everywhere : shirts, waistcoats, cotton dresses designed for comfort – dozens of colours for that acidulous effect. The prices incite you to overindulge (from 59 F to 129 F). **Other address : 11, avenue de Saxe (6th) 04 78 52 85 72.**

PHILDAR LINGERIE > 30, rue Victor-Hugo (2nd) ℂ **04 72 41 75 40.** *Phildar* doesn't just sell balls of wool, and, rest assured, their lingerie isn't knitted. The models are very comfortable, gay and colourful, and are sold at reasonable prices.

PRINCESSE TAM TAM > 38, rue de Brest (2nd) ℂ **04 72 40 98 01.** *Princesse Tam-Tam* awakes the young girl in flowers who lies dormant in all women. Most of the underwear's flowery and fruity, and the pyjamas are warm, soft and either comfortable or seductive. Don't forget the swimming suits, the wasp-waisters and the nightshirts. Very pleasant reception. **Other address : 3, avenue du Maréchal-de-Saxe (6th) 04 72 74 42 85.**

SATINATA > 2, rue Chavant (6th) ℂ **04 37 27 08 79.** You want Eva Ervimachin's Wonderbra, the same little pants as Madonna, Laetitia Casta's body stocking and certainly not your grandmother's corset – then come and look at the shelves in *Satinata*. Sexy satin, cute cotton, eternal lace, it's all here, and sod it if the purse takes a hammering, because everything's so tempting in this boutique.

WOLFORD BOUTIQUE > 1, rue Emile-Zola (2nd) ℂ **04 72 40 26 30.** Swimming suits, lingerie, tights and body stockings – the *Wolford* collection has the particularity of being stitchless, which makes it ultra-comfortable and makes women as tempting as devils. On the novelty side, there's the Fatal line : a tube-shaped dress which really hugs the body, as well as creations by the stylist *Hervé Léger,* who enhances female forms with flattering cuts and modern materials. **Other address : 2, avenue du Maréchal-de-Saxe (6th) 04 72 74 16 47.**

West Lyon

IRIS LINGERIE > 132, Grande-Rue - OULLINS ℂ **04 78 50 98 86.** Here, you'll find silk petticoats, lace nightshirts and underwear by *Huit, Lise Charmel* and *Christian Dior* – all you need to drive your man wild. For the more timid, warm pyjamas in cotton or cotton flannel.

Men's underwear

SLIPISSIMO > 14, rue Grenette (2nd) ℂ **04 78 37 44 63.** Women who want to offer their men underwear come to *Slipissimo*, where they find everything necessary to cover the bottom-half of their other half. It's not always easy to choose from all the attractive and matching outfits (shorts, tee shirts, slippers) signed by *Arthur* or *Coup de Cœur* or from the sexy underwear, like the skin-hugging pants and shorts by *Hom* or *Armani*. Why not take, both since the affordable prices allow it ? Your man will love the ultra-comfortable material (Tactel, Meryl) which fits like a second skin.

VILEBREQUIN > 7, rue du Plâtre (1st) ℂ **04 72 98 30 93.** The *Vilebrequin* label was born 30 years ago, under the Saint-Tropez sun. Since then, it's enjoyed a growing success. The range of swimming shorts inspired by Hawaiian materials, with squares, flowers and polka dots, is really attractive. In the same practical and relaxed style, you'll find a collection of Bermudas, trousers and trainers, not only for the beach.

Weddings

MAX CHAOUL > 7, rue François Dauphin (2nd) 🕿 **04 72 41 04 10.** Very, very classy. Made-to-measure, originality, in short, designer dresses. For those who don't want to look like someone else and who intend to buy a dress without looking at the price (minimum 5 figures).

◆ LEATHERWEAR

BARRET MAROQUINERIE > 21, rue de Brest (2nd) 🕿 **04 72 56 94 40.** This very beautiful and classic leather shop offers a multitude of brands and products for the whole family. Dad will find his briefcase, a classic leather wallet and a handsome umbrella. For Mum, there are bags in all shapes and sizes, all the brands and all prices. For the Little Ones, there are satchels and solid back-packs. The service is impeccable, and you can unwrap all the bags without any problem. **Other address : "La Part Dieu" Shopping Centre- Level 1 (3rd) 04 78 60 01 73.**

FURLA > 100, rue Edouard-Herriot (2nd) 🕿 **04 78 42 14 38.** A new leather boutique has opened its doors in Lyon, and we bet it's going to be an incredible success. The bags are in top-quality matt or iced leather and in classic colours – red, black, beige or brown. The models are simple, structured and perfect.

HERMES > 96, rue du Président-Edouard-Herriot (2nd) 🕿 **04 78 42 25 14.** A tiny *Post-It* holder (570 F) or an ostrich bag (39 000 F) - saddlemaker's luxury and quality have no price. But, you'll also find tableware, clothes, shoes, leather jewellery and the famous silk scarves in different sizes. The reception's up to the quality of the goods and the prices, and the expert hand of the salesgirl will unwrap the superb silk scarves to show you a thousand and one ways to knot them.

LANCEL > 16, rue de la République (2nd) 🕿 **04 78 42 13 91.** Iced leather in chocolate brown or chic beige, handbags or travel bags – who has never dreamed of slipping a *Lancel* bag under her arm ? Even if it's only for the delight of the eyes and the touch (yes, you can touch them), a visit to one of these two shops is a 'must'. **Other address : "La Part Dieu" Shopping Centre- Level 2 (3rd) 04 78 62 31 47.**

LONGCHAMP > 32, rue du Président-Edouard-Herriot (1st) 🕿 **04 78 28 14 48.** The equestrian brand now offers all colours, materials and shapes in its models so as to lose (a bit) its reputation for being too classic. Every year, there's a new range of colours for the famous canvas bags which have given a breath of youth to the brand – from the very small to the XXL at reasonable prices. A lot is in supple and solid leather, but nylon and are also used for the handbags, suitcases, travel bags, shoulder bags and wallets.

LOUIS VUITTON > 94, rue du Président-Edouard-Herriot (2nd) 🕿 **04 78 42 80 96.** Having spent years concentrating on brown, this famous establishment now has a daring stylist and is allowing itself a new wave of pastel colours and polished leather. The initials are now a little more discreet, and fashion victims can't get enough of the bags, shoes and accessories sold at incredible prices.

MAC DOUGLAS > 8, rue Gasparin (2nd) 🕿 **04 78 37 80 79.** The brand's well known, and justifiably so. You'll find elegant, light but solid bags in skin and leather, which are quite expensive but which last for a very long time. **Other addresses : "La Part Dieu" Shopping Centre- Level 1 (3rd) 04 78 60 93 96 • 13, avenue du Maréchal-de-Saxe (6th) 04 78 24 98 55.**

West Lyon

L'ELAN > 1646, route nationale 6 - LIMONEST 🕿 **04 72 17 73 90.** This friendly shop's devoted to leather goods. Here, the salesmen don't push you to buy, but offer good advice, if requested. In addition to offering all the brands, the shop also guarantees the lowest prices.

◆READY-TO-WEAR

Ladies

ANNE FONTAINE > 49, rue Edouard-Herriot (2nd) ✆ **04 78 42 07 71.** This creator's changed address, but is still in the same street, and now occupies a larger shop, decorated in white and wood. The reception's still charming, and the star is the white shirt in all its shapes – with frills, Mao collars and double cuffs, in silk cotton and lace. There's even a model in paper which can be machine-washed. There are a few models in black and grey, as well as tee shirts and little, 'futurist' jackets. From 395 F to 795 F.

BRAGANCE > 96, rue du Président-Edouard-Herriot (2nd) ✆ **04 78 42 48 86.** The sales girls in this boutique are crazy about fashion, know all the latest trends like the back of their hands and love advising the clientèle. The labels on offer couldn't be more up-to-date - *Jean-Paul Gaultier, Helena Sorel, Lacroix Jeans, Versace Sport, Fendi, Cavalli Jean*s.

CANAL FILLES > 41, rue Paul-Chenavard (1st) ✆ **04 78 29 46 01.** When they go out on the rave, girls hand out the address of this very trendy little boutique. The labels on offer are international, and come from London, like *Tim Bargeot*, or from Barcelona, like *Custo*. The tattoo tee-shirts are all the rage. The stock's renewed every week, and this is the only place in Lyon where you'll find *Acupuncture* trainers.

CHACOK > 100, rue du Président-Edouard-Herriot (2nd) ✆ **04 78 42 44 60.** *Chacok* gets its inspiration from Indai, the Far East and from Russia, and all its collections are gay and colourful, with Baroque and bright motifs. The outfits, trousers, dresses and cotton or woollen sweaters will brighten up any wardrobe and give it some taste.

DOROTHEE BIS > 35, quai Saint-Antoine (2nd) ✆ **04 78 37 89 88.** For years, the *Dorothée Bis* label has been faithful to a style which is both feminine and easy to wear, and has offered relaxed women with a bit of money elegant and relaxed outfits. All the models can be matched ad infinitum.

EDWIGE > 14, cours Franklin-Roosevelt (6th) ✆ **04 78 24 78 40.** *Edwige* offers an attractive collection of sweaters, twin-sets, skirts and dresses... from sizes 38 to 50, and including the labels *Saint-Hilaire, Mary West* and *Anne d'Aleth*.

EN FACE > 34, rue Edouard-Herriot (2nd) ✆ **04 72 07 05 39.** A very contemporary, 'minimalist' décor for the favourite labels of the trendy 20 to 60 year olds, including *Tara Jarmon, Diapositive, Tark 1, Diab'less* and *LM Lulu.* The cuts and materials are extremely trendy and sexy, and vary from the devilishly sexy to the well-structured classic, depending on the label chosen. Girls adore combining several styles, and can easily do so here because the labels on offer aren't ruinous.

GERARD DAREL > 12, rue Emile-Zola (2nd) ✆ **04 78 38 06 95.** In addition to the replica of the pearl-grey outfit worn by Jackie Kennedy, this vast and pleasant boutique offers outfits which are elegant, feminine, classic or 'younger', for active women who make a good living.

GRAPHITI FEMMES > 9, rue du Plâtre (1st) ✆ **04 78 28 57 94.** This is a very white little boutique, where the most fashionable of labels are lined up. The labels aren't numerous, but they're on exclusive offer in Lyon : *Barbara Bui* and her trouser outfits which show incredible attention to detail, *Calvin Klein*, designer or ready-to-wear *Ralph Lauren* and, by way of shoes, *Sergio Rossi* and *Michel Perry*. The clothes are elegantly cut and uncomplicated (in fashion language, we say 'minimalist'), in beautiful materials and with impeccable finishes. The shop's very fashionable and not cheap, but what do you expect from the most prestigious labels ?

INES DE LA FRESSANGE > 60, avenue du Maréchal-Foch (6th) ✆ **04 78 89 27 99.** *Inès*' logo, a small oak leaf which is now recognizable among a thousand others, decorates tableware, carpets, candles, keyrings and leather goods. On the fashion side, the label remains faithful to the "chic Parisian" style it adores : tapered outfits, Shetland pullovers and sportswear, pretty hats, close-fitting dresses, shoes and handbags. The prices are more 'designer' than ready-to-wear, and the young may find that some of the models are a bit grandmotherish.

JANE AUBERT > 79, rue du Président-Edouard-Herriot (2nd) ℭ **04 78 37 09 58.** One of the names in Lyonnais fashion, every season, *Jane Aubert* brings out a collection of the biggest designer and ready-to-wear labels : *Escada, Courrège, Jiki, Christian Lacroix, Bleu Blanc Rouge, Léonard*. The shop offers elegance and irreproachable quality, with carefully-selected, fashionable models.

KOBACCI > 21, rue Ferrandière (2nd) ℭ **04 72 40 08 58.** Kobacci sells the clothes you find in fashion shows or magazines : *Mugler, Versace V2, Claude Montana, Guess Collection, Accessoires* and *Versace* shoes… but also other labels at cheaper prices. On the corner of the *Rue du Palais Grillet* and the *Rue Ferrandière*, this is an address to note down.

LADY SOUL > 9, rue de la Fromagerie (1st) ℭ **04 72 00 27 28.** The Choupette label's logo is a large girl in built-up trainers. The clothes, which are very trendy, are inspired by the hip-hop movement, and offer feminine ready-to-wear rather than streetwear. The label targets a clientèle between the ages of 15 and 20, but the salesgirls are also used to dressing women between 30 and 40 who have fallen for the modernity of the models, the quality of the cuts and materials and the competitive prices.

LAURA ASHLEY > 98, rue du Président-Edouard-Herriot (2nd) ℭ **04 78 37 18 19.** Straight from England, *Laura Ashley* fashion's a combination of femininity and romanticism. Day and evening dresses, pretty tee-shirts and comfortable trousers, relaxed outfits… the motifs are often flowery, like the material and wallpaper sold on the first floor of the shop.

LE COMPTOIR DES COTONNIERS > 27, rue de Brest (2nd) ℭ **04 72 40 05 45.** This label's for mothers and daughters for whom fashion rhymes with affordable elegance and simplicity. In a clean and bright shop, the clothes are continuously reviewed and renewed : discreetly-plaited skirts, colourful blouses, trimmed twin-sets and modern dufflecoats. **Other address : 10, avenue du Maréchal-de-Saxe (6th) 04 72 83 50 41.**

LES CARNETS D'EDOUARD > 15, rue Edouard-Herriot (2e) ℭ **04 78 28 61 39.** The shop's been renovated, and now seems larger and more pleasant, thanks to a to large and colourful panelling and to a giant aquarium. The clothes rails, which are suspended on cables, move with the slightest draught or as soon as a curious hand slides between the clothes. The shop's faithful to its favourite labels, like *Helena Sorel* for her feminine dresses, *Eres* for its mermaid swimming suits, and *Lacroix Jeans* for its zipped and embroidered jackets. Chic and fantasy are the shop's key words.

LOLA > 24, rue de Grenette (2nd) ℭ **04 78 42 04 81.** *Lola*'s not at all flashy. Sober and simple, the shop looks like its collection : mainly skirt and trouser outfits in grey, black and beige, from 1 500 F. Very classic clothes, with fashionable cuts and in materials which hang nicely.

MAX MARA > 85, rue du Président-Edouard-Herriot (2nd) ℭ **04 72 41 72 53.** *Max Mara* allows all women to look like Italians, who are universally recognized for their elegance at all times, be it at the market, the beach or the opera. The lines combine classicism (the quality of the cuts) and modernity (the choice of materials). The long coats which have made the label's reputation, make you look like a star. Demanding clients find what they're after among the various styles on offer (city, sport and weekend).

MULTIPLES > "La Part Dieu" Shopping Centre - Level 1 (3rd) ℭ **04 78 62 26 79.** Multiple… like women's desires in fashion, like the jerseys on sale here, like the colours proposed, like the advice and the smiles offered by the salesgirls, like the collections which change because women change. *Multiples* has understood this. **Other address : "Portes des Alpes" Shopping Centre- SAINT-PRIEST 04 78 26 02 94.**

NAFNAF > 24, rue de la République (2nd) ℭ **04 78 42 99 64.** The label with the little pig knows how to keep up with fashion and, offering competitive prices, dresses all types of women, whatever their age. The collections don't lack originality, and include sportswear, dressy-wear and everyday-wear. **Other addresses : "La Part Dieu" Shopping Centre - Level 2 (3rd) 04 78 95 40 00 • "Le Pérollier" Shopping Centre - ECULLY 04 72 18 93 88 • "Portes des Alpes" Shopping Centre - SAINT-PRIEST 04 78 26 58 02 • 1-3, avenue Henri-Barbusse - VILLEURBANNE 04 78 84 62 26.**

Lyon *Fashion - Ready to wear*

PLEIN SUD > 8, rue des Archers (2nd)   ℂ   **04 78 92 81 81.** A superb shop with a simple décor and, on the clothes rails, black, lots of black : it's the label's signature. *Plein Sud*'s style is very "femme fatale" - clinging, curved and fluid. The tailored suits in stretch gabardine are a bestseller, the evening dresses are divine, and a number of accessories add the final touch to a happy client who has already become a creature of dreams.

REGINA RUBENS > 99, rue Edouard-Herriot (2nd)   ℂ   **04 72 40 97 97.** In a brand-new boutique, chic women will find classic everyday outfits and very elegant evening dresses – all in a vast range of colours, from the brightest to the more pastel, in flowing materials and with very modern cuts.

RODIER > 74, rue du Président-Edouard-Herriot (2nd)   ℂ   **04 78 42 72 80.** The *Rodier* Woman is active, city-living, elegant and relaxed at the same time, but, above all, classic. The models can be matched one with another. At *Rodier,* you can't go wrong.

SINEQUANONE > 15, rue de Brest (2nd)   ℂ   **04 72 41 75 47.** A recent arrival to Lyon, the *Sinéquanone* fashion's daring and original. The colours are gay, and the cuts are extremely fashionable : pantyhoses, stretch tee-shirts, pearls, spangles, ponchos, accessories and evening dresses – they're all here, along with very low prices and a very friendly reception. **Other addresses : 54, rue du Président-Edouard-Herriot (2nd) 04 78 42 01 11 • 16, rue Victor-Hugo (2nd) 04 78 37 97 23 • 34, rue Grenette (2nd) 04 78 37 83 56 • "La Part Dieu" Shopping Centre (3rd) 04 78 60 93 87 • 50, cours Vitton (6th) 04 72 74 13 92.**

SONIA RYKIEL > 62, rue de Brest (2nd)   ℂ   **04 72 41 01 83.** In a vast and very pleasant boutique, the red-head Sonia's collections allow Lyonnaises to have that special look – elegant, very 'evening' and incredibly feminine. The daring accessories are very popular, and beautifully match the flowing skirts and tunics, the wide trousers, the sweaters with inscriptions and the vertiginously-high shoes.

SUGAR > 52, rue du Président-Edouard-Herriot (2nd)   ℂ   **04 78 92 90 78.** The antithesis of sophistication, the tee-shirts and tops in dozens of colours, the painter's jackets in canvas and borduroy and the comfortable trousers seduce the sporty and natural woman. The fantastic reception and the quality of the goods rapidly make you forget that the shop is so small.

TARA JARMON > 10, rue des Archers (2nd)   ℂ   **04 78 38 06 81.** Between the reasonably-priced ready-to-wear (which you find everywhere) and the top end of the range (which is original but often prohibitive), there's *Tara Jarmon*, who delights coquettish women : pretty dresses, colourful knitted pullovers, simple but dressy outfits and the accessories essential to complete an outfit, like little bags, scarves and hats. The inventive and well-designed cuts are out of the ordinary, whilst the very bright colours and the materials chosen (thick cotton and fabric which looks like paper) give each item that little extra which makes it unique. **Other address : "La Part Dieu" Shopping Centre (3rd).**

VENTILO > 40, rue de Brest (2nd)   ℂ   **04 78 37 43 06.** The Ventilo Woman likes natural materials (linen, wool, cotton) which hang well and which gives her the comfort, the style and the elegance she's looking for. The skirt and trouser suits have, justifiably, made the label's reputation and can be worn with accessories like brown, black or beige moccasins, leather belts, scarves and bags. The slightly-expensive prices are fully justified by the quality of the linen and by its perfect hang – provided you follow the salesgirl's advice about the way to wash it.

VIRGINE ESPEJO > 27, cours Vitton (6th)   ℂ   **04 78 89 15 04.** In the bright and refined décor of her two boutiques, *Virginie Espejo* offers very trendy, young and colourful collections for those who are unconditional fans of designer labels, like *Montana* or *Roberto Cavalli*. **Other address : Rue Jean-de-Tourmes (2nd).**

ZAPA > 49, rue du Président-Edouard-Herriot (2nd)   ℂ   **04 78 37 34 97.** A fashion for everyday, whose aim is to magnify feminine beauty whilst remaining resolutely modern. Flowing materials, precise lines and harmonious colours characterize all the collections.

WEINBERG > 76, rue Edouard-Herriot   ℂ   **04 72 41 72 73.** Available in all sizes up to 50, well-cut, high-quality classic suits and outfits have made the label's reputation. The other part of the collection is younger, with materials which are ultra-comfortable and easy to wear, like linen, silk and cotton in yellow, coral, green, khaki and blue colours.

Mothers-to-be

BOUTIQUE FORMES > 41, rue de la Bourse (2nd) ℂ **04 78 42 49 66.** Pregnant women, forget the shapeless shorts and adolescent dungarees, and go for pretty and relaxed outfits (jeans, tee-shirts) or more dressy clothes (long and short dresses, suits and skirts), which are cleverly designed with elastic waistlines, which can be worn right up to the last month (and even after).

L'AVENUE DES BEBES > 6, rue du Président-Edouard-Herriot (1st) ℂ **04 78 39 15 66.** A charming reception and all the fashions for future mothers who want to show off their pretty, round tummies in stretchable dresses, trousers with adjustable elastic and very large, multi-coloured belt-bands to underline the tummy. The prices are very reasonable, and the very bright colours make you feel like getting pregnant.

PAPILLOTE > 3, rue du Professeur-Weill (6th) ℂ **04 78 52 16 57.** It's not because a woman's pregnant that she can't practise any sport, bathe, go to work or even get married without keeping her own style (elegant or relaxed) and without losing her sex appeal. Here, the choice is enormous, and everyone will find a dress which suits her morphology. In addition to being attractive, the outfits are made in supple material which don't put pressure on the future mother's tummy.

Large sizes for ladies

CYBELE > 23, rue Thomassin (2nd) ℂ **04 78 37 04 25.** A boutique for attractive young ladies who wear size 44 and over, and which, for once, sells something other than those potato sacks with flowery designs which are meant to pass for dresses. Rounded shapes and coquetterie go together here, and clients find their smile again. Bravo for the reception, which is incredibly pleasant and friendly.

EVYSANDLER > 55, rue Mercière (2nd) ℂ **04 78 42 03 58.** This boutique opens onto two streets and contains two areas devoted to plump women. On the *Rue de Brest* side, the creator models are designed for women who go for the latest fashions whatever their size, and the section called *"Evy's Bargains"* allows you to save money throughout the year on last season's models.

LES ARMOIRES SAINT-MARTIN > 2, rue Mulet (1st) ℂ **04 78 39 68 53.** The owner of this second-hand clothes shop knows exactly what plump but coquette women are looking for, and sells attractive collections, including all the labels, in gay colours and with up-to-date models. Everyone can deposit the clothes they're tired of, and leave with a new outfit at a very reasonable price.

SACHKA > 5, rue Paul-Chenavard (1st) ℂ **04 78 29 59 27.** The shop front is pretty, with country-green wood, and the shopwindow's equally attractive. The models on sale range from sizes 42 to 66, the clothes are simple, well-cut and with no ornament, and they're made in fluid materials

West Lyon

NANABELLE > 101, avenue Georges-Clemenceau - SAINT-GENIS-LAVAL ℂ **04 78 56 84 30.** All super-looking, plump women will find what they're after in this small but very well-stocked shop. The choice is vast and the person who runs the shop's very pleasant, which is always a plus. A specialist in sizes 46 to 52, *Nanabelle* offers the plump what they won't find elsewhere : flowing, feminine garments, linen suits, lots of skirts, shirts and pretty tops. The labels on offer are good quality : *Christine Laure, Giani Forte, Karting, Deomino...* and the prices, very reasonable.

Men

ARROW > 2, rue du Bât.-d'Argent (1st). The shop's American, which explains the very 'New York' decoration : steel and cherry wood and a giant reproduction of the Big Apple and of the Twin Towers illuminated by a thousand lights. It's in this décor that the young, or not so young, Lyonnais yuppie can dress himself from head to foot in swimming suits, suits and **87**

polonecks, ties, socks… The undisputed Star of the Show remains the shirt, which is sold in all styles, both sporty and classic, in dozens of colours, with different motifs and different sleeve-lengths. God Bless America, queen of domestic comfort : some models, from 350 F to 500 F, are guaranteed "no ironing needed".

BASIC ETHNIC > 25, rue du Président-Edouard-Herriot (1st). For his clothes, man is often as 'double' as Janus : he wants to be 'dressy' for work, but, at weekends or for the holidays, he prefers comfort. If, in addition, he carefully follows the fashions, at Basic Ethnic he'll find a sober City line for everyday, as well as a more sporty, urban line, signed by creators of all nationalities : *Olivier Strelli, Donna Karan, G Star, Paco Rabanne, Tony Martin, Dirk Bikkembergs...* For his feet, the inevitable trainers by *New Balance, Puma* and *Perry Ellis*, which can even be worn with a suit, or so the salesman says. **Other address: 14, rue Thomassin (2nd).**

BOUTIQUE OPERA-JOSEPH TAILLEUR > 9, rue Président-Edouard-Herriot (1st) ℰ **04 78 27 87 34.** Behind an old-fashioned facade surrounded by mouldings and by seven high windowpanes, this very chich boutique for men is designed like an immense dressing-room : teak parquet flooring, ash furniture, white walls and white wooden shelves. In this setting, you'll find piles of clothes beutifully lined up. Joseph Barrettara exercises his tailoring talents, snips his scissors for the made-to-measure, and represents the *Ermenegildo Zegna* label for classic ready-to-wear and sportswear. The superb suits (count between 5 500 F and 12 500 F) are always manufactured tailor-fashion, that is to say, stiffened. The lines combine impeccable cuts, fibre mixtures for high technicity, and fine-quality detail in the finishes. The welcome's royal, and men can dress themselves here from head to foot. Gentlemen, don't forget you'll always look your best in an Italian suit.

CRAVATERIE TIVAN > 63, rue du Président-Edouard-Herriot (2nd) ℰ **04 78 38 04 19.** This small boutique's recommended for all elegant men who know that class depends on that refined little detail and on the well-chosen accessory. This shop is the temple of masculine fantasy : very elegant waistcoats are matched with ties and with silk cravates. To make the style perfect, gentlemen choose cufflinks, braces (for the Wall Street effect), and very soft Cashmere sweaters at very reasonable prices.

FACONNABLE > 30, rue du Président-Edouard-Herriot (1st) ℰ **04 78 28 10 48.** Wood panelling, carpet, leather armchairs – the shop's luxurious and the reception, classy. This temple of masculine elegance dresses all men, both the classic and the sporty. Ties, shirts, trousers, coats, pullovers and accessories, you'll find everything you need.

GRAPHITI HOMMES > 104, rue du Président-Edouard-Herriot (2nd) ℰ **04 72 56 09 08.** *Ralph Lauren, Calvin Klein, Hugo Boss* – lots of stylish names for a style which, covering shirts, suits, coats and shoes, will transform any Homo sapiens into a real picture of elegance and virility. **Other address : 26, rue de la Charité (2nd) 04 78 42 29 64.**

SMART > 46, boulevard Brotteaux (6th) ℰ **04 78 24 56 93.** With labels like *Paul Smith, Ralph Lauren* or *Georges Rech,* this boutique's at the top of ready-to-wear range. Ths owner's installed a bar so that, between a fitting and an alteration, clients and those accompanying them can sit down for a moment and drink a tea or a coffee. Thanks to Channel Jimmy in one of the corners of the boutique, children stay well-behaved. A practical and pleasant concept, which pleases modern men and their families.

TRAMPS > 4, rue de l'Ancienne-Préfecture (2nd) ℰ **04 72 77 51 47.** This is a place where modern man's wishes are perfectly understood. He wants to be both elegant and comfortable in his clothes ? No problem, he'll find what he's been dreaming of at average or top-range prices among the collections of raincoats and parkas by *Allegri*, the leathers by *Serafin*, the chain-knitwear by *Kenzo* and the jeans by *Armani, Trussardi* and *Paul Smith*. Also on display are classy wedding suits for the modern groom.

VETEMENTS CHARLES > 5, Grande-Rue-de-la-Croix-Rousse (4th) ℰ **04 78 27 04 08.** Chez Charles, the reception's very traditional : the client's welcomed, listened to and advised, and the measurements are correctly taken for immaculate turn-ups. The collections are classic, but modern and fashionable, as are the labels on offer : the two *Pierres, Cardin* and *Clarence* for suits and ties, *Levi's, Lee Cooper* and *Lacoste* for jeans, canvas trousers and multi-coloured polonecks, and *Hanes* for cotton tee-shirts. **Other addresses : 32, rue de la République - OULLINS 04 78 51 30 91 • Auchan Shopping Centre - ST-GENIS-LAVAL 04 78 56 41 11 • Continent Shopping Centre - FRANCHEVILLE 04 78 59 89 19.**

West Lyon

PIERRE MICHEL > 125, Grande-Rue - OULLINS ℭ **04 78 50 79 19.** This is a comfortable, large and airy place, where the elegant man will find what he's after in the *Pierre Cardin* label. It's worth noting that, here, they're happy to unwrap all the ties and let you think quietly (and as long as you like) about the one you prefer.

Mixed

AIGLE > 62, rue du Président-Edouard-Herriot (2nd) ℭ **04 78 42 11 22.** Sporty types, adventurers, travellers and ramblers know that, at *Aigle*, they'll find comfortable and modern clothes for sports, strolls and relaxation. The parkas are waterproof and lined with polar wool, the sweaters are soft, the clothes' stitching, tight, the shoes, comfortable, and the trousers, sturdy. The clothes on offer are stylish and easily adapted to life in the city.

ALAIN MANOUKIAN > "La Part Dieu" Shopping Centre - Level 1 (3rd) ℭ **04 78 62 73 90.** *Alain Manoukian* boutiques are vast and pleasant, so that customers don't walk on each other's feet when they want to try the clothes on. Men can dress 'classic' or sporty, and women will find classic outfits for work. The collections have their fans, but are, otherwise, very conventional. There's no eccentricity in this shop. **Other addresses : 22, rue Victor-Hugo (2nd) 04 78 42 07 79 • 10, Grande-Rue-de-la-Croix-Rousse (4th) 04 78 28 15 02 • 18, cours Vitton (6th) 04 78 24 99 15 • 92, avenue des Frères-Lumières (8th) 04 78 00 30 37 • 6, Grande-Rue-de-Vaise (9th) 04 78 83 77 24.**

ARMAND THIERY > 1, place des Jacobins (2nd) ℭ **04 78 42 55 03.** This immense boutique in *Part Dieu* is mixed, whilst the one in the *Place des Jacobins* is exclusively for men. The collections are designed for all sorts of public : the young, the classic, the sporty, the trendy…Men are spoilt by an impressive choice of shirts, sweaters, suits, trousers and swimming trunks. The boutique offers pleasant services : one minute alterations to a turn-up or a sleeve, the possibility of paying by instalments thanks to a fidelity card, and the exchange throughout France of goods bought in the same shop. **Other address : La Part Dieu Shopping Centre - Level 3 (3rd) 04 78 62 64 14.**

BENETTON > 64, rue de la République (2nd) ℭ **04 78 37 61 75.** Everyone knows *Benetton* sweaters, sold in all colours, with round or V-necks. They're quite expensive and not very resistant to wild or repeated machine-washes. The label also sells collections which follow the year's trends and a superb collection of very colourful baggage, from vanity cases to cabin-cases. **Other addresses : 9, rue des Archers (2nd) 04 78 37 78 00 • 67, Grande-Rue-de-la-Croix-Rousse (4th) 04 78 30 68 03 • 10, cours Vitton (6th) 04 72 74 22 97.**

BURBERRY FRANCE > 106, rue du Président-Edouard-Herriot (2nd) ℭ **04 72 40 00 01.** This illustrious, English establishment has just shed a few years by hiring the services of the very famous model, *Kate Moss*. Of course, there's no question of abandoning the the famous square design (now to be found on bikinis), which can be spotted three miles off, or the trench coats, but the cuts are now more modern and fashionable. It's a huge success with the young and well-off.

CACHAREL > 7, rue Emile-Zola (2nd) ℭ **04 72 41 82 28.** The Cacharel salesgirls have always been the friendliest there are, and the fashion they offer you is gay, simple and feminine. The label has very successful variations on flower models, with little daisies and large, colourful tulips. The shop's pleasant, bright and spacious. In short, it's not at all the sort of place where people tread on your feet. The dressy outfits on the upper floors are definitely worth a look. **Other address : 16, rue Emile-Zola (2nd) 04 78 37 31 17.**

CAMAIEU > 6, rue Victor-Hugo (2nd) © **04 78 38 11 01.** For very modest prices, the whole family's entitled to more colour and more prints, in decent and comfortable cuts which follow the fashions. **Other addesses : 44, place de la République (2nd) 04 78 42 01 84 • "La Part Dieu" Shopping Centre (3rd) 04 78 60 16 06 • "La Part Dieu" Shopping Centre (3rd) 04 78 62 37 79 • "La Part Dieu" Shopping Centre (3rd) 04 78 60 43 23 • 6, cours Vitton (6th) 04 72 75 00 20 • "Le Pérollier" Shopping Centre - ECULLY 04 78 33 00 73.**

CERRUTI > 16bis, rue Gasparin (2nd) © **04 78 37 14 67.** The same Italian architect has signed the decoration of all *Cerruti* shops throughout the world, and Lyon's no exception to this rule. The lighting's flattering, the walls are of an incredible whiteness, the floor's in stone and marble, and the furniture's made with dark wood, glass and metal. Nothing frilly or gaudy, but a concept of luxury and modernity which matches the collections. The *Cerruti 1881* and *Arte Femme* lines combine elegance, simplicity, discretion and beautiful fabrics. The reception's discreet and efficient, which sums up this Italian fashion.

CJB > 24, place Bellecour (2nd) © **04 78 42 05 18.** In Lyon, *CJB,* alias *Christian Johan Bégot,* is one of the biggest fashion-makers when it comes to the very latest trends. His beautiful boutique, which gives onto the nicest part of the *Place Bellecour,* just opposite the cafés, offers very chic evening and day outfits *Paul Smith* and *Irié,* as well as indispensable accessories, including pocket-emptiers, scarves and cufflinks for Him, and scarves, silver, steel and hematite jewellery for Her, signed by *Desanti* or *La Molla.* It's quite expensive, but very fashionable and beautiful.

CYRILLUS > 64, rue du Président-Edouard-Herriot (2nd) © **04 78 37 46 02.** The salesgirls have the patience of angels, and valiantly put up with the unruly behaviour of well-brought up children, whilst taking care of their mothers. Madame chooses some attractive pyjamas, a kilt or some classic moccasins for herself or for her children, and buys a shirt for her husband. **Other address : 7, avenue du Maréchal-de-Saxe (6th) 04 72 74 98 19.**

DONALDSON > 40, rue de Brest (2nd) © **04 78 42 77 16.** Here, trousers, jackets, shirts and other items are as classic in their shape and colour as they possibly could be. What makes them interesting are the numerous Walt Disney characters which decorate every item. Both the young and the old, for who Mickey and Minnie, Pluto and Donald are the best of friends, come to *Donaldson* to indulge in their love of the cartoon character.

EDEN PARK > 1, rue Jean-de-Tourmes (2nd) © **04 78 37 09 96.** The famous label with the pink butterfly bow tie logo dresses elegant, stylish and sporty men and women. For Him, the rugby shirt or the classic shirt. For Her, the tapered dress and the swimming suit. For Him again, the suit and blazer, and, for Her, the tapered suit and Ladies' blazer.

GAP > "La Part Dieu" Shopping Centre - Level 1 (3rd) © **04 72 84 97 70.** Made in America, the *Gap* fashion's universal. In cool, sporty, urban and comfortable clothes, men and women resemble each other in khakis and sweatshirts signed with a big G. To smell clean and good, there's a line of eaux de toilettes and unisex beauty products with amusing fragrances ("*Grass*", for example, which smells of… freshly-cut grass !).

H2O > 15bis, rue d'Algérie (1st) © **04 78 27 01 35.** This breath of oxygen sells London style. From skirts to bags, there are a host of jungle prints (zebra, leopard). You'll find, shiny, fringed and crocheted trousers…which change. For those of both sexes who like techno clothes and the young and friendly welcome which goes with them. On Mondays and on Saturday mornings, there's an excellent idea – Fashion Hour (10% off everything).

JOSEPH > 17, rue Auguste-Comte (2nd) © **04 72 40 01 56.** This is a colourful, bright shop for fashion fans, offering the famous trousers which made the label's reputation. They're in perfect cuts and a variety of materials, but the shop also sells collections of sweaters, dresses and tapered shirts, as well as, big, soft and warm items for the winter. *Joseph*'s is a very modern way of dressing.

LACOSTE BOUTIQUE > 91, rue du Président-Edouard-Herriot (2nd)   ℃   **04 78 92 84 37.** It's easy to follow a *Lacoste* man, woman or family... the hyper-famous crocodile logo leaves its trace everywhere, particularly on tee shirts, shirts, trousers, jackets... Not to mention the range of perfumes and fragrances, the line of baggage, and the glasses and shoes.

LEVIS STORE > "La Part Dieu" Shopping Centre - Level 2 (3rd)   ℃   **04 78 62 73 52.** How do you choose the right number ? 501 or 510 ? Buying jeans is a serious business, which is made easier, here, by the professionalism of a sales staff who know their products by heart, and who know how to recommend such and such a model, depending on the sex, weight and height of the customer. **Other addresses : 47, rue de la République (2nd) 04 78 42 49 10 • "Le Pérollier" Shopping Centre- ECULLY 04 78 33 60 92.**

MEXX > 2, rue Thomassin (2nd)   ℃   **04 78 42 34 22.** *Mexx* dresses all the family from head to foot - men, women and children. The outfits are generally comfortable, fashionable, sexy, pleasant and relaxed. Nice accessories are sold to go with them.

NEW MAN > 10, rue Jean-de-Tournes (2nd)   ℃   **04 72 40 24 05.** The label offers clothes which are always elegant, with a tendency towards sportswear and relaxed clothes. There are two lines, one for the week and the office, the other for the weekend and leisure activities.

OLD ENGLAND > 53, place de la République (2nd)   ℃   **04 78 37 70 80.** This large, beautiful and very English shop, on the majestuous *Place la République*, offers a large choice of elegant and well-cut clothes at substantial prices for those who want to play Hugh Grant, give themselves the style of a gentleman-farmer, and acquire a very English elegance.

OLIVER GRANT > 93, rue du Président-Edouard-Herriot (2nd)   ℃   **04 78 92 94 95.** The décor's luxurious and inspired by a yacht cabin. The clothes offered are like the boutique, that is to say, top of the range. Men and women leave, elegantly dressed in skirt or trouser suits, impeccable white shirts, beautifully-cur parkas and leather goods, like belts and shoes. **Other address : 44, rue Victor-Hugo (2nd) 04 78 37 47 77.**

SAM RANCH'WEAR > 25, cours Franklin Roosevelt (6th)   ℃   **04 78 17 28 00.** For Camel Trophy men, at the *Sam Ranch'wear* shop, Carol and her team will reserve the best of welcomes for you. Accessories, shoes, styled clothes signed by *Tony la Marca* or *Batiste* – fashion's come to the Left Bank.

STUDIO AVENTURE > 37, rue de Brest (2nd)   ℃   **04 72 56 06 59.** Cartoon characters out of the Warner Brothers' studios have attractive big cheeks or look like nasty wolves. This is a good reason for putting them on tee-shirts, sweatshirts, shirts, jackets, sweaters and caps.

SURPRISE > 72, rue Mercière (2nd)   ℃   **04 72 77 93 53.** Bang in the middle of a street famous for its restaurants, *Surprise* is a factory shop. The clothes sold at interesting prices are relaxed in style and, sometimes, very sporty.

TRAMPS > 5, rue de l'Ancienne-Préfecture (2nd)   ℃   **04 72 77 51 47.** If you like London fashion, if, in terms of look, excess is never too much for you, if the combination of flashy colours doesn't frighten you, and if the mixture of stripes and squares is, for you, the height of good taste, come and have a look round this boutique – you won't be disappointed. The stylists really let themselves go, the accessories are every bit as daring, and fashion has no limits.

UN HOMME A SUIVRE... ET UNE FEMME > 1, rue du Bât-d'Argent (1st)   ℃   **04 72 00 25 33.** Nothing's more convivial than a coffee as you try on your clothes. This very fashionable boutique, which opens onto two streets, has a modern-looking bar (chrome and high stools) separating the men and women's shelves, where customers can take a break before deciding between collections by *Dries Van Noten, Mac Queen, Ferragamo, Armani (Le Collezioni, Mani et Jeans), Prada, Miu Miu, Jil Sander* and *Donna Karan.*

Lyon *Fashion*

ZARA INTERNATIONAL > 71, rue de la République (2nd)   ℂ   **04 72 41 14 15.** For 10 years now, the giant of Spanish fashion has been dressing the Gauls. It's a big success if you judge by the location, the number of visitors and the size of the shops. You'll find classic or trendy sportswear, with new models every week, which, once exhausted, aren't renewed. Hence, the quasi-hysterical ambiance on Saturdays and during the sales. **Other address : "La Part Dieu" Shopping Centre- Level 2 (3rd) 04 72 84 99 00.**

West Lyon

JUMFIL > 200, route de Lyon (Solaize exit) - VERNAISON   ℂ   **04 78 46 10 01.** For nearly 50 years, *Jumfil* has been equipping fans of riding, fishing, Nature and 4 x 4. Nearly 160 people work behind the scenes (manufacturing workshop above the *Vernaison* shop) so that every appointment you fix with Nature is a success. From the most heavily-built to the slightest (from 36 to 66), from the most prudent to the most daring. You enter the shop after ringing, the reception's friendly and the products very attractive. Another address in Limas.

TANDEM > 2, rue Voltaire - OULLINS   ℂ   **04 78 86 08 69.** There are two small shops side by side, one for men and the other for women, but the choice of clothes on offer and the friendliness of the reception is every bit as good as larger establishments. You'll find the most fashionable labels, like *Jean-Paul Gaultier* or *Montana,* very classy clothes and an extremely attentive service. *Tandem* has everything it needs to roll on for a long time.

◆ DISCOUNT AND REBATE STORES

ACTE 1 > 29, cours Franklin-Roosevelt (6th)   ℂ   **04 78 99 83.** For the last 4 years, *Acte 1* has been a real reference in matters of unsigned clothes in Lyon. Throughout the year, the biggest names in chic fashion-sportswear deposit clothes here, and you'll find everything – from the dressy outfit to the *haute couture* evening dress you haven't even dared to dream about, as well as cooler but equally chic lines. The choice is enormous and the prices incredibly interesting for the biggest French, Italian and German labels on display. The reception's friendly, and the shop's set out in such a way that you almost forget that this is a discount store where you can dress luxuriously for prices you'd never have expected.

MISTIGRIFF > 273, cours Lafayette (6th)   ℂ   **04 78 52 92 50.** *Internet : www.mistigriff.com* You have to rummage around the disordered containers without being discouraged by the size of the task : the shop's very large and, at the end of the day, it's true that the shelves are in a hectic state. Ther are known labels (*Caroll, Kookaï, Cacharel...*), and a few good bargains for those who have the time or patience, but there are too many old-fashiones items which may drive away even the most valiant. **Other address : 140, avenue Maréchal-de-Saxe (3rd)** ℂ **04 78 62 62 17.**

SOLDERIE DES JACOBINS > 2, rue Childebert (2nd)   ℂ   **04 78 42 55 34.** Smart buyers know the shop for its large choice of top-range labels (*Karl Lagerfeld, Versace, Dona Karan*), which are sold at half or even a third of the price than in the boutiques. Some models are a bit dated, particularly in the shoes section, but, if you come regularly, you're bound to find some bargains. There are also ski-clothes, bags and accessories.

TATI > 9, rue Grenette (2nd)   ℂ   **04 78 38 43 50.** In this 'Temple of the Working Classes', Sloane mothers, trendy youngsters and housewives of all ages rub shoulders in search of lingerie, tableware or make-up at rock-bottom prices. You have to earn the bargains, and it's only after rummaging in the containers and queueing at the cashier's that you'll leave, happy to have spent so little.

Second-hand shops

KILO SHOP > Rue Lanterne (1st). Boys and girls, you'll find everything at the *Kilo Shop*, be it in the new goods section in the first part of the shop, or in the second-hand section in the large room at the back. For 100 F a kilo, second-hand clothes include a lot of jeans, leather and suède, dufflecoats, bags, knitted waistcoats, hippy skirts, American dance dresses... It's ideal for a theme evening when you've limited means and when you want to play it kitsch.

NUEVA PLAZA > 7, rue de la Platière (1st) ℰ **04 72 07 79 39.** *Nueva Plaza* is THE trendy second-hand shop in Lyon, the one which sells articles which are in pretty good condition and fairly trendy. Since fashion repeats itself, you'll find 70's items, grandma's bags updated for modern trends, psychedelic scarves, hippy skirts, leather jackets worthy of Huggy Bear, and disco dresses for the evening. All this at low prices.

◆CREATORS

CHARLY S > 26, rue René-Leynaud (1st). Originally from Martinique, Charly S lets us discover natural and original materials like bouano, a sort of crash, which he softens and transforms into unique items with cool and original cuts.

IL ETAIT UNE FOIS DES CREATEURS > 21, rue Sergent-Blandan (1st) ℰ **04 78 30 46 08.** Once upon a time there was a modern princess who liked to muffle herself up in mini-capes, long and light skirts, and shine during the evening in unstructured dresses. In spite of a tight budget, she created her personal style by hitching up part of her skirt and by wearing a skirt over her trousers. Dressed entirely in black, today's princess doesn't resemble a witch.

JEANNETTE ET JEANNOT > 1, place Croix-Paquet (1st) ℰ **04 78 39 98 87.** *Jeannette and Jeannot* are two young creator friends who decided to set themselves up in their favourite district in Lyon. Their boutique is easily recognizable by the large, amusing characters painted on the shopwindow. Not only are their creations out-of-the-ordinary, but they're also comfortable and wearable at any time of the day. They express their creativity in their clothes without ignoring the technical side, and they've perfectly mastered the art of pleating, embroidering and double-lining. They work a lot on made-to-measure, willingly allow their customers to give precise instructions, and make it a point of honour of carrying them out exactly. The prices are very reasonable for made-to-measure creations.

LUKA > 23, rue René-Leynaud (1st). The label's named after its creators : *Luka* for *Lu*dovic and *Ka*rine. Their favourite materials are the ultra-modern fabrics used in skate- and snowboarding clothes. This gives a look which is both sober and sexy, for a very low budget of 300 F to 500 F. A clever idea – their dresses, tops, jackets, skirts and windcheaters consist of models which are adjustable from sizes 36 to 40.

TODO Y NADA > 11, rue Romarin (1st) ℰ **06 61 43 84 19.** *"All or Nothing"*, the shop's name is too modest ; "All, All, All" would suit it better. Miss Ortega selects and sells a mass of diverse objects – clothes, bags, jewellery, decoration. The ensemble reminds you of Madrid, Barcelona and the *movida*. There's a total mixture of styles, and each item is unique. There's a second-hand section with Hawaiian shirts, flowery skirts, hippy tunics, 70's dresses and creators' works carefully chosen for their "never seen it elsewhere" style. An unusual mixture of furniture allows items to be put away, but they can also be bought : cushions and multi-coloured poofs in inflatable plastic, psychedelic lamps, wire shelves – everything's unusual and sold at affordable prices.

MULTI-MEDIA
AND COMMUNICATION

◆INTERNET

LE BAR@THYM > 1, rue Dumont d'Urville (4th) ℰ **04 78 28 01 14.** *Le Bar@thym* is, first and foremost, a bar and then a restaurant – all this with a terrace and a friendly atmosphere. Then, it's a cybercafé where you can come and consult the world net, or take courses for surfing on the Internet. You can even play on line. Still hesitant ?

www.petitfute.com

Lyon *Multi-media & communication - Internet*

CONNECTIK CAFE > 19, quai St Antoine (2nd)   ✆   **04 72 77 98 85.** *Connectik* was Lyon's first cyber-café. At first sight, it's a bar like all the others. But, if you go further into the place, you go down a few steps and find yourself in the computer room. Access to the Internet and to on-line games at the end of the week. It's practical for discovering the Internet for the first time or for sending e.mails once a month, but that's all. Because the price (60 F/hour or 40 F with a subscription) is absolutely prohibitive. You'd do better to put a bit of money aside to buy your own computer !

D-STAB > 14, rue Valentin Couturier (4th)   ✆   **04 78 27 95 12.** *D-Stab* offers to set up your electronic business, open 24h/24. So as no longer to limit an Internet site to a catalogue of products, and to turn it into a real shop, *D-Stab* has developed the Easy Compact Specialized Internet Tool, which is devoted to e.-trade. In addition to creating websites, *D-Stab* is also capable of other productions – 3D movies and videos on CD ROM or VHS cassette, for example.

FRANCE TELECOM – LA STATION INTERNET > 4, rue président Carnot (2nd)   ✆   **0 800 69 2001.** A hyper-modern setting and computers for consulting the Internet (40 F an hour payable by the minute or 30 F for students). Training courses are also sold : from 100 F for two hours of introductory course to 4 500 F to learn how to set up your own website.

LSI > 14, rue Jules Vallès (Villeurbanne)   ✆   **04 72 74 01 44.** *LSI* is, above all, an access to the Internet. In a small and quiet location, which is far from the hustle and bustle which often reigns in high-tech places, you can surf for 40 F an hour or work at a computer with a subscription of 175 F for 5 hours (150 F for students). As a sideline, *LSI* also distributes computers made by the *Vobis* brand and sells spare parts and accessories (CDR for example) at attractive prices.

PANI MANI CENTER > 16, rue Cavenne (7th)   ✆   **04 72 71 31 04.** Originally, *Pani Mani* was a minuscule snackbar selling sandwiches. Then it became a large and modern snackbar-café with access to the Internet. For the last few years, it's been a large, bright and pleasant snackbar/café with, nextdoor, a computer room : general computer work, the Internet and on-line games. People are always ready to help you.

REZONE > 2, place Ambroise Courtois (8th)   ✆   **04 78 76 96 15.** With 20 computers available, *Rezone* is Lyon's largest on-line games room. With its powerful computers and, for experts, its *GeForce 256* video cards, it's impossible not to have a good time on *Half-life*, *Quake III* or *Unreal*. For the cerebral, you can compete with friends on *StarCraft* or *Age of Empires* II. At *Rezone*, you can also play on-line games thanks to a hyper-rapid connection, the ADSL. Open 7/7 days, from midday to midnight.

SMILEY > 4, rue de la Doua (Villeurbanne)   ✆   **04 72 44 06 46.** No bar, just the Internet and the computers, but there's plenty of advice and loads of computers, so that you don't have to wait for someone to finish. It's professional and it's just nextdoor to the *Doua*.

Websites

ANNUAIRE LYONNAIS > *www.lyon-web.net.* There are more than 200 Lyonnais websites referenced in search motors. It's in this jungle that lyon-web, Lyon's Internet directory, comes into action. In the same way as the Yahoo system, lyon-web offers the choice between numerous themes listing a series of links to most of Lyon's sites : institutions, companies, districts, students, special themes… Also available, Yahoo dispatches and forums.

COURSES A DOMICILE > *www.cmescourses.com.* The Casino chain of shops now comes directly to the customer to deliver his shopping. You just have to connect yourself to the site, enter the coordinates and do your shopping, virtually. You put a cross against the products and quantities wanted in the lists, check that they've been included in your shopping trolley, and then send the order. All that remains to be done is to choose the date and time of delivery, and everything's finished. The delivery cost varies between 30 F and 50 F, depending on the time of the day, and it's free for more than 900 F of purchases. You pay on delivery. No hassles.

CYBERGONE > *www.cybergone.com. Cybergone* is the Lyonnais site which is part of the *Webcity* concept. This concept, developed by a young entrepreneur who was just 20 at the time, consists of creating in every large city a site dealing with cultural activities, fashion and practical information, like cinema times. Today, *Cybergone* also offers a press review, AFP news flashes and an e.mail subscription to receive information.

GLOBAL NATIVE > *www.globalnative.com.* For those who want to put NTIC at the heart of their company strategy, *Global* is specialized in e-business and e-trade. Intranet, extranet, the creation and handling of data banks, communication and information shopwindows, the re-vamping of websites - *Global Native* carries out a company audit in order to propose the most efficient means of selling, communicating or informing.

GRAND LYON > *www.grandlyon.com.* Practical information, weather reports, road traffic, administrative procedures, opinion polls, major projects and news items – all this and much more on this beautiful and clear site, which you'll visit with a lot of interest.

OFFICE DU TOURISME > *www.lyon-france.com.* This site contains a list of hotels, and gives an oversight of different aspects of the city and its region. The presentation of each theme is summary, but all you have to do is click on a connection to land on a specialized site.

LE PETIT FUTE > *www.petitfute.com.* All *Petit Futé* publications are now on the Internet : 22 French City Guides, 14 Departmental Guides, 43 "Destination" and "Thematic" Guides, all on a clear and attractive site with cultural Lyonnais news and travel offers.

SOFTY > *www.softy.fr.* The multi-media shop at *14 Avenue de Saxe* is also on the Internet for everything to do with computer accessories. You choose the type of product and/or a constructor in order to obtain a reference list (on which you can even read a commentary). Then, you can order, and have the goods delivered to your home or shop.

TCL > *www.tcl.fr.* The *Transports en Communs Lyonnais* (Lyon Public Transport System) had the good idea of putting a programme on the Internet which gives you a metro or bus itinerary for going from one spot to another. You choose a precise departure and arrival point, and you validate to get your route. The only problem is that the programme's not very sophisticated and that it's not able on its own to choose a route involving several changes. So, the interest's very limited.

VILLE DE LYON > *www.mairie-lyon.fr.* This site belongs to the City of Lyon and is also the on-line version of the newspaper, *"Lyon Cité".* You can find out about Lyon's history, its economy, the Municipal Assemblies and the budget, and you can also read press releases and enquire about events. It's not as attractive to look at as the *Grand Lyon* site, but the explanations are every bit as clear.

WHERE TO STAY

◆ECONOMICAL

CLIMAT DE FRANCE > 9, rue Antoine Lumière (8th) © **04 78 77 50 50.** *Rooms for 2 people from 280 F to 315 F.* In all *Climat de France* hotels, rooms are identical. If the prices vary, it's above all in function of the hotel's geographical location – whether it's in the town centre, in a pleasant area or in the outskirts of Lyon. The rooms are extremely pleasant and attractive, decorated in warm and bright colours (banana, vanilla) with nice, round, modern furniture. The lighting's soft and shaded for a cosy look. Each room has its own bathroom. If you want to eat late, the *La Soupière* restaurant's open till 2 in the morning, and offers menus from 90 F to 130 F. **Other addresses : 48, rue Hénon (4th) 04 72 00 22 22 • Lyon Saint Exupéry Airport – BRON 04 72 23 90 90 • Lyon Bron Eurexpo Airport – BRON 04 78 26 50 76.**

WRITE TO US
info@petitfute.com

Lyon *Where to stay - One star*

ETAP HOTEL > 154, Grande-Rue de Saint-Clair – CALUIRE ℂ **04 78 23 01 91.** *Rooms from 170 F to 210 F for 1, 2 or 3 people.* All located on the city outskirts, near major roads, these hotels, which are very practical for those who are broke or in a hurry, offer reasonably spacious rooms which can take up to 3 people (double bed with single bed superimposed), showers and private WC, TV (Canal + and satelite TV). Automatic sale of rooms by banker's card, which is practical for late arrivals and for illicit liaisons, and as much breakfast as you want for 24 F only. All rooms look alike, so that, once you know them, there are no good or bad surprises. **Other addresses : 58, rue Paul Teste – VAULX EN VELIN 04 72 04 56 76 • Porte de Lyon – DARDILLY 04 72 17 70 02 • 165, route de Vourles – SAINT GENIS LAVAL • ZA des Clochettes-RN7 15, allée de la Grange – SAINT FONS • 163, allée du Riottier-le péage Limas – VILLEFRANCHE SUR SAONE.**

◆ ONE STAR

HOTEL DE LA MARNE > 78, rue de la Charité (2nd) ℂ **04 78 37 07 46.** *Rooms from 1 to 4 people, from 120 F to 240 F.* A nice little hotel, which is really inexpensive, and which is located in a lively district, full of shops, attractive boutiques and nice restaurants. The rooms are characterized by their quiet, which is unusual in the city centre, and have showers and private WC's, as well as phone and TV. A nice surprise – the private garage to avoid driving round for 20 minutes to find a space. Another plus is that the hotel's just 5 minutes walk from the station.

HOTEL DES FACULTES > 104, rue Sébastien Gryphe (7th) ℂ **04 78 72 22 65.** *Rooms from 135 F for 1 person to 155 F for 2 people, breakfast included.* The hotel's motto is "satisfied or reimbursed", and the dissatisfaction can be related to the cleanliness of the rooms or to the quality of the reception. Students spending just a few days in the city to present a thesis, and those on summer courses, can take advantage of the degressive prices, which depend on the duration of the stay. The decoration won't strike you, because it's pretty banale, but the friendly welcome and the low prices are such that this hotel's developed a faithful clientèle.

◆ 2 STARS

AU PATIO MORAND > 99,rue de Créqui (6th) ℂ **04 78 52 62 62.** A quiet hotel in a residential area. *Au Patio Morand* is well located, and you go by foot to the cultural centre, the *Parc de la Tête d'Or*, the Contemporary Art Museum or to *La Part-Dieu* in just a few minutes. The hotel's a pretty house, with stone walls, with its original architecture, with two little terraces, and with very pleasant patio where you can take breakfast or a nap in summer. The little salon on the ground floor is ideal for relaxing, having a drink and discussing. The 22 rooms have their own style, and they're spacious and comfortable with bright, modern bathrooms.

ELYSEE HOTEL > 92, rue du président Edouard Herriot (2nd) ℂ **04 78 42 03 15.** *29 rooms. For 2 people, 380 F with bath, 360 F with shower. Breakfast 42 F.* Recently renovated, the *Elysée Hotel*'s a cosy place in a vaguely English style, which is made warmer and more comfortable by the carpeting everywhere, the attractive curtains, and the bouquets of flowers to be found throughout the hotel. Situated right in the city centre, it's a favourite spot for tourists (which we can understand). The ultra-comfortable rooms have a slightly elaborate decoration, and are equipped with shower or bath (your choice), a hairdrier, TV and direct telephone.

◆ 3 STARS

GRAND HOTEL DES TERREAUX > 16, rue Lanterne (1st) ℂ **04 78 27 04 10.** *56 rooms for 1 person at 385 F and at 420 F for 2, 3 or 4 people. Breakfast : 50 F.* A gem of an hotel, with soothing, pastel colours. Paintings by Kandinsky and Vuillard add a touch of colour to the walls. The rooms are all large and really pleasant, decorated with painted wooden furniture. It's so nice, you could spend your stay in Lyon without leaving the hotel, going from your room to the swimming-pool, which is located in the basement and surrounded by stone walls. On the other hand, that would be a pity, because the hotel's well located, a stone's throw from the Fine Arts Museum, the Opera and the *Place des Terreaux*. Nearby, there are several car parks belonging to *Lyon Parc Auto*.

HOTEL CHARLEMAGNE > 23, cours Charlemagne (2nd)   ℂ   **04 72 77 70 00.** *Rooms for 1 person at 395 F and 48 F. Rooms for 2 people at 435 F and 545 F. Breakfast : 52 F.* The differences in price are explained by the fact that the hotel's divided into two parts, each with a separate rating. The first price offers rooms of a normal size, with bath and with straightforward furniture - modern and quite nice. For the higher price, you get more spacious rooms, with balcony, small salon, separate bathroom and WC. Business clients take advantage of the 9 conference rooms, which are entirely equipped with audiovisual equipment for marketing presentations. The hotel car park is free, which is always a plus

HOTEL DES BEAUX-ARTS > 73-75, rue du président Edouard Herriot (2nd)   ℂ   **04 78 38 09 50.** *75 rooms. Single rooms at 540 F, 620 F and 670 F. Double rooms at 590 F, 670 F and 720 F. Suite at 810 F. Breakfast : 61 F.* In a fine building which is typical of Lyonnais architecture – tall, majestuous and entirely illuminated after nightfall – the *Hotel des Beaux Arts* offers excellent service to its clients. A stone's throw from the *Place Bellecour*, its central geographical location allows you to get to the *Presqu'île* by foot. Rooms are in different categories. All are air-conditioned, soundproof and comfortable, whilst some are even specially decorated by contemporary artists. In the evening, it's pleasant to have a drink in the bar.

HOTEL LE RICHELIEU > 25, rue Lalande (6th)   ℂ   **04 78 24 76 45.** *40 rooms, singles at 280 F, doubles at 290 F, triples at 335 F. Breakfast : 35 F.* Green carpet in the doorway, flowers everywhere in the hall, and a discreet and cosy atmosphere – the hotel promises well as soon as you push the door open. This first impression is confirmed at the first contact with the staff, who do their best to offer a personalized welcome and service. It's true that the rooms look a bit old, but they're comfortable and pleasant to stay in, so that your first reaction is quickly forgotten. The good surprise comes when you pay the bill and discover that the hotel's very good value for money.

◆ 4 STARS

GRAND HOTEL CHATEAU PERRACHE > 12, cours Verdun-Rambaud (2nd)   ℂ   **04 72 77 15 00.** At the very heart of the *Presqu'île*, between the Rhône and the Saône, this is a splendid-looking hotel – both majestuous and enormous, it hasn't aged a bit since the beginning of the century. Built in 1906, today it's an historical monument and is the only example of the Art Nouveau style in Lyon. The superb entrance, decorated with a wrought-iron canopy, plunges the visitor into an old-fashioned and luxurious ambiance. The wood-panelling and mural paintings throughout the hotel have natural, floral and botanical themes. Most of the glass, furniture and ironwork are period, and have been carefully maintained. There's still many a treasure in the hotel basement, like the recently-exhumed silver fruit stands, decorated with the Three Graces. You can easily imagine yourself in the Orient Express or in the Titanic, murder and shipwrecks aside. The service is like the building itself – royal ! A night's stay in one of the superb rooms is like a refined and dream-like journey through time.

GRAND HOTEL CONCORDE > 11, rue Grolée (2nd)   ℂ   **04 72 40 45 45.** *140 rooms and 3 suites at 780 F, 920 F, 1040 F and 1240 F. Breakfast : 80 F. Parking : 100 F per vehicle. Free for children under 12 in their parents' room.* The *Hotel Concorde* is large, imposing and majestuous, and is located in a 19th century building which is magnificently decorated and which combines elegance and tradition. The rooms and suites combine the charm of the old and modern comfort in a pampered and refined world. All the rooms are air-conditioned, soundproof, and equipped with private safe, Satellite TV channels and minibar. The service is impeccable, and you can change money and send a fax on the spot. At reception, they listen to the requirements of a demanding clientèle, and propose personalized sports, excursion and show programmes.

HOTEL HILTON > 70, quai Charles-de-Gaulle   ℂ   **04 78 17 50 50.** *201 rooms (from 1 300 F to 1 500 F) of which 23 suites (from 1 800 F to 3 800 F).* At the heart of the *Cité Internationale*, between the Rhône and the *Parc de la Tête d'Or*, this hotel's well located for welcoming, amongst others, numerous international businessmen. Moreover, the rooms are classified as *Business, Executive and Deluxe*, and are equipped with magnetic keys, Internet and modem plugs. In short, up-to-date technology. The decoration's a success : on the Rhône side, the strong colours (red, bordeaux, dark wood) were chosen in function of the natural light and to add warmth, whilst, on the side giving onto the street, light and honey colours brighten the rooms. The building's entirely in terracotta, glass and aluminium. Targeting an international clientèle, the *Hilton* chose Belgian and Thai gastronomy for its two restaurants, the *Brasserie Belge* and the *Blue Elephant*. For inveterate gamblers, the casino looks like an Egyptian temple in a very Las Vegas style. The fitness centre allows you to get over the journey and to unwind before the next business meeting.

HOTEL ROYAL > 20, place Bellecour (2nd) ℂ **04 78 37 57 31.** *80 rooms.* Ideally located in the city centre, this hotel allows tourists passing through Lyon to make the best of the city, and to shop in the nearby antiques district. The rooms are luxurious, and all are decorated differently with great refinement : mahogany and bronze for the *Clipper Room,* currents and eddies in the *Balneo Room,* hangings and canopies in the *Rotonde Room*. This hotel's a real cocoon, where everything's done (successfully) to make clients feel at home : smiling and deferential reception, car valet service. Comfort, intimacy and discretion are the key words. The Beatles even stayed here in 1969, as did the G7 team in 1996.

HOTEL SOFITEL > 20, quai Gailleton (2nd) ℂ **04 72 41 20 20.** *167 rooms of which 29 suites from 980 F to 1 400 F. Breakfast : 90 F.* Lovers of Lyon detest the architecture of this building, which is rather 70's and ugly. This is rapidly forgotten when you get into the hotel, which, perhaps to excuse itself for its exterior, is carefully decorated inside with beautiful marble floors and magnificent chandeliers. The rooms on the Rhône side are the best for the view they give over the quays and the old buildings on the other side of the river. Even if you're not staying here, you can have a drink in the bar, located at the top of the hotel, to the sound of jazzy music, or you can come early in the morning to have a delicious breakfast. The hotel also has a gastronomic restaurant, Les Trois Dômes, and a brasserie.

LA VILLA FLORENTINE > 25-27, montée Saint-Barthélémy (5th) ℂ **04 72 56 56 56.** *Rooms from 1 300 F to 2 100 F, suites from 1 600 F to 2 100 F. Breakfast : 100 F.* A member of the *Relais et Châteaux,* this superb hotel on the *Colline de Fourvière* offers a panoramic view over the city stretching out at its feet. Everything here is refinement *à l'italienne* : a beautiful villa in ochre, gold and orange colours. Inside, a play between light and shade makes the best of the warm colours. The 16 rooms and 3 suites are sunny, and decorated with a mixture of contemporary Italian furniture and of Renaissance-style furniture which is both Baroque and heavy. The hotel's luxurious and, in summer, the swimming-pool makes the place even more of a 'fairy world'.

LE MERIDIEN > 129, rue Servient (3rd) ℂ **04 78 63 55 00.** *245 rooms from 950 F to 1 050 F. Breakfast : 85 F.* At the heart of Lyon's business district, *Le Méridien* is the tallest hotel in Europe. It offers businessmen the chance to relax agreeably in luxurious rooms and, above all, to take advantage of the panoramic view of the whole of the city. At nightfall, when the city shines with all its lights, the spectacle's marvellous. More than 100 metres above the ground, you forget your fear of heights. *Le Ciel de Lyon,* the hotel's friendly, English-style bar, is located on the 32nd floor and desrves its name. The service is impeccable, discreet, professional and worthy of a 4-star hotel.

◆GUEST ROOMS

LES BALCONS PART DIEU > Allée de la Fontaine - 41, rue Maurice Flandrin (3rd) ℂ **04 72 13 99 35.** Two minutes from the station and from the shopping centre, this a friendly family lodging-house, which offers an alternative to staying in an hotel, and is devilishly cheap. The rooms are clean, well-kept and pleasant to stay in. The tariffs : 180 F for 1 person, 260 F for 2 people for a room with double bed, private bathroom, TV, video and breakfast. 150 F in a single room and 230 F in a double if you share the bathroom.

◆BED & BREAKFAST

BED & BREAKFAST IN LYON > 13bis, rue de la Garenne (5th) ℂ **04 72 16 95 01.** *Open from Monday to Friday from 11.00 to 19.00. Tariffs depnding on the comfort, count 200 F for 1 person and 300 F for 2 people.* Some 60 addresses in and around Lyon give you a better overall idea of Lyonnais life. As this formula is becoming more and more popular in France, it's best to reserve in advance, especially at weekends.

◆TEMPORARY LODGING

LA REINE ASTRID > 24, boulevard des Belges (6th)   ℂ   **04 72 82 18 00.** This 4-star tourist residence allows visitors to stay for a night, a week or more. A refined setting, a warm and intimate ambiance, a garden full of greenery (something to be appreciated in the centre of the city), from a studio to a 3-room flat. The rates are a bit high, but the rooms are spacious, luxurious, prettily laid out, and decorated in bordeaux and dark red. The height of luxury – the sheets are changed daily. You have to count around 775 F and 1 250 F for a studio and 2 350 F for a 3-room flat with salon and equipped kitchen. The residence has a fitness room, with a sauna, a hammam, a jacuzzi and body building equipment.

RESTAURANTS

◆1ST *ARRONDISSEMENT*

ADONYS > 13, rue Puits-Gaillot (1st)   ℂ   **04 72 00 95 15.** *Open 7/7 days. Service till 01.00. A la carte, count around 50 F. See our chapter "Cooking from elsewhere – Lebanon".*

AU TEMPS PERDU > 2, rue des Fantasques (1st)   ℂ   **04 78 39 23 04.** *Open everyday except at midday on Saturdays and on Sundays. Service till 22.00. A la carte count around 110 F.* This is an old-fashioned bistro, where time seems to have broken its flight in order to perch on the old paintings, on the Doisneau portraits, and on the red and green benches. In addition, there's a magnificent view of Lyon and of the roofs starting at the *Croix Rousse.*The cook, Ghislaine, prepares an 'ocean' cuisine, with shrimps and ginger or red mullet with olive oil and basil, as well as a few variations on typically-Lyonnais themes. From the dining-room you can see her toiling in the kitchen. Like the weather, the cuisine varies with the seasons. The restaurant's classics are always on the menu : veal's kidneys with Madeira and a gratin of macaroni.

BISTROT VERDI > 2bis, rue Verdi (1st)   ℂ   **04 72 00 00 95.** *Open everyday.* Franck Vernet, who's an inventive chef, is the maestro of the *pastilla d'agneau* (a lamb-flavoured pie, a Moroccan speciality), the *brick de canard* (another Moroccan speciality, made with duck) and a lot of other delicacies. Yellow, stone walls, wooden panelling…you feel good, warm and serene in this attractive litle restaurant. Smiles and attentive service – the sensation of well-being grows stronger. The dishes arrive, and your tastebuds are given a treat. More smiles, and you're now feelng very good…you don't want to leave. A big hand for the reception given by Franck Vernet and all his team !

CAFE CUBA > 19, place Tolozan (1st)   ℂ   **04 78 28 35 77.** *Open everyday except on Sundays. Service till midnight. Tapas from 18 F to 35 F. See our chapter "Cooking from elsewhere – Spain and Portugal".*

CAFE DES FEDERATIONS > 8-10, rue du Major-Martin (1st)   ℂ   **04 78 28 26 00.** *www.lesfedeslyon.com • See our chapter "Regional Cuisine – Lyonnais Cuisine".*

CAFE DES TABLES CLAUDIENNES > 41, rue des Tables-Claudiennes (1st)   ℂ   **04 78 28 99 76.** *Open everyday except on Sundays.* This pleasant bistro has a speciality – mussels with cream. Perfectly perfumed with herbs and aromatics, accompanied by crisp and light chips, the dish is, quite simply, delicious. On the menu as well, frog's legs which, for once, aren't swimming in fat, *magret de canard* (breast of duck) and pieces of beef – a traditional, family cuisine you never tire of. On Friday evenings, the room gets livelier from 21.00 onwards, and the invited singers launch into a classical or highly original repertoire of French songs – to the great joy of the clients, who don't hesitate to join in the refrains.

CAFE LEFFE > 1, place des Terreaux (1st)   ℂ   **04 78 27 27 07.** *Open everyday till 01.00. Dish of the Day 45 F. Starter, main dish and dessert 72 F, mussels and chips from 48 F, salad from 36 F, dessert from 18 F.* Situated on the very busy *Place des Terreaux*, near the Town Hall and opposite the Saint-Pierre Museum, the *Café Leffe* is a favourite haunt. It offers quality food which is served rapidly. But, depending on what time you come, you may have to wait, because the very pleasant waiters aren't numerous. As in all Belgian establishments, it's a 'must' to drink beer and eat mussels and chips. However, the menu also contains other dishes, and the Dishes of the Day are copious. If you want to sit on the terrace, choose midday because, in the evening, the square isn't peaceful… the inside's decorated with the help of mirrors, wall-lights and attractive seats, and the ensemble gives a warm feeling. The vaulted, basement room is a bit noisy because of the washing-up going on nextdoor. After your meal, order a coffee because, here, it's excellent… we said "excellent !".

CAPPADOCE > 4, rue Constantine (1st) ℂ **04 78 29 20 05.** *Open everyday from 11.00 to 01.00. Kebab sandwiches to take away 23 F, on the spot 25 F, with chips 27 F, dishes from 40 F, pâtisseries 10 F. See our chapter "Cuisine from elsewhere – Turkey".*

CHEZ CARLINO > Rue de l'Arbre-Sec (1st). *Open 7/7 days. A la carte count 100 F. Service till 22.00. See our chapter "Cuisine from elsewhere – Italy".*

CHEZ HUGON > 12, rue Pizay (1st) ℂ **04 78 28 10 94.** *Open everyday except on Saturdays and Sundays. Service till 22.30. A la carte count 140 F. See our chapter "Regional Cuisine – Lyonnais Cuisine".*

CHEZ PAUL > 11, rue du Major-Martin (1st) ℂ **04 78 28 35 83.** *See our chapter "Regional Cuisine – Lyonnais Cuisine".*

COMPTOIR DU SUD > 10, rue Rivet (1st) ℂ **04 78 28 01 74.** *Open everyday except on Saturday evenings and on Sundays. Service till 22.00. A la carte count 90 F.* The *Comptoir du Sud* offers a pleasant and friendly stop, in a room with a Provençal décor mixing wood and stone. There's no menu, but a menu written on a blackboard which offers a French family cuisine. It's not expensive, since salads begin at 32 F, Dishes of the Day at 42 F, and you'll also find sandwiches, omelettes, tartares and steaks. Dishes vary with the season. The upper room can take groups of up to 40 people. In the afternoon, local grandmas and granddads come to play cards, and it's a more than pleasant place for a quiet coffee.

EL PORRON > 6, rue Désirée (1st) ℂ **04 78 28 79 22.** *Open everyday except on Sundays. A la carte count 60 F. Service till 00.45. See our chapter Cuisine from elsewhere – Spain".*

EL SOMBRERO > 9, rue Pizay (1st) ℂ **04 78 30 90 79.** *Open everyday except on Sundays and on Saturdays and Mondays at midday. Menus at 69 F at midday and 100 F to 135 F in the evening. See our chapter "Cuisine from elsewhere – Tex-Mex".*

EL TEX MEX > 3, rue Pizay (1st) ℂ **04 78 29 23 23.** *Open everyday except on Sundays, and on Saturdays and Mondays at midday. Menus 69 F (midday), 100 F, 120 F and 135 F. See our chapter "Cuisine from elsewhere – Tex-Mex".*

L'ALANDIER > 3, rue Constantine (1st) ℂ **04 78 29 56 37.** *Open from Monday to Saturday except on Monday evenings. Dish of the Day 42 F, Dish of the Day and cheese or dessert 50 F, pizza from 27 F, pasta from 22 F, salads from 20 F, maxi-salads from 40 F. Salad and Lasagna Formulae 44 F, pasta and dessert 55 F, entrée, pizza and dessert 70 F. Desserts from 18 F.* A simple, unpretentious address which is worth coming to, firstly, for its value for money. *L'Alandier*'s pizzas are good, made with thin pasta and well-garnished. The Dish of the Day changes every day and is made with market produce because Brice, the young owner, goes there every morning. True, the setting's simple, but the reception's warm, and that counts more, doesn't it ? In short, *L'Alandier*'s a good address, worth writing down for a midday break or for a meal with no frills between friends.

L'ARROSOIR > 25, rue de l'Arbre-Sec (1st) ℂ **04 78 39 57 57.** *Open everyday except on Sundays and Mondays. See our chapter "Salad Places".*

L'ETAGE > 4, place des Terreaux (1st) ℂ **04 78 28 19 59.** *Open everyday except on Sundays and Mondays. Dish of the Day 70 F at midday only. Menus at 100 F, 150 F and 280 F (based round a lobster, for 2 people). A la carte around 150 F. Service till 22.30. L'Etage* (The Floor) could have been called The Flat. Having climbed the staircase of a fairly average building, the door opens onto an attractive room whose two windows give onto the *Place des Terreaux* : illuminated at night, it's a real sight. There are no more than a dozen tables for an intimate and refined atmosphere, so that it's essential to reserve, sometimes several days in advance. All around, polished wood panelling, stretched red velvet, heavy red curtains embroidered with golden bees, subdued lighting and soft, classical music. The service is discreet, efficient and welcoming, although a little timid. The cuisine offers a festival of tastes and aromas. The menu's deliberately limited : three entrées and three main dishes are more than enough to satisfy the gourmet. The entrées, from 75 F to 95 F, are foie gras, snails and fresh cod. The main courses, at 90 F and 95 F, consist of grilled pavé of beef, knuckle of lamb and fillet of plaice *meunière*. Main dishes are accompanied by a poetic selection of vegetables : *mirepoix d'échalotes* (diced shallots), *duxelles de champignons* (chopped mushrooms), *croquant aux noisettes et au parmesan* (crisp vegetables with hazelnuts and parmesan) and *polenta crémeuse et carpaccio d'ananas* (creamy polenta and pineapple carpaccio).

L'ETOILE OPERA > 26, rue de l'Arbre-Sec (1st)　℃　04 72 10 10 20. *www.etoile.opera.com •*
Open everyday except on Saturdays at midday and on Sundays. Service till 23.00. Menus at 89 F and 120 F. A la carte around 120 F. A new bar, with the ambiance of a fashionable restaurant, has opened its doors and terrace in the *Rue de l'Arbre-Sec*. Run by Patrick Di Folco, this very popular place combines comfort and extreme modernity. The walls are in a beautiful, tropical blue, and the prevailing atmosphere's warm. Well-padded velvet benches can be found alongside very 'designer' stools. In the mezzanine, where the atmosphere's more intimate, you can have a drink in a soft armchair or a comfortable sofa. On the menu, pasta takes pride of place, which is excellent news for those who are connoisseurs of *fusilli al pesto* or *caramelone aux épinards* (caramalone with spinach) or with *Ricotta* cheese. Alternatively, you can try the fillet of beef with a *Saint-Marcellin* sauce, the *pavé* of salmon with lime, the *aiguillettes de volaille* (thinly-sliced poultry) or the beef *tartare*. L'Etoile Opéra promises to shine in the firmament.

L'OISEAU DE PARADIS > 4, rue Guiseppe Verdi — Corner of Rue de l'Arbre-Sec (1st)
℃　04 72 00 83 80. *Open everyday except at midday on Saturdays and Sundays. Menus at 73 F, 79 F, 83 F and 93 F and à la carte. See our chapter "Cuisine from elsewhere – Thailand".*

L'OXALIS > 23, rue de l'Arbre-Sec (1st)　℃　04 72 07 95 94. *Open from Tuesday to Saturday.*
Menus at 65 F, 120 F and 280 F. Service till 22h30. The *Oxalis* is a small flower you find in the undergrowth and which has a subtle taste, so that it's also known as "little sorrel". It also happens to be an elegant restaurant with an elegant, feminine and refined décor in soft and pastel hues. The tables are beautifully arranged with pretty, white tablecloths and padded chairs, whilst the paintings on the walls make this the perfect restaurant for an intimate dinner. Sonia Ezgulian, who officiates in the kitchen, stupefies her guests when she tells them that her original profession had nothing to with restaurants, because her cooking is quite remarkable. Among other delicious dishes, you'll find her *fleurs de courgettes farcies à l'orge crémé* (flower-shaped courgettes with preserved lemons), her *filet de rouget poêlé accompagné de calissons de citrons confits* (fillet of red mullet accompanied by *calissons* of preserved lemons), her *supions en fricassée d'asperges* (small squid in a fricassee of asparagus) and her *poulet de Bresse aux échalotes confites au jus de banyuls* (Bresse chicken with preserved shallots in a Banyuls juice).

LA GUILOUTE > 5, rue de la Martinière (1st)　℃　04 72 00 28 40. *Open everyday except on*
Sundays and Mondays. Service till 23.00. Dish of the Day 49 F (at midday), 78 F and 140 F. A la carte around 90 F. A *guiloute*, which is a very personal term in so far as it was entirely invented by the owner and his friends, is a small glass. It's also the name of this very attractive restaurant, which has lovely curtains, subdued lighting and dozens of bouquets of dried flowers hanging from the ceiling. You eat all sorts of dishes here at a very reasonable price : fish, salads, pieces of meat, like knuckle of beef, and other very fresh produce which varies in function of what took the chef's fancy at the nearby market. The menu at 78 F is really a bargain : entrée, copious main course, cheese (including an excellent *cervelle de canuts*) and dessert. Jean-François and Vincent always receive you in a friendly and hospitable way.

LA KAZ KREYOL > 4, rue Verdi (ex petite rue Pizay) (1st)　℃　04 78 29 41 70. *Open everyday.*
Service till 22.30. Menus at 89 F, 98 F and 145 F. A la carte around 100 F. See our chapter "Cuisine from elsewhere – The Islands".

LA MERE BRAZIER > 12, rue Royale (1st)   ©   **04 78 28 15 49.** Dark wood, velvet, silver, intimate atmosphere and personalized welcome – this restaurant has everything you expect of a fine restaurant. It's distinguished, but not stiff, luxurious without being pretentious. There are no frilly dishes, but the very best family cooking - simple and tasty. You'll find rack of lamb, quenelles, pan-fried *foie gras* and gratin of macaroni. The cherry on the cake is Miss Brazier, who welcomes all her guests like VIP's.

LA RANDONNEE (THE RAMBLE) > 4, rue Terme (1st)   ©   **04 78 27 86 81.** *Open everyday except on Mondays and at midday on Tuesdays. Service from 11.30 to 14.30 and from 18.30 to 23.00. At midday : formulae with two dishes : 35 F and 40 F, with 3 dishes : 49 F, 58 F and 85 F. In the evening : formulae at 45 F, 48 F and 55 F, menus at 65 F and 75 F. Children's menu : 32 F.* "Copious dishes at the most attractive prices" is this restaurant's motto, and, what's more, it's true ! Here, the Lyonnais, family cooking is served with a smile, and the plates are really well garnished. The dining room reminds you of a ramble, because of its collection of unusual objects, and the ambiance is simple but warm. In the evening, a piano adds a musical ambiance, and the establishment's generosity stretches as far as offering you the car park in *Les Terraux.* Finally, the prices are really exceptional – there's no need to ruin yourself to eat well !

LA TABLE D'EUGENE > 18, rue Royale (1st)   ©   **04 78 39 57 00.** *Open everyday except on Mondays, on Wednesday evenings and on Sundays. Service till 22.00. Dishes of the Day at 49 F and 69 F. A la carte around 80 F.* Eugène Varlin was a worker- bookbinder and a *communard* who launched the workers' restaurants. *La Table d'Eugène* pays him tribute by offering enormous menus at very low prices. The dishes change frequently, in function of the season and of what's available at the market – a guarantee of freshness. In winter, the recipes are borrowed from the north of France, with the use of beer and sweet wines. In summer, olive oil predominates, as it does in Provence. Throughout the year, the food's tasty and the stomach's well-filled.

LA TABLE D'HIPPOLYTE > 22, rue Hippolyte-Flandrin (1st)   ©   **04 78 27 75 59.** *Open everyday except on on Saturdays at midday, on Sundays and on Mondays.* Whatever the season, clients feel good here, and they're coddled, pampered and sometimes surprised with the quality of the food. Contrary to what you might believe, *La Table d'Hippolyte*'s chef is a woman, Pascale Boissier, who wields the heavy saucepans in the kitchen, whilst her brother runs the dining room. She has no equal for preparing a *daurade royale en crapautine* (spatchcocked sea bream), prawns with garlic, veal's liver deglazed with Frontignan wine or, more simply, a *tablier de sapeur* (literally, a 'fireman's apron', consisting of strips of marinated tripe dipped in egg and breadcrumbs and fried or grilled) or an *andouillette* (chitterling sausage) with mustard. The restaurant's attractive, the food's always tasty, and the smiling welcome makes you feel like coming back.

LA TABLE DES ECHEVINS > 12, rue Major-Martin (1st)   ©   **04 78 39 98 33.** *Open from Monday to Saturday except on Monday evenings. Service from 12.00 to 13.30 and from 19.30 to 22.00, on Saturdays from 12.30 to 14.00 and from 19.30 to 22.30. Menus at 98 F, 138 F and 158 F.* Going back ten centuries simply by walking through a door is possible just a stone's throw away from the *Les Terreaux.* Here, the desserts are called *Yssues*, the prices are in *ecus*, and you pay in hard cash. Yes, that's it, you're back in the Middle Ages. So, if you want to taste food cooked on spits, or slabs of meat, *La Table des Echevins* is for you. A fine cuisine, with original and forgotten savours. *La Table des Echevins* also organizes thematic mediaeval evenings. Reservation advised.

LE BALMORAL > 14, rue Lanterne (1st)   ©   **04 78 28 72 53.** *Open everyday except on Tuesdays. A la carte around 100 F. Service till 23.30. See our chapter "Cuisine from Elsewhere – Italy".*

LE BEVERLY > 8, place des Terreaux (1st). *Open everyday but food served only from Monday to Saturday. Salads from 32 F, pizzas from 38 F, hot dish from 40 F, dessert from 12 F.* Situated on the Place des Terreaux, Le Beverly enjoys the sort of setting you dream about. In the evening, the large diningroom's ceiling is superb – luminous effects guaranteed ! Come the summer, the terrace comes into its own, with the Town Hall, the Palais Saint-Pierre and the Bartholdi Fountain within arm's reach. "And what about the food", you ask ? It's not forgotten either, and there's a special mention for the pizzas – with their thin crust, generous garnishes and large diameter, they make a good meal. The menu also contains a number of different salads, including Greek salads, 'Ocean' salads and salads with warm goat's cheese. The welcome's friendly, and, if you dawdle a bit at the table, the owner offers you a second coffee – a fact so rare that it's worth drawing your attention to ! Impossible to reserve because *Le Beverly*'s number is ex-directory.

BEAUJOLAIS REWARDED (READ IN MODERATION)

Beaujolais is an integral part of Lyonnais life. The 3rd Thursday in November sees the arrival of the *Beaujolais Nouveau*, and it's served everywhere in the city. Every establishment or company organizes its public or private soirée : it's the Lyonnais Roland Garros - you have to be seen, known and recognized in these post-harvest social gatherings.

The fame of *Beaujolais Nouveau* now extends well beyond the city and even national frontiers. Indeed, every year, press photographers take pictures of case-loads of wine being loaded into aeroplane cargo holds bound for Japan and other exotic destinations. But, there remain a number of diehards who maintain that *Beaujolais Nouveau* is nothing but a vast marketing operation, carried out at the expense of quality wine... It's for each individual to judge, having drunk the wine... in moderation, of course.

But *Beaujolais* is also served throughout the year by restaurants for which quality is important, and they serve the "red gold" in jugs or in bottles, insisting on good value for money. It was to reward these restaurants that the "Lyonnais Cup for Astonishing Beaujolais" was created in 1995. Since then, it's been awarded annually by three associations – the *Amicale des Beaujolais de Lyon*, the *Confrérie des Compagnons du Beaujolais* and the *Francs Mâchons*. Having tested the Beaujolais served in some 20 pre-selected establishments, the jury awarded the 1999 "Lyonnais Cup for Astonishing *Beaujolais*" to *L'Apostrophe*, La Cave des Voyageurs - both of them in the 5th *arrondissement* – and to *Le Crayon* in the 3rd *arrondissement*. In the year 2000, the award went to *Mon Brouilly* in the 1st *arrondissement* and to *Le Saxe* in the 3rd *arrondissement*.

LE CAFÉ DU GROS CAILLOU > 180, boulevard de la Croix-Rousse (1st) © 04 78 27 22 37. *Open everyday. A la carte around 90 F. Service till 22.00.* What a magnificent terrace ! Everybody agrees, so that, when the weather's fine, there are always crowds in the shade of the plane trees. The menu entirely respects Lyonnais tradition, and you'll find the great classics on the enormous and, doubtless, very heavy slate blackboard : quenelles, *andouillettes*, Lyonnais sausages, *tablier de sapeur* (strips of marinated tripe dipped in egg and breadcrumbs and fried or grilled), tripe... *Le Café du Gros Caillou* is also a bar serving good wine, and where Beaujolais takes pride of place. Indeed, the *Beaujolais* served by Charles, the owner, is one of the "astonishing *Beaujolais*" selected by the jury for the "*Beaujolais* Cup" (see above). So, this is an excellent occasion for having a good drink as you satisfy your hunger. Charles also serves good *Gaillac, Côtes-du-Rhône* and *Mâcons*.

LE CARRE > 2, rue Verdi (1st) © 04 78 27 70 43. *Open from Monday to Saturday except at midday on Saturday and on Monday evenings. Unique price : 50 F entrée, 75 F main dish, 25 F for a dessert. Menu at 130 F.* You have to earn Le Carré : the little street it's in (the old *Petite-Rue-Pizay*) is very difficult to find. But, once you've found this restaurant in the Opera district, you'll be more than satisfied. *Le Carré* offers a traditional cuisine, consisting of Lyonnais specialities, and it's very good. The restaurant's also recommended to food-lovers for its daily dessert menu, consisting of some 15 different desserts. In short, *Le Carré* is very good !

LE CARO DE LYON > 25, rue du Bât-d'Argent (1st) © 04 78 39 58 58. *Open everyday except on Sundays. Service till 23.30. Menu at 130 F and à la carte.* Le Caro took a lot of trouble with the décor, so that the clientèle would fell good here – and they've succeeded. As soon as you arrive, there's a valet to park your car, which is something you appreciate in this very busy district. The dining room's superb. It's Italian in inspiration, with green walls, ochre wood, terracotta pots and Baroque chandeliers. The chief attraction remains the enormous library shelves, filled with real books from floor to ceiling, which gives a very personal touch to the place. The service is pleasant – discreet and very professional – and the cuisine's traditional, with a few Italian dishes. A novelty is the musical evenings : every Wednesday, there's a Russian evening with a typical meal ; on Thursday, it's a jazz evening, and, every Friday, you can hear radio *Fréquence Jazz* radio direct from the *Carode Lyon*.

Lyon *Restaurants - First arrondissement*

LE CASSE-MUSEAU > 2, rue Chavanne (1st) ℂ **04 72 00 20 52.** This bistro's unpretentious, but not lacking in ideas. *Le Casse-Museau* likes pasta and prepares them with a lot of imagination. Indeed, to change from the routine *spaghetti carbonara* or *bolognaise*, the home-made pasta here is perfumed with lamb curry, lard and prunes… For a salad, count around 19 F to 39 F. At midday the 'quick-bite' *formulae* are not expensive, and remind you that there are things other than a ham sandwich to allay a hunger. The reception's friendly, and the prices, reasonable. Go upstairs to admire the Fine Art fresco.

LE CHANT DE LAURE > 5bis, place Sathonay (1st) ℂ **04 78 30 90 25.** *Open everyday at midday and in the evening. Menus at 43 F, 57 F, 75 F, 89 F and 97 F. A la carte around 70 F. Service till 22.00. See our chapter "Crêperies".*

LE COFFEE SHOP > 27, rue Matinière (1st) ℂ **04 78 30 61 61.** *Menu of the Day at 70 F, Fish or Meat Menu at 95 F, half-a-free-range-chicken and salad at 69 F.* Brother cowboy, you who enter here, kindly refrain from spitting on the sheriff's boots, and simply enjoy the place, which will remind you of your native Texas. As soon as you've gone through the swing-doors, look up at the ceiling and you'll see Joe the Indian's teepee. Sit down at one of the round tables with 9 of your paleface friends, and order a Texan fondue, an ostrich steak or fresh pasta. For the ice-cream and coffee, go onto the terrace and sit in one of the film director's armchairs. Avoid whistling at the waitresses, even if you regret that they're not wearing miniskirts, stetsons and boots. Once you've gobbled down your meal, you can leave the saloon, jingling your spurs.

LE COMPTOIR DES LULUS > 3, Petite-Rue-des-Feuillants (1st) ℂ **04 78 39 00 93.** *Open from Tuesday to Saturday (except on Saturdays at midday). Service till 22.00. Dishes of the Day at 42 F and 58 F. A la carte around 80 F.* Here, you eat Italian-Lyonnais pizza and pasta, and drink a grappa at the bar to finish the meal. The cuisine's prepared on a wood fire, and the ambiance is warm – jazzy music and, on the walls, friendly cartoon characters. The specialities are called *tortellini* gratin, *tiramisu* and pizza with curry, and there's a mixture of Italian and exotic tastes. The salads are accompanied by *calzones*, delicious stuffed turnovers. This is a nice restaurant in a street which is less so.

LE CONNETABLE > 38, rue de l'Arbre-Sec (1st) ℂ **04 78 29 27 90.** *Open everyday except on Sundays. Service till 23.00. Menus at 79 F, 85 F and 109 F. A la carte around 70 F.* Stuffed chickens on the chimeypiece, stone walls, Provençal tablecloths and an ambiance of jazz music – this gives you an idea of the pleasant setting. On the menu, traditional French and Lyonnais cuisine : breast of duck, skirt of beef with shallots, calf's head, hot sausage, *filet mignon*… there's no lack of choice. All the menus consist of an entrée, a main dish and cheese or a dessert. It may not be great gastronomy, but the servings are generous, the prices are low and the reception's friendly, so you have an enjoyable time.

LE DOMINOTIER > 14, rue Constantine (1st) ℂ **04 78 27 48 10.** *Open everyday except at midday on Saturdays and Sundays. Service till 01.00. Dish of the Day at midday 43 F, Dish of the Day with entrée or dessert 53 F, Dish of the Day with entée and dessert 63 F, salad and dessert formula 55 F. Otherwise, menus at 90 F, fondue, tartiflette or raclette from 65 F. Fondue, Tartiflette and Raclette Menus from 94 F. See our chapter "Regional Cuisine – Savoie".*

LE LANTERNE > 12, rue Lanterne (1st) ℂ **04 78 27 48 19.** *Open from Monday to Saturday except on Monday evenings. Dish of the Day at 45 F, salad from 32 F, Salad Formula with chips and coffee 52 F, menu at 68 F and à la carte. Le Lanterne's* salads are famous – they're Perigordian, 'Ocean' or made with goat's cheese, for example, and are served either XL or XXL. This allows both those with a small appetite and the hungrier to leave satisfied, and the only menu on offer gives a real choice. The interior is charming, with stone walls, beams and old posters, unless, that is, you prefer to eat on the terrace when it's fine. The little *Rue Lanterne*, which is regrettably not yet a pedestrian street, is very attractive, and *Le Lanterne's* terrace, behind the greenery, is a plus. This is an address to note down, but be careful not to confuse it with the address of *LA Lanterne*, which is a sex shop in the same street and which has nothing to do with the restaurant…

First arrondissement - Restaurants Lyon

LE MANDARIN > 15, rue Lanterne (1st) © **04 78 28 45 66.** *Open from Tuesday to Sunday. At midday only, menu at 45 F. If not, menus at 67 F and 89 F and à la carte. See our chapter "Cuisine from Elsewhere – Asia".*

LEON DE LYON > 1, rue Pléney (1st) © **04 72 10 11 12.** *Open everyday except on Sundays and Mondays. Service till 22.00. Menus at 290 F (midday), 590 F and 720 F. A la carte around 400 F.* Known throughout the world, not only for having served a feast to the Heads of State during the G7 conference but, above all, for the excellence of its cuisine, *Léon de Lyon* is a gastronomic 'must' in Lyon. The ambiance is charming and intimate, the service is discreet and efficient, and this magical establishment's run by a chef who is one of the most capped in France.

LE PASSAGE > 8, rue du Plâtre (1st) © **04 78 28 11 16.** *Open everyday except on Saturdays at midday and on Sundays. Service till 22.00. Menus from 185 F to 240 F.* Whether it's on the terrace in the passageway or upstairs in a pampered and warm atmosphere, *Le Passage* serves a delicious and nicely-prepared cuisine. Among the chef's suggestions - *escalope de foie gras chaud au vinaigre balsamique* (escalope of foie gras with balsamic vinegar), *oeufs brouillés aux truffes* (scrambled eggs with truffles), and *filet de loup à la truffe noire du Périgord* (fillet of bass with black Perigordian truffle). Offering a tour of the finest produce to be found in France, *Le Passage* is definitely worth a stop.

LE PETIT PAILLET > 27, quai Saint-Vincent (1st) © **04 78 28 14 51.** *Open everyday except at midday on Saturdays and on Sundays. Menus at 74 F, 150 F and 180 F. A la carte around 150 F. Service till 22.30.* If you go up the *Quai Saint-Vincent*, you'll come across a pretty and quiet square under the trees. *Le Petit Paillet's* here, at the corner of the square. The dining room's large, the chairs and tables are very 'bistro', and the rest of the décor's personalized, thanks to photos and paintings on the light-orange walls, and to the chandeliers which give this place soul. The cuisine's traditional and tasty, the *pavé* of beef with Saint-Marcellin sauce melts in your mouth, the fish varies depending on what's available at the market, and the 'fresh salads' more than deserve their name.

LE PETIT PERSAN > 8, rue Longue (1st) © **04 78 28 26 50.** *Open everyday except on Sundays and Mondays. Menus at 59 F at midday, 85 F, 125 F and 255 F. A la carte around 120 F. Service till 22.30. See the chapter "Cuisine from Elsewhere – Persia".*

LE POTAGER DES HALLES (THE *LES HALLES* KITCHEN GARDEN) > 3, rue Thomassin (1st) © **04 72 00 24 84.** *Open everyday except on Saturdays at midday, on Sundays and on Mondays. Menus at 85 F at midday, 120 F and 150 F. A la carte around 110 F. Service till 22.30.* The setting's pleasant and the service, efficient, but the restaurant owes its name more to its location near *Les Halles* (Covered Market) than to its menu, which doesn't particularly consist of vegetables. The very friendly owner doesn't hesitate to joke with his clients (without ever going too far) if he feels they're not very receptive. The cuisine's traditional, from Lyon and elsewhere. As an entrée, the choice varies between, for example, fish terrine, goat's cheese, lentil salad, song *foie gras* or the *salade souflette*, consisting of delicious pan-fried *quenelles*. By way of fish, the salmon *rillettes* are a success. Meat-fans will opt for the stuffed hen or the *andouillette*. The desserts are home-made : chocolate pavé, lemon pastry cream, praline tart, soft coconut meringue or seasonal fruit 'soup'. If the owner takes to you, you'll have the right to a glass of his best *calvados* as a digestive.

LE POTIQUET > 27, rue de l'Arbre-Sec (1st) © **04 78 30 65 44.** *Open everyday except at midday on Saturdays and on Sundays. Service till 22.00 during the week, midnight at weekends. Menus at 110 F, 130 F and 160 F. See the chapter "Fish".*

LE RENDEZ-VOUS DES GASTRONOMES > 20, rue Terme (1st) © **04 78 30 86 44.** *Open from Monday to Saturday, except at midday on Saturdays. Dish of the Day 38 F, Menu of the Day : entrée, main dish and dessert for 55 F, menus at 80 F, 98 F, 139 F and 169 F. Le Rendez-Vous des Gastronomes* amply deserves its name, because it knows how to marry refined and rich menus (particularly with its specialities of snails and frog's legs) with simpler menus and very affordable prices. The sober décor and pleasant service make it a place to be recommended, just a short walk from *Place des Terreaux*. In summer, the terrace only adds to the restaurant's charm.

Lyon *Restaurants - First arrondissement*

LE SAINT ALBAN > 2, quai Jean-Moulin (1st) ✆ **04 78 30 14 89.** Behind the drawn, white curtains hiding the dining-room from the street and the quays, hides a charming restaurant. The setting's warm and comfortable, and the subdued lighting make the stone vaulting and wooden beams even more attractive. The place is run by Jean-Paul Lechevalier, who prepares the cuisine of a *meilleur ouvrier de France*. The result is up to the expectations of the most demanding, and the menu's both sober and imaginative.

LE SANTORIN > 10, rue Pleney (1st) ✆ **04 78 28 33 92.** *Open from Monday to Saturday except on Monday evenings. Dish of the Day 45 F, menus at 82 F and 102 F. Entrées or main dishes from 37 F, desserts from 18 F. No banker's cards. See the chapter "Cuisine from Elsewhere – Greece".*

LE TIAFE > 14, rue René-Leynaud (1st) ✆ **04 78 27 85 88.** *Service till 23.00. Formulae at 45 F and 65 F.* Le Tiafé's a bric-à-brac of unusual objects. You feel that the place is lived in, and that every object, painting, vase or poster has a history, a personal link with the restaurant or with its owners. The dining room's old-fashioned, with high ceilings and a dozen tables, and there's a bar behind, where Jean-Paul and Alain go efficiently about their business. There are fresh flowers on the tables, table-sets and napkins in multi-coloured paper, and there's a lot of taste in the way the room's set out and decorated. The restaurant has a large number of regular clients, and this can be felt in the prevailing ambiance : people laugh, discuss and exchange cracks with other tables, to a background music of French songs. The owners have a pleasant word for all their clients. The cuisine's traditional, and the chef's as much at ease with salmon in mousseline, *andouillette*, flesh of scallop or breast of duck. There's no attempt to impress – just a healthy, delicate and nourishing cuisine. A big "Thank you" to *Le Tiafé* for welcoming large and small, young and old, with the same friendliness.

LES DEMOISELLES DE ROCHEFORT > 31, rue René-Leynaud (1st) ✆ **04 72 00 07 06.** *Open from Tuesday to Saturday evening. Service till 22.30. A la carte only, count around 90 F.* Dark, lacquered red predominates and creates an intimate atmosphere and a pleasantly 'underground' ambiance. The unusual décor reinforces the restaurant's charm : bookshelves and loads of paintings on the walls. The music's pleasant and the cuisine's delicious : lamb *tajine* with honey and plums (75 F), andouillette, brick with *Saint-Marcellin* cheese and a selection of 'country *tartines*' (different 'spreads' on country bread), like the "*Ardèche and its Mysteries*" with warm goat's cheese, ham and courgettes, the "*OK Corral*" with beef and mushrooms *à la crème* or the "*Jaws*", with lumpfish eggs and smoked salmon.

LES FILAOS > 1, place F.-Rey (1st) ✆ **04 78 28 67 60.** *Open everyday except on Mondays. Unique menu at 115 F. Service till 23.00. See the chapter "Cuisine from Elsewhere – The Islands".*

LYON OPERA > 8, rue Désirée (1st) ✆ **04 78 30 72 12.** It would be a pity to miss this brasserie, which is hidden beneath the arcades. The reception's impeccable, worthy of a big brasserie, and combines speed (for those in a hurry) and friendly service. Dishes of the Day, large salads, *andouillettes* and desserts – all prepared like at home. The nice little plus : the fidelity card (12 meals and the 13th is free).

MIMI EN EUROPE > 21, rue du Bât-d'Argent (1st) ✆ **04 78 27 74 50.** *Open everyday except at midday on Saturdays and Sundays. Entrée of the Day 38 F ; Entrée of the Day, Dish of the Day and coffee 69 F ; Dish of the Day, fruit tart and coffee 69 F. Otherwise, menu at 98 F, European or Lyonnais Menu at 129 F and à la carte.* Mimi en Europe offers refined Lyonnais and European cuisine. The setting's as elegant as the cuisine is fine, and the décor's sober but not at all sad, thanks to a rich collection of bottles and other recipients. More than a place for a quick bite, Mimi en Europe is a restaurant where you should enjoy a long meal.

MON BROUILLY > 27, rue de l'Arbre-Sec (1st) ✆ **04 78 28 37 74.** *Open from Monday to Friday at midday and in the evening and on Saturday evenings. Dish of the Day, entrée or dessert for 57 F ; entrée, Dish of the Day and dessert for 67 F. Menus at 87 F and 118 F.* At the foot of the Opera, you'd nevertheless think you were eating at your aunt's place in the Beaujolais Mountains, with its period tapestry. The regional and traditional cuisine is as generous as the owner's whiskers. Difficult not to drink (with moderation) a bit of… *Brouilly* (8 F a glass).

OKAWALI > 3, rue Louis-Vitet (1st) ℂ **04 72 07 82 61.** *Open everyday except on Sundays. Service till 22.30. Menus at 98 F, 124 F and 138 F. A la carte around 120 F. See the chapter "Cuisine from Elsewhere – Japan".*

RESTAURANT CHEVALLIER > 40, rue Sergent-Blandan (1st) ℂ **04 78 28 19 83.** *Open everyday except on Mondays and Tuesdays. Dish of the Day and salad 69 F ; salad, Dish of the Day and dessert 98 F (at midday only) ; menu at 175 F.* Le Chevalier is halfway between two styles of restaurant – the chic 'Sunday restaurant' and the simple restaurant where you eat well but simply. The cuisine (the menu announces a creative, seasonal cuisine), its presentation (very *Nouvelle Cuisine*) and the bill make you think of the first category of restaurant, whilst the décor (a bit fake) and 'radio-musical' ambiance break away from the chic – it's rather bizarre !

UN PETIT TOUR EN CAMARGUE > 14, rue Royale (1st) ℂ **04 78 39 32 33.** *Open everyday except on Mondays, on Saturdays at midday and on Sundays. Service till 22.30. Unique menu at 99 F. See the chapter "Regional Cuisine – Provençal Specialities".*

VERT OLIVE > 9, rue Saint-Polycarpe (1st) ℂ **04 78 28 15 31.** *Open from Monday to Friday at midday. Service till 14.00. A la carte around 90 F.* The chef here is no rookie – he knows how to transform and bring out the flavours of turnips, green beans and other sad vegetables, so that they become a real feast for the tastebuds and the eyes, and your mouth waters over a simple carrot. To accompany these little marvels, there's steak *tartare*, *pavé* of salmon, steak with shallot, *andouillette*…all delicately prepared and prettily presented. If you feel like staying longer and ordering another and yet another coffee, nobody pushes you towards the door. It's open at midday only, and, since the place is very popularl, you're advised to reserve.

◆ **2ND *ARRONDISSEMENT***

ALCATRAZ > 44, rue Mercière (2nd) ℂ **04 78 42 21 69.** *Open everyday, non-stop service from 11.30 to midnight. Hot dish and entrée or dessert at 43 F (at midday), 59 F (in the evening) ; hot dish and dessert at 49 F (at midday), 68 F (in the evening) ; entrée, hot dish and dessert at 58 F (at midday) and 89 F (in the evening).* The name's American, but the cuisine isn't at all. On the other hand, everything here's based round the theme of the famous Californian prison. Hence, the salads are called "*The Escapee*" or "*The Al Capone*", whilst the decoration on the walls gives you the impression that you're carrying out a long sentence. Fans of this sort of décor shouldn't hesitate, particularly since the food's good and copious.

ARIZONA GRILL > 8, rue Ferrandière (2nd) ℂ **04 78 42 35 02.** *Open from Monday to Sturday except on Monday evenings. Entrée, Dish of the Day and dessert 59 F at midday only. Otherwise, menus at 79 F and 99 F, Mexican dish from 65 F.* If somebody says "South-West" to you, you immediately think of breast of duck, *foie gras*, the Gers and the Bordelais regions… in other words, happiness ! But no, because the South-West isn't just the South-West of France ! And the *Arizona Grill's* really typical of the American South-West, on the Mexican border. The Grand Canyon's to be found in *Rue Ferrandière* because America's more than hamburgers ! The décor's superb – in wood from the floor to the ceiling´– and you could almost imagine yourself in a saloon in the middle of the Mexican desert. The menu offers French and Mexican cuisine. But, keep a bit of room for the desserts, which are particularly tasty.

AU BON CRU > 8, place Gailleton (2nd) ℂ **04 78 37 09 72.** *Open from Monday to Saturday (but no food on Saturdays). Dish of the Day at 45 F and 50 F, salads from 38 F and dessert 15 F.* The restoration-work on the superb *Place Gailleton* has now finished, and *Le Bon Cru's* terrace can now breathe again and recover its charm. In the shade of the imposing monument in honour of Lyon's mayor, *Le Bon Cru* offers a simple and traditional cuisine. It's the ideal spot for a lunchtime break. The menu has no speciality or anything particularly original to recommend it, but this is compensated for by the warmth of the reception. Here, they bend over backwards for you, and even go off to look for a table in the cellar if none is free on the terrace. That's not something they do everywhere, and it's a real pleasure to feel welcome !

AU MANGE SANS FAIM > 6, rue Laurencin (2nd) ℭ **04 72 41 79 66.** *Open from Tuesday to Sunday at midday and in the evenings. Dish of the Day 42 F ; Dish of the Day and entrée or dessert 56 F ; entrée, Dish of the Day and dessert 65 F at midday only ; menus at 78 F, 93 F and 128 F. A la carte around 130 F.* The cuisine's good and the setting's pleasant. The menu offers chicken liver salad, fricassee of *boudin*, *quenelles*, salmon steak *à la méridionale*... All the produce is fresh and the dishes, home-made. Smokers and non-smokers are mixed together and, if you want to change table, there's no way. So you eat with little appetite...

BÂN THAÏ > 3, rue Ferrandière (2nd) ℭ **04 78 37 44 06.** *Open everyday. At midday, entrée, main dish and dessert 68 F. Otherwise, menus at 98 F, 128 F, 138 F, 158 F and 178 F. A la carte.* See the chapter "Cuisine from Elsewhere – Thailand".

BISTRO ROMAIN > 75-76, rue de la République (2nd) ℭ **04 78 38 44 70.** *Open everyday, service from Sunday to Thursday from 11.30 to 15.00 and from 18.30 to 23.00, on Fridays from 11.30 to 15.00 and from 18.30 to 24.00 and on Saturday from 11.30 to 24.00 non-stop. At midday, Dish of the Day 49.90 F. Otherwise, menus at 59.90 F, 74.90 F, 109 F and 149 F. Children's Menu 45 F.* Le Bistrot Romain *is a chain of restaurants implanted in mant cities and towns in France, so there are no surprises. If you've decided not to look for novelty, here, you know exactly what you're going to get, especially the unlimited beef or salmon* carpaccio *(72.90 F) which made the restaurant's reputation. So, fans of* Le Bistro Romain *can eat to their heart's content. And if that's not enough for them, they can always order the maxi-chocolate mousse (small appetites, beware !). In addition, some of the menus offer unlimited garnishes. However, people also come to* Le Bistrot Romain *in* Rue de la République *for the setting. Don't sit in the room in the front, but ask to be put in the room at the back, where you'll find a large and impressive vaulted ceiling which reminds you of a theatre or a cinema. There's also a* Bistrot Romain *in* Rue Mercière.

BISTROT DES ARTS > 20, rue Auguste-Comte (2nd) ℭ **04 78 38 35 43.** *Open from Monday to Saturday at midday and from Thursday to Saturday in the evening. A choice of two Dishes of the Day 49 F, Dish of the Day and dessert 68 F ; entrée, Dish of the Day and sessert 78 F. Everyday, mussels, chips and beer for 60 F.* A stone's throw from the *Place Bellecour*, a quick service in a setting which has recently been renovated. Today, the décor's sober but elegant, and there are several rooms to eat in as you do your shopping in the neighbouring *Rue Victor-Hugo*.

BLEU DE TOI > 51, rue Mercière (2nd) ℭ **04 78 37 24 65.** *Open everyday at midday and in the evening. Formula at 55 F at midday from Monday to Friday, hot dishes from 64 F to 73 F, crêpes from 42 F, Children's Menu at 45 F, cocktail 14 F.* Le Bleu de Toi *is a little corner of the wide ocean at the heart of the* Presqu'île. *It's successfully decorated to resemble a fisherman's cabin, and you can easily imagine yourself miles from the city, listening to the sound of the seagulls. Consequently, the menu's entirely devoted to the sea : mussels, tuna... and the fish is served in all its forms :* carpaccio, *skewers, etc. In addition, the staff is welcoming and friendly. In short, if you can't wait for your holidays by the ocean...* Le Bleu de Toi *will offer you a moment of relaxation.*

BRASSERIE PAULANER > 4, rue de la Barre (2nd) ℭ **04 78 42 06 37.** *Open everyday. Dish of the Day at 50 F ; Dish of the Day with entrée or dessert for 70 F ; menu at 85 F ; salad from 40 F ; choucroute from 60 F ; Lyonnais specialities from 52 F. See the chapter "Brasseries".*

CAFE LEONE > 8, rue de la Monnaie (2nd) ℭ **04 78 92 93 70.** *Open everyday at midday and in the evening. Hot/cold tapas from 18 F ; hot dishes from 49 F ; Paella from 69 F (59 F at midday) ; desserts from 19 F. See the chapter "Cuisine from Elsewhere – Spain and Portugal".*

CAFE PERL > 47, Président-Edouard-Herriot (2nd) ℭ **04 78 37 56 56.** *Open everyday except on Sundays at midday. At midday : Dish of the Day at 49 F. salads from 48 F, maxi-salad from 62 F and dessert from 22 F.* If somebody tells you that the *Café Perl* is in the *Rue du Président-Edouard-Herriot*, on the *Place Francisque-Regaud*, that probably won't ring a bell ; but if the same person adds that it's the little place in front of *Virgin*, with the cherry trees which are so lovely in spring, then you'll know exactly the place he's talking about. An additional reason for coming to the *Café Perl* is that they offer not one Dish of the Day, but a number of them. The day we visited the café, there were 14 of them – all at the same price and varying from *tartiflette* to mussels and chips... You can choose between the dining room, the mezzanine (with its typical chairs), the verandah (to see and be seen) and, only when it's fine, the terrace, under the famous cherry trees. It would be easy to conclude that the café is a pearl. Ho, ho, ho ! But why not try it, since it's true ?

CAFE THOMASSIN > 33, rue Thomassin (2nd) © **04 78 37 10 90.** *Open from Monday to Saturday. Dish of the Day at 44 F, dessert from 15 F, snack (omelettes, croque monsieur, i.e. a toasted cheese sandwich) from 21 F to 32 F.* If you're looking for a little bistro where you can have a nice snack standing at the bar or sitting at a table, then look no further. *The Café Thomassin* is really a good place to come to. The reception's warm, relaxed and 'authentic' ("And what will the little lady have ?"), the service is rapid, and the family cooking allows you to rediscover some of those 'forgotten' little dishes – rabbit, polenta... The friendly ambiance leads to discussion between one table and the next. In this respect, if it's true that the Café Thomassin's frequented by numerous regulars, it's equally true that clients passing through are rapidly adopted into this large family. *The Café Thomassin* – a lunchbreak that really bucks you up !

CANBERRA GRILL > 68, rue de la charité (2nd) © **04 72 41 77 77.** *Open every evening from 19.30. Buffet salads 59 F, buffet skewers 99 F, buffet salads and skewers 119 F, buffet salads and desserts 89 F, buffet skewers and desserts 119 F, buffet salads, skewers and desserts 139 F, buffet salads, skewerzs, desserts, wine and coffee 159 F. See the chapter "Cuisine from Elsewhere – Australia".*

CHEZ MOSS > 2, rue Ferrandière (2nd) © **04 78 42 04 09.** *Open everyday. Service till midnight. Menus from 95 F to 738 F. Seafood platter. A la carte around 200 F.* Located at the corner of the *Rue Ferrandière* and the *Rue Mercière*, the *Moss* restaurant particularly attracts fans of line- or dip-net fishing. In a setting which is both prestigious and 'authentic', fresco characters scrutinize gourmets who've come to taste the seafood and shellfish. The sheer size of the menu and the freshness of the produce which comes from Les Halles (the Covered Market) make the restaurant a 'must'. One of the city's best-known restaurants, *Moss* stretches onto the pavement to make room for take away sales.

D'UN SOLEIL A L'AUTRE > 5, place Gailleton (2nd) © **04 78 42 59 67.** *Open from Tuesday to Saturday. Dish of the Day 55 F, Dish of the Day and entrée or dessert 80 F from Monday to Friday at midday. A la carte. Tagines, couscous,* king prawns... the cuisine's Mediterranean, like the decoration. The mosaic tables, the natural-coloured sofa and the small pieces of wooden furniture give the place a warm feeling, and you can imagine yourself in the cool of the interior of a Provençal cottage in summer – unless, that is, you've decided to sit on the terrace which gives onto the very beautiful *Place Gailleton*, with its greenery and water.

EDEN ROCK > 68, rue Mercière (2nd) © **04 78 38 28 18.** *Open from Monday to Saturday till 01.00. Dish of the Day at 49 F, salad from 35 F, dessert from 25 F.* Eden Rock's one of the most popular places on the *Rue Mercière*. The 'concept' is both modern and young. The ground floor has a bar and cocktail area, whilst the 1st floor is reserved on Thursdays, Fridays and Saturdays (from 21.00 onwards) for concerts : pop rock, funky, disco and blues. There's something for every taste, and the restaurant deserves its name. The trendy, American cuisine is served in copious portions.

GAMBA'S HOUSE > 9, rue Mercière (2nd) © **04 72 41 70 00.** *Open everyday except on Sundays at midday and on Mondays. Menus from 80 F to 89 F. Service till midnight. See the chapter "Fish".*

GRAIN DE SEL > 2, rue David-Girin (2nd) © **04 78 42 77 19.** *Open everyday except on Sundays and Mondays. At midday, 'formulae' at 48 F and 58 F ; in the evening, à la carte and 'formulae' at 79 F. From 15.00 to 18.00, crêpe room. See the chapter "Crêperies".*

HIPPOPOTAMUS > 48-50, rue de la République (2nd) © **04 78 38 42 42.** *Open everyday, non-stop service till 00.30 during the week, 01.00 at the week-end. Midday 'formula' : 1 dish and coffee 52 F ; otherwise, dish and drink 67 F ; dish, entrée, dessert and coffee 98.50 F ; entrée, dish, dessert and coffee 115 F ; 'formula' with cinema ticket 139 F ; Children's Menu 47 F.* Hippopotamus is known to everyone as *Hippo*, so we're going to call it *Hippo*, as well ! Hippo's the temple of good meat, served in all possible ways – grills, *carpaccio, tartares,* lovely, red steaks… What's more, the decoration's predominantly red ! But *Hippo*'s open-minded, so you'll also find fish dishes. Dishes are garnished notably with chips and haricot beans, which are served in unlimited quantities for "no extra charge" (it's marked on the menus in bold print, so it must be important !). Prices are a bit high (but that's the case in all restaurant chains of this type), it's impossible to change the slightest thing in the 'formulae', there's only a single non-alcoholic drink on offer, and you're out of luck… it's got bubbles (impossible to have a fruit juice). The same applies to the desserts… So then, *Hippo*'s not a lot of fun, but it's good !

KIOSQUE BELLECOUR > Place Bellecour (2nd). *Open everyday except Sundays. Salads from 38 F ; hot dish from 37 F ; hot dish, drink and dessert 59 F ; salad, drink and dessert from 60 F ; sandwiches at the table 20 F. No banker's cards.* The place is rare… You'll never be able to eat more in the middle of the *Place Bellecour* unless you picnic on horseback with Louis XIV. So, as you'd expect, the restaurant's extremely popular. For its success, *Kiosque Bellecour* gambled on the site and on nothing but the site. The menu's simple, because this is a snackbar, and the salads, chicken or sausages and chips are sufficient for a simple food-break. Since people don't come here for the menu, you'd expect to eat your simple dish quickly. Well, if that's what you expected, you're wrong, because you have to count on a good quarter-of-an-hour before you even get the menu, and another 15 minutes to see your chicken and chips actually arrive. And then, what a surprise ! Your chicken had to wait as long as you did, so it's cold. Above all, don't feel like mustard or bread, because the waiter will walk past you dozens of times before he gives you what you're entitled to… Then, it's the chips' turn to be cold. Even if it's not a gastronomic restaurant, you've the right to expect to be treated with a bit more consideration you get here !

L'ENTRECOTE > 10, rue de la République (2nd) ℂ **04 78 28 16 64.** Toothless meat-eaters, this is your restaurant. The meat here is so tender it literally melts in the mouth. Forget your dietetic resolutions – the famous, secret sauce which generously covers the meat seems to consist largely of… butter, and it's delicious ! In spite of a unique 'formula' at 85 F (salad with nuts, a generous portion of ribsteak, unlimited but rather plain chips), the bill turns out to be quite high once you've added the wine, dessert and coffee. There's no hanging around, because profitability seems to be the key word. Indeed, the service is so expeditious, it's mind-boggling.

L'ESPACE > 26, place Bellecour (2nd) ℂ **04 78 37 45 43.** *Open from Monday to Saturday . At midday : Dish of the Day 52 F ; entrée and cheese or dessert 65 F ; Dish of the Day and entrée 80 F ; entrée, Dish of the Day and dessert 89 F. Otherwise, menus at 89 F, 109 F, 149 F and 169 F.* L'Espace is also called "The Blue Brasserie" because of the dominance of this colour as soon as you enter, under the sheeting which shelters the terrace along the *Place Bellecour*. It's ideal for studying the last chestnut trees on what is supposed to be the largest square in Europe ! This restaurant harmoniously combines the elegant and the relaxed. Elegance, with a refined and elegant cuisine, including *jarret d'agneau en cocotte* (knuckle of lamb stewed in a casserole), *foie gras* with prunes marinated in Armagnac, and relaxation, with waiters in blue Bermudas. An address to note down !

LA BRASSERIE VICTOIRE > 5, place Carnot (2nd) ℂ **04 78 37 37 24.** *Open 7/7 days. Menus at 55 F, 65 F, 75 F, 95 F and 120 F. A la carte around 120 F. Service till midnight. See the chapter "Brasserie ".*

LA CREPE D'OR > 1, rue Laurencin (2nd) ℂ **04 78 92 90 54.** *Open everyday from midday to midnight. Banker's cards not accepted. At midday : 'formula' 3 dishes at 45 F. Otherwise, menus at 58 F, 69 F and 85 F, Group Menu at 75 F (more than 6 people at midday and 9 in the evening). A la carte. See the chapter "Crêperies".*

LA CUVEE > 38, rue Sala (2nd) ℂ **04 72 77 79 01.** *Open everyday except on Sundays. Buffet of hors-d'œuvre or Dish of the Day and cheese or dessert for 69 F (at midday only), buffet and Dish of the Day for 83 F (at midday only). Menus at 99 F and 145 F.* In a very pleasant, vaulted cellar, the 'formula' offering an unlimited buffet is popular with many – including President Chirac, who came to eat here. On the other hand, the beautiful, vaulted ceiling leaves little pure air for non-smokers.

LA HOUBLONNERIE > 1, rue Thomassin (2nd) ✆ **04 78 37 90 80.** *Open everyday at midday and in the evening. At midday : Dish of the Day 49 F ; Dish of the Day and dessert 69 F ; mussels and chips and dessert 79 F. Otherwise, mussels and chips from 69 F to 98 F, entrées from 34 F, desserts from 28 F. Menus from 89 F to 170 F, Children's Menu 48 F.* The Belgian restaurant in the pedestrian *Mercière* district has the originality of possessing an immense verandah, so that throughout the year you can take advantage of the street's Renaissance and contemporary setting. The verandah, which extends as far as the street, along with the teak garden furniture, give you the impression of eating in the open air all year long. The large, round tables are paricularly convivial. *La Houblonnerie's* menu allows you to discover that mussel and chips can be eaten *à la flamande, à la provençale*, with green pepper or with mustard. Finally, leave some space for the desserts and the chocolate... liégeois, obviously.

LA MANILLE > 33, rue Tupin (2nd) ✆ **04 78 37 35 93.** *Open from Monday to Saturday. Dish of the Day 50 F, Dish of the Day and entrée 85 F, salad from 38 G, dessert 18 F, Lyonnais specialities from 50 F. Service from 11.30 to 15.00. See the chapter "Regional Cuisine – Lyonnais Cuisine".*

LA MERE COTTIVET > 20, rue Palais-Grillet (2nd) ✆ **04 72 40 96 61.** *Open from Monday to Saturday. At midday, Dish of the Day at 50 F ; Dish of the Day and entrée or dessert 68 F. Otherwise, menus at 90 F, 118 F and 130 F, à la carte entrées 48 F, dishes 74 F and desserts 26 F. See the chapter "Regional Cuisine – Lyonnais Cuisine".*

LA MERE JEAN > 5, rue des Marronniers (2nd) ✆ **04 78 37 81 27.** *Open from Monday to Friday from 12.00 to 14.00 and from 19.00 to 22.00. Menus at 69 F (midday), 83 F, 96 F, 114 F, 149 F and à la carte. See the chapter "Regional Cuisine – Lyonnais Cuisine".*

LA MERE VITTET > 26, cours de Verdun (2nd) ✆ **04 78 37 20 17.** With more than 40 years' experience, this typically Lyonnais brasserie offers a very friendly welcome. The staff are polite and professional, and you sense that they are attached both to the establishment and to the clientèle, which makes the place even more human. Dark wood on the ceiling and walls, tables which are spaced well apart, white tablecloths – what does it matter if the décor isn't very 'high tech', you feel at ease here. Moreover, it's a restaurant where people come for Sunday lunch, for birthdays, and where grandparents take their grandchildren. The cuisine's essentially 'brasserie-style': Lyonnais specialities, seafood, tartares, foie gras, frog's legs and choucroute – they all live up to the restaurant's good reputation.

LA PASSERELLE (THE FOOTBRIDGE) > 36, quai Saint Antoine (2nd) ✆ **04 78 37 61 32.** *Open everyday from 05.00 at week-ends and 05.30 during the week. At midday : Dish of the Day 49 F, Dish of the Day and dessert 74 F.* This is a good address for those who love Lyon. Located on the quays of the Saône, provided you sit just beside a window or, even better, on the terrace, *La Passerelle* offers you a magnificent view of the *Colline de Fourvière* and of *Saint-Jean*, just opposite the... footbridge (astonishing, isn't it ?) leading to the 'Palace of 24 Columns', that is to say, the Law Courts. If you're not lucky enough to have one of these seats, you can always admire the mural fresco inside. This is an address for those who get up early or go to bed late : *La Passerelle* serves food from 5 o'clock in the morning onwards, and not just a breakfast, but a real meal with red meat. Enough to set you up after a mad night... or to put you in the right frame of mind for a day in the office !

LA GRANDE TAVERNE MIDI MINUIT > 83, cours Charlemagne (2nd) ✆ **04 78 37 67 95.** *Open everyday. Dish of the Day (at midday) 45 F, choucroute, dessert and beer 80 F, oysters from 41 F, seafood menu from 117 F, dessert from 32 F. See the chapter "Brasseries".*

LA TIRELIRE > 14, rue de la Monnaie (2nd) ✆ **04 78 37 37 42.** *Open from Monday to Saturday (except Monday evenings). Dish of the Day 49 F, Dish of the Day and dessert 69 F. A la carte. La Tirelire is the place for eating quickly thanks to a rapid and efficient service. Quickly... but well !* La Tirelire, situated in the *Mercière* district, offers a simple but good cuisine... in short, traditional or Lyonnais cuisine, with dishes like hot sausage and steamed potatoes. The décor's original – large wooden barrels pay tibute to a number of different wines : *Saint-Joseph, Côtes-du-Rhône*... Finally, before leaving, take the time to visit the WC's, which are worth a detour because, with hundreds of mirrors everywhere, they're rather kitsch but original.

Lyon *Restaurants - Second arrondissement*

LE BARYTON > 30, rue de l'Arbre-Sec (2nd) Ⓒ **04 78 28 34 41.** *Open from Monday to Friday. Dish of the Day 47 F ; Dish of the Day and entrée or dessert 60 F ; entrée, Dish of the Day and dessert 75 F ; salads from 40 F.* Below a magnificent French ceiling, you can eat either at the bar or at a pedestal table, unless you choose the back-room, where you eat at normal tables. For that, it's best to reserve, because *Le Baryton's* a popular eating place. The service is rapid and efficient, but also friendly – something which is too often forgotten elsewhere, and the owner's "ça va ?", as she comes to see you in the middle of your meal, may even astonish you because we've quite simply lost the habit of coming across this sort of politeness. In addition, the restaurant's frequented by the local, national and international press : *Le Baryton's* such a pleasant place to eat, particularly since the cuisine's simple, traditional and Lyonnais. But, why's it called *"Le Baryton"* ? Because, in the evening, the brasserie transforms itself into a temple of jazz, and the music played is transmitted on *Radio Fréquence Jazz.* However, because these evenings inevitably create noise which sometimes disturbs the neighbours, they've become increasingly rare, and now only take place once or twice a month.

LE BISTROT DE LA PLAGE > 40, rue de la Charité (2nd) Ⓒ **04 78 42 25 12.** *Open from Monday to Saturday, food service at midday only. Dish of the Day 43 F ; Dish of the Day, entrée or dessert and coffee 64 F ; salad 43 F ; dessert 18 F ; Suggestion of the Day from 50 F.* A 'holiday feeling' at the heart of the *Presqu'île*, a stone's throw from the offices and shops – this is the ideal place for a lunchbreak to change your ideas and set yourself up ! The bistro's a pleasant and attractive place, and the décor's modern and inviting. The cuisine at *Le Bistrot de la Plage* is good and original. The large board which serves as a menu proposes no less than a dozen salads and as many desserts. The food, served on square plates, is presented with refinement. As for the service, it's dynamic and friendly. You can also have breakfast here (café, *croissant*, orange juice for 13 F), or a drink in the evening. Is there sand under the floor-tiles ?

LE BISTROT DE LYON > 64, rue Mercière (2nd) Ⓒ **04 78 37 00 62.** *Open everyday. Service till 01.00. Menus at 65 F (child) and 120 F. A la carte around 140 F.* This restaurant was one of the first to open in the *Rue Mercière.* When (no less than 25 years ago) Jean-Paul Lacombe decided to offer himself a recreation between two dishes served in the gastronomic restaurant, *Léon de Lyon*, he inherited from his father, he opened *Le Bistrot de Lyon.* Firmly anchored in the Lyonnais tradition, and benefiting from the owner's knowledge and experience, the restaurant's success was virtually guaranteed. Frequented more by well-off Lyonnais than by tourists, the place is 'well-to-do' and very pleasant for a lunch or for an apéritif in the evening, before dinner with friends.

LE BISTROT SAINT-NIZIER > 12, rue Longue (2nd) Ⓒ **04 78 28 43 12.** *Closed all day on Sundays and on Monday and Tuesday evenings. Dish of the Day 43 F ; Dish of the Day and entrée or dessert 57 F ; menu 65 F ; choucroute from 59 F.* A friendly and smiling welcome, and a cuisine which is good, copious and... cheap. So, jokers might say that the bill's not as long as the street ! The *choucroute's* particularly good. The only criticism – the place is a bit dark.

LE BOUCHE A OREILLE > 9, rue Claudia (2nd) Ⓒ **04 72 40 94 22.** *Open everyday except on Saturdays at midday and on Sundays. Service till 23.00 during the week and till midnight on Fridays and Saturdays. Menus from 57 F to 125 F. A la carte around 130 F.* People have been eating here for around 150 years. Upstairs, on the terrace or opposite the bar, José and his team receive their guests with friendliness and enthusiasm. When you read the menu, you may be one of the many who choose one of the 'formulae' on offer. These include dishes like mussels and chips with a beer, frogs legs *à la provençale*, 'duo' of *foie gras* and smoked salmon, *confit de canard* and sautéed potatoes, or steak with shallots. Because the chef's generous, the plates are well-garnished, and, because the owner likes to please his clients, he celebrates birthdays by offering a cake and the song that goes with it.

LE BOULEVARDIER > 5, rue de la Fromagerie (2nd) Ⓒ **04 78 28 48 22.** *Open everyday. Service till 23.30. menus at 120 F and 150 F. A la carte around 130 F.* This restaurant-café has changed hands and look. What remains from the old place is the old, wooden bar, the mirror behind it reflecting the bottles, the shiny leather seats, the 'bistro' tables and chairs...in short, the nicest items. The rest of the décor's simple, sober and colourful, thanks to the walls, which are green and orange-yellow. On the menu, you'll find a well-prepared, traditional cuisine : a lot of fish (salmon *tartare*, *pavé* of tuna, pike quenelle, fish skewer) and a fair amount of meat (*tartare, andouillette*, thinly-sliced beef). The sauces are delicious – seasoned, spicy and tasty. The charming young brunette who officiates here doesn't lack humour, and she often teases her clients in the politest way possible. On Thursday, Friday and Saturday evenings, the superb, vaulted cellar, which has recently been renovated, welcomes jazz groups and other musicians. After the concert, everyone gets up to dance and have a good time till late into the night.

LE CAVEAU (THE CELLAR) > 5, place Antonin-Poncet (2nd) ✆ **04 78 37 35 04.** *Open from Tuesday to Sunday. Service from 11.45 to 14.30 and from 18.45 to 23.30. At midday only : Dish of the Day 49 F ; Dish of the Day and entrée or dessert 63 F ; entrée and dessert 49 F. Otherwise, salads from 59 F ; assiette anglaise (cold meat platter), salad and chips 65 F ; Lyonnais specialities from 48 F ; menus at 74 F, 86 F, 98 F and 128 F.* In winter as in summer, *Le Caveau*'s a pleasant place - either inside, under real vaulting (because *Le Caveau*'s not simply a name, but a real cellar), or on the terrace in summer (and in the winter, too, because the terrace is heated under the red awning which covers it). The view, here, is superb - onto the pedestrian *Place Antonin-Poncet*, with its lawns, fountains and the La Charité Bell-tower. The cuisine's good and traditional, and an entire menu pays tribute to Lyonnais cuisine. What's more, the reception's friendly, so that all the necessary ingredients are united for making this a restaurant you'll want to come back to.

LE CIRQUE > 14, rue Grôlée (2nd) ✆ **04 78 42 15 00.** *Open from Monday to Saturday. At midday : Dish of the Day or Pasta of the Day at 58 F ; Dish of the Day, entrée or dessert at 85 F ; entrée, Dish of the Day and dessert at 98 F. Otherwise, menu at 130 F. A la carte around 154 F. Children's Menu 48 F. Le Cirque* isn't just a name, but a real 'concept' (as it's trendy to say nowadays) ! Here, everything's been designed to pay tribute to the circus. In the main dining room, you'd think you were under the big top : fairy lights, projectors and paintings all help to create this ambiance. At the bottom of the main room, the small dining room's more intimate, and, with its mirrors, looks rather like a dressing-room. The cuisine's modern and daring, and doesn't hesitate to combine the sweet and the sour. All this is served on superb plates, decorated with designs from... the circus. And, as in every circus worthy of its name, the kids aren't forgotten, and there's a menu reserved for them. On Fridays and Saturdays, a magician comes and, every evening, there's candyfloss.

LE COMPTOIR SAINT-HELENE > 39, rue Sainte-Hélène (2nd) ✆ **04 72 77 69 35.** *Open everyday except Sundays. Service till 16.30. Starter of the Day 35 F ; Dish of the Day 46 F ; Dish of the Day and entrée or dessert 65 F ; entrée, Dish of the Day and dessert 75 F.* In the shade of the imposing Gailleton Fountain, which is spanking new since its renovation, *Le Comptoir Sainte-Hélène* marries the culinary and pictorial arts, because, from time to time, artists come to exhibit in the restaurant's dining room. So, it's the ideal spot for uniting the pleasures of the taste and the sight. The good, family cooking and the warm welcome are such that you'll have an excellent meal beside the Gailleton !

LE DECK > 5, rue Tupin (2nd) ✆ **04 78 42 38 12.** *Menu at 135 F, Dish of the Day 65 F at midday only. A la carte around 180 F. Service till 22.30. See the chapter "Fish".*

Lyon *Restaurants - Second arrondissement*

LE FABRIZIO > 24, quai Saint-Antoine (2nd) ✆ **04 78 38 00 11.** *Dish of the Day 50 F ; Dish of the Day, entrée and dessert 69 F ; 'formula' 65 F at midday only. Salads from 47 F ; fresh pasta from 48 F ; pizza from 48 F. Menus at 110 F and 125 F. See the chapter "Cuisine from Elsewhere – Italy".*

LE FLAM'S > 12, rue Tupin (2nd) ✆ **04 78 37 51 61.** *Open everyday till 23.30 during the week and midnight at the week-end. Express 'formulae' at midday : 43 F, 46 F, 50 F and 56.50 F. Flam's Dessert 'Formula' at 73.50 F ; Flam's entrée at 76.50 F ; 'All Flam's' at 99.50 F. Children's Menu at 35 F. See the chapter "Regional Cuisine – Alsace".*

LE GORMEN'S CAFE > 12, quai Maréchal Joffre (2nd) ✆ **04 78 38 48 38.** *Open 6/7 days.* The old *All Sports Café* has been completely changed, with a restaurant part which is more inviting. As we go to press, *Le Gormen's* is putting the final touches to its menu, and is concocting numerous surprises based on Savoyard specialities – ideal for an evening meal between friends. There's a superb terrace, which is unique in its type, beside the Saône. The establishment also has three bars : a Beer Bar, a Rum Bar and a Tequila Bar.

LE GRENETTE > 2, rue Grenette (2nd) ✆ **04 78 42 27 04.** *Open everyday, but no food served at midday on Sundays. Dish of the Day 45 F ; entrée and dessert 52 F ; Dessert of the Day 18 F ; salad from 37 F.* At the corner of the *Rue Grenette* and the *Quai Saint-Antoine, Le Grenette* enjoys a spectacular view on the *Colline de Fourvière* and its basilica. Their creates a striking relief, and leaves you the time to admire this exceptional setting. Provided you can stand the noise of the traffic heading down the quay to the bridge, you can install yourself on the terrace. If not, Le Grenette's interior is a traditional bistro, offering an equally traditional menu, including its Dish of the Day and similar brasserie-type dishes. There's also a fresco at the bottom of the dining-room. This is common enough, but, at the same time, frescoes are still not sufficiently commonplace (and they're so beautiful !) for us to tire of mentioning them !

LE JARDIN DE BERTHE > 3, rue Fleurieu (2nd) ✆ **04 78 38 24 46.** *Open from Monday to Saturday from 12.00 to 14.00 and from 19.30 to 22.30. Salad, dessert and coffee 55 F at midday only ; entrée, main dish and dessert or cheese 72 F and 85 F ; entrée, main dish, cheese and dessert 98 F. See the chapter "Salad Places".*

LE JEAN MOULIN > 22, rue Gentil (2nd) ✆ **04 78 37 37 97.** *Open everyday except at midday on Saturdays and on Sunday evenings. Menus at 88 F and 140 F. A la carte around 130 F. Service till 23.00.* On the quays of the Rhône, somewhat removed from the hustle and bustle of the *Arbre Sec* district, Philippe Pelisson holds the reins of this refined and sober restaurant. Sober, like the décor – in shades of white with wood. On the tables, you'll find white tablecloths and fresh flowers. The seats are, infact, comfortable, padded chairs, which incite you to taste your food slowly. In the entrance hall, there's a friendly bar, with staircases leading up to the restaurant. Those in a hurry will opt for the 'formula' at 88 F. The cuisine's sunny and, in the main, southern : marinated, fresh tuna, *poulet confit* with lemon and herbs, chicken carpaccio, stuffed mussels, *confit* of cod with tomatoes… As for the desserts, they're pure marvels for sugar-lovers, and all are home-made, of course.

LE MERCIERE > 56, rue Mercière (2nd) ✆ **04 78 37 67 35.** *Open everyday. Menus at 80 F, 119 F and 140 F. Service till midnight on Saturdays, and till 23.00 other days. A la carte around 180 F. See the chapter "Regional Cuisine – Lyonnais Cuisine".*

LE MUNDO CAFE > Corner of Rue Thomassin and Rue Grolée (2nd) ✆ **04 78 92 60 20.** *Non-stop food from 11.30 to 18.00. No-smoking establishment. Dish of the Day 55 F.* This is a cybercafé, located on the first floor of the *Raconte-moi la Terre* Bookshop. It serves a simple but quality cuisine which allows you to eat rapidly. The food's very cosmopolitan, with dishes like gaspacho, *mezze, sushi* (from 25 F to 40 F), *assiettes fraîcheurs* (45 F), bagels and green salads (50 F), as well as *Ben & Jerry*'s ice-creams. Depending on your mood, you'll eat at the table, at the bar or on the sofas. Throughout the day, you can drink tea, coffee or other international beverages.

LE P'TIT COMTE > 17, rue Auguste-Comte (2nd) ℭ **04 72 41 06 09.** *Open everyday except on Sundays and on Monday evenings. Dish of the Day 49 F ; Dish of the Day and entrée or dessert 67 F ; menus at 76 F and 88 F ; evening menus at 149 F.* Good accounts make for good friends, and little bills make for small dishes ! OK, the popular saying's a bit simple, but this version of it is absolutely true. The cuisine's traditional, and the presentation, refined, with prices which are very correct for the area. What's more, if you ask for it, the service can be rapid.

LE NORD > 18, rue Neuve (2nd) ℭ **04 72 10 69 69.** *Open everyday. Service till midnight. Dishes of the Day at 75 F and 88 F. Menus at 48 F (child's), 115 F (except on Sundays and Public Holidays) and 130 F (including a drink – except Sundays and Public Holidays). A la carte around 190 F.* This brasserie's existed since 1907. In the old days, the entire Lyonnais bourgeoisie had to come here. For the last 5 years or so, Paul Bocuse and his associates have written their names at the bottom of the registers, and are pursuing the tradition with success. Hence, the walls are green and red, whilst wood gives a refined and warm touch to the ensemble. It's a good place for a meal, especially since the service is irreproachable and the cuisine, fine. Lyonnais specialities and traditional dishes are entwined without, however, making knots, under the attentive gaze of Bruno Brugière, the *chef de cuisine*. On the terrace, in the main room, or upstairs in one of the private salons (recently renovated, with room for 5 to 60 people), *Le Nord* is Bocuse's first brasserie, as is pointed out on the menu, and the atmosphere's 'brasserie' – as we all like them.

LE PETIT LYONNAIS > 5, rue Ferrandière (2nd) ℭ **04 78 42 20 24.** *Open from Monday to Saturday (except on Monday evenings), possibility on Sundays and on Monday evenings of group reservations. Dish of the Day 46 F ; Dish of the Day and entrée or dessert 58 F ; entrée, Dish of the Day and dessert 68 F. Menus at 79 F, 99 F and 129 F. At midday on Thursdays, 'formula' with frogs.* Le Petit Lyonnais deserves to be *grand*, because its welcome, its cuisine and its prices are good, but really good. How many restaurants do you know at the heart of the *Presqu'île* which offer a 'formula' including salad, frogs, dessert and coffee for just 68 F ? Well, we've found it, and, now, so have you ! For the moment, this little pleasure is reserved for Thursdays at midday, but may shortly be extended to Thursday evenings, and, from there, who knows ? But, *Le Petit Lyonnais* isn't just that. Everyday, there's a rich menu and a fine cuisine. For all that, the place is without pretention, and you can sit yourself down on the small (but, very small) terrace, unless you prefer to go inside to admire the temporary exhibitions.

LE PICCADILLY > 10, rue des Marronniers (2nd) ℭ **04 72 77 56 39.** *In summer, open 7/7 days. In the low season, closed on Monday evenings and on Tuesdays. Dish of the Day and dessert 62 F (at midday) ; buffet of unlimited entrées, Dish of the Day and dessert 71 F ; menus at 85 F, 98 F and 158 F.* Le Piccadilly enjoys an incredible location on the pedestrian Place Antonin-Poncet, right next to Bellecour. In summer, the play of the fountains creates a refreshing ambiance, and, in winter, the heated verandah allows you to take full advantage of the setting, in spite of the weather. The cuisine's traditional, but the service, a bit slow. The day of our visit, the buffet plates weren't very clean, and there was a hair in the Dish of the Day. All right, it was only once, but, all the same : two problems the same day…But, let's not draw any hasty conclusions, you just have to look before you eat !

LE ROND DE SERVIETTE > 6, rue des Marronniers (2nd) ℭ **04 78 61 11 40.** *Open everyday. Close on monday. At midday : Dish of the Day at 50 F ; Dish of the Day, entrée or dessert at 67 F ; entrée, Dish of the Day and dessert at 75 F. Otherwise, menus at 85 F, 95 F, 98 F, 110 F and 158 F. A la carte at least 149 F.* In the other Lyonnais street which is devoted to restaurants, two dining rooms await you at *Le Rond de Serviette*. At *Le Rond de Serviette*, the cuisine's essentially Lyonnais – something which will please its fans.

Le Rond de Serviette
Restaurant - Lyonnais Bouchon

Service at midday and in the evening

Open all day around

6, rue des Marronniers - 69002 Lyon
Tel. 04 72 41 81 22 - Fax 04 78 61 11 40

115

Lyon *Restaurants - Second arrondissement*

LE SHANTA > 23, rue de la Charité (2nd) ℂ **04 78 42 98 80.** *Open from Monday to Saturday. In the evening only on Fridays and Saturdays or by reservation for 5 people or more. At midday : Dish of the Day 54 F, salad 39 F, buffet of hors-d'œuvre 38 F. In the evening : menu at 69 F. Le Shanta*'s a vegetarian restaurant, but don't expect to find a cuisine for over-aged hippies : here, the vegetarian's gay and modern. The Ali Baba's Cave of fruit and vegetables offers different dishes everyday, and the produce comes straight from the Croix-Rousse Market everyday. Because vegetarian doesn't rhyme with sadness, the desserts are numerous. So, for once in your life, try a vegetarian restaurant. Like 90% of the clientèle, you'll have come to give it a try, and, who knows, you may never be able to eat meat again.

LE SUD > 11, place Antonin Poncet (2nd) ℂ **04 72 77 80 00.** *Open everyday. Service till midnight. Menus at 48 F (Children's Menu), 115 F and 130 F. A la carte around 190 F.* Between Provençal terracotta lamps and objects straight from the medina, the waiters serve a Mediterranean cuisine. The South honours a sunny cuisine, under the watchful eye of Paul Bocuse, who used to be the brasserie's chef. The basil, *aïoli*, mozzarella, *tajines, lasagnas, osso bucco* and gaspacho are prepared in the kitchen by Eric Pansu, *Meilleur Ouvrier de France* in 1997. A total success !

LES 3 TONNEAUX > 4, rue des Marronniers (2nd) ℂ **04 78 37 34 72.** *Open from Monday evening to Saturday evening. At midday : Dish of the Day 43 F ; Otherwise, menus at 79 F, 89 F, 159 F. See the chapter "Regional Cuisine – Lyonnais Cuisine".*

LES FABLES > 4, rue Fleurieu (2nd) ℂ **04 72 40 00 35.** *Open from Monday to Saturday except on Tuesday evenings. Dish of the Day or giant salad 48 F ; Dish of the Day, dessert and coffee 64 F. Otherwise, menus at 89 F, 99 F and 109 F.* The Crow and the Fox, the Frog who wanted to be as big as an Ox, the Cricket and the Ant… Had you noticed how Lafontaine's fables all talk about food ? The Crow's camembert, the Cricket who found himself short of food when winter arrived… and there are a host of others we won't mention now. So, it was only natural that, in its turn, a restaurant should pay tribute to the Lafontaine's fables. Several, paintings, engravings and statuettes are displayed in the dining room… and you eat a traditional and copious cuisine.

LOLOQUOI > 40-42, rue Mercière (2nd) ℂ **04 72 77 60 90.** *Open everyday. Salads from 48 F ; pasta from 68 F ; desserts from 40 F ; at midday, 'formula' of pasta and salad at 68 F. Loloquoi*'s unique. Its 'concept' is resolutely modern, and the result's a success. The décor is very trendy. The sober and black walls contrast with the originality of the accessories : stone chandeliers, 'bouquets' of leaks on the the bar and, in the window, a large ice cube slowly melting during the meal. As for the basins in the WC's, they deserve a visit ! Fine, but a restaurant's, above all, for eating in… Good news : the same originality and creativity displayed in the restaurant's décor is to be found in a refined and modern cuisine. Loloquoi's a restaurant devoted to fans of pasta…*Loloquoi*, a name on everybody's lips !

MC DONALD'S > 68, rue de la République (2nd). *Open everyday from 07.30 to 01.00. Menu at 32 F (hamburger, chips and drink) with several variations possible : minced beef, chicken, cheese, etc.), dessert from 6 F. Breakfast from 17 F served till 11.00.* What more can we say about *Mc Donald*'s ? To eat quickly, on the spot or take away, the place on the *Place Bellecour* is a favourite meeting-place for young Lyonnais, at the foot of the métro station, opposite the cinema and the *FNAC*. It has a terrace which you can use all year round (well-sheltered from the winter wind) and one of the best views of the Place Bellecour ! It should, however, be pointed out that this restaurant was closed by the authorities in July 2000 because of a lack of hygiene. We'd grown to expect better of the Clown.

MAMMA MIA > 66, rue de la Charité (2nd) ℂ **04 72 56 10 52.** *Open from Tuesday to Saturday. One dish 42 F, two dishes 54 F, three dishes 68 F. See the chapter "Cuisine from Elsewhere – Italy".*

MARGUERITE > 41, rue Franklin (2nd) ℂ **04 78 37 71 21.** *Open from Tuesday to Saturday. Service from 12.00 to 13.45 and from 19.00 to 21.45. Menus at 76 F, 89 F, 96 F, 148 F and 169 F. Frog 'formula' at 89 F.* Here, they no longer know why the restaurant's called "*Marguerite*". They just tell you that it's always been called that, and memories of the restaurant go back to 1943. However, since then, owners have come and gone, but the name's remained. The new generation wanted to change it, which explains the error made on the outside awning – there's an 'e' missing in the name *Marguerite*. Time has passed since then, but the error hasn't been rectified… so, it's still *Marguerit*' outside… So much for the little story. As far as the cuisine's concerned, it's traditional. Note the Frog '*Formula*' and, on the drinks' side, the list of whiskies. The décor allows you to admire a few pictures of Lyon in an air-conditioned climate, which is good news when the summer heat installs itself into the little streets of the *Presqu'île*.

MONNA LISA > 44, cours Charlemagne (2nd) ℂ **04 78 37 85 25.** *Open everyday in season, but closed on Sundays in winter. At midday : Dish of the Day 48 F ; Dish of the Day, entrée or dessert 65 F. Otherwise, pizza at 42 F, menus at 85 F, 120 F and 150 F. Service till 23.00.* See the chapter "Cuisine from Elsewhere – Italy".

NEW YORK STREET > 20, rue Mercière (2nd) ℂ **04 78 42 33 55.** *See the chapter "Cuisine from Elsewhere – Yank Specialities".*

O'BRASIL > 3, rue de la Fromagerie (2nd) ℂ **04 78 28 49 59.** *Open everyday except Sundays. Menus at 198 F, 260 F, 310 F and 395 F. Service till midnight.* See the chapter "Cuisine from Elsewhere – Brazil".

PETIT GRAIN > 19, rue de la Charité (2nd) ℂ **04 72 41 77 85.** *Open from Monday to Saturday from 10.00 to 20.00 non-stop. Dish of the Day 43 F, salads from 43 F, desserts from 16 F.* If you're looking for a place where the reception's friendly, warm and smiling ; if you're looking for a place combining Asian and French cuisine ; if you're looking for a place where the servings are copious ; if you're looking for a place where the service is rapid and energetic ; if you're looking for a place with an original décor (the bar's composed of old, wooden letter boxes from the halls of blocks of flats, as well as five clocks showing the time from Hawaii to Saigon) ; if you're looking for a place with a small terrace between *Bellecour* and *Perrache* and for a place where the bill won't knock you out… look no further ! *Le Petit Grain* is just what you've been looking for, and is just waiting for you.

PITADINE > 10, rue Grenette (2nd) ℂ **04 78 37 45 50.** *Open everyday except on Sundays at midday. Air-conditioned room. Pita and entrée 75 F, maxi-salad from 52 F. Other addesses : 61, Rue Garibaldi (6th) and 134, Rue Dedieu in Villeurbanne.* The *pita*'s a dough of Byzantine, Greek and Armenian origin. An old recipe which goes back 3000 years, it's eaten today throughout the Near and Middle East. The *pita* (the word means "flattened") is the same shape as a *galette*, and *Pitadine* offers an assortment of garnished *pitas*.

PIZZA PINO > 106, rue Président-Edouard-Herriot (2nd) ℂ **04 78 38 30 15.** *Open everyday. Non-stop service from 11.30 to 03.00. Salads from 38 F ; pizzas from 48 F ; beef carpaccio 59 F ; Dish of the Day 49 F ; desserts from 26 F ; ice-creams from 29 F.* See the chapter "Cuisine from Elsewhere – Italy".

PIZZAPAPA > 34, rue Tupin (2nd) ℭ **04 72 40 02 99.** *Open everyday. At midday : hot dish and entrée or dessert 59.90 F. 'Formula' with 2 carpaccio dishes 49.90 F. Menus at 79.90 and F 89.90 F, Children's Menu at 39 F. See the chapter "Cuisine from Elsewhere – Italy".*

PIZZERIA NAPOLI CHEZ NICOLO ET VITO > 45, rue Franklin (2nd) ℭ **04 78 37 23 37.** *Open from Monday to Saturday, service from 12.00 to 14.00 and from 19.00 to 23.00. Pizzas from 32 F to 68 F, meat dishes from 54 F to 71 F, desserts from 15 F, ice-cream from 25 F. Menus at 69 F and 74 F. See the chapter "Cuisine from Elsewhere – Italy".*

POLO CLUB > 9, rue des Quatre-Chapeaux (2nd) ℭ **04 78 42 83 10.** The place is really cute – in an English style, with flowery, chintz tablecloths, antique porcelain and old teapots – although the cuisine's vaguely Indian. The reception's charming, and Penelope, an eternal smile on her lips, takes good care of her guests. In the morning, breakfast is served with an assortment of scones, muffins, crumpets, pancakes and toast, with fresh butter and jams. At midday, there's a varied choice between fresh salads (chicken curry, tandoori, sea salad), Lebanese *mezzes* and Club sandwiches. In the afternoon, the restaurant becomes a tea room and serves superb cakes with the entire range of teas from Mariage Frères. On Sundays, from 11.00 to 15.00, three well-garnished buffets allow you to keep going for the day : brunch 'formula' at 140 F.

POMME DE PAIN > 87, rue de la République (2nd) ℭ **04 72 41 93 43.** *Open everyday from Monday to Friday from 08.00 to 21.00, on Saturdays from 08.00 to 21.30, and on Sundays from 11.30 to 19.30. Sandwich from 16 F ; dessert from 14 F ; sandwich, potato and drink 35 F or 42 F : sandwich, dessert and drink 45 F. In summer : salad from 28 F ; salad, cheese and drink 42 F.* Pomme de Pain is the rapid restaurant with the crusty bread and the regional cuisine. Here, the sandwiches are called *Niçois, Bressan, Strasbourgeois,* or *Villageois* and, of course, *Lyonnais*... Because 'regional' doesn't rhyme with 'sectarian', the menu also offers Oriental and Norwegian tastes. So as to vary the food, P*omme de Pain* also offers different menus depending on the season. The service is, obviously, rapid, but lacks a bit of smile… Pity, because the place is attractive. There's a lovely stone vault inside, whilst, outside, the terrace giving onto the busy R*ue de la République* makes this an exceptional location ! *Pomme de Pain*'s also an address for breakfast at 10 F and 21 F, as well as for breaks during the day – pastry and drink 20 F. Finally, good clients are rewarded with a fidelity card !

RESTAURANT BRUNET > 23, rue Claudia (2nd) ℭ **04 78 37 44 31.** *Open everyday except on Sundays and Mondays. A la carte around 120 F. Service till 23.00. See the chapter "Regional Cuisine – Lyonnais Cuisine".*

RESTAURANT TAKEYAMA > 6, rue Thomassin (2nd) ℭ **04 72 40 29 18.** *Open from Monday to Saturday. At midday : menus at 65 F, 85 F and 89 F. Otherwise, menus at 99 F, 139 F, 149 F and 199 F. See the chapter "Cuisine from Elsewhere – Japan".*

RESTAURANT TUNIS > 9, rue des Marronniers (2nd) ℭ **04 78 37 37 01.** *Open everyday. Menus at 69 F, 76 F, 79 F and 99 F, couscous from 52 F to 115 F, tagines 65 F. See the chapter "Cuisine from Elsewhere – Maghreb Countries".*

SIMPLE SIMON > 13, rue Thomassin (2nd) ℭ **04 72 41 04 98.** *Open without interruption from 11.00 to 18.00. See the chapter "Regional Cuisine – So British".*

TANTE ALICE > 22, rue des Remparts-d'Ainay (2nd) ℭ **04 78 37 49 83.** *Open from Thursday to Monday from May to July. At midday, except on Sundays and on Public Holidays : Dish of the Day 55 F ; salad, Dish of the Day and coffee 75 F ; menu at 95 F. Otherwise, menus at 130 F, 160 F and 220 F. Tante Alice* is a *Beaujolais* near Brouilly, but, in Lyon, Aunt Alice really existed and, in the post-War period, served hens which her old clients remember to this very day. Aunt Alice is no longer with us, but Véronique and Raphaël, who have been at the helm of this restaurant for the last two years, perpetuate the restaurant's renown by marrying tradition and modernity in a cuisine which is sometimes daring in its combination of the sweet and savoury, but always tasty. The décor in the two dining rooms is traditional, even old-fashioned, with a genuine No Smoking corner. *Tante Alice* also offers cooked dishes to take away. An address to note down for a lunch break : rapid service (never was the expression "No sooner said than done" more amply deserved) and a traditional cuisine.

THE SALMON SHOP > 54, rue Mercière (2nd)   ℭ   **04 78 42 97 92.** *Open everyday till midnight. Menus from 67 F to 77 F. See the chapter "Fish".*

◆**3RD** *ARRONDISSEMENT*

L'ARISTO BAR > 67, rue Moncey (3rd)   ℭ   **04 78 60 46 98.** *Open everyday, but food served from Monday to Friday only. Dish of the Day 45 F to 48 F ; Dish of the Day and entrée or dessert 65 F ; entrée, Dish of the Day and dessert 80 F ; Entrecôte 'Formula', chips and salad 75 F.* This is a dream location - in the pedestrian part of the *Rue Roncey*, just opposite the Labour Exchange which, after its successful renovation, has become one of Lyon's most popular 'show places'. *L'Aristo* offers an unpretentious, but good and copious cuisine, which is served rapidly and with a smile. It also proposes a pre-show dinner, served from 18.30 onwards. In summer, sit on the shaded terrace, which climbs in several banked steps as far as the bushes and is next to the busy, modern fountain… called the *"Buisson ardent"* (Burning Bush). It's impossible to describe this fountain, so, satisfy your curiosity by going to have a look. The bar's open all week.

L'OCTOPODE > 2, quai Augagneur (3rd)   ℭ   **04 72 60 93 06.** *See the chapter "Fish".*

LA BARTAVELLE > 132, rue Tête-d'Or (3rd)   ℭ   **04 78 60 10 26.** *Open from Monday to Friday, in the evening from Wednesday to Friday. Service till 22.00.* On the walls, the yellow, Provençal sun, on the plates, a traditional cuisine, with southern specialities like salad of king prawns with *pistou*, home-made *foie gras* or *carpaccio*. In your glass, the Wine of the Month, which comes from the south. The smiling welcome given by Monsieur and Madame Pollet (and by Jean-Michel at the bar) warms the heart, whilst the Rum cocktail (Rum, dry fruit, honey, coffee, vanilla) served as an aperitif softens the gullet. Those from the South of France will feel at home.

LE MAUBERT > 85, rue Moncey (3rd)   ℭ   **04 78 62 87 43.** *Open everyday except on Saturdays at midday and on Sundays. Menus at 108 F, 125 F and 158 F. A la carte around 200 F. Service till 22.30.* In a friendly setting where you'll forget your problems for an hour or two, *Le Maubert* serves excellent meat and fish dishes, made with quality produce cooked in such a way as to bring out all its taste. As far as the fish is concerned, the fillet of John Dory is poached, the *aoli* sauce tastes as it does along the Mediterranean, whilst the salmon comes from Scotland and the *carpaccio* from Norway. Cows, pigs and lambs are served up on your plate in the form of *duo de bavette d'aloyau et d'onglet confit* (duo of sirloin and hanger steak *confit*), which is tasty and simply melts in the mouth (a real feast !), *rosette* of breast of duck and *pavé* of lamb.

LE VAL D'ISERE > 64, rue de Bonnel (3rd)   ℭ   **04 78 71 09 39.** *See the chapter "Regional Cuisine – Lyonnais Cuisine".*

LES ALIZEES > Place Beraudier (3rd)   ℭ   **04 72 13 13 60.** *Open from Monday to Friday from midday to 14.30. Main dish from 85 F, entrée from 40 F, dessert from 35 F, 'formula' at 135 F.* This is a 'business' restaurant located in *La Part Dieu* Station. But, because station doesn't necessarily rhyme with "*SNCF* sandwiches", *Les Alizées* offers a real menu and service worthy of businessmen : the carpet's thick, the tablecloths are beautiful, and there are lots of glasses on them. In short, the works ! It's also practical, because TV screens show which trains are shortly going to leave, so that you don't miss your train. What's more, there's a lift which takes you up to the restaurant, which is always useful when you've got too much luggage…

PUB O'GORMAN'S > Place Beraudier - La Part Dieu Train Station (3rd)   ℭ   **04 72 13 13 60.** *Open everyday from 05.30 to 01.00, food service from 11.00 to 22.00. Dish of the Day 60 F, entrée from 28 F, dessert from 22 F, 'formula' at 68 F. Breakfast 35 F.* A bit of exoticism just before leaving ? Or, if you're unable to take leave, a trip abroad whilst staying in Lyon ? Whichever, the *Pub O'Gorman*'s will take you to Ireland. The décor's superb – you can choose between eating on stools, chairs or benches and, in the entrance, there's a "typical" phone booth. A small point to bear in mind – you need two 1 F coins to use the cabins in the WC's. However, to come back to the food, this Irish pub offers typical Irish fare, as well as 'European' dishes like *choucroute*. Every week-end, groups play Irish music in the evening.

Lyon *Restaurants - Fourth arrondissement*

◆ 4TH *ARRONDISSEMENT*

BRASSERIE LYON PLAGE > 85, quai Joseph-Gillet (4th) ℂ **04 72 10 44 44.** *See the chapter "Brasseries".*

CANUT SANS CERVELLE (BRAINLESS SILK-WEAVER) > 4bis, rue de Belfort (4th) ℂ **04 78 30 10 20.** *Open everyday, on Sundays from 10.00 to 14.00. Menu at 100 F, 'formulae' at 65 F and 80 F at midday. Service till 23.00.* Brainless he may be, but this silk-weaver nevertheless knows how to welcome and satisy his guests. You come in through the bar, before heading to a large and pleasant dining room with nicely-laid tables in bordeaux-coloured wood. You can also head to the left, go through the kitchen (a common practice in the *Croix-Rousse*) and install yourself in a smaller room with yellow walls. Clients are welcomed as if they've been coming here for years, even if it happens to be their first visit. Very much at ease, guests then enjoy *pierrade* and *raclette*, or *tartares* made with salmon, beef or breast of duck. Other excellent and popular dishes include small frogs, the impressive *jambon au foin* (ham in hay) and the *confit de canard* (preserved duck). The beautiful smell of these dishes hits you as soon as sit down. Here, fresh produce is prepared simply, but with a lot of skill, and is served in portions large enough to satisfy even those with a very healthy appetite. On Sundays, you can have brunch with the family or between friends.

LE PREMIER > 3, rue d'Austerlitz (4th) ℂ **04 72 98 39 08.** *Open everyday except on Sundays. At midday, Dish of the Day at 48 F and 'formula' at 68 F. Menus at 89 F, 94 F and 129 F. A la carte roughly 120 F. Service till midnight.* In the *Croix-Rousse*, there's a lot of activity at night in the *Rue d'Austerlitz*, and *Le Premier* is one of the reasons for it. The dining room is large, has a high ceiling, and is, quite simply, superb. The bar's made with wooden planks, and beams on the ceiling and stone walls give the place a special 'feel'. Large windows, surrounded by curtains, give directly onto the street. The owner, Tony, receives all his guests like stars, and this personalized welcome continues throughout the evening. He asks you if everything's fine, and makes sure that everybody has an excellent time. On the walls, you'll find paintings by his favourite artists. The menu combines a southern cuisine, with spicy, Martiniquais dishes and Lyonnais preparations, and all of these are served by a charming young lady, who's amusing, friendly and very natural. The ambiance (assisted by the music, ti-punch and intimate lighting) incites you to dance, flirt and generally enjoy yourself.

PIZZA PUCE > 5, place du Commandant-Arnaud (4th) ℂ **04 72 00 00 40.** *Open 7/7 days. Menus at 39 F, 49 F and 59 F. A la carte roughly 90 F. Service till 23.00. See the chapter "Cuisine from Elsewhere – Italy".*

◆ 5TH *ARRONDISSEMENT*

CAMPAGNE > 20, rue Cardinal-Gerlier (5th) ℂ **04 78 36 73 85.** *Menu at 139 F. A la carte roughly 100 F.* This restaurant was well named ! From the street, who would think that, behind these doors in the middle of the city, hides such a peaceful spot ? The best part of the place is, of course, the beautiful summer garden, which is vast and shaded, with trees, bar and wine barrels. You'd think you were in the middle of the country ! In winter, you can dine in front of a wood fire. The menu, too, is country-like and good : pan-fried wild mushrooms, fricassee of chicken with morel mushrooms and a home-made country terrine. To make the very best of the place, try the home-made desserts, and stay for a while at the bar after your meal.

COCO D'OR > 3, rue Soufflot (5th) ℂ **04 78 42 39 66.** *Open from Tuesday to Sunday in the evening only and on Sundays at midday. Menu of the Day 100 F. Otherwise, menus at 118 F, 158 F, 195 F and 210 F. See the chapter "Cuisine from Elsewhere – The Islands".*

LA GARGOUILLE > 70, rue Saint-Jean (5e) ℂ **04 78 38 27 57.** *Open everyday, but food is served only at midday from Monday to Saturday. Dish of the Day 38 F, entrée 36 F, hot dishes from 42 F, dessert 20 F. La Gargouille* is the unpretentious address you come across by accident but which you return to for a number of reasons. The traditional cuisine, including steak, escalope of veal and *andouillette*, is good and served in generous portions. The interior of the restaurant's pleasant : numerous black and white photos allow you a glimpse of Lyon as it used to be. The room at the bottom is quieter, and owes its charm to the stone walls and wooden ceiling. *La Gargouille* is fortunate enough to have a terrace on the *Place Saint-Jean,* at the foot of the impressive Saint John's Cathedral. Hence, throughout the meal, you can admire the facade, its fine stone sculptures and... gargoyles. Even though you're at the heart of historical Lyon (the *Eglise Saint-Georges* bell-tower is just opposite), you can get a real breath of fresh air as you gaze at the trees on the *Colline de Fourvière* and listen to the murmuring of the waterfall on the *Chemin Neuf.* A lunch here allows you a real break, a stone's throw from the *Saint-Jean* métro station !

LA MACHONNERIE > 36, rue Tramassac (5th) © **04 78 42 24 62.** *Open every evening and on Saturdays at midday, open on Sundays at midday from September to Easter. Menus at 100 F, 130 F, 150 F, 180 F and 250 F. A la carte around 120 F. Service till 22.30. See the chapter "Regional Cuisine – Lyonnais Cuisine".*

LE BEAUJOLAIS > 48, rue Saint-Georges (5th) © **04 78 37 84 13.** *Open from Monday to Saturday. Dishes of the Day at 48 F and 52 F, salad 39 F, dessert from 17 F.* This snackbar in the middle of *Saint Georges* is like the district – unpretentious and 'authentic'. So, if you want to get away from the hordes of people strolling around *Saint-Jean,* or simply spend a pleasant afternoon or evening, come to *Saint-Georges.* It's not fancy in this area, but so what ? Just beside the *Eglise Saint Georges,* Maryse and André will welcome you to their bar which reminds you of days gone by. The formica bar, the horn-radiator, the dog poster and the triangular water carafe with the name of a famous aniseed manufacturer on it... we told you, it's all authentic. In Paris, this would become a trendy place very quickly. The cuisine's simple, 'family' but good, and it even has a few surprises in store, like the apple tart served surrounded by *crème chantilly* (sweetened, whipped cream) and caramel. In summer, the little terrace allows you to enjoy the calm reigning in the paved *Rue Saint-Georges.* Then, after a stop here, you can go for a gentle stroll to digest, either on the nearby *Saint-Georges* Footbridge over the Saône, or, for the bolder, a climb up to Fourvière along the pedestrian *Montée des Epiés.*

LE BŒUF D'ARGENT > 29, rue du Bœuf (5th) © **04 78 43 21 12.** *Open from Tuesday to Saturday. At midday, Dish of the Day and entrée or dessert 80 F, or menus at 99 F, 148 F and 199 F.* Situated in the Old Quarter, *Le Bœuf d'Argent* was taken over by a new owner a few months ago. There's also a new chef. The cuisine served is delicate and refined. It's both traditional and Lyonnais. This isn't a place where you stuff yourself silly ! Here, quality has replaced quantity, and it's very *"Nouvelle Cuisine".* But, you'll really enjoy the dishes. The setting, too, is stylish, with a fine, vaulted dining room and a terrace. The service is equally good – your glass is topped up and the breadcrumbs swept away. In short, *Le Bœuf d'Argent* is a classy establishment, where the prices are, nevertheless, affordable. To be tried !

LE CAFE DE LA FICELLE > 33, rue de Trion (5th) © **04 78 36 39 48.** On the *Colline de Fourvière,* Jean-François, the really pleasant owner, welcomes all those who cross the threshold of his returant. With no frills or messing about, he serves a small glass of white wine, a grilled *andouillette* with no fat, giant salads, tender meat, delicious vegetable gratins and desserts which are as good as any you've ever eaten at home. The atmosphere here's really friendly, and owes much to the warm personality of the owner and to tables which are lined up together, so that everyone can talk to one another. The restaurant's small, with an 'authentic' décor (a copper bar-top, a piece of old furniture), and it's often full in the evening. So, reserve your table.

LE JARDIN DE SYLVIE > 2, rue des Trois-Maries (5th) © **04 78 37 95 93.** *Open from Monday evening to Sunday midday. At midday, Menu of the Day (entrée, main dish and dessert) 69 F, menus at 98 F, 118 F and 145 F, Children's Menu 45 F, à la carte roughly 145 F.* In the *Saint-Jean* quarter, near the Law Courts, *Le Jardin de Sylvie* has been under new management for a bit over 18 months, and is definitely worth a visit. Firstly, the setting's magnificent. As in many restaurants, the dining room's decorated with a mural fresco, but it also has a magnificent French ceiling, stone walls and soft lighting. The ensemble is a great sucess, and the ambiance is discreet. The place is also worth a visit (and this is more important) for its fine, really traditional cuisine, which includes a number of Lyonnais specialities. If you happen to come on a day when there's *boudins aux pommes,* you may even write to us about it ! The service isn't rapid, but that's explained by the fact that, in the kitchen, dishes are prepared with every order, and not in advance. So, it's worth waiting a bit, because you'll enjoy your food even more when it arrives. Finally, the restaurant's to be visited for the warm and friendly reception. *Le Jardin de Sylvie* can also take up to 8 people in its little cellar, for an intimate soirée or birthday party. After a meal here, you can head off on a visit of Lyon's Old Quarter.

LE PANIER A SALADE > 1, place Neuve (5th) ✆ **04 78 37 22 85.** *Open 7/7 days. Menus at 95 F, 140 F and 195 F. A la carte roughly 120 F. Service till 23.30.* The chairs in this restaurant are high and padded, doubtless to encourage the clients to sit up straight, so that they can enjoy the delicious dishes served here. The rest of the décor's inspired by the Italian Renaissance, perhaps to match the square the restaurant's located in, which is one of the most beautiful in Old Lyon. For nearly 30 years, lovers of French cuisine have been coming here to enjoy lobster in a seafood glaze with *confit* of lemon, genuine Lyonnais *andouillette* or *ragoût de noix de Saint-Jacques aux morilles* (ragout of scallops with morel mushrooms). It's wise to reserve, because the restaurant's often full.

NAMASTE INDIA > 17, quai Romain-Rolland (5th) ✆ **04 78 42 38 20.** *See the chapter "Cuisine from Elsewhere – India".*

RESTAURANT DE FOURVIERE > 9, place de Fourvière (5th) ✆ **04 72 57 90 12.** *Open everyday. At midday, menu at 70 F. Otherwise, menus at 110 F, 145 F and 180 F.* You just have to come to the *Restaurant de Fourvière,* right next to the basilica ! The cuisine here is good and the portions, generous, which isn't surprising when you know that the menu consists principally of Lyonnais dishes. You have to come for the service : a discreet, efficient and pleasant team. You also have to come for the view. Sitting either inside, in front of an impressive bay window, or on the terrace in summer, you've got the whole of Lyon at your feet, and we're not talking metaphorically. During the day, you can try and situate your hotel or another building, and, in the evening, the lights of the city are at their very best from this vantage point. It's a beautiful and unique sight, and *Le Restaurant de Fourvière* is an exceptional address.

◆ **6TH** *ARRONDISSEMENT*

CELTI ROME > 275, cours Lafayette (6th) ✆ **04 78 52 07 56.** *Open at midday from Monday to and in the evening on Thursdays and Fridays. Dish of the Day at 45 F ; unlimited buffet of entrées or dessert and Dish of the Day for 56 F ; buffet of entrées, Dish of the Day and dessert for 68 F ; menus at 66 F, 85 F and 98 F.* With a name like this, you'd expect a pizzeria, but it's nothing of the sort ! Quite simply, the owner has Nordic and Latin origins, and his restaurant is named in honour of these roots. Judging by the number of people paying with luncheon vouchers, judging by the speed of the service, judging by the copious dishes (the buffet alone is enough to satisfy your hunger), and judging by the opening hours, the *Celti Rome* has to be *the* address in this district at midday. But, in the evening it's quieter, and you can take more time to enjoy a cuisine which is every bit as generous and good.

COULEUR SAUMON > 73, rue Masséna (6th) ✆ **04 37 24 15 66.** *Open at midday from Monday to Friday and in the evening from Thursday to Saturday. At midday, 'formulae' at 65 et 68 F, in the evening, menus at 78 F, 88 F and 98 F. A la carte roughly 130 F. See the chapter "Fish".*

IL RISTORANTE > 25, rue Bossuet (6th) ✆ **04 78 52 60 93.** *Open from Monday to Saturday except on Monday evening, Tuesday evening and Saturday at midday. Dish of the Day 59 F ; Dish of the Day and entrée or dessert 79 F at midday only. Otherwise, à la carte, entrée from 40 F, main dish from 70 F and dessert from 30 F. Il Ristorante,* as its name suggests, is an Italian restaurant, but one which doesn't just serve dishes from the other side of the Alps. The food's refined, and the menu contains creative dishes, like the duck simmered in red wine with blackcurrant seeds. The ambiance is intimate and warm, with a lot of red – in the chairs, the curtains and the tablecloths – contrasting with the many black and white photos in honour of Italian cinema. At the bottom of the dining room, there's also a large juke-box. Music's important at *Il Ristorante*, and, the first Wednesday of every month, there's a Musical Evening.

KEY BISCAYNE > 88, cours Vitton (6th) ℂ **04 78 24 01 00.** *Menus at 130 F and 160 F. See the chapter "Fish".*

L'EST > 14, place Jules Ferry - Gare des Brotteaux (6th) ℂ **04 37 24 25 26.** *Open everyday. Service till midnight. Menus at 115 F and 145 F. A la carte roughly 190 F. L'Est, according to Paul Bocuse, is a brasserie serving nothing but a 'travel' cuisine. Located in the old Brotteaux Station, the ovens are in the middle of the dining room, so that, as they sit at their tables, delighted clients can watch the chefs put small portions of food into large dishes and casseroles. It's chic and relaxed at the same time. In addition, it's really good.*

LA BRASSERIE DES BROTTEAUX > 1, place Jules-Ferry (6th) ℂ **04 72 74 03 98.** *Open from Monday to Saturday. Menus at 92 F and 130 F, dishes from 89 F. See the chapter "Brasserie".*

LA BUVETTE DES CYGNES > Parc de la Tête-d'Or (6th) ℂ **04 78 89 11 27.** *Open everyday except in the event of rain. Sandwich from 17.50 F, croque-monsieur 24 F, plate of chips and ham or sausages 41.50 F. In the shade of the plane trees and beside the superb lake in the Parc de la Tête d'Or, you couldn't find a more romantic spot. The snackbar's terrace is right over the water, and you can gaze at the island, make out the rose garden, or look at the passing boats or swans after which the snackbar's named. You won't find gastronomy here, just menu allowing a snack before heading off on a tour of the park by foot, rollerblade or pedal craft. Throughout the day, La Buvette des Cygnes sells drinks, ice-creams and snacks.*

LA CABANE A HUITRES > 128, rue Boileau (6th) ℂ **04 78 52 61 35.** *See the chapter "Fish – Seafood".*

LA GAUFRERIE DU PARC DE LA TETE D'OR > Place du Théâtre-de-Guignol (6th) ℂ **04 78 94 03 39.** *Open every week-end and on Wednesdays and during School Holidays (and during the week, depending on the weather). Crêpes and waffles from 10 F to 18 F. See the chapter "Crêperie".*

LA MOZZARELLA > Place de l'Europe (6th) ℂ **04 78 52 25 49.** *Open from Monday to Saturday except on Monday evenings. Salads from 23 F, pizzas from 35 F, pasta from 40 F and desserts from 20 F. See the chapter "Cuisine from Elsewhere – Italy".*

LE DOLIVIER > 125, rue de Sèze (6th) ℂ **04 78 24 41 26.** *Closed on Sundays and Mondays. Menus at 71 F and 115 F.* A traditional and delicate cuisine in a dining room with a rustic décor. The wine cupboard at the bottom of the room is as beatiful as the mousseline of fish and mushrooms is good. A good address, a stone's throw from *Les Brotteaux.*

LE GRAND CAFE DE GENEVE > 10, avenue de Saxe (6th) ℂ **04 78 52 18 96.** *Open from Monday to Saturday, food served only at midday. Entrée and drink 55 F ; hot dish 65 F ; meat and vegetables 75 F ; dish, dessert, crink and coffee 100 F.* A name, an address ! Alain Barge's restaurant and terrace are always full, thanks to the establishment's reputation. And you pay for the name, which, incidentally, is written everywhere – on the waiters' shirts and on the restaurant's blinds. So, you can be sure that you're really at Alain Barge's place. The cuisine's good – a steak and chips with a few leaves of green salad for 75 F... It's a name and an address ! *Le Grand Café de Genève* is entirely decorated in yellow, and offers a traditional cuisine. *Le Petit Genève*, just nextdoor, is open in the evening till 22.00 from Monday to Saturday at midday. The latter restaurant's decorated in green and offers traditional Lyonnais dishes.

LE KABUTO > 169, rue Cuvier (6th) ℂ **04 72 74 93 28.** *Open everyday except on Sundays and at midday on Mondays. Menus at 54 F and 74 F at midday, 79 F, 98 F, 125 F, 150 F and 198 F in the evening. A la carte roughly 120 F. Service till 22.00. See the chapter "Cuisine from Elsewhere – Japan".*

LE MARTINI > 12, avenue Foch (6th) ℂ **04 78 93 16 61.** *Open from Monday to Friday, in the evening till 22.30. At midday : Dish of the Day 60 F ; entrée, Dish of the Day and dessert 90 F. Otherwise, menus at 130 F and 185 F. In the evening, fondues from 80 F.* The *Avenue Foch* is nothing like the *Rue Mercière*. Here, restaurants are few and far between, and some maintain that this bourgeois area is rather sad, or even dead. However, a short visit will allow you to discover an address worth knowing. Inside, you can sit on the velvet-covered benches under the mirrors, in front of the stained-glass windows or on the terrace with its laurel trees and enjoy the terrine of fresh vegetables or the '*Cannibal Plate*'. In the evening, there are *raclettes* and *fondues* (both Burgundian and Savoyard). After a meal like this, you'll need to digest, and you may fancy a stroll in the *Parc de la Tête d'Or*, which is just a few hundred metres away.

LE PARADOXE > 49, rue Masséna (6th)   ℂ   **04 78 52 13 17.** *Open from Monday to Friday. Dish of the Day and coffee 47 F ; Dish of the Day and entrée or dessert 68 F ; entrée, Dish of the Day and dessert 71 F ; salads from 48 F. Service from 11.45 to 13.30. Banker's Card from 100 F.* A stone's throw from the Les *Brotteaux* district, this address has existed for more than a century. In 1899, the restaurant was called *"Au bouillon du XXe siècle"*, although the menu's been changed a few times since then, and the current restaurant offers a delicate and traditional cuisine, with dishes like *blanquette de veau* (veal stew in white sauce) or *pavés* of salmon with basil. The décor creates a lot of atmosphere in the 'high-celinged' dining room : false balconies and windows make you think for a second that you're on a small village square. You can also come here in the morning from 06.30 onwards for breakfast and pastries, or in the afternoon for the tea room.

LE POT DES GONES > 90, rue Masséna (6th)   ℂ   **04 78 24 46 00.** *Open from Monday to Saturday. At midday and in the evening : Dish of the Day 48 F ; Dish of the Day and entrée or dessert 68 F ; entrée, Dish of the Day and dessert 85 F ; menus at 95 F and 100 F.* Since 1995, this very Lyonnais restaurant has been the headquarters of the *Compagnons de la Tête de Veau* (Companions of Calf's Head), who are a group of locals who come here for a bite to eat every morning. This is a guarantee, if ever there was one, that the cuisine here is 'authentic'. The traditional cuisine includes Lyonnais dishes like hot sausage and *andouillettes*. The restaurant's décor's equally traditional : Guignol in his puppet-theatre presides over the large dining-room, to which old irons, coffee-grinders and lace curtains add their share of charm. When we tell you that the reception's very friendly and that, in the courtyard at the back, there's a flower-decked terrace where you can sit on fine days, you'll have understood that *Le Pot des Gônes* is an address to write down.

LE SPLENDID > 3, rue Jules Ferry (6th). *Open everyday from 12.00 to 14.15 and from 19.00 to 23.30. Menu of the day at 110 F every midday except Sundays and Public Holidays. 150 F (menu carte), 230 F (Entre Bresse et Dombes) and 250 F (Saveurs de Saisons Menu with two main dishes).* As this guide is going to press, *Le Splendid* is getting ready to open, so the restaurant more than deserves the sign reading "New" which you'll find outside ! But, Georges Blanc's arrival in Lyon is well worth this little scoop. Be it on the terrace, in the dining room (a refined brasserie atmosphere), or in one of the private rooms, you'll taste a modern cuisine which changes with the season, and part of which is dedicated to famous Mothers and their recipes. Run by Dominique Lagnier, who's been one of G. Blanc's faithful friends for years, this establishment will certainly feature in next year's *Le Petit Futé* guide.

LE TROCADERO > 16, cours Vitton (6th)   ℂ   **04 78 52 71 30.** *Open from Monday to Saturday. Menus at 100 F, 170 F and 240 F.* Le Trocadéro was the name of the thoroughfare designed by the architect, Morand, which, from the days of the July Monarchy to the 19th century, linked the west to the east via the *Place Kléber* (now called the *Place Vitton*). But, Trocadéro's, above all, the name of a restaurant which deserves to be known. The owner and chef, Gérard Duc, offers a delicate, refined cuisine, with desserts which are particularly creative and delicious. The setting's up to the standard of the food : you can either eat in the lower dining room, beneath a kimono embroidered in gold thread (which the owner brought back from Japan, where he worked for a time), or on the mezzanine. There, a large, round table can take up to 10 guests. On Thursdays and Fridays, the white grand piano is played during musical evenings. Dishes served include an escalope of hot foie gras with pears and dry fruit. Every month, a theme dominates one of the restaurant's menus, so that, for example, a recent Tour of the World Menu allowed guests to discover tastes from elsewhere.

LES CIGALES > 31bis, rue Ney (6th)   ℂ   **04 78 52 29 24.** *At midday, from Tuesday to Friday and, in the evening, from Tuesday to Saturday. At midday, 3 menus : Dish of the Day for 50 F ; Dish of the Day and dessert for 60 F ; entrée, Dish of the Day and dessert for 67 F. Evening Menu at 120 F and à la carte. See the cahpter "Regional Cuisine – Provençal Cuisine".*

LES JARDINS DE MADO > 77, cours Vitton (6th) ℂ **04 78 89 11 52.** *Open on Mondays at midday, from Tuesday to Friday in the evening. At weekends by reservation for groups only. 'Formulae' at 47 F, 58 F and 69 F (at midday) and 53 F, 73 F and 93 F (in the evening).* Mado is someone who lives for her work, and, to enable us to share her culinary passion, she's invented a new food formula. You only eat *à la carte* for a minimum of 47 F at midday and for 53 F in the evening (this entitles you to either an entrée, a main dish or a dessert). Thereafter, you can add additional dishes for 11 F at midday and for 20 F in the evening. In real terms : at midday, you order a main dish for 47 F, then an entrée for 11 F, and then a dessert for another 11 F. Total for three courses 69 F. You see how it works ? But, if you haven't got it, Mado's always there to explain her magic formula to you.

LES TROIS ORANGES > 47, avenue Foch (6th) ℂ **04 78 89 58 73.** *Open everyday except Monday evenings. At midday from Mondat to Friday : 'Market Dish' and coffee 56 F ; entrée, 'Market Dish' and dessert 71 F. Otherwise, menus at 77 F, 91 F and 121 F.* You might have expected it – inside, the colour orange dominates and brightens the beautiful stone walls. The place is very elegant. The small, square and round tables, and the numerous frames surrounding black and white photos, bathe in a soft light created by wooden, Venetian blinds. The mezzanine, with the stone railing around it, give the restaurant a certain class. The menu lives up to the quality of the décor, and is both imaginative (the *millefeuille* with salmon *tartare*), traditional (the gizzard salad) and regional (the Bressan Menu and the frogs, which are served in the evenings only).

PIERRE ORSI > 3, place Kléber (6th) ℂ **04 78 89 57 68.** *http://www. pierreorsi.com - E-Mail : orsi@relais.chateaux.fr. Open everyday except on Sunday. Service till 22.00. Menus at 200 F (at midday only), 320 F, 400 F and 500 F. A la carte roughly 450 F.* Pierre Orsi is one of the restaurants which really count in the city. Awarded the title of *Meilleur Ouvrier de France* in 1972, the Chef concocts recipes in function of the season. They're always beutifully-presented, well-prepared and delicious. No-one will regret having come to eat here – either because of the food or because of the refined décor of this *maison bourgeoise*. To note down in your business diary. Absolutely.

RIVE GAUCHE (LEFT BANK) > 31, cours Franklin-Roosevelt (6th) ℂ **04 78 89 51 21.** *Open from Monday to Saturday except on Monday evenings. Dish of the Day 59 F ; Dish of the Day and entrée or dessert 79 F at midday. Otherwise, menus at 129 F and 149 F.* The Lyonnais Left Bank is not as well known as its Parisian cousin, but *Rive Gauche* is also the name of a restaurant you should come to. Be it on the terrace (only when it's fine) or in the dining room, you'll enjoy a good and traditional cuisine. There's a menu and a 'formula', but the restaurant always pays attention to its guests' wishes, and it's always a pleasure to be able to 'negotiate' a bit of *ratatouille* because you simply detest broccoli, which just happens to be the vegetable which was meant to accompany the Dish of the Day. It makes a change fom the large restaurant chains, where the client's nothing more than a table number or, even worse, a ticket... It's a shame, all the same, that, at the *Rive Gauche,* you have to leave the terrace so that the team can lay the tables at the end of the afternoon, because it would be really nice to have an apéritif there ! If you choose to eat inside, then ask for a table in the third and final dining room, where the mural fresco, the benches and Voltaire-style armchairs make up a very warm ensemble. The Parisian Left Bank had better watch out !

◆7TH *ARRONDISSEMENT*

A LA GUILL'ON DINE > 59, Grande-Rue-de-la-Guillotière (7th) ℂ **04 78 69 39 16.** *Open from Tuesday to Saturday. At midday : Dish of the Day at 85 F ; Dish of the Day, entrée or dessert at 70 F ; entrée, Dish of the Day and dessert at 85 F. In the evening, menus at 155 F and 180 F.* At the heart of the *La Guillotière* district, you arrive in the restaurant, only to be welcomed by the *Livre d'Or* (Visitors' Book), signed by the artists who have exhibited their work here. In contrast, there's no menu, but a large tableau at the bottom of the dining room. It's not easy to make a choice. When it comes to paying, the banker's card isn't accepted for less than 100 F, which is, in itself, proof that, at midday, you can't use it unless you invite all the colleagues in your office ! Good, traditional cuisine, a good effort at decoration and, every three months, an exhibition by young painters.

CAFFE MILANO > 35, rue de l'Université (7th) ℰ **04 37 28 97 98.** *Open everyday except on Sundays and at midday on Mondays. Service till 22.30. 'Formulae' at 50 F, 68 F and 78 F. A la carte roughly 120 F.* The food's Italo-Provençal and the décor's New York. From this, you'll understand that it's sober, chic and so popular that it's often crowded. In a pleasant, 'designer' setting, you'll find bottles of red wine lined up along the walls. On the menu, there's *carpaccio*, wood-fired pizzas, fresh pasta, grilled meat, 'slimming' dishes – tasty food at interesting prices. Reservations are essential because the place is so popular. As you wait, you can sip an apéritif at the bar and admire the numerous pretty girls. In summer, there's also a shaded terrace in the middle of abundant vegetation. Edouard and his team really know how to receive you.

CARNEGIE HALL > 253, rue Marcel-Mérieux (7th) ℰ **04 78 58 85 79.** *Open everyday except on Sundays. Service till 22.30. A la carte around 100 F.* Vegetarians, abstain ! Lovers of red meat, welcome – the *Carnegie Hall* offers you the chance to dig your teeth into all sorts of meat : lamb, veal, horse, beef, pork... The portions are monumental, like the dining room – immense and somewhat noisy. A large panel shows the picture of a cow, so that you can identify which part of the beast you're about to eat, with the help of a system of lights, similar to those you find on métro maps in Paris. The meat which is about to be prepared can be seen from the dining-room, and it's tasty, tender and perfectly-prepared. One regret, however – the service, which is sometimes rather expeditious and not always attentive. Is the client being treated like cattle ? **Other address : 4, rue Mont-Blanc - CORBAS 04 78 21 81 10.**

CHEZ MICHEL > 231, rue Marcel-Mérieux (7th) ℰ **04 78 72 62 46.** *Open everyday. Menus at 70 F, 91 F, 99 F and 124 F. A la carte around 120 F. Service till 22.30. See the chapter "Regional Cuisine – Lyonnais Cuisine".*

EN METS, FAIS CE QU'IL TE PLAIT > 43, rue Chevreul (7th) ℰ **04 78 72 46 58.** *Open everyday except on Tuesday evening, Saturday and Sunday. Service till 22.00. A la carte around 150 F.* A little, wooden house (rather like a little log cabin) at the corner of the street – it's here ! The tables and chairs are blue, like in Greece. The décor's sober but cleverly chosen, with amusing figurines instead of stauettes, Pop Art plastic lamps and plaster paintings in relief on the walls. As far as food's concerned, the menu's fairly limited, but quite sophisticated : stuffed neck of duck , pork ribs grilled in their skin and fat 95 F, various fish (from 65 F to 120 F), cheese and desserts at 45 F. For visual pleasure, all the dishes are artistically presented, and the fresh vegetables contribute their splash of colour. Food-lovers are spoilt here because everything's delicious and beautifully seasoned.

FOOD CONTINENTAL CAFE > 147, avenue Jean-Jaurès (7th) ℰ **04 37 27 00 96.** *Open from Monday to Friday at midday only. A la carte around 60 F.* At last, here's a little café which is original, innovative, straight from the States, and totally unlike other places of its type. The café offers dishes from the four corners of the world : American, Scandinavian, African, Asian and Italian. So, fans of pasta, of Cantonese rice or of salmon can now all sit happily around the same table. No time-wasting : the nearby car park (which is enormous) means that you don't have to drive round for 20 minutes in search of a parking space. With regard to the food, the dishes are ready – all you have to do is order and eat. There are varied salads (Caesar, Greek, *taboulé*) from 19 F to 35 F, hot dishes from 28 F to 65 F, and your purse will appreciate your eating here. For once, international food takes pride of place, which is a good thing.

L'AMPHI > 65, rue de Marseille (7th) ℰ **04 72 80 07 13.** *Open everyday except on Saturdays and Sundays. Service till 21.00 from Monday to Wednesday, till 23.00 on Thursdays and Fridays. A la carte roughly 90 F.* Eating at *L'Amphi* is like developing a habit. You relax behind the star-shaped bar, or on the green leather benches, and begin to take root in front of a glass served by the indescribable Yvan. In the kitchen, the truculent Pierrot delights in simmering little family-style dishes, at prices which are more than reasonable : veal birds, *tournedos*, fish in parcels, giant salads... from 45 F. His gratins and ratatouille are home-made – a point of honour ! As for the seafood *lasagna*, you have to taste it to believe it.

Seventh arrondissement - Restaurants **Lyon**

L'AROMATE > 94, Grande Rue-de-la-Guillotière (7th) ℂ **04 78 58 04 56.** *Open everyday except on Wednesday evening and on Sundays. Service till 22.00, after 22.00 by reservation. Menus at 85 F and 125 F. Midday 'formula' at 58 F. A la carte aound 90 F.* Françoise and Guy know how to receive their guests warmly in their little restaurant – *Table d'hôte*. Having worked for years in some of the big Lyonnais restaurants, sailed the oceans as a chef and lived in the Camargue, Guy set up shop in the 7th arrondissement. He proposes a sunny, Mediterranean cuisine : Camargue bull, lots of very fresh fish (marlin, sea bream, shark *à la créole*, barracuda, king prawns with *pastis*), *aïoli*, Arlesian and Saintois 'platters'… You immediately sense that there's knowledge, experience and imagination in this cuisine. When the dining-room's full, clients install themselves in the room nextdoor, even if they don't know one another (this is the very principle of the *table d'hôte*). The warm, Camarguais décor (on the walls, Van Gogh, bulls and toreros) make you feel as if you're eating at a friend's place, except that, at the end of the meal, you're not asked to help clear the table !

LA CHOUCROUTINE > 6, rue Challemel-Lacour (7th) ℂ **04 78 69 06 30.** *Service till 22.00, 23.00 on Match Days or when there are events at the Halle Tony Garnier. Menus at 74 F, 84 F and 99 F. A la carte around 110 F.* See the chapter "Regional Cuisine – Alsace".

LE JARDIN DE FEDORA > 249, rue Marcel Mérieux (7th) ℂ **04 78 69 46 26.** *Open everyday except at midday on Saturdays and on Sundays. Service till 21.30. Menus from 139 F to 420 F. A la carte roughly 350 F.* Here, the cuisine's principally turned towards the Ocean. In this restaurateur's nets, you'll find *rillettes* of tuna with pistachio nuts, tuna in *tartare* with lime, bass and tuna marinated in vodka, lobster salad with herbs and preserved lemon, bass in a Guérande salt crust. Always fresh and nicely-prepared, the dishes here are extremely tasty. For this and for other reasons, your meal in *Le Jardin de Fédora* will be a memorable one.

LE SAINT LAURENT > 82, rue Béchevelin (7th) ℂ **04 78 58 75 15.** *Open everyday except on Sundays and Public Holidays. Dish of the Day 48 F at midday only, Menu of the Day 80 F, pizza from 39 F and dessert from 24 F, Chef's Menu 138 F.* See the chapter "Cuisine from Elsewhere – Italy".

LE SEVENTH'AT ARGENSON > 40, allée Pierre-de-Coubertin (7th) ℂ **04 78 72 64 53.** *Open 7/7 days. 'Dégustation' Menu at 330 F. A la carte around 180 F. Service till midnight.* La Maison Argenson, which is virtually 100 years old, has changed its name by incorporating "Seventh" into it, perhaps as a 'tribute' to the arrondissement which houses it, and which is going up, up, and up… and getting younger as it does so. From the outside, no-one would guess that there's so much tranquillity and harmony (bordering on the luxurious) inside. Three rooms have been decorated in different ways. The largest, which is swimming in light filtering in through large bay windows, serves as the restaurant where Patrick d'Ambrosio, the talented chef, serves a varied cuisine combining traditional and international tastes. The striped salon, with its more intimate ambiance, is more appropriate for receiving private parties and groups. The bar's batheing in Provençal colours. In summer, a verandah and terrace allow you to get a tan as you hide behind your sunglasses. Well-known, this restaurant's clintèle includes the local Jet Set. It's the last fashionable place where it's 'suitable' to be seen.

LES DEUX GARCONS > 198-200, rue de Gerland (7th) ℂ **04 72 71 93 76.** *Open from Monday to Friday at midday and from Thursday to Saturday in the evening (the other evenings by reservation for a minimum of 20 people). At midday : Dish of the Day 45 F ; Dish of the Day and entrée or dessert 65 F. Otherwise, menus at 85 F, 110 F and 140 F. Salads from 41 F, desserts from 18 F, ice-creams from 20 F. In the evening : 95 F, 120 F and 150 F.* The sports world is to be found in *Gerland*. It's just a stone's throw from the stadium and from the *Palais des Sports*, so it comes as no surprise. *Les Deux Garçons* broadcasts sports news and major sporting events live by cable, but it's also, and above all, a restaurant. In a décor where blue and yellow predominate, the cuisine's refined, and includes dishes like breast of duck with peaches and corn pancakes, or king prawns flambéed with whisky or pastis. There's a terrace, but you should opt to eat inside, near the large aquarium, where you can relax and dream at the foot of the mural fresco. A very rich wine list, with some exceptional wines.

PIZZA LATINO > 243, rue Marcel-Mérieux (7th) ℂ **04 78 72 62 97.** *Open 7/7 days from 06.00 to 01.00. Dish of the Day 45 F. A la carte roughly 90 F. See the chapter "Cuisine from Elsewhere – Italy".*

RENE GAMBONI > 241, rue Marcel Mérieux (7th) ℂ **04 78 72 62 48.** *Open everyday except in the evening on Saturdays and on Sundays. Service till midnight. Menus from 80 F to 125 F. A la carte around 200 F. Gamboni* likes meat, and it shows. On the wall, there's an old photo of the Tony Garnier Hall, which dates from the time when cows mooed there for the last time before being carved into different pieces. The slaughterhouse no longer exists, and the site's now a Festival Hall where there's a succession of concerts, salons and…works (the latter are closed to the public !). This doesn't prevent the restaurant from serving rumpsteaks, T-Bones, *entrecotes* and other cuts of meat with a lot of professionalism. It's been that way for 30 years, and the arrival of a new millennium has changed nothing. So much the better.

UNE FAMILLE, UN CAFE > 32, rue de l'Université (7th) ℂ **04 78 73 34 11.** *Open from Monday to Friday. Dish of the Day 43 F ; Dish of the Day and entrée or dessert 55 F ; entrée, Dish of the Day and dessert 65 F. salads from 35 F, desserts from 15 F.* One family and one café are to be found at the corner of the *Rue de l'Université* and the *Place du Prado*. Now that the works have finished (goodbye to the large lorries and barriers !), this little square now looks like a village or a holiday-spot. The restaurant's terrace, which is shaded by plane trees, is a refreshing and pleasant place ! The interior's almost as inviting, with a discreet but modern décor. The cuisine's good, and the menu offers a large variety of salads and desserts.

◆ **8TH** *ARRONDISSEMENT*

CHEZ DON VITO > 154, avenue des Frères-Lumières (8th) ℂ **04 78 09 22 88.** *Open from Tuesday to Sunday midday. Dish of the Day 40 F, salads from 20 F, pasta and pizzas from 39 F, desserts from 18 F. See the chapter "Cuisine from Elsewhere – Italy".*

L'AUBERGE SAVOYARDE > 72, avenue des Frères-Lumière (8th) ℂ **04 78 00 77 64.** *Open everyday except on Sundays. Service till 22.30. Menus at 88 F, 125 F and 225 F. A la carte roughly 150 F. See the chapter "Regional Cuisine – Alsace".*

L'HIRONDELLE > 102, avenue Albert-Thomas (8th) ℂ **04 78 74 06 30.** *Open everyday except on Sunday and Monday evenings. Dish of the Day and entrée or dessert 65 F ; entrée, Dish of the Day and dessert 87 F (served at midday from Monday to Friday). Otherwise, menus at 137 F and 172 F.* A strange idea, going to a restaurant in the 8th *arrondissement* ? Not at all ! Firstly, by métro, it's barely 10 minutes from *Bellecour* (*Montplaisir-Lumière* métro station). In addition, parking in the 8th is a hell of a lot easier than on the *Presqu'île* ! What's more, here they nourish your body with a traditional cuisine, but they also feed the soul : "The destiny of nations is determined by the way they eat" (Anthelme Brillat-Savarien), the menu announces. The welcome and service are friendly, which takes nothing away from the pleasure of eating here.

AND WHAT ABOUT THE TASTE ?

Whilst all school canteens in France are trying, after advice from eminent dieticians, to develop our children's taste by the use of varied menus, we can't help noticing that a large number of restaurateurs are making no effort to concoct "Children's Menus". Those that exist are incredibly boring, and the poor kids are systematically subjected to the eternal ham and purée or chicken and chips – often the favourite evening dishes of tired mothers who are simply not feeling inspired. The cherry on the cake remains the dessert, consisting of ice-cream in a tub with a little plastic spoon. In the meantime, their parents are feasting themselves on salmon *tartares,* prawn *gratins* or chicken with crayfish. Dear Restaurateurs, a bit of imagination, for God's sake ! Children can have an excellent meal with a (small) portion of steak with shallots, accompanied by a smooth *gratin dauphinois*, and followed by an unctuous home-made flan – and these are just simple dishes. Dear Restaurateurs, your profits won't be any the less, and you really should think about training your future clients.

L'ILOT CORSAIRE (THE PIRATE ISLAND) > 64, avenue des Frères-Lumière (8th) ℂ **04 78 75 00 00.** *Open everyday except Sundays and Mondays. Service till 22.30. Menus at 98 F, 128 F and 145 F. Children's Menu 35 F. A la carte around 90 F.* The setting's really pleasant, and this place specializes in mussels and chips : *cabane de marin pêcheur* (Trawlerman's Cabin), *galion de corsaire*.(Corsair's Galleon)... it's up to you to choose. There's a large terrace at the bottom of the garden, which is lovely in summer and less noisy than the dining rooms. A nicely thought-out décor makes you think of adventure on the high seas. On the menu, some 40 dishes : oysters, salmon, sea bream, bass grilled with thyme, shelled prawns, crab... but also meat and salads. Some evenings during the week, *Le Corsaire* even gives 'presents' to its clients : on Tuesdays, 50% more oysters, on Wednesdays, a cocktail for the ladies, on Thursdays, unlimited mussels and, on Saturdays at midday and on Tuesday evenings, a free *Ti Pirate Menu*. The prices are amazingly attractive, and the waiters are always smiling and friendly. Two hours of parking are offered every midday, there's a real No Smoking room, and, inside, there's a cabin for the kids to play in (toys, video games).

◆9TH *ARRONDISSEMENT*

LE MALAGA 2 > 26, rue du Bourbonnais (9th) ℂ **04 78 47 29 07.** *Open everyday. Service till 23.00. A la carte roughly 120 F. See the chapter "Cuisine from Elsewhere – Spain and Portugal".*

◆EAST LYON

Bron

LA BRAISE GOURMANDE > 158, rue de la Pagère ℂ **04 72 14 06 65.** *Open at midday only from Monday to Saturday and at the week-end by reservation. Dish of the Day 42 F. Menu of the Day : buffet of entrées, choice of Dishes of the Day and dessert 64 F.* A really nice place ! *La Braise Gourmande* is the ideal address for chatting in the little corner of a good restaurant. Unless you happen to live in the area, you'd think that there's no reason for coming to Bron for a meal. But, you'd be wrong ! This restaurant has something very special. Situated in the town, it really feels like the country, here. It's so nice to eat good, diced, spring vegetables with a a piece of steak – just like your mother used to make. Very good value for money. In addition, once a month, *La Braise Gourmande* offers (by resevation only) special evenings, like the Spanish Evening, with a paella and guitar music.

RESTAURANT L'ALPAGE > 12, rue Maryse-Bastié ℂ **04 72 37 01 14.** *Open everyday from 12.00 to 14.00 and from 19.00 to 21.45, on Saturdays from 19.30 to 22.00 and closed on Friday evenings, at midday on Saturday and on Sundays.* Ten minutes from Lyon, heading towards La *Porte des Alpes*, in the *Parc Saint-Exupéry*, this restaurant (whose name already takes us towards the nearby mountain-tops), welcomes you in a friendly atmosphere, and allows you to taste Savoyard specialities. To get your strength back, we recommend the *Assiette du Montagnard* (Highlander's Platter), which includes slices of buttered bread, fondues, *tartichèvre*, *raclons*, and other melting delicacies.

◆WEST LYON

Brignais

LA RONDE > 9, place Emile-et-Antoine-Gamboni ℂ **04 72 31 05 90.** On the Church square, Madame Campo and the chef, Matthieu Brand, invite you to discover a combination of traditional French cuisine and 'travel' cuisine in an attractive restaurant (yellow walls and a pleasant décor) with a 'family' ambiance. On fine days, you'll enjoy the terrace, whilst the 1st floor can take up to 35 people. Everyday, the ultra-fresh, market produce is carefully turned into delicate, perfumed dishes, like the home-made foie gras, the *pavé* of salmon with saffron sauce, or the *grande assiette gourmande*.

Lyon *Restaurants - West Lyon*

Champagne-au-Mont-d'Or

LA CHAUMIERE > 11, avenue du Général de Gaulle ✆ **04 78 35 10 60.** *2-star hotel with 16 rooms. Parking.* For the last 15 years, this excellent establishment has been serving a traditional cuisine made with regional produce. You'll taste a *tourte bressane*, or a *tournedos* with fennel before going for a well-deserved rest in this quiet and practical hotel.

Chaponost

LE CROUTON > 27bis, avenue Paul Doumer ✆ **04 78 45 06 47.** *Open everyday except on Wednesdays. Menus at 68 F, 79 F and 90 F during the week and at 128 F, 155 F and 210 F at the week-end.* In this establishment, Patrice Genin and his team offer a creative cuisine, prepared only with the very best quality produce. Apart from an efficient service (much appreciated by many businessmen), the restaurant also offers excellent value for money. Depending on the season, you may eat thinly-sliced salmon with walnut oil and a fresh salad, a salad of fricasseed lobster with dill and a slice of *foie gras*, or an *assiette du boucher*, with 5 different meats and a fricassee of browned shallots.

Charbonnières-les-Bains

CAP OUEST > 78bis, route de Paris ✆ **04 72 38 02 87.** *Open from Monday to Friday. On Saturdays and Sundays, banquets, Communions and Christenings. Menus at 65 F and 140 F.* Steer a westerly course for a complete break in a magnificent décor, consisting of a mixture of material (glass, metal, island wood) in blue shades, and with a very simple design. You immediately feel at ease in this marine universe, whilst enjoying a magnificent view. On the menu, there's fish, of course, with a *brick de la mer au coulis d'écrevisse* (sea *brick* with a crayfish sauce), a *viennoise de rascasse au vieux parmesan et coulis de tomates fraîches* (breaded scorpion fish with mature parmesan and a thin, tomato sauce), copious and refreshing salads and delicious desserts, including a lovely peach and blackcurrant tart. An elaborate and delicate cuisine.

Collonges-au-Mont-d'Or

LA SILA > 12, quai Illheusem ✆ **04 72 42 21 21.** A large, white building at the side of the road, an enormous car park, an immense dining room – the *La Sila* pizzeria is also a karaoke joint. The owner's decorated the walls in a pretty yellow, and has added wooden sculptures, which makes for a Venetian décor. A pleasant terrace makes this a good place to stop when the weather's fine. As far as the food's concerned, there's a large menu of fresh pasta and pizzas, grilled meat, fish and a number of home-made dishes. As you come into the restaurant, you come face to face with a superb presentation of home-made ice-creams. Yves Bentata, the boss, makes them himself. It's his hobby. In doing so, he adds no artificial flavours, but uses nothing but fresh fruit which he has carefully selected himself. He has no equal when it comes to testing new flavours or trying new and unusual recipes. His *tiramisu* ice-cream is a pure marvel.

LE CRUSOE > Ile Roy ✆ **04 78 22 11 69.** *Open everyday from April to September. Service till 22.30. Menus at 100 F, 150 F and 200 F. A la carte around 100 F.* "If you're in a hurry, keep going" is this charming little café's motto. City man, if you miss the country air, if you need to see a bit of greenery and Nature, then come to *Le Crusoë* and watch time drift by. The clientèle's a mixed one (families celebrating a birthday, night owls come for a peek at the sun, lovers out for a drink), which is all part of the charm. You have to take the ferry to get to the island, where you'll discover a real country cottage, with a landing-stage, a shady terrace and a vast solarium. There's a large lawn with deck chairs, a small volleyball court, toboggans and a table tennis table. There's even a forest for a little stroll. The ambiance is friendly, and there's dancehall music in the background. You'll eat fried whitebait, frog's legs, a pot of snails, chicken with vinegar or crayfish, fillet of pike-perch in red wine, *foie gras* and melon with parma ham. To finish on a sweet note, fresh seasonal fruit and home-made desserts.

PAUL BOCUSE - L'AUBERGE DU PONT DE COLLONGES > 50, rue de la Plage ✆ **04 72 42 90 90.** *Open everyday. Service till 22.00. menus at 410 F (at midday only), 510 F, 610 F, 710 F and 740 F.* Four kilometres north of Lyon, you'll find one of the world's most famous restaurants.

Recognizable by its multi-coloured paint, it houses a luxurious décor, an impeccable service, and recipes which take your breath away. Paul Bocuse is omnipresent in the restaurant – his face can be seen on the tableau at the entrance, on the napkin rings, the matches and on the tableware. At least you can be sure of being in the right place ! As soon as you taste the appetizers, you know you're living an exceptional moment. Cooking's an art, and *L'Auberge du Pont de Collonges* confirms the fact. Till the very last moment of the dessert, you enjoy the privilege of eating in the gastronomic restaurant *par excellence*. It's purely and simply an unforgettable feast for the eyes and the tastebuds.

RIGOLETTO > 1, quai de la Libération © **04 72 42 04 14.** *Open everyday except on Sundays and Mondays. Menus at 78 F and 98 F.* On the banks of the Saône, opposite the Aquatic Centre, you may be tempted to sing an Italian air. The place is all the more charming because this traditional establishment has a warm and family-style atmosphere. So, when it's fine, sit yourself down on the terrace or in the green - and pink coloured dining room, and enjoy a pizza between friends, or choose one of the 20 Italian dishes on the menu.

Craponne

RESTAURANT LE PESAGE > 26, rue du 11 Novembre 1918 © **04 78 57 83 40.** *Restaurant closed on Mondays. Hotel Best-Western Le Longchamp.* The *Le Pesage* restaurant offers you country charm, just 10 minutes from the centre of Lyon. It's a pleasant establishment, with a shady terrace giving onto a swimming pool where you can go and relax after a meal consisting of traditional dishes. Brunch on Sundays.

Dardilly

LES FEUILLANTINES > 3, place de l'Eglise © **04 78 66 19 57.** *From May to September, closed on Saturdays at midday, on Sunday evenings and on Mondays. From October to April, closed on Saturdays at midday and on Sunday and Monday evenings.* At *Les Feuillantines*, you'll be seen by everyone, thanks to a sumptuous, panoramic terrace. For the last 4 years, M. Roche, who has worked in some of the region's finest restaurants, has been treating his guests to a creative and tasty cuisine.

Irigny

AU VIEUX PORT > 6, impasse du Vieux-Port © **04 78 51 71 50.** *Open everyday except on Sunday evenings and on Mondays. Menus from 72 F to 198 F.* In summer, nothing's more pleasant than lunching or dining out of doors, in the fresh air and on a shady terrace under plane trees. In winter, the two dining rooms can take up to 100 people, so that it's the ideal place for a very, very large family, banquets, birthdays or business dinners. The cuisine's French, traditional and good. In season, adults and children alike can feast themselves on assorted fried dishes and frog's legs, which are the house speciality.

Limonest

LE HOME CATALAN > 168, avenue Général de Gaulle © **04 78 35 10 41.** *Closed on Sunday evenings and on Mondays.* A very beautiful "home" (the décor's spanking new), but not as "sweet" as that ! Indeed, there's something of a spicy southern wind blowing through this establishment (which has two dining rooms and room for 80 to 85 guests), where you'll be served *paella* and *zarzuela*. So, you don't come here to fall asleep in front of your plate, but to discover the warm atmosphere of "Home Spice Home".

Montagny

LE RELAIS DE MONTAGNY > Place de Souzy © **04 78 73 58 68.** *Closed on Sunday evenings and on Mondays. Menus at 38 F, 50 F, 60 F and 95 F at midday and during the week and at 125 F, 150 F, 190 F and 240 F in the evening and at week-ends.* Having worked in several prestigious restaurants, Patrice Louiset proposes an original and varied menu, based on market produce. He prepares fish and regional specialities (piece of beef with a red wine sauce, home-made *foie gras*) with a lot of talent. Catherine Louiset reserves a very warm welcome for you. There's a nice terrace, and for all occasions (weddings, business meals, family meals, seminars, etc.), *Le Relais de Montagny* offers a pleasant setting.

Lyon *Restaurants - West Lyon*

Oullins

LE VESUVE > 17, rue de la République ℂ **04 78 50 52 39.** Over the 18 years that this restaurant has existed, it has conquered a faithful clientèle with the friendliness of its welcome and with the genuine human warmth each client cannot fail to feel. From Italy, *Le Vésuve* brought its name, as well as the secret of its pizzas, which are cooked over a wood-fire and whose incredible size (they're larger than the plates they're served on) will satisfy the largest of appetites – all at very low prices. In addition to being enormous, the pizzas are delicious and crusty. The other House Specialities are the *andouillette*, the *saltimbocca*, the escalope of veal with ham and the breast of duck with pepper. There are many reasons for coming back often to *Le Vesuve*.

Saint-Genis-Laval

LE MITHAN > 19, rue de la Ville ℂ **04 78 56 83 56.** *Open everyday except on Sunday evenings.* A quiet little street in an old town, behind the main avenue, an old-fashioned and welcoming dining room – you're here. But, what happens in this dining-room is a lot less quiet : 'theme evenings' are organized on a regular basis, so that you have a really enjoyable time as you eat your meal. At *Le Mithan*, you feast (for very little money) on a fresh, traditional and inventive cuisine : taboulé with seafood, roast pork with mushroom sauce and a pasta *gratin.*

LES DEUX PLATANES > 134, rue Henri-Barbusse ℂ **04 78 51 54 02.** *Open everyday except on Saturdays and Sundays. Menus at 58 F and 80 F. A la carte around 90 F.* At midday, three large dining rooms, decorated in a Provençal style, welcome starving locals and all those who know the address. The service is ultra-rapid, but you can also take your time, if you prefer. The dishes aren't at all expensive, and you'll be served a family-style cuisine : veal's kidneys and *purée, choucroute*, grilled meat, various salads... In summer, the terrace behind the restaurant is like a little corner of the countryside, with a bit of lawn and a fountain in the middle.

Tassin la Demi-Lune

RESTAURANT COTE JARDIN > 13d, avenue Victor Hugo ℂ **04 78 64 68 69.** *Novotel Hotel Lyon Valvert (Porte Lyon Valvert exit).* It's well known that the Novotel hotels often conceal little pearls in the shape of their *Coté Jardin* restaurants. This Novotel hotel's no exception to the rule, and offers a gastronomic treasure, thanks to the culinary talent of Marie Cécile Bernard. She's a very promising young lady, because she won 1st Prize in the 1998 *"Marmite Beaujolaise"* Competition for the most promising young chef in the region. So, this is a place to stop at.

Villeurbanne

LA BRUNOISE > 4, rue Alexandre-Boutin ℂ **04 78 52 07 77.** *Open at midday from Monday to Friday and in the evening on Thursdays. Menus 125 F and 230 F. A la carte around 150 F.* Built into an old, vast and bright garage, which has been magnificently renovated, this very pleasant place is one of Villeurbanne's rare gastronomic restaurants. The cuisine's light and tasty, and is prepared by the expert and imaginative Josette and Guy Jandard, who have been cooking for 22 years. They prepare foie gras, lobster, pan-fried scallops, roast saddle of hare, cardoons (a vegetable, similar to artichoke), and semi-cooked salmon which they've smoked in their own smoke-house, using only traditional methods. At the end of the meal, when the bill arrives, you discover with no small pleasure that you can eat here for less than in a vulgar pizzeria.

LE PRISCA > 11, rue Prisca ℂ **04 78 89 29 49.** *Menus at 85 F, 120 F and 180 F. A la carte around 100 F.* In Villeurbanne, in a slightly isolated street, you'll find a very pleasant little place - *Le Prisca*, a restaurant offering you tasty food, emotion and music. The large dining-room can take up to 120 people, and it has a garden where, in summer, there are jazz bands for dinner-concerts (160 F) or dessert-concerts (80 F). Thursday and Friday evenings are Theatre Evenings. The quality of the entertainment is equal to the finesse of the cuisine. The menu borrows the best from various regions of France : Lyonnais tripe and brains, Corézian salad and smoked breast of duck, as well as fillet of red mullet with anchovy butter and pavé of steak with morel mushrooms. Music fans will enjoy themselves here.

MELI MELO > 54, rue Gabriel-Péri   ☎   **04 78 93 70 49.** *Open everyday except on Sundays. Unique menu at 69 F. Groups only. Service till 23.00.* Crêpes are good, very good, but they're such a pain to prepare ! Even if you're with just two or three friends, you have to count on three good hours in the kitchen, turning and re-turning the batter to make dozens of crêpes. What's worse is that, even if you think you've been generous in your calculations, there never seem to be enough, because you can eat mountains of them. This nice restaurant resolves your problem by proposing to make the crêpes for you, and by organizing on the spot an enormous Crêpe Party at prices defying all competition. Only groups are allowed, and, for 69 F, everyone can eat as many sweet and savoury crêpes as they want.

PIERRA PASTA > 57, rue Racine   ☎   **04 78 03 09 67.** *Open everyday except on Sundays. Gourmand Menu at 89 F, Express Menus at 65 F and 78 F. Dish of the Day in the evening at 49 F.* Are you fed up with sandwiches, and do you fancy some real hot dishes on a table worthy of its name ? Here's exactly what you're looking for. This Italian restaurant serves rapid and elaborate Mediterranean dishes. From 29 F to 50 F, you can eat pasta with tomato, *à la bolognaise*, with salmon, etc., or some Italian charcuterie, salads or an *escalope milanaise* accompanied by Italian wine. Depending on what's available at the market (an expression which is always reassuring for consumers), you'll also find fish on the menu.

◆ AROUND LYON

CHATEAU DE CHAPEAU CORNU > Vigneu (38)   ☎   **04 74 27 79 00.** *Open everyday except on Sunday evenings. Menus at 149 F, 179 F, 199 F and 269 F. Children's Menu at 59 F. Menu of the Day (served at midday from Monday to Friday) at 99 F. Dauphinois Menu at 89 F. 21 rooms including 3 suites from 390 F up to 750 F for a suite.* Built in the 13th century, this château's strategically located between Lyon and Grenoble (roughly 1 hour from each city). It offers a panoramic view over the valley, and has a park with shady alleyways for visitors. You can sit beside the fire in the stone dining room (old Arms Room) or on the terrace when it's fine, and eat menus which evoke some of the great names you'll have come across in your tour circuit : Stendhal, Claudel or Ravier… Home-made, semi-cooked foie gras with its sparkling "Saint Chef" jelly, breast of duck with honey and quince (from the château grounds) and Saint Savin trout are just a few of the dishes you'll find on the menu. And, to digest, several walks are signposted from the château, and there are tennis courts (there's even a sports ground) at your disposal.

LA GRILLE - L'ESPACE RESTAURANT > On the Grenoble Road - MORESTEL (01)   ☎   **04 74 80 02 88.** *Hotel restaurant open all year, everyday except on Sunday evenings. Menus from 60 F to 180 F. Children's Menu 60 F. Car park.* In an old and carefully-restored house with a bright verandah where it's very pleasant to eat, the gourmet will be able to taste a fine and generous cuisine which, for a number of years, has made the establishment's reputation. It's worth noting that the restaurant also offers an excellent catering service.

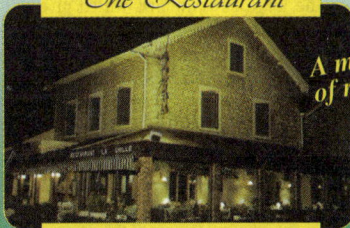

The art of receiving
LA GRILLE
The Restaurant

A moment of relaxation

58, route de Grenoble - **38510 MORESTEL** - Tel. **04 74 80 02 88** - Fax : 04 74 80 05 10

RESTAURANT LA MALADIERE > Domarin (38) ✆ **04 74 93 04 29.** *Open everyday except on Wednesday evenings and on Thursdays. Menus at 67 F, 98 F and 125 F.* Let's never forget that the Isère is on Lyon's doorstep, and that all it needs is a short drive to discover beautiful countryside. This establishment offers a beautiful, shady terrace, as well as a 'relaxation area' for kids who won't stay at the table. On the different menus, you'll find specialities like the *escalope savoyarde*, the chicken with lime, the breast of duck with raspberry vinegar, and lots of fish.

◆ BRASSERIES

LA BRASSERIE DES BROTTEAUX > 1, place Jules-Ferry (6th) ✆ **04 72 74 03 98.** *Open from Monday to Saturday. Menus at 92 F and 130 F, 'plates' from 89 F.* This establishment has been welcoming clients in an exceptional setting since 1913. Here, you come into a real living museum. The sculpted, wooden bar is period, just like all the ceramics, the opalines and the circular window. Lise Igolen Faucon and her son, Emmanuel, have been serving a reputed cuisine for the last ten years, and continue to keep up this magical site. Everything in the restaurant, including the coat-rack, is a little piece of history. There are plans to make a second room, which will be a Music Room for listening to French songs. *La Brasserie des Brotteaux*, which is located in a district round the old station destined to become a gastronomical centre, is an address you have to come to, particularly since it enjoys the title of European Heritage Historical Café.

FANS OF EUROPEAN HERITAGE HISTORICAL CAFÉS

This is a distinction which goes beyond the quality of the food. *"Fans of European Heritage Historical Cafés want to defend sites where human exchange and communication offer potential answers to the problems of anguish which so trouble the beginning of the new millennium. You say "Good Morning", you lend the newspaper to the person at the next table, conversations start up which break the cycle of solitude. These sites are real Living Museums, they're part of our heritage, they constitute that Way of Life where friendliness, the understanding of your neighbour, and the respect of the foreigner or of the tourist are both a rule and a tradition"*, explains their President, Jean-Pierre Boccard. There are now 125 of these cafés (which Jean Jaurès called "People's Salons" and which Edouard Herriot cited as models of social life) to be found in France, Austria, Belgium, the United Kingdom, Italy and Switzerland. In Lyon, establishments which have been awarded this title are : *Le Bar Américain-Café Anglais, Le Grand Café des Négociants, La Brasserie Georges, Le Jura, Le Musée* and *La Brasserie des Brotteaux* (see above).

BRASSERIE LYON PLAGE > 85, quai Joseph-Gillet (4th) ✆ **04 72 10 44 44.** Don't look for the beach, there hasn't been one here for ages. Goodbye, towels, parasols and sandcastles. Far from Palavas-les-Flots, *Lyon-Plage* is more like Deauville or Saint-Tropez when it comes to the clientèle. The décor's very classy, with exotic wood and sea-blue colours – all brightened by the light filtering through the large bay windows which give onto the terrace and the swimming pool. In the kitchen, the chef simmers Lyonnais specialities and Southern dishes, like *bouillabaisse*, grilled lobster and seafood. We strongly recommend that the dozens of businessmen lunching here take their ties off, relax and really enjoy the food they're being served. In short, this is a very pleasant restaurant, where the service is more than perfect.

BRASSERIE PAULANER > 4, rue de la Barre (2nd) ✆ **04 78 42 06 37.** *Open everyday. Dish of the Day at 50 F ; Dish of the Day and entrée or dessert at 70 F ; menu at 85 F ; salad from 40 F ; choucroute from 60 F ; Lyonnais specialities from 52 F.* If there's a Golden Triangle when it comes to restaurants in Lyon, it's not necessarily to be found on the *Presqu'île* because quantity doesn't always rhyme with quality. However, there are exceptions, and the *Brasserie Paulaner* is one of them ! Its menu offers considerable diversity at reasonable prices, and its location, near shopping- and office areas and cinemas, makes it a very handy spot.

LA BRASSERIE VICTOIRE > 5, place Carnot (2nd) © **04 78 37 37 24.** *Open 7/7 days. Menus at 55 F, 65 F, 75 F, 95 F and 120 F. A la carte roughly 120 F. Service till midnight.* Here, they like football, and they loudly proclaim it on the walls and behind the bar. There are photos of Florian Maurice everywhere, and the reason for it becomes clear when you learn that he created the place himself, and now leaves his brother, Max, to run it efficiently. People come here to have a drink in a relaxed atmosphere, to have a simple bite from the kitchen, or to watch the games being played on the football table which, in itself, is worth the detour. On Match Evenings, atmosphere's guaranteed – particularly when the Little Florian's team wins. In summer, the pleasant terrace gives both onto the pedestrian street and onto the *Place Carnot* and its big trees. People also stop here between shops.

LA TAVERNE MIDI MINUIT DE MAITRE KANTER > 83, cours Charlemagne (2nd) © **04 78 37 67 95.** *Open everyday. Dish of the Day (at midday) 45 F ; choucroute, dessert and beer 80 F ; oysters from 41 F ; Seafood Menu from 117 F ; dessert from 32 F.* Do you know the story of Maître Kanter ? Hans Kanter, born in 1874, discovered that the quality and purity of Bavarian water, mixed with barley and hops, gave a special taste to his beer, which has been called *Kanterbrau* since then. Today, whilst the manufacturing process is still a closely-guarded secret, *Maître Kanter* is also the name of a chain of breweries. In the *Cours Charlemagne*, a series of rooms allows enough space for 400 diners, but the clever design of the rooms is such that each keeps a certain intimacy and has a genuine No Smoking section. The menu offers a wide range of *choucroute*, but *La Taverne Midi Minuit* is also famous for its seafood. Finally, you should know that, every fortnight, *La Taverne* proposes organized evenings, with jazz, accordeon music or magic shows. So, there's something for every taste !

◆CREPERIES

GRAIN DE SEL > 2, rue David-Girin (2nd) © **04 78 42 77 19.** *Open everyday except on Sundays and Mondays. At midday, 'formulae' at 48 F and 58 F. In the evening, menus and 'formulae' at 79 F. From 15.00 to 18.00, Salon de Crêpes.* If, in addition ot the pinch of salt, the team could add the tiniest, sincere smile, that would make the place much pleasanter. Particularly because all the crêpes ae very good, the prices reasonable, and the location of the crêperie ideal during your shopping spree on the nearby P*lace de la République*, or as you come out of the cinema. There's an original décor, and, in the mezzanine, a water basin's home to our friends, the turtles.

LA CREPE D'OR > 1, rue Laurencin (2nd) © **04 78 92 90 54.** *Open everyday from midday to midnight. No Banker's Cards accepted. At midday : 'formula' with 3 dishes at 45 F. Otherwise, menus at 58 F, 69 F and 85 F, Group Menu at 75 F (more than 6 people at midday and 9 in the evening). A la carte. La Crêpe d'Or*, which opened in 1978 and is one of Lyon's oldest crêperies, proudly displays a sign reading, "Nothing is more necessary than the superflous", and it's true to say that the place is rather different from other 'Breton establishments'. The menu contains some original compositions, like crêpe with *ratatouille* or with tomato and mustard... You have to admit that it's a bit of a change from the traditional ham and gruyère or strawberry jam ! But, if novelty frightens you, you'll also find the classic. As far as the décor's concerned, the traditional bagpipes have given way to numerous photos of Australia. So, as we said, it may not be your normal crêperie, but it's definitely an address worth (re)discovering !

LA GAUFRERIE DU PARC DE LA TETE D'OR > Place du Théâtre-de-Guignol (6th) © **04 78 94 03 39.** *Open every week-end, on Wednesdays and during School Holidays (and in the week, depending on the weather). Crêpes and waffles from 10 F to 18 F.* Right in the middle of Lyon's 'Green Lung', opposite the famous Guignol Theatre, *La Gaufrerie du Parc* offers crêpes and waffles to take away (no tables here). There are more than 20 flavours of jam for the crêpes and waffles which are prepared in front of you, on 32 waffle-griddles and 5 pancake-griddles. You'll find some original and unforgettable accompaniments, such as white chocolate. La Gaufrerie has lovely frescoes on its walls, reminding us of how Lyon and the Park used to be in 1900. For a pleasant, family break, or for a quick bite as you tour the park in your trainers or on your bike or rollerblades.

LE CHANT DE LAURE > 5bis, place Sathonay (1st) ℂ **04 78 30 90 25.** *Open everyday at midday and in the evening. Menus at 43 F, 57 F, 75 F, 89 F and 97 F. A la carte around 70 F. Service till 22.00.* No larger than a pocket-handkerchief, this crêperie is, nevertheless, pleasant. In summer, the minuscule terrace allows you to enjoy the *Place Sathonay*, which is quiet, shady, and frequented by pétanque-players or by locals strolling under the large trees. On the menu, you'll find refreshing and varied salads, buckwheat *galettes* (with *Saint-Marcellin* cheese, *à la carbonara*, with a*ndouillette*...) and sugared crêpes, accompanied by the inevitable sweet or dry Breton cider. The charming lads who run the place have the gift of the gab, and don't hesitate to chat with their clients or to tell them stories about the district. A really friendly reception – very like the district, where everyone knows each other.

LE DOMINOTIER > 14, rue Constantine (1st) ℂ **04 78 27 48 10.** *Open everyday except at midday on Saturdays and Sundays. Service till 01.00. At midday, Dish of the Day 43 F ; Dish of the Day and entrée or dessert 53 F ; entrée, Dish of the Day and dessert 63 F ; salad and dessert 'formula' 55 F. otherwise, menus at 90 F ; tartiflette or raclette from 65 F ; Fondue, Tartiflette or Raclette Menus from 94 F. See the chapter "Regional Cuisine – Savoie".*

◆ FISH AND SEAFOOD

MELI MELO > 54, rue Gabriel-Péri ℂ **04 78 93 70 49.** *Open everyday except on Sundays. Unique menu at 69 F. Groups only. Service till 23.00. See the chapter "Villeurbanne - Fish and Seafood".*

CHEZ ANTONIN > 102, cours Lafayette (3rd) ℂ **04 78 62 39 10.** *A la carte between 150 F and 200 F.* Here, you'll find oysters, clams, lobsters and shellfish, which you can eat either rapidly, or in the dining room with a glass of Mâcon. Eric Giraud and his team give a warm and friendly welcome to their clients.

COULEUR SAUMON > 73, rue Masséna (6th) ℂ **04 37 24 15 66.** *Open at midday from Monday to Friday and in the evening from Thursday to Saturday. At midday, 'formulae' at 65 and 68 F, in the evening , menus at 78 F, 88 F and 98 F. A la carte roughly 130 F. Couleur Saumon* isn't just a name, but a reality ! Obviously, although the salmon's, first and foremost, to be found on your plate, the colour salmon is everywhere : on the tablecloths, lampshades, paintings, coat-racks, and even on the tulips in the restaurant window. So, obviously, those who don't like the colour aren't going to like the place at all, but the others will have a really good time. Since the service is a bit slow, you can really study the décor. *Bonne cuisine !*

GAMBA'S HOUSE > 9, rue Mercière (2nd) ℂ **04 72 41 70 00.** *Open everyday except on Sundays at midday and on Mondays. Menus from 80 F to 89 F. Service till midnight.* In this place, king prawns and other fish are the Stars of the restaurant – after the superb, wooden décor. The famous king prawns are eaten grilled, pan-fried or spicy (they're really spicy !), the paella's quite simply royal, there's an assortment of fish, and the pasta's only there to accompany the seafood. The *parillada,* an enormous casserole of fish for two people, is a real marine feast.

KEY BISCAYNE > 88, cours Vitton (6th) ℂ **04 78 24 01 00.** *Menus at 130 F and 160 F.* Key Biscayne's an island in Southern Florida, so there's no need to draw a picture – the cuisine and décor are, essentially, marine. On the walls, they've hung magnificent models of yachts, a giant marlin, a parrot... The bar's in brown wood, of the sort you find in schooners, and the walls are in white wood, like an American holiday house. In short, the place is superb, and a simple read of the menu's enough to make fish-lovers' mouths water. When the dishes arrive, they're excellent, and you're not disappointed : the Lyonnais salad has a marine touch, thanks to the addition of tuna, the fish *choucroute* and *couscous* are remarkable, the tuna's served as *carpaccio*, the salmon as a *tartare*, whilst the codfish acras give a Creole touch. After this feast, clients pay their bill without a grimace, even if it's nearly as salty as the Dead Sea.

LA CABANE A HUITRES > 128, rue Boileau (6th) ℂ **04 78 52 61 35.** A cute, cabin-like restaurant in sea blues and white, where the oysters and other produce on display come straight from the Charente, where the owner's father is an oyster-breeder. So, freshness is guaranteed, and connoisseurs of seafood will immediately recognize the quality of the produce served. Corinne Robert gives advice to her clients, and orientates them towards a typically Charentais meal : oysters with a corn pancake with Cognac and accompanied by a glass of dry, white wine (the Cousinaud, for example). All the additional savours go together very pleasantly, and the combination simply serves to bring out the freshness of the seafood. The shrimps, the oysters and the *moules marinières* are also fresh, excellent and simply-prepared : the taste of the sea, and nothing else.

LE DECK > 5, rue Tupin (2nd) ✆ **04 78 42 38 12.** *Menu at 135 F, Dish of the Day at 65 F at midday only. A la carte roughly 180 F. Service till 22.30.* The décor, firstly, is magnificent, and harmoniously combines modernity and 'authenticity', warmth and refinement. You'd think you were really on a ship, especially if you're sitting at the tables at the bottom of the restaurant. The chef beautifully prepares fish and seafood, and invents new dishes everyday, without being afraid of daring combinations which, in the main, come off very well. What a good idea to combine king prawns, morel mushrooms and raw ham, saffron potatoes and fish for a marine version of the Alsatian *bæckeofe*, or sea bream, tuna and salmon for a *Three Fish Plate* ! In the name of quality, ultra-fresh produce is delivered every morning, and, from 10.00 onwards, you can taste oysters.

LE POTIQUET > 27, rue de l'Arbre-Sec (1st) ✆ **04 78 30 65 44.** *Open everyday except on Saturdays at midday and on Sundays. Service till 22.00 during the week, till midnight at week-ends. Menus at 110 F, 130 F and 160 F.* The tables are round, the lights, dimmed, and the walls, made of stone. Who could ask for more to have an enjoyable time, unless it's the sound of the sea ? In addition, Le Potiquet, which is a fish restaurant, offers a tasty and original cuisine, very fresh produce, and delicate dishes which are based on fish in all its shapes and forms : scorpion-fish salad with a thin, sweet red pepper sauce, pan-fried shellfish, roast scallops, marlin, anglerfish and halibut. Those who are not over-keen on fish will also find dishes to their liking among the salad of preserved pig's cheek, the fillet of beef or the *filet mignon.*

L'OCTOPODE > 2, quai Augagneur (3rd) ✆ **04 72 60 93 06.** This yellow and blue barge, anchored on the quays of the Saône, offers a choice between fish and fish. Well, that's not entirely true, because there's also frogs and meat, but the fish is really worth the detour. The menu varies depending on the catch and the mood of the chef, who has a talent for inventing new and successful recipes with new combinations : gâteau of chicken's liver with king prawns, red mullet salad, fillet of sea burbot barded with bacon, anglerfish with morel mushrooms... When the weather's fine, it's a pleasure to dine outside, on the bridge, in the fresh, Rhône air, opposite Lyon's bridges, the Hôtel Dieu and the illuminated Operahouse. In addition, there's no problem parking, because the car park on the quays is enormous, and there's always room.

THE SALMON SHOP > 54, rue Mercière (2nd) ✆ **04 78 42 97 92.** *Open everyday till midnight. Menus from 67 F to 77 F.* Be it the décor (a sort of Canadian lumberjack's cabin), the rapid, smiling and efficient service, or the dishes, everything here's North American – you know, where it gets really cold, and where it's so good to be inside. *The Salmon Shop*, it's a bit like that. You're warmly received, even if the place is often jam-packed (well done, girls !). Here, salmon's eaten in all its forms (*tartare*, grilled on the barbecue, as a fillet in a parcel, half-cooked with olive oil) and is ritually accompanied by toast, unlimited home-made chips and coleslaw. The dessrts also have a Yank accent, and are called cheesecake and brownies.

◆SALAD PLACES

LE JARDIN DE BERTHE > 3, rue Fleurieu (2nd) ✆ **04 78 38 24 46.** *Open from Monday to Saturday from 12.00 to 14.00 and from 19.30 to 22.30. salad and dessert and coffee 55 F at midday only ; entrée, main dish and dessert or cheese 72 F and 75 F ; entrée, main dish, cheese and dessert 98 F.* In a garden, you find salads ! At *Le Jardin de Berthe*, there are a lot of salads. The menu offers 36 different salads : sea salad, chicken salad and cheese salad are just a few possible 'themes'. The lay-out's original : as you come in, you walk past the open kitchens, so that you can have a glance at the food to whet your appetite. Then, once you've sat down, you can admire the attractive, vaulted ceiling above the cellar where you'll find the restaurant.

L'ARROSOIR > 25, rue de l'Arbre-Sec (1st) ℂ **04 78 39 57 57.** *Open everyday except on Sundays and Mondays.* This extremely pleasant café-salad place has the particularity of exhibiting works by invited artists all year long : all the paintings on the walls are for sale (the prices are marked above, and you can always try to bring them down) if they haven't already been sold. So, it offers the ideal opportunity for falling in love with a work of art whilst you eat. In a very friendly atmosphere, everyone can choose between bricks, salads or delicious home-made chips. The bricks, which are originally Oriental, are served here *savoyardes,* *bolognaises* or *océanes.* The copious and varied salads are fresh and full of imagination. It's an address worth noting down because it offers low prices in a lively area.

◆REGIONAL CUISINE
Alsace

LA CHOUCROUTINE > 6, rue Challemel-Lacour (7th) ℂ **04 78 69 06 30.** *Service till 22.00, 23.00 on Match days or when there's an event at the Tony Garnier Hall. Menus at 74 F, 84 F and 99 F. A la carte around 110 F. Carte compter 110 F.* Everything makes you want to come in and try this restaurant : the attractive, red, yellow and green facade, and the prospect of feasting on a good *choucroute,* prepared by a specialist. Benoît Delabays, the owner, is, quite simply, the son of a cabbage- and *choucroute*-producer. It seemed only natural that he should follow the family tradition and add his own personal and creative touch, in the form of specialities which are probably unique in the world : fish *choucroute, choucroute* with preserved duck, *choucroute bourguignonne* with snails, which you can even take away to eat at home. The rest of the menu, from 59 F, gives pride of place to Lyonnais specialities, with the *petit salé aux lentilles* (salt-cured pork belly with lentils), the *entrecôte* and the *andouillette vigneronne* (chitterling sausage with a wine sauce). The reception's charming, attentive and warm. In summer, you'll enjoy the small, shaded terrace.

LE FLAM'S > 12, rue Tupin (2nd) ℂ **04 78 37 51 61.** *Open everyday till 23.30 during the week and till midnight at the week-end. Express 'Formulae' at midday : 43 F, 46 F, 50 F and 56.50 F. 'Flam's Dessert Formula' at 73.50 F, Flam's Entrée Formula at 76.50 F, All Flam's Formula at 99 F, children's menu at 35 F.* The *flammeküeche* is a bread dough, enriched with a mixture of fresh cream, onions and bacon pieces, cooked in the oven at 400°C for 1H30 on a wooden plank and... it's good.. Alsatian cuisine has to be tried, and the fidelity card will, doubtless, make you want to come back and become a real regular.

Daniel et Denise, Le Garet, Chez Georges-le petit bouchon, Les Gônes, Hugon, Le Jura, Chez Marcelle, Le Mercière, La Mère Jean, La Meunière, Le Morgon, Le Musée, Le Novelty, Le Pasteur, Chez Paul, Le Val d'Isère, A ma Vigne and Le Vivarais. To receive this valuable title, these authentic Lyonnais bouchons had to fill a certain number of criteria with regard to the menu, the quality of the service and the conviviality in the restaurant. The official Charter, which is dated 24th March 1997, contains no less than 10 detailed articles, setting out what an authentic Lyonnais *bouchon* should be. "It must serve Lyonnais dishes, like *tablier du sapeur* (marinated strips of tripe dipped in egg and breadcrumbs and either fried or grilled), although other dishes are not excluded. Wine should be served preferably in a jug. Cloth napkins are obligatory, and coffee cups with advertising on them are not desirable", explains the Association's President Chabanel. A criticism sometimes made of *bouchons* is that they're expensive and not accessible to all ! The President's reply : "A *bouchon* is expensive because the title is awarded in function of quality. However, prices should not be allowed to take off. For between 120 F and 150 F, you can eat very well". The result of this new, "Made in Lyon" label – the turnover in these establishment has increased by 20% to 30%. So, having published a book, entitled "Recipes of Authentic Lyonnais *Bouchons*", the Association wants to launch a "Cuisine Day", along the lines of the Music Festival.

Lyonnais Cuisine

CHEZ HUGON > 12, rue Pizay (1st) ✆ **04 78 28 10 94.** *Open everyday except on Saturdays and Sundays. Service till 22.30. A la carte around 140 F.* You don't come here for the décor and the lay-out – this is a real local bistro, which is both old and the size of a pocket handkerchief. It deserves its title of authentic Lyonnais *bouchon*, and hasn't changed an iota since it was opened in 1937. Forget the surroundings (which aren't very attractiveor fashionable), and concentrate on what's on the plate. You'll find an authentic Lyonnais cuisine which varies everyday. Today, it may be the gâteau of chicken's liver, the chicken with vinegar, the *andouillette* tied with string, the quenelles, the parsley ham... everything's served simply, in large casseroles which are placed on the table and are copiously garnished. It's hugely amusing to listen to the conversations of the locals, who hail each other from one corner of the room to the next, and are not in the least embarrased about being overheard by other clients. On the other hand, don't expect to make any savings here, because, if the place has stayed the same, the prices haven't forgotten to rise with the cost of living.

CAFE DES FEDERATIONS > 8-10 rue du Major-Martin (1st) ✆ **04 78 28 26 00.** *www.lesfedeslyon.com.* Sausages hanging from the ceiling, tablecloths with red and white squares, bistro tables and chairs, stuffed benches in shiny leather... here, we are in a Lyonnais *bouchon*, but a real one, which has kept its feet on the ground, in spite of its growing success. It continues to prepare and serve Lyonnais specialities, pork produce and other delicacies for solid appetites.

Lyon *Restaurants - Regional cuisine*

CHEZ MICHEL > 231, rue Marcel-Mérieux (7th) ℂ **04 78 72 62 46.** *Open everyday. Menus at 70 F, 91 F, 99 F and 124 F. A la carte roughly 120 F. Service till 22.30.* This Lyonnais *bouchon* has a long history. Opened in the 1940's as a grocer's, it was subsequently changed into a bar, where you could have a little nibble before heading off to the restaurant. Renovated in 1994, it now offers a Lyonnais cuisine. This is served in two large dining rooms, which can take up to 120 people, and, in summer, the restaurant also has a quiet and shady terrace. The service is rapid, zealous and friendly, and all you have to do is concentrate on your plate. The cuisine's essentially Lyonnais : calf's head with *gribiche* sauce (a sauce made with mayonnaise and capers, herbs and chopped hard-boiled egg), chicken liver *gâteau*, pike *quenelles, tablier de sapeur* (strips of marinated tripe dipped in egg and breadcrumbs and fried or grilled), tripe, pig's tail and trotters, fillet of pike-perch with red wine, salad, *andouillette* (chitterling sausage) with mustard... all of it served with the inevitable *gratin dauphinois* and the only-too-rare *gratin* of cardoons.

CHEZ PAUL > 11, rue du Major-Martin (1st) ℂ **04 78 28 35 83.** A very typical Lyonnais bouchon, with a very simple décor and an easy-going atmosphere. The dining room's, quite frankly, ugly, but who gives a damn - we're here to eat, not to look stylish. You grab a seat where you can, wherever there's room, beside total strangers to whom you pass (having served yourself to them, first) bowls of ham, saveloys, *charcuteries*, lentil salads and muzzle. Then, the hot dishes arrive. These are more Lyonnais than ever, and go from sole to *tablier de sapeur*. When it's time for cheese, it's the same story – the cheese platter and the jar of *cervelle de canuts* (a soft cheese) are handed round from table to table. It's a great place for those with a healthy appetite and for those who enjoy this sort of 'local' atmosphere.

LA MACHONNERIE > 36, rue Tramassac (5th) ℂ **04 78 42 24 62.** *Open every evening and on Saturdays at midday, open on Sundays at midday from September to Easter. Menus at 100 F, 130 F, 150 F, 180 F and 250 F. A la carte around 120 F. Service till 22.30.* La Mâchonnerie isn't a *bouchon*, but a restaurant where they serve an authentic Lyonnais cuisine and where terrines, quenelles, chicken's liver *gâteau* and other specialities are made on the spot. The surroundings are comfortable, the two dining rooms are intimate and warm (thanks to bouquets of flowers and dim lighting), and you feel as if you're eating at a friend's place – a feeling which the friendly reception reinforces : if you fancy a chat with the waitress, she'll willingly oblige, but, if you prefer, she'll leave you to yourself. The owner loves good food, obviously, but is also a connoisseur of wines and beers, and talks enthusiastically about them. As an opener, you'll find crackling, grilled bread and cheese on the tables, and the Gnafron (a cocktail made with *Beaujolais*, cream of blackcurrant and *marc*) promises to kill any germs which may be incubating inside you. The Lyonnais salad, for 35 F only, is a marvel and is served in unlimited quantities in a salad bowl. Then, the choice is difficult between the casserole of pork produce, which is as lean as it can be (!), the *andouillette* (chitterling sausage), the smoked salmon, the tripe and the guineafowl stuffed with mushrooms – all accompanied by a gratin of leaks in Gargantuan proportions. To resume, here, you're served basic Lyonnais dishes, which are beautifully-cooked and as good as you'll find anywhere.

LA MANILLE > 33, rue Tupin (2nd) ℂ **04 78 37 35 93.** *Open from Monday to Saturday. Dish of the Day 50 F ; Dish of the Day and entrée 85 F ; salad from 38 F ; dessert 18 F ; Lyonnais specialities from 50 F. Service from 11.30 to 15.00.* Plate of pork produce, *tablier de sapeur* (strips of marinated tripe dipped in egg and breadcrumbs and fried or grilled), tripe, hot sausage, veal's head or *andouillette* – either you know them and adore them or, perhaps, you're trying them for the first time ? Whichever, don't hesitate to take the *Rue Tupin* and come into this establishment, which has been open since the 1860's. The menu offers dishes other than Lyonnais specialities, and the service is rapid, so that it's ideal for a midday break. *La Manille* only serves food at midday, unfortunately, but the room on the 1st floor takes groups in the evening by reservation.

LA MERE COTTIVET > 20, rue Palais-Grillet (2nd) ℂ **04 72 40 96 61.** *Open from Monday to Saturday. At midday, Dish of the Day at 50 F ; Dish of the Day and entrée or dessert 68 F. Otherwise, menus at 90 F, 118 F and 130 F, à la carte entrées 48 F, dishes 74 F and dessert 26 F.* An institution ! An address you have to visit ! A really good place ! There's no end of good things you can say about this address, which is right in the middle of the *Presqu'île*, and all of them are justified. Here, everything's good, very good. The cuisine is totally Lyonnais, with dishes like the 'Croix-Rousse Caviar' – lentils with hot sausages. The reception's friendly, the service rapid and efficient, and the setting exceptional. The *rosette* (Lyonnais pork sausage) hung from the ceiling, the newspapers which serves as carpet, the tables in iron and wood – the place has a soul. Here, the kitchen's as small as the chef's talent is great ! If you come here once, you should do as many others do, and bring your napkin for the pigeon-hole designed for this purpose. Excellent value for money, marvellous cuisine and generous portions. A bouchon which doesn't knock you out when it comes to paying the bill – a rare treat !

LA MERE JEAN > 5, rue des Marronniers (2nd) ℂ **04 78 37 81 27.** *Open from Monday to Friday from 12.00 to 14.00 and from 19.00 to 22.00. Menus at 69 F (midday), 83 F, 96 F, 114 F, 149 F and à la carte.* An institution since 1923 ! An authentic Lyonnais *bouchon*, just as we like them, with hot sausage and potatoes, just as we like them, and a period décor, just as we like them. Not a false old décor! Here, you really feel the country. As for your diet, never fear because the owner used to be a doctor !

LE MERCIERE > 56, rue Mercière (2nd) ℂ **04 78 37 67 35.** *Open everyday. Menus at 80 F, 119 F and 140 F. Service till midnight on Saturdays and till 23.00 on other days. A la carte around 180 F.* Jean-Louis Manoa, nicknamed The Viking, welcomes all clients to his darling *bouchon*. Having worked pretty well everywhere, he set up shop in this pleasant and lively street. A talented and experienced chef, he likes traditional tastes, as well as the 'authentic' dishes he cooks as simply as possible. His dishes vary with the seasons and with the produce available at the market. Game takes pride of place with the Bresse poultry and cream. But, you'll also find andouillettes, charcuteries (pork produce)and tablier de sapeu (strips of marinated tripe dipped in egg and breadcrumbs and fried or grilled). The pike quenelles are seasoned with *Nantua* sauce (crayfish sauce with butter and cream), and he serves a good knucle-joint of lamb.

LE VAL D'ISERE > 64, rue de Bonnel (3rd) ℂ **04 78 71 09 39.** Despite its somewhat 'highland' name, *Le Val* is an authentic Lyonnais *bouchon*, where you feast opposite a giant Guignol painted on the walls, and where, from 8 o'clock in the morning, you can eat mâchon (a Lyonnais term for snacks), including calf's head with *Ravigote* sauce, *Bobosse andouillette* (chitterling sausage), *tablier de sapeur, sabodet* (thick pork sausage served hot in slices), skate wing, stuffed or grilled pig's trotter and pike-perch. The chef, Jean Abade, has a lot of experience. Everyone eats marvellously, which makes the atmosphere convivial.

LES 3 TONNEAUX > 4, rue des Marronniers (2nd) ℂ **04 78 37 34 72.** *Open from Monday evening to Saturday evening. At midday : Dish of the Day ; entrée, dessert at 45 F ; Dish of the Day and entrée or dessert at 52 F ; entrée, Dish of the Day and deseert at 59 F. Otherwise, menus at 69 F, 82 F, 85 F, 97 F, 149 F. Les 3 Tonneaux* is an address to write down. Since 1930, this Lyonnais *bouchon* has been serving good food. Moreover, the reception's warm and friendly. If you request it, the service is rapid, and, since the menu's more than affordable (including frog in the menu at 85 F), you really must try *Les 3 Tonneaux* – on your birthday, for example, when the aperitif or the cake will be offered free of charge. We told you it was an address to write down !

Lyon *Restaurants - Regional cuisine*

RESTAURANT BRUNET > 23, rue Claudia (2nd) ✆ **04 78 37 44 31.** *Open everyday except on Sundays and Mondays. A la carte around 120 F. Service till 23.00.* Brunet has existed since 1934, and is well-known to all Lyonnais and lovers of good food. When *Les Halles* (The Covered Market) were still in *Les Cordeliers*, where you now find that dreadful multi-storey car park, a certain Mr. Brunet was running this restaurant, which still has its 1930's décor – bistro furniture, tablecloths with red and white squares, Guignol and Gnafron painted on the wall-mirrors. Unfortunately, *Les Halles* were rased to the ground in 1969. Fortunately, on the other hand, *Restaurant Brunet*'s still here, and, today, it's Gilles Maysonnave who runs the place. The aromatic herbs come straight from his garden. The menu's as long as your arm, and is full of Lyonnais specialities, but also includes oysters and fresh frogs. The *gâteau Brunet*, made with apples and pralines, is an absolute marvel. In the morning, *mâchon* (a Lyonnais term for snacks) is served from 09.00 onwards, along with salad of lentils and muzzle, or pig's cartillage and trotters. The pleasant verandah which, in summer, opens onto the street, is heated in winter. The cherry on the cake's the golden service – professional, friendly, warm and… Lyonnais !

Provençal Cuisine

LES CIGALES > 31bis, rue Ney (6th) ✆ **04 78 52 29 24.** *From Tuesday to Friday at midday and from Tuesday to Saturday in the evening. At midday, 3 menus : entrée, Dish of the Day for 50 F ; Dish of the Day and dessert for 60 F ; entrée, Dish of the Day and dessert for 67 F. In the evening, menu at 120 F and à la carte.* The ideal place for getting ready for, or prolonging, your holidays. The Provençal cuisine, the smiling staff and the restaurant's décor will give you the feeling that you're already (or still) in the South of France, by the coast. The bouquets of lavender may even incite you, before you leave, to buy some of the regional produce which is on sale in the restaurant.

UN PETIT TOUR EN CAMARGUE > 14, rue Royale (1st) ✆ **04 78 39 32 33.** *Open everyday except on Mondays, at midday on Saturdays and on Sundays. Service till 22.30. Unique menu 99 F.* In softened lighting and to the sound of a gypsy guitar and a flinty voice, everyone squeezes together at large, wooden tables. This detail is important. Because of the noise and the proximity of strangers, this restaurant is definitely not to be recommended for a romantic dinner – at the risk of a serious squabble. You can't order *à la carte*, and there's a unique menu at 99 F : 10 entrées (squid, mussels, oysters…) served in (very) small earthenware dishes. Once the aperitif, the wine, the dessert and the coffee have been added to the bill, you have to count on around 120 F a head. It's a place you'll remember for its great atmosphere, which is worthy of a southern *féria*.

Savoie

L'AUBERGE SAVOYARDE > 72, avenue des Frères-Lumière (8th) ✆ **04 78 00 77 64.** *Open everyday except on Sundays. Service till 22.30. Menus at 88 F, 125 F and 225 F. A la carte around 150 F.* With the smallest amount of imagination, you'll forget the town, the pollution and the traffic in the nearby street and think you're at the mountains when you eat in this comfortable and friendly dining room. This impression is reinforced by floral wallpaper, the parquet flooring and the copper pans hanging on the walls. The restaurant serves *fondues* and *tartiflettes* (70 F), *raclettes* and *pierrades* (92 F) among the many Savoyard specialities. There's a vast choice of French and Lyonnais dishes and an impressive wine list (all regions of France are represented). To round it all off, the restaurant has 40 years of experience, and provides a service which is friendly, professional and attentive.

LE DOMINOTIER > 14, rue Constantine (1st) ✆ **04 78 27 48 10.** *Open everyday except at midday on Saturdays and Sundays. Service till 01.00. At midday, Dish of the Day at 43 F ; Dish of the Day and entrée or dessert at 53 F ; entrée, Dish of the Day and dessert 63 F ; 'formula' with salad and dessert 55 F. Otherwise, menus at 90 F or fondue, tartiflette or raclette 65 F ; Fondue, Tartiflette or Raclette Menus from 94 F.* Le Dominotier calls itself a crêperie, looks like a crêperie, but is more than that. The retaurant's under new management, but has kept the menu with all the crêpes, and has added *fondues, raclettes* and *tartiflettes*. The mountain feeling is heightened by the cauldrons at the entrance, the tablecloths with red and white squares, the stone walls and the wood everywhere in the upper dining-room. Moreover, you can choose between the mezzanine or down below, beside the aquarium, for example, to make the most of the contrast with the busy *Rue Constantine*. At midday, you can eat a Dish of the Day which has nothing whatsoever to do with crêpes.

◆CUISINE FROM ELSEWHERE

Asia

LE MANDARIN > 15, rue Lanterne (1st) ℂ **04 78 28 45 66.** *Open from Tuesday to Sunday. At midday only, menu at 45 F. Otherwise, menus at 67 F and 89 F and à la carte.* The smiling, Asian reception isn't just a legend, and a visit to *Le Mandarin*, a stone's throw from the *Place des Terreaux* (on the Saône side), allows you to confirm that, here, you're really welcome. The restaurant's nicely decorated – sober, but typical. The thick tablecloths, the wall tapestries and the lighting create a warm and intimate atmosphere. The menu offers a large diversity of Asian dishes, as well as a few treasures. To try absolutely : the frog's legs. Because they're not always cooked à *la provençale* (with tomatoes, garlic and olive oil), you can taste them here à *la mode asiatique* (Asian-style) in dishes like frogs in soya leaves – delicious !

Australia

CANBERRA GRILL > 68, rue de la charité (2nd) ℂ **04 72 41 77 77.** *Open every evening from 19.30. Buffet salads 59 F ; buffet skewers 99 F ; buffet salads and skewers 119 F ; buffet salads and desserts 89 F ; buffet skewers and desserts 119 F ; buffet salads, skewers and desserts 139 F ; buffet salads, skewers, desserts , wine and coffee 159 F.* At *Canberra Grill*, a change of scene is guaranteed : adventure begins in the Perrache Quarter, so there's no point in taking a long flight since, here, you'll find the exotic restaurant you may have been dreaming about. It's just waiting for you ! All you have to do is cross a little wooden bridge to find yourself in the Australian outback. You feel like eating ostrich, kangaroo and cooking your own skewers on the brbecue ? Then, the *Canberra*'s for you ! All the 'formulae' can be eaten in unlimited amounts, so you'll eat to your fill. In addition to these exotic meats, you can also eat poultry, beef or ham with *boudin* (blood sausage), pineapple or bananas, and the combination's pleasant. Part of the fun is that you prepare your own skewer, and start again – as many times as you want. The buffet of entrées is also varied and copious. *Le Canberra*'s an address to eat *en tête à tête* (if you promised her a honeymoon at the other end of the world, a trip here won't cost you very much!), or between friends because a barbecue's a relaxed and friendly way of eating.

Brazil

O'BRASIL > 3, rue de la Fromagerie (2nd) ℂ **04 78 28 49 59.** *Open everyday except on Sundays. Menus at 198 F, 260 F, 310 F and 395 F. Service till midnight.* There's a tropical heat in the *Rue de la Fromagerie*, and *O'Brasil* sets the place alight like only Brasilians know how. During a meal consisting of typically South American dishes, including the delicious grilled meat, client-spectators enjoy a superb show of scantily-dressed girls who dance like Rio Carnival Queens, assisted by supple male acolytes performing extraordinary feats of acrobatics. The show takes place on the stage in the dining room, where there's an atmosphere of samba and lambada. The multi-coloured lamps, the painted wood and the highly colourful frescoes provide a trip to the other side of the Atlantic. Baïla, baïla !

Spain and Portugal

CAFE CUBA > 19, place Tolozan (1st) ℂ **04 78 28 35 77.** *Open everyday except on Sundays. Service till midnight. Tapas from 18 F to 35 F.* To go with your *Cuba Libre* or your *Mojito* (cocktails), there's nothing like eating a few *tapas* at the bar or in the nicely-decorated dining room. Hot, cold, sweet or savoury, everything's allowed and even highly recommended. Many of the recipes come from Spain and Latin America (Serrano ham, *tortilla, guacamole*, squid, gazpacho), but others (and not the least of them) come from elsewhere (marinated salmon, tiramisu). The portions are generous, and having nibbled, eaten or devoured, connoisseurs will let themselves be tempted by a good cigar which comes directly from the *Café Cuba*'s cellars.

Lyon *Restaurants - Cuisine from elsewhere*

EL PORRON > 6, rue Désirée (1st) ✆ **04 78 28 79 22.** *Open everyday except on Sundays. A la carte around 60 F. Service till 00.45.* Bart, the owner, isn't Spanish. Nevertheless, his bar-restauarant, where you can dance, is just like an authentic Andalusian *tapas* bar – both for the décor and for the dishes served. The tiles on the floor, the beams on the ceiling, the corrida posters, the wooden or ceramic tables and the food on display at the bar – everything's here. Bart's travelled round all the bars in Spain, and has kept only the best of them : bread rubbed with garlic and tomato and sprinkled with olive oil, stuffed squid, potato or cheese *croquettes*... The top of the tops is the beautiful, tender and tasty charcuteries – lomo and soubressade are served on slices of grilled bread. From 14 F to 25 F, you're tempted to taste everything. To stay in the atmosphere, you drink large quantities of *sangria* at 50 F for a jug, Spanish or Cuban cocktails, or *manzana*, which is a delicious digestive made with green apples, and which you drink ice-cold, either neat or in a long drink.

LE CAFE LEONE > 8, rue de la Monnaie (2nd) ✆ **04 78 92 93 70.** *Open everyday, midday and evening. Service till midnight. A la carte around 80 F.* Are you missing the hot and electric ambiance of Spanish nights since your last holiday on the Costa Brava ? Then come and visit this pleasant restaurant to enjoy the best Spain has to offer – conviviality, fiesta, a mixed and noisy crowd which discusses, exchanges and dances together to Flamenco rhythms. Olé ! There are sunny specialities on the menu : king prawns, *paella,* all sorts of *tortillas,* sweet peppers marinated in olive oil, meat balls, *zarzuela*... which you can eat as a main dish or in tapas, accompanied by a *chato* (a small wine glass) of red or white wine, of *sangria* or of *daiquiri.*

LE HOME CATALAN > 168, avenue Général de Gaulle - LIMONEST ✆ **04 78 35 10 41.** *Closed on Sunday evenings and on Mondays. See the chapter "Cuisine from Elsewhere – Spain".*

LE MALAGA 2 > 26, rue du Bourbonnais (9th) ✆ **04 78 47 29 07.** *Open everyday. Service till 23.00. A la carte roughly 120 F.* For the last 18 years, this has been a favourite restaurant of entire generations in the *Part Dieu* Quarter. In a warm décor, and in a musical ambiance which is unique in Lyon, the restaurant has now found its place on the other side of the Sâone. This is the perfect moment to come and taste our Spanish and Portuguese friends' delicious specialities. You've probably tasted *tapas* and cod specialities, but you should know that Spanish and Portuguese gastronomy has many other dishes to reveal to you. In summer, the quiet terrace lets you appreciate the musical evenings even more. On Fridays and Saturdays, well-known groups and artists (Flamenco and Fado singers) come to play to the delighted clients. The evening continues into the early hours with a *soirée dansante.*

Greece

LE SANTORIN > 10, rue Pleney (1st) ✆ **04 78 28 33 92.** *Open from Monday to Saturday except on Monday evenings. Dish of the Day 45 F. Menus at 82 F and 102 F. Entrées or main dishes from 37 F, desserts from 18 F. Banker's cards not accepted.* Santorin's the name of one of the Greek Cyclades Islands, an island famous for its very high cliff. *Le Santorin* in Lyon is equally famous, but for the quality of its welcome. In this place, they recognize you the second time you come, and they greet you like an old friend. This is the sort of reception you find very rarely these days. Furthermore, Greek cuisine is full of sun, and, in addition to *moussaka* and vine leaves, you'll find less-known recipes based round lamb and shellfish. The setting's warm – mural frescoes and photos transport you to Greece – and you can sit either in the main dining room or in the mezzanine. *Le Santorin*'s a restaurant to visit for a foretaste, or for souvenirs of, your holidays.

The Islands

COCO D'OR > 3, rue Soufflot (5th) ✆ **04 78 42 39 66.** *Open from Tuesday to Sunday in the evening only and on Sunday at midday. Menu of the Day 100 F. Otherwise, menus at 118 F, 158 F, 195 F and 210 F.* A change of scene guaranteed ! To put the island sun on your plate, to travel by proxy or, on the contrary, to prepare yourself a Seychellian dish... *Coco d'Or* is made for you. The interior looks like a small cabin : the green, the wood, the light and the plants transport you, and the large, mural fresco makes you imagine you're thousands of miles away under the Indian Ocean sun. And yet, you're in the middle of Old Lyon. The second change of scene : a quiet street in *Saint-Jean* ! A stone's throw from the *Place du Change,* the *Rue*

Soufflot is free of the hordes of tourists you find elsewhere in the area. In summer, the *Coco d'Or*'s terrace is opened up, and it allows you to dine in the open with flowers on the table... all that's missing is the sound of the waves. There's a Menu of the Day with three dishes, including king prawns (for 100 F), offering very good value for money ! The menu at 195 F allows you to discover nine different dishes which are typical of Seychellian cuisine. Connoisseurs of fish, shellfish and spicy sauces will love it here. On request, *Coco d'Or* can also organize musical evenings.

LA KAZ KREYOL > 4, rue Verdi (1st)   ©   **04 78 29 41 70.** *Open everyday. Service till 22.30. Menus at 89 F, 98 F and 145 F. A la carte roughly 100 F.* As the song says, "It smells of bananas, vanilla, cumin, sugar cane, mango and tamarin". In the district where you'll find the Lyonnais bistros and *bouchons*, Le Kaz Kreyol has found its little niche, and brings a touch of exoticism and sunshine. A little culinary trip : for curious novices, it's the opportunity to discover tasty, foreign cuisine, whilst connoisseurs come here for the friendly reception and the simple, exotic and spicy dishes with poetic names, like Christophine, Chicken Colombo, Creole Boudin, stuffed crab...

LES FILAOS > 1, place F.-Rey (1st)   ©   **04 78 28 67 60.** *Open everyday except on Mondays. Unique menu at 115 F. Service till 23.00.* This restaurant's a real tribute to the Island of Reunion. They love their beautiful island, and it shows because there are maps of the island everywhere – on the restaurant's facade, on the tablecloths, the napkins, and even on the waitresses' aprons. In summer, the terrace under the trees, with the coconuts and the large, white parasol, is extremely pleasant. In winter, two large dining rooms can take large families and groups. As an aperitif, you have to try the house punches, made with island fruit : coconuts, lychees, pineapple, lime… The entrées vary from *achards* (slices of raw, marinated and spicy vegetables) to crispy and freshly-prepared *samosas*. As fish, there's squid and king prawns, and there's a huge choice of meat : chicken curry, sausages, *cabri massalé* etc. – all eaten with rice, red haricots, lentils and peppers. The place is always full, so that it's essential to reserve. As for the service, it's cool, relaxed and faithful to the rhythm of life in Reunion.

Italy

CHEZ CARLINO > Rue de l'Arbre-Sec (1st). *Open 7/7 days. A la carte around 100 F. Service till 22.00.* This is one of Lyon's oldest pizzerias and has lost none of its dynamism. From the street, the dining room's hidden by ugly curtains, and nothing tempts you to push the door open. Once inside, you find an unpretentious but pleasant décor, a dining-room with a mezzanine above, a ceiling painted *à la Michaelangelo* with a blue sky and cotton-like clouds, photos of Stars and family photos on the walls. At midday, the restaurant's often full, and the service is rapid and efficient. The ambiance is nice and lively, and there are a number of regular customers. On the menu, you'll find most of the pizza 'Classics' : fresh pasta from 35 F to 50 F, wood-fired pizzas from 44 F to 54 F, meat and a large choice of desserts, including a perfect tiramisu. The waiters – genuine Italians with a real accent – are friendly, and wear attractive red shirts which match the tablecloths and napkins. They enjoy talking to the clients and are always polite – even if there's a big football match between France and Italy the following day ! Air-conditioned dining-room.

Lyon *Restaurants - Cuisine from elsewhere*

CHEZ DON VITO > 154, avenue des Frères-Lumières (8th) ℂ **04 78 09 22 88.** *Open from Tuesday to midday on Sunday. Dish of the Day 40 F, salads from 20 F, pasta and pizzas from 39 F, desserts from 18 F.* If children's happiness exists, it's probably to be found on the *Avenue des Frères-Lumières*. Not only are games awaiting them (such as a castle stronghold, where they can play whilst their parents take too much time at the table), but, what's more, they're invited. At midday on Sunday, the children's menu is on the house (for the under-12's and with a maximum of 4 accompanied children), and this sort of generosity merits congratulations ! In addition, the reception given to adults and children alike is extremely friendly. The salads and pizzas are very copious and the prices affordable. Two dining rooms (French ceiling, wooden pillar, copper pans make up the décor) and a terrace are waiting for you, so come to *Chez Don Vitto*!

LA MOZZARELLA > Place de l'Europe (6th) ℂ **04 78 52 25 49.** *Open from Monday to Saturday except on Monday evenings. Salads from 23 F, pizzas from 35 F, pasta from 40 F and desserts from 20 F.* If you've ever dreamt of sharing your pizza with a player on the *Olympique Lyonnais* football team, *La Mozzarella*'s your restaurant. Is it for the sportsman's diet (starch = slow sugar), for the dream of a European Cup (as they wait for the title they have to be satisfied with the square with the same name), or for the friendship they have for this supporter's establishment ? Whichever, from time to time some of the Lyon football players come to eat here and, every time they come, they leave souvenirs of their visit on the walls. The dishes are really copious and, unless you, too, are a serious athlete, you'll have trouble finishing them. In summer, the terrace allows you to take advantage of this beautiful and quiet pedestrian square, its fountain and its trees, close to the very busy *Cours Lafayette*.

LA SILA > 12, quai Illheusem ℂ **04 72 42 21 21.** *See the heading "West Lyon - Collonges to the Mont d'Or".*

LE BALMORAL > 14, rue Lanterne (1st) ℂ **04 78 28 72 53.** *Open everyday except on Tuesdays. A la carte around 100 F. Service till 23.30.* Le Balmoral's a little corner of Italy at the heart of Lyon. Its seven, large round tables are waiting to welcome you – be you just two or in a group of six – and to reveal the savours of Italy rather than a simple steak and chips. This must be the reason why students don't seem to like the place. You'll find pasta and pizzas, as well as more refined Italian dishes. The reception's typical and worthy of southern character. At weekends, the evening ends with a dance in the cellar.

LE FABRIZIO > 24, quai Saint-Antoine (2nd) ℂ **04 78 38 00 11.** *Dish of the Day 50 F ; Dish of the Day and entrée or dessert 69 F ; 'formula' 65 F at midday only. Salads from 47 F, fresh pasta from 48 F, pizza from 48 F. Menus at 110 F and 125 F.* Even before you sit down, you're introduced to Italian customs and traditions, because, here, they don't want you to leave rapidly in order to free the table for the next client, but, on the contrary, they leave you the chance to appreciate the cuisine. And what you find here will make you want to stay at the table because "Italian" doesn't simply mean "Pizzeria". Le Fabrizio is a restaurant offering all sorts of Italian cuisine. Inside, you can sit near the window, below the French ceiling, or in the mezzanine, behind the imposing stone columns. Unless, in fine weather, you prefer the terrace. The view's superb onto the Palais des 24 Colonnes and the ochres and reds of Saint-Jean, through the plane tress which line the Quai Saint-Antoine.

LE SAINT LAURENT > 82, rue Béchevelin (7th) ℂ **04 78 58 75 15.** *Open everyday except on Sundays and on Public Holidays. Dish of the Day 48 F at midday only ; Menu of the Day 80 F ; pizzas from 39 F and desserts from 24 F ; Chef's Menu 138 F.* This is a very beautiful restaurant with stone walls decorated with paintings. There's a dining room and a mezzanine, where you can choose from 19 sorts of pizzas, *escalope milanaise*, pan-fried and flambéed king prawns with cinnamon, House lasagna and Sicilian *farfalle*. Faithful clients are rewarded – the menu named after them allows them to win free meals, a bottle of *Dom Perignon* champagne, and even a dinner-show in the *Lido* in Paris.

LE VESUVE > 17, rue de la République ℂ **04 78 50 52 39.**

146 *See the heading "West Lyon – Oullins".*

MAMMA MIA > 66, rue de la Charité (2nd) ℂ **04 72 56 10 52.** *Open from Tuesday to Saturday. One dish 42 F, two dishes 54 F, three dishes 68 F.* Rarely has the expression, "Mamma Mia, it's good !" been so well-deserved ! *Mamma Mia* is the temple of pasta. All colours, all shapes, eat on the spot or take away – the choice is yours. The pasta's made in the restaurant everyday and served the same day. On the table, you'll find twisted forks and instructions on how to use them. But *Mamma Mia*'s more than that because the menu also offers *crouties* ! *Crouties* are large slices of bread made with yeast and garnished with different things. Different *crouties* are on offer, but you can modify their composition. You'll stuff yourself with them ! The quality and friendliness of the reception is the cherry on the cake. If you really don't feel like going to the *Perrache* district, *Mamma Mia* delivers by rollerblade, either to your home or to your office.

MONNA LISA > 44, cours Charlemagne (2nd) ℂ **04 78 37 85 25.** *Open everyday in season, but closed on Sundays in winter. At midday : Dish of the Day at 48 F ; entrée, Dish of the Day and dessert 65 F. Otherwise, pizza at 42 F, menus at 85 F, 120 F and 150 F. Service till 23.00.* Italian style and spirit reign here. The style is everywhere on the walls of this pizzeria, which is entirely pink and decorated with paintings. As for the spirit, it's on your plate. The pasta's home-made, and there's an enormous choice of pizzas, along with ice-creams and crêpes, which allow you to finish your meal on a sweet note.

PIZZA LATINO > 243, rue Marcel-Mérieux (7th) ℂ **04 78 72 62 97.** *Open 7/7 days from 06.00 to 01.00. Dish of the Day at 45 F. A la carte around 90 F.* Before or after the match, this is the ideal pizzeria (right next to the stadium and large enough to take crowds of fans) to set yourself up with a pizza cooked over a wood fire in front of you, or with some spaghetti or an *escalope milanaise*. The place is pleasant, the service ultra-rapid, and the servings more than generous. The red walls put you in the right frame of mind for supporting your favourite football team. There are two very kitsch Roman statues in the entrance, and the restaurant boasts a terrace and a heated verandah.

PIZZA PINO > 106, rue Président-Edouard-Herriot (2nd) ℂ **04 78 38 30 15.** *Open everyday. Non-stop service from 11.30 to 03.00. salads from 38 F, pizzas from 48 F, beef carpaccio at 59 F, Dish of the Day at 49 F, desserts from 26 F and ice creams from 29 F.* An institution ! The meeting-place ! In short, a restaurant which is always full. It's impressive to see the queues every evening at the weekend until very late (even in the winter when it's cold). Si si ! It's true, and it's been like this for years. It's true that Pizza Pino has the advantage of an incredible location at the corner of the Place Bellecour, that the cuisine is good and that the portions are generous. Special mention has to be made of the beautiful, salads and profiteroles : aïe, aïe aïe, they're delicious and enormous ! The décor's colourful but not overloaded. In winter, the verandah allows you to see and be seen, and is replaced in summer by the terrace, which is beautifully decorated with exotic plants. Pizza Pino also celebrates special occasions and, for example, is particularly attractive at Russian New Year.

Pizzeria Restaurant

Don Vito

ℂ **04 78 09 22 88**
154, av. des Frères Lumière
69008 Lyon

Lyon *Restaurants - Cuisine from elsewhere*

PIZZAPAPA > 34, rue Tupin (2nd) © **04 72 40 02 99.** *Open everyday. At midday : hot dish and entrée or dessert 59.90 F. 'Formula' with two carpaccio dishes 49.90 ; menus at 79,90 F and 89,90 F ; Children's Menu at 39 F.* Pizzapapa's more than a pizzeria – it's a whole family of pizzerias, and this has its advantages and disadvantages. Like in most restaurant chains, there's never any surprise, even if the menu's large and well-presented. Each dish is photographed, and that helps you to choose and whets your appetite ! In addition, there's a small margin for manouevre in the 'formulae', and you can normally negotiate a fruit juice instead of an American soda. There's a large diversity of pizzas, meats, Italian hams and, of course, pasta. At midday, the *'Rapid Formula'* allows you to be served within 20 minutes, so it's perfect for a quick lunch break.

PIZZA PUCE > 5, place du Commandant-Arnaud (4th) © **04 72 00 00 40.** *Open 7/7 days. Menus at 39 F, 49 F and 59 F. A la carte around 90 F. Service till 23.00.* Pizza Puce has been serving pizzas in the *Croix-Rousse* for 13 years. But now, it also sells its produce in the *Tassin* district as well. The pizzas are simple (from 35 F to 73 F) or more 'complicated' (from 71 F to 79 F), and there's an infinite variety for every taste. They're cooked over a wood-fire, the pasta's freshly prepared, and the tomato sauce is home-made. On the menu, you'll also find salads from 20 F to 24 F which are served by an attentive team. If you don't fancy leaving the house, the pizzas can be delivered to your home provided that you live in or around the Tassin area, in the 1st or 4th arrondissements or in *Calioure*. **Other address : 46, avenue Victor-Hugo - TASSIN-LA-DEMI-LUNE 04 72 59 09 09.**

PIZZERIA NAPOLI CHEZ NICOLO ET VITO > 45, rue Franklin (2nd) © **04 78 37 23 37.** *Open from Monday to Saturday. Service from 12.00 to 14.00 and from 19.00 to 23.00. Pizzas from 32 F to 68 F, meat dishes from 54 F to 71 F, desserts from 15 F, ice-creams from 25 F. Menus at 69 F and 74 F.* Chez Nicolo et Vito has been serving Italian specialities and grills since 1966. It's the Star's pizzeria. Yes, yes, the Stars ! Tennis players, cyclists, singers... everyone comes to *Nicolo et Vito* ! And every celebrity who comes here during his stay at the nearby Sofitel Hotel is photgraphed, and the photo's hung on the wall. So, there are lots of photos... The pizzas are served in three sizes – small, medium and large, which is practical and lets you gauge your appetite. The meat's incredibly tender – to be recommended.

RIGOLETTO > 1, quai de la Libération © **04 72 42 04 14.** *Open everyday except on Sundays and Mondays. Menus at 78 F and 98 F. See the heading, "West Lyon - Collonges to the Mont d'Or".*

India

NAMASTE INDIA > 17, quai Romain-Rolland (5th) © **04 78 42 38 20.** This gastronomic restaurant's specialized in Indian and Pakistani cuisine. It offers the opportunity to discover new tastes in an authentically-Indian décor – even the waiters are in colourful, traditional dress. The ambiance is warm, and India offers you one her most beautiful smiles. The Indian cuisine is refined, delicate, perfumed and light. As entrées, the choice is difficult between the *samosa*, the *raita* and the *kalegi tikka* (a House Speciality, consisting of liver skewers in spices). Then, the chicken, lamb and prawns are prepared with *balti, vindaloo, Madras* or *biryany* recipes. The fish and meat is accompanied by Basmati saffron rice and vegetables, like spinach, aubergines and mushrooms. *Namasté* also runs a catering activity, and delivers to your home, or prepares the food for banquets, birthday parties, weddings and other special occasions.

Japan

LE KABUTO > 169, rue Cuvier (6th) © **04 72 74 93 28.** *Open everyday except on Sundays and at midday on Mondays. Menus at 54 F and 74 F at midday, and at 79 F, 98 F, 125 F, 150 F and 198 F in the evening. A la carte around 120 F. Service till 22.00.* There's no need to take the plane to find yourself in the Land of the Rising Sun. You just have to open the door of *Le Kabuto*, and you're in a different world. Everything here's authentically Japanese. A host of *sushi* and raw fish dishes are on offer. Everyone sits on the floor on tatamis, and the meal's eaten off low tables. You'd better know how to use chopsticks because there are no knives and forks – it's difficult to start with, but you quickly learn. The décor's strictly Japanese and makes you forget that Lyon's the city of andouillette, so that everyone rapidly converts to the *Sushi* religion.

OKAWALI > 3, rue Louis-Vitet (1st) ℭ **04 72 07 82 61.** *Open everyday except on Sundays. Service till 22.30. Menus at 98 F, 124 F and 138 F. A la carte around 120 F.* The Japanese décor's soft and harmonious – a lot of wood, particularly for the tables, the chairs and the benches, but also for the beams on the ceiling, the screens and, of course, the chopsticks and even a bit of crockery. Soft lighting, attractive bouquets of flowers, bamboo plants in plots – it's simple, but in very good taste. The service is extremely smiling and friendly and, what's more, many of the clients are Japanese (nothing but men – where are the Japanese women ?), which is a guarantee of quality. In Japan, it's customary to drink beer during meals, so that you have a chance to try the *Kirin Ichiban* to go with the very light cuisine served here. The famous *miso* soup is drunk throughout the meal to accompany the fillets of mackerel and salmon, or the steak with *tofu,* served with rice and raw, marinated vegetables. Everything's eaten in attractive oval or rectangular stone plates and the dishes are served in a host of little bowls. As a dessert, the chocolate cake, one of the restaurant's best desserts, is worth its weight in cocoa. The curious will try the House Ice-Creams made with red haricot beans and green tea.

RESTAURANT TAKEYAMA > 6, rue Thomassin (2nd) ℭ **04 72 40 29 18.** *Open from Monday to Saturday. At midday : menus at 65 F, 85 F and 89 F. Otherwise, menus at 99 F, 139 F, 149 F and 199 F.* It's difficult to talk about Japanese cuisine without talking about the inescapable *sushis* : little balls of rice covered with layers of raw fish. But, if you want to discover less-known Japanese dishes, *Takeyama* offers other treasures : *surimi* salads and a large variey of skewers, for example. This new Japanese restaurant has three dining rooms, each separated by a step. The decoration's traditional – pure, white with wood. Raw fish and chopsticks – a complete change of scene on the *Presqu'île* !

Lebanon

ADONYS > 13, rue Puits-Gaillot (1er) ℭ **04 72 00 95 15.** *Open 7/7 days. Service till 01.00. A la carte around 50 F.* The two Lebanese brothers who welcome their clients and do the cooking have brought back from their native country a series of delicious recipes, made with fried aubergines, parsley-green *taboulé,* very fresh salads and small pasta with sesame seeds. Everything's delicious, delicate and fresh, because it's all prepared the same morning. To discover – the hot galettes stuffed with chicken's liver, fillets of turkey or lamb. The spices and herbs – thyme, cinnamon, parsley and mint – will delight the most refined of palates. As a dessert, you have to try the Oriental pastries with honey, almonds or walnuts. This is a good address, which makes a change from the *shish-kebab* places which are full of chips and vast amounts of mayonnaise. In addition, the prices are very low, and you only pay 17 F for a sandwich or 49 F for an *assiette dégustation.*

Maghreb

RESTAURANT TUNIS > 9, rue des Marronniers (2nd) ℭ **04 78 37 37 01.** *Open everyday. Menus at 69 F, 76 F, 79 F and 99 F, couscous from 52 F to 115 F, tagines 65 F.* In the middle of the *Rue des Marronniers,* which is home to many famous restaurants and shops, you'll find this authentic little address. As you go in through the door, you're transported to the Maghreb countries. The setting's not up to much, but that's what it's like down there ! In summer, a few tables can seat clients outside, in the pedestrian street. The menu offers numerous Tunisian specialities : *couscous,* skewers, *bricks* and *tagines,* as well as North African wines. Don't forget to leave room for the pastries, which are particularly good and which you can choose from the dessert tray. Every Friday, the *Tunis* proposes a *paella.*

Persia

LE PETIT PERSAN > 8, rue Longue (1st) ℭ **04 78 28 26 50.** *Open everyday except on Sundays and Mondays. Menus at 59 F at midday, 85 F, 125 F and 255 F. A la carte around 120 F. Service till 22.30.* Once you've crossed the threshold, you find yourself elsewhere, and Monsieur Massoud takes you warmly under his wing and talks to you enthusiastically about his sunny cuisine. He gives marvellous advice to his clients, recommending (depending on your tastes) the caviar from the Caspian Sea, the duck with nuts in a sweet-and-sour sauce or the beef skewers with saffron.

149

So British

SIMPLE SIMON > 13, rue Thomassin (2nd) ℂ **04 72 41 04 98.** *Open without interruption from 11.00 to 18.00.* The setting's charming, very cosy and cute. The produce is fresh, since it's made on the spot everyday by Monsieur and Madame Régnier, who may not be English but who prepare delicious specialities like salmon turnover, Indian meat loaf, cheese and onion pie and Cornish pie. At tea time, the scones, cheesecake and cakes are eaten with a nice cup of tea, of course, and with the little finger in the air, if you please.

Yank Specialities

NEW YORK STREET > 20, rue Mercière (2nd) ℂ **04 78 42 33 55.** The décor's 100% Made in the USA : red, padded benches, photos of the Big Apple on the walls, glasses and carafes in transparent plastic. The waitresses are all foreign students, preferably blonde with a charming little accent, and they serve you with an unfailing smile. Dishes include Caesar salad, enormous pizzas, hamburgers and cheeseburgers, marinated chicken legs and grilled pork ribs. At the week-end, they abandon their trays long enough to perform a little choreography for the delighted clients on the mezzanine.

Tex-mex

EL SOMBRERO > 9, rue Pizay (1st) ℂ **04 78 30 90 79.** *Open everyday except on Saturdays, Sundays and at midday on Mondays. Menus at 69 F at midi and 100 F to 135 F in the evening.* As you walk into the restaurant, you're transported 12 000 kilometres from the *Rue Pizay*. Mexico ! Here, you'll find chilis, beef and chicken *fajitas,* cactus salads, *guacamole,* cumin and peppers. If you want to taste a bit of everything, try the *Discovery Menu* at 120 F. As an apéritif, don't forget the tequila paf (the waitress makes a little vocal demonstration along the lines of "aïe, aïe, aïe, ariba" at the moment you have to down it it one, but don't be embarrassed, everyone gets the same treatment) and, if you like wine, don't hesitate to order the Chilean wine, because it's excellent. The menu's presented like a Mexican newspaper, the owner and staff are dressed in desperados, and the music gives a lot of ambiance. This restaurant's a 'must', and it's so popular that it's always full. Don't forget to reserve.

EL TEX MEX > 3, rue Pizay (1st) ℂ **04 78 29 23 23.** *Open everyday except on Sundays and at midday on Saturdays and Mondays. Menus : 69 F (midday), 100 F, 120 F and 135 F.* The Mexican adventure begins well : between the yellow walls, you'll find lots of little corners in a succession of intimate and convivial rooms which are in no way like a noisy cantina. On the menu, there are giant cocktails (up to 1 litre) and mezcal, classic *tacos, enchilladas, burritos* and *chili con carne,* tasty meat and delicious avocado and red bean purées. Watch out, when the waitress tells you it's spicy, you'd better believe her !

Thailand

BAN THAÏ > 3, rue Ferrandière (2nd) ℂ **04 78 37 44 06.** *Open everyday. At midday, entrée, main dish and dessert 68 F. Otherwise, menus at 98 F, 128 F, 138 F, 168 F and à la carte.* The *Bân Thaï*'s a superb place. All three dining rooms have their own charm. The large dining-room downstairs is warmly decorated in wood and houses a wooden painting which is sculpted in relief – it's magnificent. If you go to the dining room between the two floors, you'll be surprised to discover an aquarium at your feet – a unique experience in Lyon. The room on the first floor's more intimate, but equally pleasant. As for the cuisine, when you learn that the *Bân Thaï* team "is honoured to serve the Thai Royal Family", you'll have understood that the address is to be classed in the top category of restaurants for the subtle sweet-and-sour blends of Asian cuisine. The quality of the service is worthy of the legendary Thai hospitality. It's worth noting that the midday 'formula' offers excellent value for money ! We repeat one last time – *Bân Thaï* is a restaurant you have to visit.

L'OISEAU DE PARADIS > 4, rue Guiseppe Verdi - Angle rue de l'Arbre-Sec (1st) © **04 72 00 83 80.** *Open everyday except at midday on Saturdays and Sundays. Menus at F, 79 F, 83 F and 93 F and à la carte.* L'Oiseau de Paradis *is a little corner of exoticism and of escape, just a stone's throw from the Opéra, at the heart of a district which is very lively in the evening. Thai cuisine includes recipes based on beef, king prawns, frogs and duck, and* L'Oiseau de Paradis *has perfectly mastered them all. It's not for nothing that the Confrerie of Asian Gastronomy awarded it the Golden Lotus Prize in 1996. A small word for connoisseurs – the menu's entirely steamed. The decoration prolongs your exotic journey, and the traditional calligraphy, picture frames and chandeliers provide a moment of escapism. When it's fine, you can also sit on the terrace, in the pedestrian section of the* Rue de l'Arbre Sec.

Turkey

CAPPADOCE > 4, rue Constantine (1st) © **04 78 29 20 05.** *Open everyday from 11.00 to 01.00. Kebab sandwiches to take away 23 F, on the spot 27 F, 'plates' from 40 F, pastries 10 F.* If the *Rue Constantine* is the realm of the kebab, the *Cappadoce* restaurant is, without doubt, its king. This is an address which doesn't empty until late into the night but, please, don't park on the bus stop like so many people. All the tastes of Turkish cuisine await you at the Cappadoce, and, in addition to the well-garnished kebab sandwiches, the restaurant offers *galettes*, 'plates' and skewers. You won't be able to resist the *Kofte Platters*, which combine meat balls, chips, rice and raw vegetables (48 F). Take the time to sit down at the end of the room, which has been turned into an Oriental salon with benches and low tables and a mural fresco of the banks of the Saône. The *Cappadoce* proudly displays its Year 2000 Hygiene Certificate, as well as the certificates for earlier years – an address you can be sure of ! It's a pity that the TV music's a bit loud... and you won't park on the bus stop, will you ?

◆'DANCING' RESTAURANTS

JAMBALAYA > 1, quai Jean-Baptiste-Simon - FONTAINES-SUR-SAONE © **04 78 22 41 26.** *Open 7/7 days. Menu 165 F.* There's a large room, a large terrace and a choice place allocated to the dance floor in this 'dancing' pub. You have to come around 20.00 during the week and at 21.00 at the weekend to be able to dine and then let yourself go to the music organized by the DJ, Antonio. The ambiance is festive every day of the week. Groups are welcome, but you can also come in smaller numbers. The menu includes an entrée, a main dish, a dessert, coffee and wine, and the chef can even concoct a special menu on request.

LE BALMORAL > 14, rue Lanterne (1st) © **04 78 28 72 53.** *Open everyday except Tuesdays. A la carte around 100 F. Service till 23.30. See the heading, "Cuisine from Elsewhere – Italy".*

LE MONTE CRISTO > 52, quai Clémenceau - CALUIRE-ET-CUIRE ✆ **04 78 29 45 92.** *Open every evening from Tuesday to Saturday. Menus from 195 F to 315 F. Le Monte-Cristo welcomes you to a sumptuous décor, and proposes a refined cuisine and a variety of music. Those who want a candle-light dinner or a party between friends are guaranteed to have an excellent time.*

LES ANNEES FOLLES > 13, quai Romain-Rolland (5th) ✆ **04 78 42 44 14.** *Unique menu at 225 F.* If John Travolta or the Clodettes were passing through Lyon, they'd certainly come to pay a visit to *Les Années Folles.* Betwwen the kir, the peanuts and the starter, you can have a little turn on the dancefloor to warm yourself up. The menu includes fish and traditional Lyonnais dishes, like andouillette. After some cheese, a dessert and a short rest, you're set up for the entire night. You won't be able to resist the call of the DJ, and even less the call of Frankie Vincent or the *Compagnie Créole.* Good Lyonnais food, rapid service, festive music, friendly ambiance – all dance-lovers, come and move your body and bury the office life.

TAPA'S CLUB > 110, quai Pierre-Scize (5th) ✆ **04 72 00 09 13.** *Open everyday. Unique menu at 200 F.* At *Tapa's Club*, a restaurant-cum-karaoke bar-cum-dancehall, you have to reserve your table, because there's a real party every evening ! groups come here to celebrate birthdays, stag nights, office parties... people mix, chat, sing and dance together. It has to be admitted that karaoke's a good way of bringing people together. The menu includes an aperitif of your choice, a salmon or hot goat's cheese salad, a steak, a breast of duck or the Fish of the Day, cheese or *faisselle* (drained soft fresh cheese), dessert, coffee and a carafe of red or rosé wine per person.

GOING OUT

LIVING IT UP

Contrary to what certain disgruntled people say, there's a lot to do in Lyon and, when it comes to going out, you've got a huge choice of things to do. The proof can be found in this *Petit Futé* guide – dozens of pages of addresses which constitute just a small percentage of the establishments in the city. Several styles of soirées can be envisaged. An improvised drink between students which might end at 2 o'clock in the morning at *L'Amphi*, an organized "booze up" in the inevitable *Rue Sainte-Catherine*, a quiet and relatively sober evening on the Quays of the Saône (5th and 9th arrondissements) with dinner in a restaurant in *Saint-Jean* followed by a visit to a pub and, perhaps, by a nightclub. You can also spend a good evening in three establishments which are just a few metres from each other in the Rue Terme (1st) : firstly, an institution, the *Palais de la Bière* ; then, a fashionable and original place, the 2P+C and, finally, a karaoke bar/nightclub, the *Opéra Rock*. For those who want everything in the same place, there's no contest – it has to be the *Bahia Impérial* in Estrablin. But, you can also start with an aperitif at the *Rouge-Gorge*, then go to eat, head off to play billiards at *66 Road Café*, do a bit of bowling in *La Part Dieu* and finish the evening in a nightclub like *Le Fridge* (for those who like techno music). Alternatively, you can mix things a bit by starting at *Le Bus Café*, eating at *Caffé Milano*, having a digestive at *Le KGB*, before moving off to dance at *Le First* or *Le Box Office*. You must absolutely go to *Le Kart* and *Le Mégazone*. But, if you do, you should go and have a drink afterwards. Infact, there are endless solutions for spending 2 hours or the whole night, for spending a fortune or less than 100 Francs.

FIND US ON THE NET
www.petitfute.com

◆**CINEMAS**

LE PATHE > 79, rue de la République (2nd)   ✆   **08 36 68 20 22.** *Le Pathé* was entirely renovated a few years ago. It's the 'American concept' in the city centre. There's an immense popcorn-soda bar at exorbitant prices, escalators, 3 storeys, immense cinemas, unbelievable screens, and seats with popcorn-holders built into the arm-rests. In short, the works (fortunately, because it costs 50 F for a place), with, sometimes, a few problems with the air-conditioning.

When you see "VO" next to the title of a film, it means that the film's being screened in the Original Version (that is to say, the language it was filmed in) with sub-titles in French. Be careful, the original title of the film is often changed, so that the title in French is rarely a literal translation of the original title. In Lyon, films are rarely screened in the original version in the big cinemas. Here are a few addresses where you've got more chance of finding what you're looking for :

AMBIANCE > 12, rue de la République (2nd) 08 36 68 20 15 • **ASTORIA - UGC > 31, cours Vitton (6th)** 0 892 700 000 • **CIFA SAINT-DENIS > 77, Grande rue de la Croix-Rousse (4th)** 04 78 39 81 51 • **CNP BELLE COUR > 12, rue de la Barre (2nd)** 08 36 68 69 33 • **CNP ODEON > 6, rue Grôlée (2nd)** 08 36 68 69 33 • **CNP TERREAUX > 40, rue Edouard Herriot (1st)** 08 36 68 69 33 • **COMEDIA - UGC > 13, avenue Berthelot (7th)** 0 892 700 000 • **FOURMI LAFAYETTE > 68, rue Pierre Corneille (3rd)** 08 36 68 05 98 • **LE CINEMA > Impasse St-Polycarpe (Terreaux, 1st)** 04 78 39 09 72 • **LE CINEMA OPERA > 6, rue Joseph Serlin (1st)** ✆ 04 78 28 80 08.

LES 8 NEFS > 20, rue Thomassin (2nd)   ✆   **08 36 68 00 29.** The only cinema in the city centre to offer such low prices : 30 F for all, all the time (except at midnight on Saturdays). Cinema halls with 50 places classed as Historic Monuments, several medium-sized and one large cinema hall with a balcony and a screen which may not be as big as its compeitors', but which is more than sufficient. The halls aren't always very clean (although they're not catastrophically dirty), but you never have to queue for too long and the price, the price ! Morning showings at 20 F ! Amazing !

UGC CINE CITE > Quai Charles-de-Gaulle (Cité Internationale) ✆ **08 36 68 68 58.** This is the multiplex *par excellence*. Difficult to imagine a cinema which is larger... or more expensive (51 F). You'd think you were in Beaubourg. Walls in glass, and escalators which never seem to end. Incredibly large cinemas and screens, a bar... and it's impossible to miss the Ciné Cité when you arrive in Lyons — the luminous beams which move across the city sky aren't invaders from outer space, but incredibly powerful projectors installed on the UGC roof !

Lyon *Going out - Cafes-Theatres*

UGC PART DIEU > "La Part Dieu" Shopping Centre ✆ **08 36 68 68 58.** The only cinema to offer these prices (*Les 8 Nefs* costs 30 F, but isn't in the same central area) : 29 F a showing for all, all the time and on two levels. The only problem is that you have to be willing to walk here in the evening…

◆ CAFES-THEATRES

ESPACE GERSON > 1, place Gerson - Saint-Paul (5th) ✆ **04 78 27 96 99.** *Mondays and Tuesdays : 'Discovery Shows' (professionals come to present their shows which are due to be programmed in the near future). Wednesday to Saturday : there are a series of comedians, and the programme changes every three weeks.* A pure café-theatre in the finest tradition, where the public first discovered so many talents who have subsequently become famous. It's the reference in the Rhône-Alpes, since all selections for Comedy Festivals take place in this convivial theatre. The atmosphere's friendly and, after the show, you can have a drink in the bar or billiards-room and meet the comedians. It's worth noting that, at the Espace Gerson, you can also hire rooms to organize private soirées in cellars fitted out for this purpose (350 m²).

LE BOUI BOUI > 7, rue Laurent-Mourguet (5th) ✆ **04 78 37 40 30.** You laugh and drink at *Le Boui Boui*. A young and very popular café-theatre where the Lyonnais troupe, *Les Astrobaldings*, got their first experience. Admission fee 60 F.

◆ DINNER-SHOWS

L'ANE ROUGE > 11, rue Juiverie (5th) ✆ **04 78 39 37 55.** At *L'Ane Rouge*, for 220 F, you get a decent meal and a comic show. What more does the people want ? In an underground room, you begin to eat, and wait impatiently for the artist who's performing here, just 1.5 metres away, on the little stage. Infact, the young owners wanted everyone to finish their main dish and cheese before starting the show. There then follows 1h30 of hilarity, after which dessert is served, and you leave, delighted with your evening.

LES PIEDS DANS L'PLAT (THE FEET IN THE DISHES) > 18, rue Lainerie (5th) ✆ **04 78 27 13 26.** The place is surprising when you don't know it. The name gives a clue... but only when you know the place. Here, apart from having a good time eating and laughing at the comedian's sketches (count at least 250 F), the originality of the place derives from its design : the entrance is at plate-level, so that, when you're sitting at your table, you can… see which of the girls coming in isn't wearing any knickers.

◆ BARS - PUBS

BRASSERIE GEORGES > 30, cours Verdun (2nd) ✆ **04 72 56 54 54.** This is a real brasserie. Rows of benches, monumental *choucroutes* and, above all what interests us, real brasserie beer – *Rinck* beer. A family beer, named after the owner, and which is now brewed by *Heineken* in Alsace.

CAFE CUBA > 19, place Tolozan (1st) ✆ **04 78 28 35 77.** *Open everyday except on Sundays. Service till midnight. Tapas from 18 F to 35 F.* To go with your *Cuba Libre* or your *Mojito* (cocktails), there's nothing like eating a few *tapas* at the bar or in the nicely-decorated dining room. Hot, cold, sweet or savoury, everything's allowed and even highly recommended. Many of the recipes come from Spain and Latin America (Serrano ham, *tortilla, guacamole*, squid, gazpacho), but others (and not the least of them) come from elsewhere (marinated salmon, tiramisu). The portions are generous, and having nibbled, eaten or devoured, connoisseurs will let themselves be tempted by a good cigar which comes directly from the *Café Cuba*'s cellars.

CAFE ANGLAIS BAR AMERICAIN > 24, place de la République (2nd) ✆ **04 78 42 52 91.** A few dozen metres from the *Grand Café des Négociants*, the *Café Anglais* attracts the same clientèle – a clientèle corresponding with the prices and the interior decoration, top bracket. As soon as the sun peaks through the clouds, the terrace giving onto the *Rue de la République* is packed, and, throughout the year, you can taste waffles and crêpes, made with batter containing a hint of rum.

GNOME ET RHONE > 157, avenue Jean-Jaurès (7th) ℂ **04 78 60 27 86.** A bar and a pub, the *Gnome* is open day and night. The ambiance and lay out are more bar than pub, but that doesn't make the place any less attractive, and it's frequented by a relatively young clientèle. A choice of beers and a billiards table help you to spend a pleasant evening.

KGB > 2, rue des Bons-Enfants (7th) ℂ **04 37 28 63 36.** A new and hyper-Sloane establishment. It's very dark, very classy, very large, full of boxes to eat in privacy, and there's a vodka bar with cigars, a valet parking service and a courtyard where you can dine. The red signs and the walls decorated with shards of broken glass and barbed wire are, perhaps, there to remind you of a certain communist luxury.

L'AMBASSADEUR > 22, quai Romain Rolland (5th) ℂ **04 72 41 83 79.** *Open from 18.00 till dawn.* A luxurious ambiance for a refined pub ofering numerous cocktails (with or without alcohol), which you can drink either at the bar or comfortably installed in little, purple-coloured salons. Throughout the year, 'Theme Evenings' are organized with the sponsorship of alcohol suppliers. To prolong the evening, you just have to go down a few steps in order to dance in the cellar.

L'ARLEQUIN > 1, quai des Célestins (2nd) ℂ **04 78 37 41 80.** Since the *Country Rock Café* was replaced by *L'Arlequin*, the establishment's lost much of its flavour. The record covers, the motor-bike... all this has disappeared and hasn't been replaced. Along with that, the menu's banale. All that's worth noting is the milkshakes, which are very good and not at all expensive.

L'EDEN ROCK CAFE > 68, rue Mercière (2nd) ℂ **04 78 38 28 18.** Since it changed management a few years ago, *L'Eden* has become a concert specialist. Unfortunately, the room the groups play in is quickly full. Nevertheless, you can spend just a short while here, and then go and eat a hamburger with a beer, like the average American. Because, sometimes, with a lot of ketchup, being an average American's not that bad.

L'ETOILE OPERA > 26, rue de l'Arbre-Sec (1st) ℂ **04 72 10 10 20.** This very recent bar-restaurant relies heavily on its very "in" décor. Very stylized and simple, the room's very modern and successful. Outside, you'll find a few tables in the street. Everyday, there's a 'two-star apéritif' from 18.00 to 20.00.

L'OXXO > 7, avenue Albert-Einstein - VILLEURBANNE ℂ **04 78 93 62 03.** Without doubt, one of the establishments selling the largest quantity of beer in the whole of Gaul ! (It has to be admitted that the half of beer's incredibly cheap). *L'Oxxo* is a festive temple for thousands of students who live in, or close to, the *La Doua* Campus. Every evening, the ambiance is "Let's get pissed to forget the studies". In short, folly reigns well into the night, and many students come out not knowing what to hang on to, unless it's the aeroplane wings which decorate the establishment's entrance.

LA BRASSERIE DES BROTTEAUX > 1, place Jules-Ferry (6th) ℂ **04 72 74 03 98.** *La Brasserie des Brotteaux* proposes something of a return to the past. A return to the beginning of the century. The décor hasn't changed much since then, and it's quite pleasant.

Lyon *Going out - Bars & pubs*

LA BRASSERIE VICTOIRE > 5, place Carnot (2nd) ✆ **04 78 37 37 24.** A brasserie in shades of blue and with a decoration based on football (see the giant football table). Nothing surprising when you know that it belongs to Florian Maurice and his brother, Max. A nice team, a pleasant terrace in summer, the perfect spot for the third half.

LA FACADE > 45, rue Mercière (2nd) ✆ **04 72 42 98 13.** Some tend to say that *La Façade* is a bit middle-class and a bit dear. Maybe, but so what ? It's not bad, and there's always good music, either taped or live during the Concert Evenings.

LE 110 VINS > 3, rue Saint-Georges – Vieux Lyon ✆ **04 78 37 99 64.** *M° Vieux-Lyon. Open from Monday to Thursday from 18.00 to 01.00 and on Saturday from 11.00 to 01.00.* This wine bar's in a very old house, lacated in Saint-Georges (the Old Town). Here, you can sit in a charming cellar and taste a range of wines accompanied whith typical food (French cheese and Lyon sausage). You can also buy bottles of the wine which took your fancy to take home as gifts or for your own cellar.

LE 203 > 9, rue du Garet (1st) ✆ **04 78 28 66 65.** Le 203 is the fashionable bar of the moment. All the 20 to 30 year olds come here. It's typical of the "switched on – convivial" trend. An original theme – the 203, of which you'll always find several parked in front of the door or not far away. You'll find some modified 203's, one of them made to look like a pick-up – a bit bizarre. So, the theme's original, the bar's a bit small, the décor changes, because it consists of works by exhibiting artists (very, very, very trendy, this idea of exhibitions in bars), the street's a bit busy, the meal's are a bit expensive, the owner knows how to talk about everything and nothing... but it all works !

LE BARTHOLDI > 6, place des Terreaux (1st) ✆ **04 72 10 66 00.** At *Le Bartholdi* (the name of the sculptor who made the statue in the square), something's always happening. Three weeks per month, the soirées are nearly all devoted to culture and discussion. There are "Café-Philosophy" soirées for which *Le Bartholdi*'s become famous over the last 5 years, but also "Science" soirées, general 'meet-ups', concerts... all this while you eat for around 50 F. The atmosphere's very often intellectual, but always interesting, fun and inexpensive.

LE BISTROT DE LA PASSERELLE (THE FOOTBRIDGE BISTRO) > 36, quai Saint-Antoine (2nd) ✆ **04 78 37 61 32.** New owners. A place where you can bet on the horses when you've finished your shopping in the market. It's not very big, but *Le Bistrot de la Passerelle*'s nevertheless a place where you feel at ease. It's located opposite the footbridge which leads to "24 Columns" (The Law Courts). Hence, its name.

LE BISTROT DE LA PECHERIE > 1, rue de la Platière (1st) ✆ **04 78 28 26 25.** There's been a bar on this site for 70 years. Originally, it was the *Bar des Pêcheurs*. Then, last spring, it became *Le Bistrot de la Pêcherie*. It's filled with more or less unusual objects and some superb mural paintings. *Le Bistrot* has also decided to let its clients dance, so that there's Argentinian Tango on Mondays, Flamenco on Wednesdays, Exotic music (Cuban, Brazilian or African) on Fridays and Saturdays. Avoid the terrace (beside the quays) during rush hours.

LE BISTROT DE LA PLAGE > 40, rue de la Charité (2nd) ✆ **04 78 42 25 12.** The doorway into *Le Bistrot de la Plage* is a 'spatial-temporal' short-cut to the South. However, there's no need to come in swimming trunks. Pastis and conviviality are sufficient to create the ambiance. The cuisine here's simple but popular. L*e Bistrot*'s jam-packed at midday !

LE BUS CAFE > Face au 18, quai Sarrail (6th) ✆ **04 72 74 40 91.** A pub on one of the pavements along the quays of the Rhône with a superb, shady terrace. The idea's original, provided you can still see the Rhône after a heavy night. Since alcohol should be drunk in moderation, there should be no problem. In the evening, the place is often full of serious students who have a lecture the following morning on the quays and who set a good example.

LE CAFE CHANTECLER > 151, boulevard de la Croix-Rousse (4th) ✆ **04 78 28 13 69.** There are two good reasons for stopping for a moment at the *Chantecler*. Firstly, the quiet and shady terrace, which is very pleasant in summer. Secondly, and above all, for the home-brewed beer, which you absolutely have to try. There are three colours, three different tastes, but only one

price for a half - 13 F.

LE CAFE DE LA MAIRIE > 4, place Sathonay (1st) ℰ **04 78 28 08 67.** *Le Café de la Mairie*'s a café for regulars. Some have been coming for tens of years to this real local café which serves the *pétanque* players on the *Place Sathonay*. It's charming because the square is now very beautiful and pleasant, the half of beer's among the cheapest in Lyon (12 F, like the *pastis*) and, finally, you're well away from the traffic.

LE CAFE DU MARCHE > 25, quai Saint-Antoine (2nd) ℰ **04 78 38 06 31.** Bright, spacious and new, *Le Café du Marché*'s a pleasant spot. The clientèle's mixed, the drinks served are classic, and the prices are correct. So, you can't criticize this bar, situated opposite one of the city's nicest markets (open 7/7 days). Many Lyonnais come here for lunch and for an apéritif.

LE CAFE 100 TABAC > 23, rue de l'Arbre-Sec (1st) ℰ **04 78 27 29 14.** The promise has been kept - *Le Café 203* now has a little brother. You'll find the same ambiance as at the elder, but this one's reserved for Non-Smokers. This may be THE concept for the 21st century, for all those who are fed up with having to share other people's toxic and smelly tobacco smoke.

LE CHARLES'INN > 50, rue Mercière (2nd) ℰ **04 72 40 08 19.** This place has a new owner. No, there aren't just restaurants in *Rue Mercière*, there's also *Le Charles'Inn*. The bar's a gourou of whiskies (an unbelievable choice) and of beers, and its location in this busy street is such that it's often difficult to find a place.

LE CINTRA > 43, rue de la Bourse (2nd) ℰ **04 78 42 54 08.** There's an intimate ambiance and a piano in the evening. It's the sort of place for a good cocktail, surrounded by smart people.

LE FBI > 11, quai Pierre-Scize (9th) ℰ **04 72 53 02 11.** Who wouldn't love to be held for questioning for 24 hours in the *FBI Café* ? You'll find sexy policewomen, an improvised décor, and you can be sure you won't be arrested for drinking a bit too much.

LE FIRST CLASS VIP APERO > 15, place Jules-ferry (6th) ℰ **04 37 24 19 46.** *Le First Class VIP Apéro Club* rises out of the waves from 19.00 to 01.00 (from Tuesday to Saturday). The bar's decorated like a yacht, with a series of little, Mediterranean salons. Immediate boarding for a trip to the realm of pleasure, but, watch out, it's a trip in first class. If you haven't yet understood, the place is very fashionable.

LE FOOD CONTINENTAL CAFE > 147, avenue Jean-Jaurès (7th) ℰ **04 37 27 00 96.** *Le Food Continental Café* is well-known as a restaurant (see this heading), but it's also a pleasant and spacious bar, where there's sometimes a DJ at aperitif-time.

LE FUNAMBULE > 29, rue de l'Arbre-Sec (1st) ℰ **04 72 07 86 70.** It's sometimes difficult to find a seat at *Le Funambule*. So, if you succeed, you'll want to stay for a while, because it's enjoyable - at least, more enjoyable than standing up in a queue.

LE GORMEN'S CAFE > 12, quai Maréchal-Joffre (2nd) ℰ **04 78 38 48 38.** Fancy a change of air ? Then, head to *Le Gormen's*, which offers a complete change, right in the centre of Lyon. Initially, you're not tempted to come here. You have to drive down quays, and you tell yourself that it's going to be noisy. But, not at all. Along the Saône, beside the barges, the café's terrace is well-protected from the urban pressure, and the best of it is that you sip your drink in a deckchair, with, at drinks time, a few crisps. Inside, there are three bars – a Beer Bar, a Rum Bar and a Tequila Bar. Throughout the year, the café organizes Students Evenings, Theme Evenings and concerts, and screens major sporting events. It's also a restaurant.

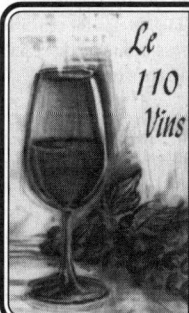

LE GRAND CAFE DES NEGOCIANTS > 2, place Régaud (2nd) ✆ **04 78 42 50 05.** This place is a bit starchy, very Parisian and very middle-class at tea time. It's different on the terrace where you'll find all sorts of clientèle. The café's become a popular place for the Intelligentsia of the *Presqu'île*. Recordings for *Radio Scoop* and TV programmes hosted by Michel Field are made at *Le Grand Café des Négociants.*

LE HOT ROAD > 58, quai Pierre-Scize (5th) ✆ **04 78 27 37 38.** *Le Hot Road* is the fashionable pub for Lyon's Golden Youth. Apart from that, the establishment's very pleasant and, since 2000, the new owners have done a lot to make the atmosphere enjoyable.

LE NEW ORLEANS > 12, quai Romain-Rolland (5th) ✆ **04 78 38 11 31.** This is a Jazz and Blues pub. The Chippendales appear on Friday nights, on Wednesdays there's a Latino Evening, there's karaoke on Mondays, Jazz, Rock and Boogie-Woogie on Thursdays, as well as Theme Evenings, concerts... a great ambiance for all ages to have a good time.

LE PALAIS DE LA BIERE > 1, rue Terme (1st) ✆ **04 78 27 94 00.** When it comes to drinking beer, it's impossible to do better than Le Palais de la Bière. The figures are impressive – 300 bottled beers and 13 draughts. You wonder if there's a single country in the world which doesn't brew this drink, which was invented by the Egyptians at a time when they still hadn't fully understood the role played by yeast. It's really THE international drink for those who like to 'travel hard'. *Le Palais* also has some 50 whiskies on sale. At meal times, *Le Palais* is also known for its mussels and chips... with beer, obviously !

LE 2 PIECES + CUISINE (TWO ROOM FLAT + KITCHEN) > 3, rue Terme (1st) ✆ **04 78 30 02 01.** Normally, you hear, "Let's go into the drawing room for a drink". Here, it may be the drawing room, but also the kitchen, the bathroom, the dining room, the bedroom... in short, every room in the flat can be used for a drink, and there's no-one to stop you smoking in the toilet or drinking whisky in the bath – quite the opposite. In addition, you dance in the corridors ! It's going to be a real mess when the parents get home !

LE REPUBLIQUE > 19, rue Professeur-Louis-Paufique (2nd) ✆ **04 78 42 59 56.** People normally refer to "*Le Rep*" when they talk about this place in the city centre which is both trendy and chauvinist. The mixture of types is such that you always feel at ease in *Le Rep*, where the clientèle is, mainly, young. You eat simply but correctly (pasta, chips...), you drink, you play chess (watch out, there are some very good players) and you listen to music, either played by groups in concert, or taped and projected onto a large TV screen. For drinking your beer, there's either the terrace (relatively quiet), the room on the first floor or the room at the bottom, which is vaulted, in stone, and has rustic, wooden tables.

THE ALBION > 12, rue Sainte-Catherine (1st) ✆ **04 78 28 33 00.** This is the English pub *par excellence*. The dark and protected (almost austere) ambiance is so British. With the barmen, it's best to talk in pints and half-pints rather than in large and small glasses. Rugby and football matches are shown on a large screen, there are concerts at the week-end, and you'll also find the sacrosanct game of darts.

THE BARREL HOUSE > 13, rue Sainte-Catherine (1st) ✆ **04 78 29 20 40.** Opposite *The Albion, The Barrel House* belongs to the same owner and welcomes young groups for concerts during the week. In the legendary R*ue Sainte-Catherine*, *The Barrel House* is another beer pub (but home-brewed beer), which is often crowded and where the atmosphere's over-excited.

Discothèques

BOX OFFICE > 30, rue Eugène-Deruelle (3rd) ✆ **04 78 95 37 02.** *On Wednesdays and Thursdays, free admission. On Fridays and Saturdays, admission 60 F.* To stay at the top of the charts, the *Box Office* is enjoying incredible success with its Theme Evenings (disco's still trendy, and famous artists pull in the crowds) and with Student Evenings. It's the most popular club among all sorts of night-owls, particularly because of its late hours which mean that you don't have to move off for an "after". The *Box Office VIP's* a club within a club, a sort of leopardskin cocoon where, behind tinted glass, you get served as you eye up the nightclubbers. Then, there are tigresses and leopards to chase into the nocturnal jungle...

DANCING NEW HOLLYWOOD > 6, rue Henri-Barbusse (8th) © **04 78 69 42 77.** *Open on Mondays, Thursdays and Sundays from 14.30 to 20.00 as well as on Thursdays, Fridays and Saturdays in the evening.* Tango, waltz, two-step... the New Hollywood has an entire programme. Here, you dance in twos on the dancefloor, body to body to the sound of devilish rhythms. Move, baby, move !

FIRST CLASS > 13-14, place Jules-Ferry (6th) © **04 37 24 19 46.** Built into the old *Les Brotteaux* Station, *First Class* is the trendiest and most fashionable club in town. The DJ's perched up in the clouds and, from this vantage point, he conducts the assembly till the early hours. Excellent address for Very Important People only.

L'ALIBI > 13, quai Romain-Rolland (5th) © **04 78 42 04 66.** *Open everyday from 22.00. Admission fee : 80 F with a drink.* Beside *La Grange au Bouc*, *L'Alibi* welcomes a similar public. By that you must understand that you can only get in if you've already undergone a face-lift or a hair implant. The establishment recommended for those who are at least 30 years old. At least. On Tuesdays, it's disco fever, on Wednesdays, it's girl's night and, on Thursdays, the Theme Evenings change all the time.

L'OPERA ROCK > 7, rue Terme (1st) © **04 78 39 99 88.** *Open from Tuesday to Saturday from 22.30 onwards.* This is a karaoke discothèque and a lot more besides... It's in a festive spirit that *L'Opéra Rock* offers people of all tastes the chance to have a good time. During the week, Philippe proposes evenings combining the intimacy of the karaoke bar and the atmosphere of a discothèque. At the bar, Tony serves his cocktails and, on Wednesdays, offers one free to all the girls. Things heat up at the weekend and, if you succeed in calming the two presenters, you may just be able to get to bed before sunrise. Warm, musical ambiance.

LA COUR > 4, rue Mulet (1st) © **04 72 00 84 00.** *Open from Thursday to Saturday and the evening before Public Holidays from 22.30 onwards. On Thursday, Student Evening. On Friday, African Evening. Admission fee : 80 F with a drink, except on Saturdays : 70 F with a drink.* There are a lot of young people (students especially) and lots of Theme Evenings in this establishment which, as is necessary on the *Presqu'île*, has a very classy décor, partly because of its stone walls, and partly because of its recent renovation. Good music, good ambiance, good décor. No hesitation, a good place for an evening with friends.

LA GRANGE AU BOUC > 9, quai Romain-Rolland (5th) © **04 78 37 41 55.** *Open from Tuesday to Saturday from 23.00 onwards. Correct dress obligatory.* This is certainly one of the best-known establishments in town, and is even known to many non-Lyonnais. You'll find a 'mature' clientèle, Erotic Evenings, karaoke, and a door which isn't necessarily closed to young people, because 'mature' people like the young. After all, you have to please the client ! Except, of course, that the clients often find pleasue on their own.

The best addresses in the four corners of France

www.petitfute.com

LA MARQUISE > 20, quai Augagneur (3rd) ☎ **04 72 61 92 92.** *From Wednesday to Saturday from 19.00 onwards. Free admission.* This is a barge on the Rhône, where you spend a good evening between friends.

LA SALSA DISCOTHEQUE > 10, rue Pizay (1st) ☎ **04 72 07 79 32.** *Open everyday except on Mondays from 22.30 onwards (18.00 on Sundays). Admission fee : 30 F except on Fridays and Saturdays : 80 F with a drink.* So, there's a salsa ambiance, but not always. Sometimes it's African, American, West Indian (yes, with rum), Jamaican – but it's always hot, exhausting and really good !

LE BAHIA IMPERIAL > The Abbaye Crossroads - ESTRABLIN (38) ☎ **04 74 57 25 02.** *Open only on Fridays, saturdays and the night before Public Holidays. Admission fee : 45 F or 70 F with a drink. How to get here : Motorway A7 heading towards Marseille, Vienne exit. Then, direction L'Isle d'Abeau, it's 4 kms away.* Le Bahia's a large, multi-activity complex and is, quite simply, great. There's a traditional dancefloor and a techno dancefloor (which rotates), a restaurant, a snackbar, a karaoke club and a bowling alley... all this at the same price as elsewhere. Don't miss an outing here.

LE FISH > Opposite 21, quai Augagneur (3rd) ☎ **04 72 84 98 98.** *Open from Thursday to Saturday from 10.00. Free admission (without drink) till 11.00. Thereafter, 60 F (during the week) or 80 F (Saturdays) with a drink.* The large, blue boat opposite the *Hôtel Dieu*, that's *Le Fish*. And *Le Fish* is the top/trendy/in/smart nightclub of the moment. The concept's great. There's a bar-room right down the length of the boat, with a view of Lyon's illuminated bridges. There's a terrace for summer evenings (when it's not reserved for a private soirée), and the dance-floor's just below. You'll come across 20 to 25 year olds, 25 to 30 year olds, sometimes in suits, older guys with their girlfriends, rich businessmen, and, of course, there's always techno music. You should note that there are 'Special Evenings' with well-known DJ's. In summer, the Thursday Evening Drinks are a 'must' if you want to meet everyone who is anyone in the city.

LE MOULIN ROUGE > 49, quai Barbusse - ALBIGNY ☎ **04 78 91 30 38.** *Open on Fridays, Saturdays and the night before Public Holidays. Admission fee : 50 F on Fridays and 70 F on Saturdays with a drink. Bus 43 leaving from Vaise and the Quai de la Pêcherie.* This is Lyon's first musical multi-pole, occupying more than 2 700 m². It's complete, spacious and beautiful (the vaulting). Four theatres, six DJ's and six dance-floors : techno, disco, funk-groove, a summer dance-floor with a swimming-pool and two dance-floors at the club for over-25's. You'll find all ages. Watch out for the radar on your way back to Lyon !

LE PALACIO > D51 - QUINCIEUX ☎ **04 78 91 18 04.** Between Neuville and Anse, *Le Palacio* plays trendy music at the weekend. Young people come to the bar and the dance-floor, where they throw themselves about. As the night advances and fatigue begins to set in, people head for *Le Spaghetti Bar* or for the sweet-distributor to recover a bit of energy. Classic but efficient.

LE PARADISO CLUB > 24, rue Pizay (1st) ☎ **04 78 28 07 85.** *Open everyday from 22.30 onwards. Admission fee : 90 F with a drink. The following drink : 50 F. 'Afters' from 06.00 onwards with admission fee 50 F including a drink.* "There's always something happening at *Le Para*", the publicity reads. It's true, and there's something for every taste, even if, and it has to be said, *Le Paradiso* makes special efforts to please the girls. On Tuesdays and on the first Thursday of every month, there's a Chippendales Evening. On Wednesdays, it's Girl's Night, with free admission and one free cocktail. The last Thursday of every month, it's Singles' Night. All other Thursdays, Theme Evenings sponsored, more often than not, by alcohol manufacturers, allow you to leave with little presents or to win drinks.

LE XYPHOS COMPLEX > Route de Poleymieux - COUZON-AU-MONT-D'OR ☎ **04 78 22 31 55.** *Open on Fridays, Saturdays and the night before Public Holidays. Admission fee : 50 F with a drink before 23.00 and 70 F afterwards. How to get here : head down the Saône, heading towards Rochetaillée and Couzon ; then follow the signs.* Great – a shuttle service leaves *Le Xyphos* at 05.00, and takes you back to *Les Terreaux*. Do you remember the voice of Doc in the film "Return towards the Future" (French version) ? Well, for the last few years, the same guy who dubbed that voice has been doing the radio advertisements for *Le Xyphos*. Commercially, this was an excellent idea because, now, everyone knows *Le Xyphos*. Or, more exactly, the *Le Xyphos* Complex, because it's a real complex of nightclubs on several levels. There are a number of totally different dancefloors, and each has its name, its own décor, its snackbar, and all the dance-floors are frequented by a very young clientèle. The ambiance at *Le Xyphos* is one of the best in the region, and, to get things really going, gogo dancers shake themselves sensually on the bar.

Karaoke

LE BAHIA IMPERIAL > L'Abbaye Crossroads- ESTRABLIN (38) ℂ **04 74 57 25 02.** At *Le Bahia*, everything's great : the nightclub, the bowling alley, the restaurant, the snackbar and the karaoke bar. There's a presenter, a large choice of songs and a giant screen which increases the ambiance and gets everyone singing.

L'OPERA ROCK > 7, rue Terme (1st) ℂ **04 78 39 99 88.** *Open from Tuesday to Saturday from 22.30 onwards. Admission fee : free from Tuesday to Thursday (without a drink), 50 F on Fridays and 70 F on Saturdays with a drink.* L'Opéra Rock is a nightclub but also (and especially) a karaoke bar. Infact, it's also a bit of a pub, so there's a lot of people, and not everybody comes for the same thing. So, when you sing, you'd better make it good ! Ambiance guaranteed.

TAPA'S CLUB > 110, quai Pierre-Scize (5th) ℂ **04 72 00 09 13.** *Open everyday. Unique menu at 200 F.* This is a restaurant-karaoke bar-dance hall. Think of reserving for your birthday, your best friend's stag night, your annual office get-together, your exam results, etc.

LE TRANS EUROP EXPRESS > 29, cours d'Herbouville (4th) ℂ **04 72 98 23 00.** This nightclub and karaoke bar has more than 3 000 titles in its repertoire. *Le Trans* is one of the karaoke bars preferred by connoisseurs. Following its sucess, *Le Trans* has just put one over the other karaoke bars – your performance can now be taped on CD. Quite simply great... or, sometimes, grotesque !

◆ FUN

Billiards Halls

66 ROAD CAFE > 8, place des Terreaux (1st) ℂ **04 78 27 37 42.** Here, and somewhat removed from the dance-floor, you'll find a number of tables for billiards enthusiasts – and there are plenty of them. Lots of people come here just for that. Others come here for a game or two when they're fed up with flinging themselves around the dance-floor. The temptation's great : 10 F a game. Cool !

ACADEMIE DE BILLARD DE LYON > 31, rue Martinière (1st) ℂ **04 78 27 01 59.** Here, there are 15 billiards tables and seats around a central table for competition days. A little bar's now trying to brighten up the particularly austere ambiance of the Académie. It's possible to take courses from September onwards. For 1 200 F, you have the right to two hours a week in a group in order to learn a game which is an illustration of numerous Laws of Physics.

BILLARD PUB 23 > 23, quai Perrache (2nd) ℂ **04 72 56 00 93.** The Billard Pub 23 is virtually the first establishment which the traveller from the South will see on his arrival in Lyon. It's a pub which has 19 billiards tables and is open from Monday to Thursday from 11.00 to 01.00, on Fridays and Saturdays till 03.00 and on Sundays from 13.00 to 01.00.

L'OXXO > 7, avenue Albert-Einstein - VILLEURBANNE ℂ **04 78 93 62 03.** In this exclusively-student pub, you can enjoy yourself for very little money : 10 F for a half of beer and 10 F for a game of billiards !

LA BILLE NOIRE > 17, rue Claudius-Pinchon (3rd) ℂ **04 72 13 91 84.** With 7 American billiards tables, 2 snooker tables, 1 French billiards table (few people know how to play it) and 10 pool tables, you can try all the styles, everyday from 15.00 to 01.00. It's great to be able to play all four, one after the other, but it's rarely possible because there are a lot of enthusiasts. It costs 63 F an hour (subscriptions possible), and it's certainly one of the best billiards halls in Lyon.

Lyon *Going out - Bars & pubs*

PALACE SNOOKER > "La Part-Dieu" Shopping Centre – Level 1   ©   **04 78 60 67 24.** French and American billiards, snooker – there's the choice, and the tables are regularly brushed and beautifully-maintained. But, watch out, you have to pick your moment to play billiards at the Palace Snooker. Here, you pay by the hour, and rates depend on the hour you play at. You start gently at 22 F an hour in the morning, only to finish the night at 56 F an hour. A that rate, you may prefer to have a drink at the bar or in one of the simple but pleasant rooms. There are pictures of islands on the walls, and giant portholes giving onto the billiards tables. The terrace, which gives onto the side of the library, is pleasant, because it's far away from the street and because the armchairs are comfortable.

SNOOKER CHARLEMAGNE > 84, cours Charlemagne (2nd)   ©   **04 78 37 20 73.** This enormous snooker hall's behind the much-criticized Perrache Station.

Bowling alleys

AMF BOWLING PART-DIEU > 20, rue Eugène-Deruelle (3rd)   ©   **04 78 62 64 32.** *One game at 30 F and 35 F in the evening, plus 12 F for shoe hire.* Very bright, modern and pleasant, the Part-Dieu Bowling Alley has electronic scoring with screen control for the 50 alleys available. Once you've got your shoes on and the computer set, you're off for a series of 10 times 2 bowls. And you should take your time because, if you don't, the game will be over in 10 minutes. If that should happen, there's always something else to do – have a drink at the bar, play a game of billiards or a video game.

LE BAHIA IMPERIAL > L'Abbaye Crossroads - ESTRABLIN (38)   ©   **04 74 57 25 02.** Le Bahia Impérial's a huge complex combining a discothèque, restaurant, karaoke bar and disco bowling. There are 8 alleys available for those who have paid their admission fee to the establishment. Admission to Le Bahia costs 45 F and a game of bowls 35 F (without shoe hire). To get here : as you leave Vienne, it's 4 kms away on the road to Isle-d'Abeau.

BOWLING MARIUS BERLIET > 80, rue Marius-Berliet (8th)   ©   **04 78 01 21 65.** *One game at 30 F and 39 F in the evening, shoe hire included.* Here, there are 14 'variable-speed' alleys that you have to be a pro to understand the point of this), as well as a bar to prolong your evening. Because the problem with this bowling alley is that it's isolated in the 8th *arrondissement*. It's fine for those who live in the area, except for the fact that there's nothing else in the vicinity !

Casino

LE LYON VERT > 200, avenue du Casino - LA TOUR-DE-SALVAGNY   ©   **04 78 87 02 70.** Yes, you may have seen it on progammes shown by TF1 and M6, the *Le Lyon Vert* casino's the largest in France. There's an immense car park, 400 slot machines (one-armed-bandits or card games, minimum stake 2 F), three tables for the game of *Boule* (minimum stake 5 F) and, of course, a room you have to pay to get into in order to play, like James Bond, at Baccarat or Roulette, for example (high minimum stake). The décor's rather pleasant (waterfall), and the bar prices are reasonable enough for an establishment like this. Watch out for the way you're dressed : if you come in jeans and trainers, you'll get turned away. But, you can always get by, because the casino hires out trousers (business, business !).

LE PHARAON > Cité Internationale. It took three official requests and all the weight of Lyonnais politicians to enable the casino to open its doors. This establishment also belongs to the *Partouche* Group and was built at the same time as the *Hilton* (*Partouche* property !). It's the only casino in France to be found in a town which isn't a seaside resort. Its inauguration, which included the participation of a number of Stars, cost millions. The décor's Egyptian and superb. As this guide goes to press, the slot machines still haven't arrived.

Race Courses

HIPPODROME DE PARILLY > Avenue P.-Mendès-France - BRON   ©   **04 78 77 45 45.** Yes, you may not think of it, but, in Lyon, you can also go to the races and bet on Jolly Jumper and the blue helmet. All you have to do is go to the race track, located on the same site as the park and stadium in Parilly.

SPORTS

◆STORES

General stores

DECATHLON > 21, chemin Jean-Marie-Vianney - ECULLY ℂ **04 78 43 35 32.** If *Go Sport* is remarkable for its line of clothes, *Décathlon*'s remarkable for its line of equipment (tents, rucksacks..). The *Décathlon* brand is, in fact, a guarantee of quality comparable to that of the big makers names, and it's much less expensive. All the equipment's rigorously tested before it's commercialized. When you buy it, you'll also be impressed by the competence of the salesmen, who really know their subject. **Other address : "Portes des Alpes" Shopping Centre 04 78 26 69 01.**

DEFI SPORT > 85, rue Moncey (3rd) ℂ **04 78 60 83 56.** Here, you'll find nothing but known brands for sports shoes, tee-shirts, shorts, track suits, and you look at the clothes to the sound of rap.

GO SPORT > 62, rue de la République (2nd) ℂ **04 78 42 36 03.** Here, there are three floors of equipment, accessories and clothes for sportsmen, holiday-makers or simply for those who like to wear something other than jeans and a shirt. In this field, *Go Sport* distinguishes itself by its own label of clothes, called *Wanabee*, which offers excellent value for money. Sales for these products are the deal not to be missed. As far as equipment's concerned, prices are often interesting, but not always, because, for example, there's no rebate on skis at the end of the season. **Other address : "La Part Dieu" Shopping Centre 04 72 60 00 00.**

INTERSPORT > Ecully Grand Ouest Shopping Centre ℂ **04 78 33 06 98.** In this 800 m² sales area in Ecully, you'll find all sports, all labels, salesmen who know what they're on about, and, above all, ranges where you're sure to find a good bargain. Brands and quality – you have to pay for that. So, the shop seems expensive, but it isn't any dearer than others selling exactly the same products.

INTERSPORT CARIBOU > 86, Grande-Rue-de-la-Croix-Rousse (4th) ℂ **04 78 29 50 90.** Who would have imagined that there's a shop as huge as this in *Grande-Rue-de-la-Croix-Rousse* ? Incredible ! All sports and leisure activities are covered, and you'll find equipment for beginners and for super-pro's. There's also a wide range of clothes, which are set out by label. The salesmen have to be among the most knowledgeable in town. If you like this sort of shop, you should allow an hour for a look-round.

SPORTSTOCK > 8, cours Gambetta (7th) ℂ **04 78 58 61 36.** *Sportstock* sells resolutely modern gear. Most seasonal sports are represented in this nicely-arranged, little shop. The lower level's reserved for textiles. The reception's relaxed, and the prices par for the course. To be recommended to those who don't like the department stores.

TROC SPORT > 30, avenue Charles-de-Gaulle - CHAMPAGNE ℂ **04 78 66 25 30.** *Troc Sport*'s a shop where you can buy and sell second-hand sports equipment. Hence, products are seasonal. As in all second-hand shops, you'll find the best alongside the worst. The ideal thing's to drop by often, thereby multiplying your chances of coming across a real bargain. Worth noting – the warm welcome always given by Marco.

Specialized Shops

CAP TENNIS > 31, quai Victor-Augagneur (3rd) ℂ **04 78 60 47 01.** This tiny shop's for tennis-lovers. You'll find rackets, balls, but also shoes (even for the smallest kids) and clothes : socks, shorts, tee-shirts, pullovers, small sports tops for ladies. The shop also strings rackets. For a nylon string, for example, count around 110 F to 350 F, depending on the quality. In general, the prices are not very expensive for a small shop.

FOOT LOCKERS > 26, rue de la République (2nd) ℂ **04 78 42 30 35.** Foot Lockers sells tee-shirts, shorts and caps. Infact, the shop's oriented towards all sports where you use your feet a lot. The range of shoes is one of the biggest in town, and a lot of the shoes are top of the range. **Other address : "La Part-Dieu" Shopping Centre (3rd) 04 78 62 96 13.**

INTERNATIONAL ROLLERS RIDERS > 33, rue Bossuet (6th) ✆ **06 61 95 68 90.** What sport allows you to get plenty of fresh air whilst muscling soft thighs and buttocks – rollerblading, of course ! On Friday evenings, rollerbladers get together for a major circuit through the city – all other traffic has to give way, because the city belongs to the rollerbladers. On Sunday afternoons, beginners learn how to break, stop and handle themselves on pavements, without knocking over everyone who happens to be in their way.

SCUBA > 7, place Commandant-Arnaud (4th) ✆ **04 78 27 81 43.** When you push open the door of *Scuba Lyon*, it's to buy diving equipment. The shop sells equipment to allow you to go 20 000 leagues under the sea, but it also has a training school with State-qualified teachers.

SPODE > 13, rue Tupin (2nd) ✆ **04 78 42 02 42.** Small but powerful. At *Spode*'s, there's not a large sales area, but they've, nevertheless, made the shop pleasant. Oriented towards athletics, Spode offers a large number of shorts for runners, running shoes and reviews. The reception's very friendly, but the average price is quite high, because you only find major brands.

◆ DISCIPLINES

Aeronautics

AEROCLUB DE VILLEURBANNE > Rue Clément-Ader - CORBAS ✆ **04 72 50 28 42.** It's not only at *Saint-Exupéry* that you can pretend to be a bird. At Corbas, albeit in a more modest way, you take to the sky. There are several methods at your disposal – from maiden flights to courses for your pilot's licence. There are 'formulae' for gliders and planes.

AIR AVENTURE > Bâtiment 3 - Avenue Louis-Mouillard - BRON ✆ **04 72 37 34 58.** Air Aventure offers maiden flights for some and piloting courses for others.

CENTRE DE VOL A VOILE LYONNAIS > Avenue Taillis - CORBAS ✆ **04 72 50 24 43.** To take to the air and make the most of the silence of the skies, the *Centre de Vol à Voile Lyonnais* lets you fly into the clouds suspended to a hang-glider. If you like thrills, come and try !

MBP > 48, chemin Chantegrillet - SAINTE FOY-LES-LYON ✆ **04 78 59 67 34.** You don't have to wait till Saturday to blow into the balloon. To take to the sky, all you need is gas… and an air-balloon. For about an hour, you can fly over West Lyon and, when you land, your exploit will be rewarded with a glass of champagne. To remind you of your flight, and to enable you to impress your mates, you'll be given a flight certificate. Such an unusual flight as this will cost you around 1 000 F a head (all the same !).

TRANS HELICOPTERE SERVICE (THS) > Lyon Bron Airport - Terminal H2 - BRON ✆ **04 72 81 15 15.** It's Sunday, and you don't know what to do ? The weather's fine ? What about flying over the Lyonnais region in a ? Nothing could be more simple with *Trans Hélicoptère Service*. Leaving Lyon Bron Airport, you can fly over Lyon in a Squirrel-type helicopter (maximum 5 passengers) for around 1 750 F for the day. You can also set course for a superb and picturesque site, like a *Relais et Château* hotel or a gastronomic restaurant, for a romantic dinner. You don't get more luxurious than that, do you ?

ULM DECOUVERTES > Pizay - SAIN-JEAN-D'ARDIERES ✆ **04 74 66 27 44.** All you need is a runway to pick up speed, a sail with a propellor and a hint of courage to don the helmet and launch yourself skywards. The equipment's tried and tested, and so are the instructors. There's no reason to back down. No reason not to tempt the devil, either. To do it really properly, don't hesitate to take piloting courses..

Mountaineering and Climbing

CENTRE PILOTE D'ESCALADE ET D'ALPINISME (CPEA) > 1, chemin des Vergers - VAULX-EN-VELIN ✆ **04 72 04 37 01.** If you fancy learning to climb, the *Centre Pilote d'Escalade et d'Alpinisme* is a good address to note down. Here, you'll learn how to climb in a natural environment or on artificial structures, like the 46 metre-high tower. This leisure activity's for adults, but also for **164** kids from the age of two-and-a-half (in theory).

M'ROC > 74, rue Greuse - VILLEURBANNE ✆ **04 78 85 73 04.** *M'Roc's essentially into climbing, and a 450 m² wall awaits people who like exerting themselves more than 5 metres from the ground. M'Roc also sells climbing equipment and invites people to discover the joys of canyoning and of treks in snow shoes. They offer a free testing session.*

Walls and sites to climb in and around Lyon

MUR MUR > 11, rue Lortet (7th) ✆ **04 72 71 83 84.** *Open everyday. From Monday to Friday from 12.00 to 22.30. On Saturdays, Sundays and Public Holidays from 09.30 to 18.30.* For nearly two years now, *Mur Mur* has been whispering into the ears of Lyonnais that the mountains are nearer than they had imagined. On a 'climbable' surface area of 1 300 m², novices and beginners cling to 8 000 holds, built into 200 climbing routes of between 12 and 21 metres. As climbers tackle a series of difficulties, instructors oversee operations and give advice during instruction sessions (from 200 F). So that the ropes don't break and the rock doesn't crumble, the initiators of the project took care to adapt it to the needs of the entire range of clientèle in the city. Hence, both large families and students will find prices within their budgets. For those who like thrills, without leaving the city centre.

Martial Arts

Aïkido, a martial art of Japanese origin, is a discipline which doesn't teach you to destroy the other person, but to build yourself. It regulates the rhythms of modern life, and allows everyone, regardless of age, sex or physical condition, to get out of the most difficult of situations without resorting to violence.

AIKIDO TASSIN > Gymnase des Genetières - TASSIN LA DEMI-LUNE ✆ **04 78 35 35 23.** *Membership between 700 F and 1 500 F.* What do you do when you're faced with a problem ? Do you say, "Oh, my God !" or do you think Aïkido ? For those who opt for the second solution, the only advice can be, "Come to *Aïkido Tassin*". You can enrol throughout the year, you don't have to come regularly, and you'll find a club which satisfies the wishes of all (men, women and children over 8) : self defence, relaxation for greater self-control, the discovery of another philosophy by means of a non-violent martial art.

ACADEMIE AIKIDO DU RHONE > 18, rue Bon-Pasteur (1st) ✆ **04 72 67 94 21.** You need courage and tenacity to become an Aikido champion. It's not easy and not necessarily what this place wants to turn you into. Sign on the bottom line, and you'll certainly get your money's worth.

ACADEMIE FIDESIENNES DES BOXES > 5, rue Gensoul - SAINTE-FOY-LES-LYON ✆ **04 78 59 09 07.** Here, under the watchful eye of Richard Gury, boys and girls practise kick boxing and self-defence. You'll need a lot of discipline to stick to the training sessions and become a champion. Maker of champions, Richard Gury has already seen several of his students climb onto the podium. Frank, on the other hand, gave up after a single session. Never mind, Frank, next year you can play table tennis.

CROIX ROUSSE ARTS MARTIAUX > 88, rue Hénon (4th) ✆ **04 78 07 04 51.** Judo, karate and kung fu are the main disciplines taught by this martial arts school. From white to black belt, the road is a hard one, but,along the way, the sportsman learns another way of life and to think differently. Here, you practise sport, you don't learn how to beat people up.

ECOLE INTERNATIONALE DE SHAOLIN - LA MANTE VERTE > 29, rue Colin - VILLEURBANNE ✆ **04 78 89 67 54.** *Everyday from 10.00 to 22.00.* La Mante Verte makes it a point of honour of teaching self-defence, kung-fu, Thai boxing, taï-chi-chuan-zen, nunchaku and ninjustu. All these disciIplines require a lot of concentration and physical effort. The best can prepare a National Diploma of Kung-Fu and the Martial Arts. All activities here are carefully supervised by the master of shaolin, Hoang-Cong-Luong, an 8th Dan black belt. There are both group and private lessons for men, women and children (from the age of 5).

GYMNASE LA FICELLE > 65, boulevard des Canuts (4th) ✆ **04 78 08 74 24.** Edmond Dominé, who is a State-qualified instructor, runs the lessons devoted to martial arts for adults and children. Several times a week, he initiates all who are interested to the techniques of Taekwondo, Habkido and Hamkido. These offer a surprising range of efficient gestures you may want to learn.

165

Lyon *Sports - Disciplines*

ASSOCIATION GENERALE HUNG-GAR / KUNG-FU > 16, rue Imbert-Colomès (1st)
℃ **04 78 28 88 13.** For kids who want to imitate the master, the lessons are tiring but worth it, because, at the end, they'll be afraid of nobody.

Lyonnais Boule

COMITE BOULISTE DEPARTEMENTAL DU RHONE > 86, quai Perrache (2nd) ℃ **04 78 37 16 10.** Lyonnais *boule* isn't like other sorts of boule. Larger than its beach cousins, it's rolled rather than thrown. It's more physical, and attracts both the old and the young.

Near the *Pont Pasteur*, the *boulodrome* is home to regular and famous competitions.

Basketball

ASV FEMININE > Maison des Sports - 243, cours Emile-Zola - VILLEURBANNE ℃ **04 78 85 70 66**

ASVEL BASKET ASTROBALLE > 44, avenue Marcel Cerdan - VILLEURBANNE ℃ **04 72 14 17 17.** *Internet : www.asvel.com • E-mail : asvelbasket@infonie.fr.* Born out of the merger between *Eveil Lyonnais* and the *Association Sportive de Villeurbanne*, the Club's played at a highly competitive level from the beginning. Known internationally, *ASVEL* successfully participates in European Cups, French Cups and the French Championship. Supported by some 2 000 official members, the team plays at the *Astroballe*, a unique and magical site to watch "The Greens".

Boxe

BOXING CLUB DU GRAND LYON > 1, rue Dominique-Perfetti (1st) ℃ **04 78 39 58 78.** To begin or to confirm your taste for the ring, the *BCGL* is an important address in the city centre.

RING LYONNAIS > 108, rue Pierre-Audry (9th) ℃ **04 78 25 50 52.** So as not to forget Marcel Cerdan, or because you saw Rocky Balboa and would like to spar with Hacine Cherifi (just for fun), the *Ring*'s open to all. After a bit of skipping and some physical exercise to muscle your little body, you head to the shower.

Canoeing-Kayaking/ Rowing

AVIRON UNION NAUTIQUE DE LYON > 59, quai Georges-Clemenceau - CALUIRE ℃ **04 78 23 21 92.** To discover the joys of rowing, this association regularly offers (and particularly during school holidays) introductory lessons to collective rowing for all ages.

ALPHA BATEAUX > Vallon Pont d'Arc ℃ **04 75 88 08 29.** In the Ardèche, there are circuits of 6, 24, 30 or 60 kilometres, with the possibility of bivouacing in specially-prepared areas (with WC and barbecue equipment).

CAP CANOE > Saint-Ambroix ℃ **04 66 24 25 16.** In the Gard, two hours from Lyon, these circuits of 4, 8, 14 and 30 kilometres are accessible to all. For the lazy, the less sporty or for weekend adventurers, you can cover the circuits in two days.

ESPACE EAU VIVE > Saint-Pierre-de-Bœuf ℃ **04 74 87 16 09.** 50 kilometres to the south of Lyon, on the artificial river at Saint-Pierre-de-Boeuf, thrills are guaranteed as you take lessons or follow courses in rafting, canoeing-kayaking or swimming in fast-running water. The trip's worthwhile for the thrills and for the countryside.

KAYAK VERT GARDON > Collias (30) ℃ **04 66 22 80 76.** Follow the current and end your journey under the magnificent *Pont du Gard* - this is what *Kayak Vert Gardon* proposes. Kayaking circuits cover 6, 11, 22 or 29 kilometres.

LIDO LOCATION > Saillans (26) ℃ **04 75 21 54 20.** In the Drôme, and with a magnificent view of the Vercors as a bonus, *Lido Location* proposes circuits of 7, 10, 15, 22, 30 or 50 kilometres in a canoe or aboard a raft.

Dance

ECOLE DE DANSE BRUNERIE > 16, rue Paul-Chenavard (1st) ✆ **04 78 27 71 11.** If music's made for dancing in twos, the *Brunerie* School knows the song. The rock (acrobatic or otherwise), the waltz, the tango, the paso, the salsa, the twist, the swing, the samba, the boogie-woogie, the be-bop, modern' jazz – all these types of dance are taught to dance fans. Either in groups or in private lessons, children and adults alike take their positions on the stage, in front of a large calendar showing a beautiful American limiusine. The rates charged are enough to make anyone smile – from 45 F a session (during certain periods). Nice one.

ACADEMIE DE BALLET NINI THEILADE > 9, Petite rue des Feuillants (1st) ✆ **04 78 30 56 86.** This school offers courses for tiny tots, as well as courses of classic, contemporary and jazz dance for the bigger.

ALICE ET SYLVIE KAY ACADEMY > 39, rue Franklin (2nd) ✆ **04 78 42 84 48.** From nursery school upwards, your little Sophie will spring around the stage and may develop into a Star. There are also courses for Mums at the Academy. For Covent Garden, things get more difficult...

CADANCE > 14, rue Pizay (1st) ✆ **04 78 28 18 61.** Caroline Palatin-Ginot, who has a classic and modern jazz background, puts her experience (and her patience) at your disposal during classic and modern jazz dancing lessons for both children and adults. For the keen, the professor also gives keep-fit and stretching lessons. Course times are flexible (in the morning, between 12.00 and 14.00 or in the evening from 18.00 onwards) and allow all students to combine work and well-being. Enrolment takes place between the beginning of September and mid-November. For the undecided, there's a free trial lesson without commitment. Rates depend on the formulae : from the monthly card (with one course a week) to the season subscription (36 courses for a bit more than 2 200 F), and including a quarterly subscription (12 courses only).

CENTRE DE DANSE JEAN-CLAUDE CELDRAN > 32, rue des Tables Claudiennes (1st) ✆ **04 78 28 71 85.** The Jean-Claude Celdran School teaches both beginners and professional dancers. You can discover modern dance or perfect and already-high level in contemporary jazz dance or rock. To change a bit, the school also gives lessons in tap-dancing. Free trial lessons.

CLUB 48 > 83-99, avenue des Frères-Lumière (8th) ✆ **04 78 01 24 88.** *Club 48* loves rock, and shares its passion with beginners and confirmed rockers. From time to time, exhibitions of all sorts of ballroom dances are take place in this little swing theatre. With a friendly and warm atmosphere, Elvis himself would have appreciated the reception.

CORINNE AZEGLIO > 54, cours Vitton (6th) ✆ **04 78 24 03 51.** At the front of the stage, this classical dance school seeks to turn children and adults into Stars (both local and international). Spotted young, the most talented follow courses designed to prepare them for admission to the major dance schools. There are also limbering-up lessons for adults.

RACHEL CHARMOT > 58, rue de la Charité (2nd) ✆ **04 78 38 37 80.** Children (from the age of 5) and adults (provided they have the strength) take to the stage and dance at *Rachel's*. Classical dance takes pride of place. It allows you to move and to make the body more supple. For the more motivated, the school prepares an end-of-the-year show.

RIMES > 5, rue de Castries (2nd) ✆ **04 78 37 16 12.** For the small or for the big, the dance here's classical or contemporary. Lessons are for beginners, as well as for the more experienced, and Anne-Lise Blanchard proposes workshops adapted the levels of all. It all takes place in bright and very pleasant surroundings.

STUDIO 4 UNIVERSITE > 25, quai Claude-Bernard (7th) ✆ **04 72 73 21 54.** Modern jazz, tap-dancing, rock, be-bop, boogie, street funk... this school accepts children and adults whatever their levels. You should note the interesting (and almost irresistible) prices : it's been known here that, for 10 F put on the juke box, you get a beginner's lesson in rock (10 week course, with 3 lessons a week). At that price, there's no way of escaping Elvis Mania.

Lyon *Sports - Disciplines*

Horseriding

CENTRE EQUESTRE DE L'EPERON > Cublize ℂ **04 74 89 51 36.** This centre offers numerous possibilities for learning to ride or for improving your riding level. There are several options : courses, excursions (on ponies or horses), outings. The adventurous should note that some of the excursions take place at night.

CENTRE EQUESTRE PONEY CLUB DE LA BERVILLIERE ℂ **04 72 26 42 94.** 20 minutes from Lyon, between the woods and the pans, the *Centre de la Bervillière* takes groups and proposes 'discovery' days, courses (during the holidays) and outings. On horses and ponies.

CENTRE EQUESTRE DE MALATRAY > La Rivoire - Route de Saint-Bel - LENTILLY ℂ **04 74 01 75 05.** As you go through the paddock doors, you choose between the courses preparing you for competitions, excursions, horse care or the covered ring.

CENTRE EQUESTRE "LA RIVIERE" > 46, la Rivière - SAINT-SYMPHORIEN-SUR-COISE ℂ **04 78 44 32 86.** Here, you can learn to mount a horse, but you can also go on excursions in carriages. It's certainly less sporty, but it's so much more romantic.

CENTRE EQUESTRE DU SEPEY > Montluel ℂ **04 78 91 84 73.** Everyday, the horses are harnessed and allow children and adults alike to take riding lessons. The centre organizes excursions and outings (gentler and shorter), and it also provides stabling facilities for your own horses, and organizes games of horse-ball (it's new).

CENTRE EQUESTRE UCPA > 112, chemin de Saint-Bonnet-de-Mure - SAINT-PRIEST ℂ **04 78 21 73 71.** For adults, horses ; for children, ponies. And for beginners, you get quality teaching in one of the most attractive riding centres in the area.

CENTRE EQUESTRE DU VIEUX MOULIN > Loire-sur-Rhône ℂ **04 78 73 21 83.** This centre offers lessons for all, whatever your level : excursions, horse-ball, horse jumping. For real fans, you can enrol for courses designed to prepare you for riding competitions.

CENTRE HIPPIQUE LA RANDONNEE > Pollionay ℂ **04 78 48 10 45/04 78 48 12 24.** This centre in the Lyonnais Mountains houses a riding school which includes covered rings, a cross-country course, obstacles and stabling facilities. Certain instructors prepare pupils for exams during courses which take place throughout the year, whilst others enable you simply to relax during outings in the neighbouring region.

ECOLE D'EQUITATION DE L'ABBAYE > 53, rue des Vallières - VOURLES ℂ **04 78 56 26 13.** Roland Atteli welcomes you for supervised excursions, courses for adults in the evening, for children on Wednesdays and for adults and children of all levels on Saturdays and Sundays. Just 11 kms from the *Place Bellecour*, and in an exceptional natural environment, we recommend this establishment, which offers a number of attractive formulae to convince you to stay in the saddle.

LE RELAIS DE VELIONE > Lieu dit Fontrobert - YZERON ℂ **04 78 81 03 11.** Come and discover this farm/riding centre, situated in the *Monts du Lyonnais*, 30 kilometres from the city centre. It offers excursions in the open air as well as horseback outings (on ponies for the smallest).

Football

OLYMPIQUE LYONNAIS > 3, rue Louis-Broussas (7th) ℂ **04 72 76 76 04.** *O.L.* is the club dear to all Gones. He who has never gone to a match at *Gerland* can't understand real Lyonnais fervour, even if some say that, when it comes to warmth, you can't compare Lyon with Saint Etienne (sworn enemies) or, when it comes to fanaticism, with the Marseillais crowds (the other sworn enemy). OK, we're not going to go on about the Lacombe episode or about questionable recruitment, and we just want to remind sceptics that *O.L.* often begins the championship badly, only to end in a blaze (like last year). Finally, we hope *O.L.* will win the cup this year (the last time they did so was before *Le Petit Futé* was born, so fans can now try to work out how old we are) with the support of their large fan club. *Le Petit Futé* will be there... *O.L. ! O.L. !*

Golf

GOLF CLUB INTERNATIONAL DE GRENOBLE > Route de Montavie - BRESSON ✆ **04 76 73 65 00.**
Internet : http://www.23rdstreet.com • Situated in the Belledone, Vercors and La Chartreuse Massifs, the *Golf de Bresson* golf course is undulating, wooded, technical and physical. Only the best players will get to the 18th with their nerves intact. Problems begin at the second hole – a long, 462-metre Par 5. It's a double-dog left- and right leg, stretching for 260 metres alongside a lake. The rest of hole is about as much fun, with nearly 12 bunkers leading up to the green. Good luck...

GOLF CLUB DE MIONNAY LA DOMBES > Domaine de Beau-Logis - MIONNAY (01)
✆ **04 78 91 84 84.** This is an 18-hole, 5 983-metre, Par 71 with, as a bonus, a swimming-pool and tennis courts. At the heart of a 60-hectare park, this course leads you through the bushes and pans of Les Dombes. The countryside's magnificent and, with the birds singing all round you, you'll need all your concentration to overcome the course's many obstacles, particularly at the 7th and 13th holes.

GOLF CLUB DE LYON > Villette d'Anthon (38) ✆ **04 78 31 11 33.** Here, there are no less than 36 holes. That is to say, 2 courses of 18 holes. In addition, the Golf Club has a 6-hole, pitch and putt course. The Parcours des Sangliers (Wild Boar's Course) is by far the more technical of the two, with numerous water-traps and grass bunkers. It's a course you have to try in order to test yourself against the best of them. And if, by misfortune, the deer, swans and herons have made you miss the ball, put your clubs away and, to reward yourself for all your efforts, head back to the clubhouse. There, you'll forget your ill luck as, with a glass in hand, you enjoy the view over the 3 000 of greens. That's not bad at all.

GOLF DU BEAUJOLAIS > Lucenya-Anse ✆ **04 74 67 04 44.** This is an 18-hole course which will delight all golf enthusiasts.

GOLF DE CORRENCON-EN-VERCORS > Les Ritons - CORRENCON-EN-VERCORS ✆ **04 76 95 80 42.** This is a mountain golf club, and, like all mountain courses, it's very technical. But, that's no problem, because you're very good. With one eye, you watch the ball as it flies off the tee, with the other, you take in the beauty of the Vercors Natural park. They say that, at an altitude of 1 100 metres above sea level, the air's slightly different to the air you breathe in the *Place Bellecour*. You swing through the bunkers on the 4th hole. The slope's steep. But, that's no problem, because you're very good. When you get to the end of the 18th, the view over the village below is magnificent. It has to be seen... unless you're not that good.

GOLF DU GOUVERNEUR > Château du Breuil - MONTHIEUX ✆ **04 72 26 40 34.**
www.golfgouverneur.fr • info@golfgouverneur.fr. There are those who have chosen fly fishing, swimming or tennis. There are also those who've preferred to stay in their hotel rooms (53 rooms and 4 stars, all the same). Then, there are those who take out their clubs to go round the *Golf du Gouverneur*'s 233 hectares. Two 18-hole courses and one 9-hole course will delight players of all levels. You don't have to show a green card here – anyone can play. The best will go for the *Breuil* Course, which is a genuine international-standard course (with enough water to sink a battleship), whilst others will prefer to play the *Soche* Course, which is rserved for beginners. At the end, and before leaving, you may feel you need to stop a while on the practise course (80 tees).

GOLF DE L'ISLE D'ABEAU > Le Rival - L'ISLE D'ABEAU (38) ✆ **04 74 43 28 84.** This 9-hole course is ideal for sunny week-ends in the Isère.

GOLF DE LYON-CHASSIEU > Route de Lyon - CHASSIEU (69) ✆ **04 78 90 84 77.** Here, 18 holes allow you to change your ideas whilst putting your nerves to the test.

GOLF DE LYON-VERGER > 1350, chemin de l'Allemande - SAINT-SYMPHORIEN-D'OZON
✆ **04 78 02 84 20.** An 18-hole course. What more do you need for swinging with a gloved hand and for chasing after a ball ? To prevent you from struggling on the greens and from spending half your time replacing divots, golf lessons are organized. And for those who are tempted, but not entirely convinced, by golf, there's a very inexpensive trial membership. Watch out, it's fatal...

GOLF DE SALVAGNY > 100, rue des Granges - **LA TOUR DE SALVAGNY** ✆ **04 78 48 88 48.**
Les Etangs (The Basins/Pans) is the name of an undulating and varied course. Infact, the greens are so up-and-down that they need your greatest concentration. In order to climb onto the podium, you'll have to be in top form when it comes to the putting. Water-traps are so distributed as to test the abilities of the very best. Yes, the *Golf de Salvagny* is a very interesting course to play. As for the 19th hole, it's very 'family' and a whole lot of fun.

GOLF DE LA SORELLE > Domaine de Gravagneux - **VILLETTE-SUR-AIN (01)** ✆ **04 74 35 47 27.**
18 holes for the pleasure of it…

Parachute Jumping

ESPACE CIEL PARACHUTISME LYONNAIS (ECPL) > Rue Clément Ader - **CORBAS** ✆ **04 72 50 22 15**

SILVER SKY > 11, rue Commandant-Faurax (6e) ✆ **04 78 94 04 90.** *Silver Sky* is a private free-fall school. Here, you learn how to fly in the silvery sky and to pull the cord before you become nothing but a snack in the *Place Bellecour*.

Hang-gliding

ECOLE DE PARAPENTE DES BAUGES > La Compote ✆ **04 79 54 88 63.** This school's open from 1st May to 31st October. It offers maiden flights, advanced courses, as well as 'two-seater' flights and excursions. On hang-gliders, obviously.

Ice Skating – Ice Hockey

PATINOIRE BARABAN > 52, rue Baraban (3rd) ✆ **04 72 35 92 69**

LYON HOCKEY CLUB > 100, cours Charlemagne (2nd) ✆ **04 78 38 36 30.** A lion on an ice rink, that's possible. They've been seen here. A lion which is top of the bill and which meets the best European and international teams, that's possible. They've been seen here. The Lions are the ice hockey professionals who wear the city's colours.

Diving

SCUBA > 7, place du Commandant-Arnaud (4th) ✆ **04 78 27 81 43.** *Scuba* sells underwater diving equipment, but it's also a training school which prepares divers for the various State diplomas and instructors' licence. Training course for the two qualifications : 5 sessions in the swimming pool (protected environment) of 1 hour each, theoretical courses on video and in books, a weekend at sea (between Toulon and Marseille) with 4 dives in a natural environment, insurance, the licence and a diving log for 2 770 F. Supervision is carried out by State-qualified instructors. Very good ambiance.

Quad

AMONZEVO ORGANISATION > 20, quai Fulchiron (5th) ✆ **04 72 41 81 34.** *Amonzevo* offers activities on quads (4-whell motorbikes), but also in 4x4's, buggies and motorbikes. The activites take place on a circuit or in the open. Thrills guaranteed.

Skiing

ASVEL SKI MONTAGNE > 245, cours Emile-Zola - **VILLEURBANNE** ✆ **04 78 03 84 45.** This is the *ASVEL* club's skiing and mountain section. As soon as the first snow appears on the Alps, the club offers outings on the peaks to practise downhill skiing, cross-country skiing and also snow-shoe excursions.

BOARDERLINE > 1, avenue Félix-Faure (7th) ✆ **04 78 72 10 94.** They're the specialists in snowboarding and surfboarding…

MAGIC EVASION > 22, quai Fulchiron (5th) ✆ **04 72 40 92 48**

SKIMANIA > 4, rue François Verney (5th) ✆ **04 78 30 50 00**

SLD VOYAGES PLEIN SKI > 14, place Carnot (2nd) ✆ **04 72 56 90 90.** *SLD*'s one of the big specialists in skiing activities. A day's skiing for tuppence-ha'penny is possible through *SLD*. Afterwards, it's up to you to invent the life that goes with it and to make friends with your bus companions.

UCPA > 5, place Carnot (2nd) ℂ **04 72 56 90 90.** A few mediatised scares at the top of the mountains and, sudenly, *UCPA* are meant to be losing control. Nevertheless, they remain one of the best mountain outfits.

Surfing

SURF SANS FRONTIERES > Bordeaux-Lacanau ℂ **05 56 26 36 14.** *http://www.ssf.fr* • *E-mail : surfsansfrontier@hotmail.com.* For sliding fans, this is a perfect address. This outfit offers week-ends or weeks which are 100% surfing on the beaches at Lacanau-Océan, from April to November non-stop. *Surf sans Frontières* is also surfing trips, surfing courses, equipment hire or simply lodging in a charming 30's villa. From October to April, discover the surfing trips organized to the south of Portugal, to Morocco, to Guadeloupe or the Canaries, a surfboard under your arm. All activities are supervised by guide-instructors for maximum security. So, wax your boards and let's go surfing at their place to find out a bit more.

Tennis

ASUL TENNIS DE LYON > 60, rue Pierre-Baratin - VILLEURBANNE ℂ **04 72 34 55 08.** The *ASUL* has 13 tennis courts. Beginners and confirmed players can take lessons or participate in courses which are organized internally. It's serious stuff !

TENNIS CLUB ECULLY > 2, chemin des Hautes Bruyères - ECULLY ℂ **04 78 33 37 29**

TENNIS CLUB DES AQUEDUCS > Montée des Roches - FRANCHEVILLE ℂ **04 78 59 11 83**

TENNIS CLUB DES BAROLLES > Route de Sacuny - BRIGNAIS ℂ **04 78 05 09 85.** 23 tennis courts of which 7 are indoor.

TENNIS CLUB DE CHAVRIL > 12, rue Juisseaud - SAINTE-FOY-LES-LYON ℂ **04 78 25 63 41**

TENNIS CLUB DU FORT > 271, rue des 39-Fusillés (9e) ℂ **04 78 43 85 73**

TENNIS CLUB DE LYON > 3, boulevard du 11-Novembre-1918 - VILLEURBANNE ℂ **04 78 89 49 68**

Bicycling

In Lyon, people want to boot cars out of the city. With extended métro lines, dozens of bus services covering the entire city, and a tramway which is making the news at the moment, all that's missing is to put the "Little Queen" on the throne to make things perfect. Anachronistic. For a short time now, lanes reserved for cyclists have been put into service. These cover around 5 kilometres of city road from *Grange Blanche* to *Saint-Jean*. But, they've have been badly designed, because they're often shared with buses. One of the most flagrant examples is to be found in the *Cours Albert Thomas*, at the top of the *Boulevard des Tchécoslovaques*. Here, the cycling lane is cut through by cars heading for *La Part-Dieu* by turning right. Consequently, the cyclist who wants to go straight on without risking his skin is obliged to leave the alley reserved for cyclists, and cut into the area reserved for pedestrians. These aren't genuine cycling lanes ; they're a sort of skin-graft which will never 'take', because the lanes aren't reserved exclusively for cycles.

ASSOCIATION SPORT-NATURE-CULTURE DES MONTS D'OR > Cour du Château - SAINT-CYR-AU-MONT-D'OR ℂ **04 78 22 50 44.** This association had the good idea of offering its members mountain-bike excursions every Saturday and Sunday. The excursion normally takes place in the M*onts du Lyonnais.*

ESPACE LOISIRS ACTIVERT > Saint-Laurent-de-Chamousset ℂ **04 74 26 59 00.** Situated in the *Monts du Lyonnais*, the *Espace Loisir Activert* allows everyone to hire mountain-bikes and set off on excursions along signposted itineraries. It's open every Sunday and on other days by appointment.

EVASION BEAUJOLAISE > Marchampt ℂ **04 74 02 06 84.** The complex offers 300 kilometres of signposted track. A record ! You can hire mountain-bikes on the spot. Depending on what you want to do, it's possible to cycle at night, go on outings or even participate in competitions.

Lyon *Sports - Disciplines*

LE LAC DES SAPINS ✆ **04 74 89 50 31.** In a superb setting, with a forest running alongside a lake, you can go on a beginner's circuit which is 10.7 kilometres-long and which includes a number of technical difficulties. Afterwards, to bed.

◆GYMS AND FITNESS CLUBS

Two types of club share the fitness market. On the one hand, there are the large structures, which belong to enormous chains like *Gymnase Club*, and, on the other, you'll find the small, local clubs. They have one point in common – competition between the clubs is cut-throat. Apart from that, they couldn't be more different. In the large clubs, it's a bit of a factory. Fitness machines are lined up by the dozen, there are fitness courses of up to 80 people, a host of activities and, often, a swimming pool (especially when aqua-gym courses are on offer). A multitude of services are offered, and membership is counted by the thousand - 5 000 at *Swiss Training,* for example. Often presented as the perfect place for meeting the partner of your dreams, these large structures are impersonal and, above all, very expensive (3 000 F, 4 000 F or even 5 000 F for the year, and rarely less). These clubs don't hesitate to push the client to opt for long-term membership formulae. At these prices, members often find that, at the end of the working day, there's no machine available. In contrast, the small clubs are often very convivial and relatively affordable (between 1 500 F and 2 500 F). Only, the choice of activities is more limited. Some clubs are somewhere between the two (like *Club 48*), and these may offer the perfect solution. Here's a list of the largest clubs to be found in Lyon along with a selection of small clubs :

BODY SCULPT > 42, rue d'Alsace - VILLEURBANNE ✆ **04 78 84 90 90.***Open from Monday to Friday from 09.00 to 21.00 and on Saturdays from 09.00 to 16.00.* Because fitness clubs are growing like mushrooms (many die almost as rapidly, thereby dragging their members into the dirt), you'll be happy to learn that this friendly, 'family' club was formed in 1957. But, watch out, the courses here aren't for grandads ! The club offers three different sections. Firstly, there's an area devoted to weight training, with cardio for warming up and endurance training. Then, there's an area for group courses and dance, and, finally, a 'water''area with a swimming pool, a hammam and a sauna. In addition, the club has an institute where Valérie takes you in hand with a 'combined therapy', including dietetic, aesthetic and balneotherapeutic treatment... An address where finesse and fitness go together.

CLUB PACIFIQUE > 1, avenue du Bon Pasteur (Tour Smart Roundabout) - ECULLY ✆ **04 72 189 189.** A new club has just opened its doors in Ecully. It offers high-quality services on 2 500 m². Activities include balneotherapy, personal training, 'aquatonic', fitness, slimming, beauty treatment... This fitness club is well run and supervised. Very practical – a car park with 20 spaces.

GYMSEA > 153, rue Vendôme (6th) ✆ **04 78 71 02 21.** *This is Lyon's 'up-market' Well-being- and Balneotherapy Centre. Open 7/7 days till 22.00 during the week. Private car park.* This is the ideal place for making the most of your free time, in a setting impregnated with essential oils. Hygiene here is about as faultless as is humanly attainable. The club has an osteopath and a nutritionist, and, for all mothers, there's a child-minding centre, open everyday with a qualified nanny. To relax even more, there's an 'aquatic area' with a swimming pool, jet baths, a hammam and a sauna. To perfect your beauty, there's also a Beauty Institute using the *Dauphin* range of products. For those who want to launch themselves on a 'well-being cruise', welcome aboard !

ODYSSEE > 100, cours Gambetta (7th) ✆ **04 72 73 04 49.** Three clubs, three swimming pools in Lyon and Villeurbanne. A professional team welcomes you every day of the week, and gives you advice to keep in the best of form. It offers : a a cardio/training area, body building, dance, group courses, a relaxation area (sauna, hammam, swimming pool, jet baths) and a slimming centre. **Other addresses : Lyon Vaise - 69, rue Gorges-de-Loup (9th) 04 72 20 50 00**

• **56, rue Paul-Verlaine - VILLEURBANNE 04 37 43 32 32.**

Beaujolais *Region*

Beaujolais Region

◆ USEFUL ADDRESSES

LE PAYS BEAUJOLAIS > Maison du Tourisme - 96, rue de la Sous-Préfecture   ℂ   **04 74 02 22 00.**
Both a region and a tourist structure, Le *Pays Beaujolais* replaced the **Groupement Régional Touristique Beaujolais** in1992. It groups people and organizations involved in tourism, local and regional representatives, as well as Tourist Offices and Information Bureaux throughout the region. Its objectives are fourfold : Firstly, to increase knowledge about the *Pays Beaujolais* throughout France and overseas, by means of salons, publicity drives, press relations and other communication tools. Secondly, to group and harmonize tourist offers within the *Pays Beaujolais*. Thirdly, to ensure that each small region enjoys harmonious tourist growth, by co-ordinating activities at a federal level. Finally, to commercialize tourist products (like stays and circuits), in association with the various partners throughout the *Pays Beaujolais*. By grouping the 12 Tourist Offices/Information Bureaux, the organization covers 147 communes (90% of which are rural), 12 cantons and a population of 190 000 inhabitants. It is developing its activities, with the support of the County Council, Regional Councils, local representatives and the U.I.V.B. Several initiatives already taken include the Profession Olympics in 1995 and the reception of 40 American journalists during the G7 Summit, to cite but two. Thanks to this regional dynamism, you'll learn how to be Natural, Gourmand, Curious and Fun-loving in the Beaujolais with the help of Michel Deflache (Director), Joëlle Dubois (Publicity), Françoise Girel (Group Organization), Carole Labruyère (Reception, Documentation and Individual Circuits), Véronique Demoment (Entertainments Officer), Laurent Bernier (Projects Officer) and Geneviève Bret(Administration and Accounts).

DISCOVERIES IN THE *PAYS BEAUJOLAIS*

A number of museums and wine-tasting - and tourist centres will allow you to make the most of the Pays Beaujolais.

◆ WINE-TASTING AND TOURIST CENTRES

To improve your knowledge, 4 Beaujolais wine-tasting and tourist centres have been opened. They're classed as major Beaujolais Heritage Sites and allow you to discover the region by visits to museums, châteaux and areas devoted to the winemaking industry. These four sites should allow you to find out and understand everything about the region, and, with an annual pass which is given to you on your first visit, you have the right to a reduction on all the other sites and to various presents. Adult rate around 30/35 F, depending on the site, children 15/20 F.

L'ESPACE DES PIERRES FOLLES > Saint-Jean-des-Vignes   ℂ   **04 78 43 69 20.** *With access to car park for cars and buses. Can be visited throughout the year by groups by appointment and by individuals from 1st March to 30th November from 08.30 to 12.30 and from 14.00 to 18.00. Closed on Wednesday moenings.* The *Sentier des 4 Sites Géologiques* (Path of the 4 Geological Sites) was inaugurated by Haroun Tazieff and provides a retrospective of geological history in the region. There's an aquarium with live nautili and a botanical garden, amongst other things.

LA MAISON DES BEAUJOLAIS > RN6 - SAINT-JEAN-D'ARDIERES   ℂ   **04 74 66 16 46.** *Wine-tasting area open all year from 09.00 to 22.00 (except between mid-December to mid-January), closed on Tuesday evening and on Wednesdays. Tastings lasting an hour by appointment for groups.* An introduction to wine-tasting and to regional cuisine is proposed in a large dining room seating 150 people, and in which legs of lamb and pieces of beef are grilled in front of an open chimney. There's a private salon which can take groups of 20 people. Terrace in summer. The tasting room is designed to take up to 50 people.

LES SOURCES DU BEAUJOLAIS > Maison de Pays – BEAUJEU   ℂ   **04 74 69 20 56.** *A 'Wine Trip' down history. Access to the centre of Beaujeu with car park for cars and buses. Open from 1st May to 30th September everyday, closed on Tuesdays. Then, from 1st March to 30th April and from 1st October to 31st December from 10.00 to 12.00 and from 14.00 to 18.00. Visit lasts 1h30 to 2 hours.* The ticket gives you the right to visit the Beaujeu Spring, the Marius Audin Museum (closed from 12.00 to 14.00) and to a free wine-tasting in the Beaujolais-Villages cellars. The cellar, the Maison de Pays, the Tourist Office and the church have all been renovated and are all close to one another in the village centre.

Beaujolais Region

ROCHEBONNE (or the Château of Passions) > Theizé 📞 **04 74 71 16 10.** *Access to the centre of Theizé, car park for cars and buses. Group visits all year by appointment, individuals from 30th May to 31st October. Closed on Tuesdays. Visit lasts 1h30 to 2 hours.* The ticket gives you the right to visit the château as well as the area called "The Fiancés of Autumn", the old church and the museum area in the château's vaulted cellars.

MONTMELAS

On the D44, take the Villefranche exit heading towards Hôpital. Montmelas is signposted at the roundabout and is about 8 kms away. It's just outside the Pierres Dorées Tourist Circuit, and doesn't fall within the Tourist Office's communes. On the D504 from Denicé to Rivolet, the château overlooks the road.

LE CHATEAU DE MONTMELAS > *At the Château de Montmelas you can go round the castle by foot and enjoy the panorama. Visits are for groups only on 04 74 67 32 94.* The current owner is the Comte Henri d'Harcourt. This prestigious château protects five centuries of family tradition. It was the imposing fiefdom of the Lords of Beaujeu and then of Bourbon, and is a real fortress. From the top of the hill, it dominates a 70-hectare vineyard and, on clear days, offers a view over 7 departments and of *Mont Blanc.* The château's celebrating a thousand years of history in the year 2000, since it was built in the course of the 10th century. It became a residential château from the beginning of the 17th century onwards, and its present owners are the descendants of Jehan Arod, who bought it in 1566. The Arods reinforced the defensive system with a line of trenches connecting the east wing to the north-east wing, which forms an interior courtyard. They also added fortifications on the south-west of the château. Jean-Jacques Arod built the present south wing and the first version of the gallery leading to the upper floors. In the middle of the 18th century, Montmelas became the Lords of Montelmas' permanent and official residence. In 1742, the rich mariage between the Marquis François-Marie d'Arod and Marguerite Denis allowed reconstruction to be completed. A new, covered galley was built and certain common buildings were added. In 1842, works ordered by the Marquis de Tournon and completed under the supervision of the Lyonnais architect, Louis Dupasquier, copy the style of Villet-le-Duc and give the château its present day appearance : the crenellations, the watchtower, the monumental doors (constructed from a piece recovered from the *Château du Sou de Lacenas*), the keep, the towers surrounding the Honour Staircase and the sheet-copper roofs. The *Château de Montmelas* produces a Beaujolais-Villages wine, called, not surprisingly, "*Château de Montmelas*".

CORCELLES-EN-BEAUJOLAIS

Signposted from the main road between Belleville and Romanèche-Thorins, on the Mâcon road.

LE CHATEAU MEDIEVAL DE CORCELLES 📞 **04 74 66 00 24.** *Visits from Monday to Saturday and on Public Holidays from 10.00 to 12.00 and from 14.30 to 18.30 by appointment. From March to July open everyday from 10.00 to 12.00 and from 14.00 to 18.00. Guided visits for groups by appointment.* This fortified château dates from the 12th century and was

Beaujolais Region

modified in the Renaissance. It's classed as an Historic Monument. You can visit the interior courtyard with its Renaissance gallery, the chapel with its lace friezes, the kitchens and the secret dungeon. Of the old fortress the walls with the line of trenches were kept, as were the towers and the square keep. The wells date from the 15th century. At the château, you can also taste *Beaujolais, Beaujolais-Villages*, white and rosé *Beaujolais*, as well as *Brouilly*.

SAINT-JULIEN-EN-BEAUJOLAIS

You get here quickly from the Villefranche exit heading towards the Hôpital, then turning off before the village of Arnas. This village is known to fishermen because the Marverand is full of trout. It's also famous for its *Beaujolais* and *Beaujolais-Villages*, and thanks to Claude Bernard.

MUSEE CLAUDE BERNARD ℂ **04 74 67 51 44.** *Fax 04 74 67 59 42 • http://www.fond-merieux.org. Open from 1st October to 1st March from 10.00 to 12.00 and from 14.00 to 17.00. From 1st April to 30th September open from 10.00 to 12.00 and from 14.00 to 18.00.* This museum's been part of the Marcel Mérieux Foundation since 1965, and is open everyday except on Mondays and Tuesdays. There's an annual closing in March. It's run and subsidized by the Foundation. The physiologist, Claude Bernard (1813-1878), was born in this house and became the founder of experimental medicine. A researcher, philosopher and winegrower, you'll discover this character in the different rooms of the house he was born in. The house is a testimony to literary and scientific life in the 19th century.

ROMANECHE-THORINS

Here, you'll find the wine, *"Moulin à Vent"*, which owes its name to the 300-year-old windmill which is 10 metres-high and 5.5 metres in diameter and stands in the middle of the vineyards. However, the sails didn't survive the storms of 1910 and have never been replaced.

LE HAMEAU-EN-BEAUJOLAIS > La Gare ℂ **03 85 35 22 22.** *Fax 03 85 35 21 18. Inaugurated by the Maison Georges Duboeuf in 1993, this place is open everyday from 09.00 to 18.00 except in January.* In the course of a visit which lasts at least two hours (and takes you through 10 000 m² of buildings), the world of wine is recounted to you in an original way. In a magnificent, reconstructed station hall, you take a ticket to leave on a trip through the history of wine, which is presented in a number of different rooms. You'll find a number of objects diplayed, including an impressive collection of tools, presses and other objects used in the preparation of wine. In every room, an explanation is given, sometimes by means of video presentations. The 'electronic theatre' explains the importance of the 4 seasons, the 1876 locomotive was the first motorized means of transporting wine, and you're told that Georges Duboeuf is fascinated by everything to do with trains. Noah, the first winegrower ? The history of the arc is recounted up to the planting of the first grape. Nothing's forgotten. You're told about the importance of the quality of the soil, whilst the making of wine barrels is commented by a video film, as is cork-making. There's a musical comedy in relief with, as Star participants, Bernard Pivot, Christian Marin and Paul Bocuse. This recounts harvesting and the celebrations which follow as if you were actually present !

At the Wax Museum, you meet personalities connected with the world of *Beaujolais* (like Marguerite Chabert and, more recently, Gérard Canard) in a bistro setting.

To end this unforgettable visit, which many won't hesitate to repeat, a wine-tasting is held in a magnificent room. Even if you're familiar with winemaking and with everything the winemaker's job involves, the imagination with which all the details are presented (as well as the incredible décor) simply can't be found elsewhere.

Novelties in 2000 : an evening session till 22.00 every Friday in July and August plus a roundabout and a carrousel in the courtyard for visitors' children.

At the café, whose entrance is in the courtyard, you'll find various snacks, *charcuterie*, cheese and drinks or a *Mâchon Beaujolais Menu* for 72 F.

FIND US ON THE NET

www.petitfute.com

Le Hameau en Beaujolais
The Wine Hamlet in Beaujolais
Das Weindorf im Beaujolais

La Gare - 71570 ROMANECHE-THORINS
Between LYON and MACON (RN 6)

Beaujolais Region

◆ THE VINEYARD

SARL SAINT-CYR > Les Pérelles – ANSE ℂ **04 74 60 23 69.** *Fax 04 74 60 23 26. On the A6, take the D70 exit to Limas. Les Pierres Dorées is just before Lachassagne. The cellar's open 7 days a week from Monday to Friday from 10.00 to 12.00 and from 15.00 to 19.00, on Saturdays from 09.00 to 12.30 and from 16.00 to 19.00 (with a snack of regional produce in the morning), on Sundays from 11.00 to 12.30 and from 16.00 to 19.00.* Elected Agriculturist of the Year in 1999 at the Agriculture Show in Paris, the family estate belonging to Laurence, Thierry and Sébastien does everything it can to "give wine its raison d'être : conviviality", and it offers : a recently constructed cellar, open 7 days a week, with photo exhibitions covering work on the vine, membership of the *Club Saint-Cyr*, with preferential prices and progrmmed events, a range of red and white *Beaujolais* wines (including the Club Wine for laying down), a guided visit of the vat room during the harvest, with a wine-tasting, an audiovisual presentation of work on the vine and on *Beaujolais* winemaking, and an introductory trip to discover wines from other regions in France. Groups are welcome.

DOMAINE ALBERT > Au coteau de Chalier - POMMIERS ℂ **04 74 65 12 67.** *Fax 04 74 65 92 07.* On their superb property, Eric and Chantal take care of wine sales and of wine-tasting every day of the week, preferably by appointment. From Villefranche, heading towards Liergues, near the Gleizé Cooperative Cellar, take the Saint-Fonds road. The property's signposted from there. Out of the property's 9 hectares, 8 are *Gamay* and 1 is *Chardonnay*, and the property produced a white wine which won a gold medal at Mâcon for the 1998 vintage. This Chardonnay also allows them to make a *blanc de blanc* using the Champenois method (both white and rosé) and a *Crémant de Bourgogn*e. The red wine's sold principally as *Beaujolais Nouveau*, but some of it (the *Cuvée Vieilles Vignes*, for example) is made for laying down. The wines are sold to the public during annual Open days, one during the harvest, one when the new wine comes out on the 3rd weekend in November, and one during the spring. The vat room adjoing the house is vast and serves as a reception room for roughly 150 people, for weddings, celebrations and seminars.Another room serves as a shop for the sale of a variety of wines – in bottles of 75 cl and 50 cl, with a range of red and white *Beaujolais, blanc de blanc* and *crémant*, or in gift boxes, with two bottles and a glass, for example. The property's been entirely restored, and you'll see stone everywhere – in the vaulted cellars, one of which is under the vat room and another under the building which serves as a kitchen and a dormitory for harvesters in a building adjoining the shop. The old doors have been kept, with old furniture and old barrels, as has the feeding trough in the shop which used to be a stable. The trees and greenery surrounding the buildings are perfect for apéritifs served to groups of visitors, either outside or under cover. The ground has been entirely paved to facilitate access to the various buildings.

CAVES FERRAUD > 31, rue Maréchal Foch - BELLEVILLE ℂ **04 74 06 47 60.** *Fax 04 74 66 05 50. www.ferraud.com • ferraud @asi.fr. Guided visits of 45 minutes approximately without wine-tasting at 18 F. Joint visit to the Hôtel-Dieu and the Ferraud cellars : 30 F.* Jean-Michel, who is Vice President of the Villefranche Chamber of Commerce, and his brother, Yves-Dominique, run the family estate. Since 1882, five generations have been making Beaujolais wine in 100-year old oak casks. In the course of your visit to this site, which begins with an audiovisual explanation in three languages, you'll discover winemakers' work, vine cycles and procedures for selecting wine. During the visit, which ends with a ritual wine-tasting, you'll see all phases of bottling. In order to produce and preserve top-quality wines, grapes are picked parcel by parcel, and the wine matures in separate vats. Great care is taken at all phases of winemaking – be it the bottling in new, rinced bottles, the bottle-filling at room temperature, the corking, the numbered labelling or the stocking on pallets, with the top of the bottle facing downwards.

CAVE DU CHATEAU DE LA CHAIZE > Odenas ℂ **04 74 03 41 05.** *The vat room, built in 1810, is the longest in the Beaujolais region. It's 108 metres-long, and is classed as an Historic Monument. You can taste and buy Brouilly wines.* Two other châteaux in the region are associated with winemaking estates. These are the *Château de Pierreux* and the *Château de Nervers*. Bernard and Martine Audiffred sell their *Brouilly* and *Côte-de-Brouilly* in the renovated cellar of their 10-hectare property. Martine makes humorous labels which are hand-painted.

DOMAINE DE LA GRANGE CHARTON > Domaine de la Grange-Charton - Régnié-Durette
℃ **04 74 04 31 05.** *Fax 04 74 04 36 23. www.epicuria.fr/hospices-de-beaujeuü hospices-beaujeu@epicuria.fr.* This 69-hectare estate belongs to the *Hospices de Beaujeu*. The winemaking buildings and the immense vat room form a quadrilateral around a courtyard of more than 3 000 m². The courtyard can be visited, as can the vat room by appointment. Opposite Régnié's two bell-towers, the *Grange Charton* Estate is an important part of the Beaujolais heritage, and Alain Belles and his team allow you to visit the vat room. The latter is equipped to make 5 000 hl of wine at a self-regulating temperature. Every year, on the second Sunday of December, 600 bottles are auctioned at the oldest auction in Beaujeu. *Hospices de* Beaujeu wines are made and bottled on the estate under Régnié *appellations*. They come from parcels of land on the *Grange Charton* and *La Plaigne* Estates. Régnié wines have a beautiful, ruby colour, are both structured and tender at the same time, and have a fruity (and predominantly currant) taste.The *Brouilly* wine consists of the *Cuvée Pisse-Vieille*, which is made with grapes from the legendary slopes at Cercié. It has a purple-violet robe, is tender and fleshy, and develops a perfume of cherry and raspberry. The *Morgon* wine is made with grapes growing on the finest land around the *Colline du Py*. It has an intense purple-violet robe, and develops a perfume of blackcurrant and almost of kirsch. It's a wine to lay down, because it's full-bodied and long in the mouth. The *Beaujolais-Villages* is made with grapes from the slopes between Vaugervand and Lantignié. It goes perfectly with *"Mâchon Beaujolais"* (local dishes and snacks), and has a ruby-red robe and a perfume dominated by red fruit.

WHERE TO SLEEP • OR EAT

LA MAISON DE L'ITALIEN

Georges Pedat is waiting for you in the prestigious setting of this 16th century *"Maison de l'Italien"* which is classed as an Historic Monument. You'll admire this private mansion, which is the only one to have an Honour Court on the main street. It has a polygonal turret topped with a belvedere, and the motifs carved onto the main are reminiscent of the Renaissance gallery at the *Palais Jacques-Coeur* in Bourges. A visit to the belvedere is included in the visit of Old Villefranche. Legend has it that this architectural masterpiece was the work of an Italian architect (hence, the name).

When it's fine, you'll find a brasserie menu in the Honour Court. It offers a wide choice of varied entrées and salads at 50 F or 60 F, and these are enough for a quick meal. Alternatively, you can also eat grilled meat (or *tartares*), fish (including a salmon tartare) and smaller snacks. Everyday, an entrée, a Dish of the Day and the Chef's Dessert is on offer at 80 F. The Chef's Desserts include an excellent banana tart. However, the specialities are equally delicious, and these include *flammekueche*s, mussels and chips (15 different preparations), varied *choucroutes* (6 different sorts), Lyonnais and regional specialities. You'll find all types of Beaujolais wine, beers (including the famous *Abbaye de Leffe*) and cocktails, both with and without alcohol. A large room, called " The Chapel ", has a vaulted ceiling and is perfect for get-togethers, seminars and banquets, because it can take up to 60 or 70 guests.

LE CAFE LEFFE > 407, rue Nationale - VILLEFRANCHE ℃ **04 74 09 04 04.** *Brasserie-bar-restaurant. Open from Monday to Saturday from 09.00 to 01.00 and, on Sundays, from 11.00 to 17.00.*

LE SIX > 415, route d'Anse - RN6 - VILLEFRANCHE ℃ **04 74 60 02 45.** *Restaurant and bar open from Monday to Friday from 11.00 to 15.30 and from 18.30 onwards. On Saturdays from 16.00 onwards. Closed on Monday evenings, on Saturdays at midday and on Sundays. From May to October, closed only on Monday evenings.* Just before you get to the town centre, you'll be attracted by the shady, green courtyard which faces due south and by the immense summer terrace and its large, bay windows. These are enough to make you stop, even if it's only for a look. On the other hand, you may prefer the interior, behind the bay windows. The décor's simple, but the reception's very warm and the menu, large. A whole range of prices goes from 49 F for a tempting Dish of the day to 'formulae' at 79 F, 119 F and 165 F. The cuisine's both traditional and regional, as Hervé and Laurent will explain. But, we also tried the bison in wine suace, which was delicious.

Beaujolais Region *Where to sleep or eat*

AU CHENE PATOUILLARD > Bully ℂ **04 74 26 89 50.** *Signposted before the village, follow the sign "Chambres d'Hôtes" (guest rooms) which is to be found 2.5 kms from the village, surrounded by Nature. Guest rooms (3 épis) : for one night plus breakfast : 200 F. Couple : 250 F ; for 3 people : 340 F and for 4 people : 480 F. Evening meal by reservation, wine and coffee included : 85 F.* Isabelle and Michel Biron have practically built an immense residence in a dilapidated farm, with a number of outhouses beside a water basin, and surrounded by extensive courtyards, terraces and meadows. An independent gîte for two people gives onto vineyards and a garden. To get to the 5 guest rooms at the front of the house, you enter a vast sitting cum dining room, with a solid wood table and sofas. All the rooms have one or several beds, a shower/WC area, a television and a view of the country. You'll love the furniture, because the wardrobes, chests of drawers and armchairs have been renovated by the owner, who's a cabinet maker and upholsterer. His workshop is in one corner of the estate. Isabelle adores decorating the beautiful interior, and cooks on order a goat *à la savoyarde* or an apple tart with produce from the farm. A real fairy in her own home, this superb blonde has boundless energy and looks after the gîte, her three children and the cooking at the same time as she takes care of the farm animals. In this Noah's Ark, which is beautifully decorated with wood and stone from floor to ceiling, you'll find a host of animals, including a dozen goats, a cow, two calves, two sheep, ten chickens, a couple of Guinea geese and a couple of turkeys (the list may not be exhaustive !). It's ideal for those who love the quiet and the countryside where you can isolate yourself, but it's also ideal for children, who can play around in safety. Single guests often spend several weeks here, because of the excellent value for money.

CHATEAU DE PIZAY HOTEL-RESTAURANT > Saint-Jean-d'Ardières ℂ **04 74 66 51 41.** *Fax 04 74 69 65 63 • www.chateau-pizay.com • info@chateau-pizay.com.* Set back 50 metres from the B road, this 14th and 16th century château has a facade decorated with coats of arms, and an imposing half-timbered keep. It's a private residence, but parts of it have been converted in order to house an hotel, a restaurant and seminar rooms. Hotel guests (and the general public on Heritage Days) can visit the French gardens, which are set out like a chessboard, and the chapel. **Restaurant** : When the weather's fine, you can eat on a huge terrace in front of the château. Otherwise, there's there's a comfortable dining-room, where you'll eat a gastronomic *cuisine. There's a Regional Menu at 200 F, a Gastronomic Menu at 290 F and a 'Prestige' Menu* at 360 F, but you can also eat *à la carte* or try the *'Young Guest's' Menu* at 130 F. The restaurant's specialities include a *matignon de légumes et escargots de Bourgogne au Vin du Domaine* (selection of vegetables with Burgundy snails with wine from the estate), a *poêlon de grenouilles* (fried frog's legs), a *tournedos de bœuf émincé aux escargots de Bourgogne* (thinly-sliced tournedos of beef with Burgundy snails), a *foie gras de canard confit en terrine maison* and a *gratin de queues d'écrevisses à la crème de crustacés au gingembre* (gratin of crayfish tails with a shellfish and ginger cream). The prices are reasonable for a gastronomic meal in a dream setting. **Hotel** : 14 highly-comfortable, air-conditioned rooms with private terraces on the ground floor and 48 flats with an air-conditioned mezzanine-bedroom giving onto the swimming pool and park. Each room has a salon under the mezzanine, a very comfortable bathroom, a telephone, a minibar, Satellite TV and a small, individual terrace – all equivalent to a small, luxurious flat. Prices are in line with the quality and are not unreasonable, bearing in mind the comfort and services offered. For a single room, they start at 545 F for a night in low season (750 F for half-board), and increase to 595 F and 750 F in high season for a 'park pavilion' which gives onto either the vineyard or the forest, depending on your choice. Breakfast at 75 F. Rebates for children from 3 to 6 years old 30% and for children from 70 to 12 years old 15%. Animals 55 F. For a double room, prices range from 625 F a night in low season to 715 F in high season (half-board in a double, from 525 F per person in low season to 575 F in high season). In the château wing, prices go from 735 F a night for a single in low season (885 F for half-board) to 785 F (925 F for half-board) in high season.

Au chêne Patouillard

Isabelle and Michel BIRON
5 rooms and food

Guest
Rooms

Tel. 04 74 26 89 50
69210 BULLY

A flat with two adjoining bedrooms costs from 1 640 F to 1 990 F a night per person and from 700 F to 755 F per person for half-board. A swimming pool, a 'health route' through the château forest, a tennis and a billiards room are just some of the facilities on offer. This hotel's ideal for anyone looking for an exceptional level of comfort, a pleasant setting and tranquillity – either during an idyllic holiday or for a business seminar. The surrounding gardens and the little chapel are sometimes the venue for exhibitions. When we stayed, there was a beautiful exhibition of works by the famous Beaujolais sculptor, Miguel Fernandez.

HOTEL-RESTAURANT LE CHATEAU DES LOGES > Le Perréon   ©   **04 74 03 27 12.** *The chef de cuisine is Georges Lagarde. Menus from 100 F to 275 F for a delicate but gastronomic cuisine made with regional produce. Terrace when it's fine.* In the middle of the village, this restaurant's on the 1st floor of a fine, 18th century château. It was built at the end of the 18th century by the Barons de Vauxonne, and was a private residence for more than a century. In 1960, the *Cave Beaujolaise du Perréon* became owner of the château and built its co-operative in the park, as well as the cellar in 1962. In 1989, *La Cave* began to restore the château and, in 1995, part of it was turned into an hotel/restaurant. On the ground floor, there's a dining-room for 35 people, as well as three rooms equipped for seminars, with direct telephones, fax machines and equipment for meetings. Cocktail parties can be organized on the terrace. There's a magnificent billiards room on the 3rd floor in the garret. The hotel has 10 rooms. These are decorated *à l'ancienne* and offer 3-star comfort, bathroom, telephone and TV.

REGIONAL PRODUCE

A typically Beaujolais 'discovery' : pottering around in Beaujolais-Vert !

"BILLEBAUDEZ" EN BEAUJOLAIS-VERT > Château du Bois - OUROUX   ©   **04 74 04 61 20.**
Here, you can ask for details of all members of this interesting little Association, which groups a number of regional craftsmen and producers. In the *Haut Beaujolais*, the cantons of Monsols and Beaujeu are full of greenery, pine trees, meadows, plants and animal trails. Green hills and slopes merge into one another, criss-crossed by paths. The local inhabitants, artists and craftsmen recognized that, in order to attract tourists to a region which is not easily accessible in winter, ingeniosity was required. Consequently, they formed an association which, in the year 2000, received First Prize in the Green Tourism Trophy, which is awarded by the National Federation of Departmental Tourist Committees. This rewards them for all their work.

Passionately involved in their various trades, the members of *"Billebaudez en Beaujolais Vert"* will surprise you with their creativity and astonish you with their professional skill and knowledge.

At Gérard Gauthier's equestrain farm, *Carruge d'Ouroux*, you don't win the *Prix de l'Arc de Triomphe*, but, whether you're an experienced mount or not, you can go on rides through the forest right up to Mont Saint-Rigaud, which, culminating at 1 010 metres above sea level, is the highest spot in the Beaujolais region. At the same farm, Linda offers goat's cheese made into original shapes (Beaujolais corks, pyramids, etc.).

On the road from Monsols to Ouroux, you'd better slow down, so as not to miss the sign on the right directing you to *La Serve*. This place, which is 500 metres from the road, is run by Pascal and Pascaline Patin, and proposes a romantic night in a caravan. A cabinet maker and restorer by profession, Pascal gives soul back to ancient carriages, whilst Pascaline takes care of the meals. There's a terrace and showers in a nearby building to provide that extra bit of comfort. About 3 or 4 kilometres futhter on, you'll meet Jean-Claude Hyvert, who is the association's President. He's a talented water-colourist, who sells his work, as well as offering courses. At the same site, Mireille cooks wonderful bread in an authentic, wood-fired oven. In the little hamlet of La Loire, Jean Revelin will allow you to discover work with horses. At Jorlet, Cathy Croutelle runs the *Maison des Poneys*, whilst, in Chassagnes, Jean-Paul Amin tells you all about the work of a wood-cutter and Viviane Amin makes delicious home-made jams, *"Les Savoureuses du Saint-Rigaud"*.

Beaujolais Region *Regional produce*

In Amplepuis, at the *Montchervet* Farm, the Magnin family sell authentic products made on the farm, like terrine, rolled head, paté in a crust, sausage and crackling.

At Saint-Claude, Huissel Dominique and Pierre Noyel let you taste their superb cheeses.

Farm pork produce is also sold at Saint-Just d'Avray, where Philippe and David Corgier raise their pigs with cereals.

Gisèle and Pierre Cochet reveal the life of bees at Le Fût d'Avenas. In the same village, you can admire the cabinet-making talents of Alain Bertuol and enjoy the regional menu concocted by his wife, Agnès.

Trout-fishing takes place at *Le Safari Pêche* in Saint-Didier-sur-Beaujeu, where you'll also find Jean-Marc Montegottero, an award-winning oil-producer.

In Chamelet, at *La Ferme de la Vieille Route* owned by Marick by Antoine Apruzzese, you'll find pack-mules which can be loaded up for a picnic outing, whilst figurines from the rural Beaujolais world are on sale at Françoise Ferraton's place in Propières and in the Maison du Col de Crie.

CHARCUTERIE BOBOSSE > Lieu-dit "Amorges"   ℃ **04 74 66 04 05.** *Fax 04 74 66 27 35. Open from Monday to Friday from 08.00 to 12.00 and from 14.00 to 17.00. Sale to professionals and to the general public. Very well signposted from the N 6 heading towards Mâcon, on the right.* This plant is run by Bernard Juban, with the help of 8 assistants. Here, they jealously protect the Bobosse establishment's reputation and know-how. Regional produce is prepared using only traditional methods, and you'll find, for example, the famous *andouillette* (made with 100% veal) which is often to be found on the menu in good restaurants under the mention *"andouillette Bobosse"*. Other specialities include the *sabodet* (thick, pork sausage served in thick slices), the saveloy with pistachio nuts, the Beaujolais pâté and the chicken liver terrine. In 1999, the establishment produced 100 tons of food, 80% of which was destined for restaurants and 5% for export (particularly when the *Beaujolais Nouveau* comes out). You're given an excellent welcome, especially from the friendly Bernard who talks about his profession with equal enthusiasm and conviction, and who also proposes some of his recipes. The pork produce made by the *Bobosse* establishment is mentioned in cookery books and is known everywhere.

Lyonnais *Region*

Lyonnais Region *Discovery in the Lyonnais Region*

The last cliffs in the *Massif Central*, the Lyonnais region has a long history. Its most ancient inhabitants have left us many questionmarks about the megaliths which dot the countryside and which are the subject of numerous legends. The Lyonnais region was already called this in the days of the Gauls, when it was peopled by the *Séguviaves* tribe. A bit later, the Romans constructed an extraordinary network of aqueducts in the region, in order to supply Lyon (the Capital of the Gauls) with water. Of this masterpiece, there remains a heritage which is unique in the world and which is remarkably conserved. In the course of history, the Lyonnais region was the site of territorial division and of ownership disputes between the Counts of Forez and the Archbishops of Lyon. Hence, the Lyonnais region is intimately linked with the history of Forez and of neighbouring Beaujolais. The recent history of the Lyonnais region has been marked by the transition of manual craftwork to industrialisation and by the modernization of agriculture, because, throughout history, the rural *massif* which is the Lyonnais region has taken advantage of the proximity of the major 'poles', Lyon and Saint-Etienne, and has been involved in both agricultural and industrial activity. Traces of this history are still to be found in a region which combines a multitude of various professions and skills, not the least of which is the perpetuation of an 'Art of Living' which has been lovingly conserved.

DISCOVERY IN THE LYONNAIS REGION

MAISON DE L'ARAIRE > 23, rue de la Cascade – IZERON ✆ **04 78 45 39 09.** *Open from May to October, on Fridays, Saturdays and Sundays from 14.00 to 18.00. Other days, by appointment. Free admission. Leaflets in English are available at the reception desk.* L'Araire is an association which focuses on the history and the heritage of the *"Pays Lyonnais"*. Originally, an *"araire"* was an antique plough without a wheel, and was used to till the land and extract its wealth. L'Araire has two main activities : the writing and publishing of a quarterly magazine about local history and the running of the Exhibition House in Yzeron. The four exhibitions on display in the house are entitled 'Old Trades', 'Silk and Velvet Weaving', 'Lyon's Roman Aqueducts' and 'Old Watermills in the Pays Lyonnais'.

CHATEAU DE LA POUPEE (THE DOLL'S CHATEAU) > Domaine de Lacroix-Laval – MARCY-L'ETOILE ✆ **04 78 87 87 00.** *Open from Tuesday to Sunday from 10.00 to 17.00.* A prestigious and old collection invites you to discover the special and little-known world of the porcelain doll, from the second half of the 19th century onwards. For those who want it, an accompanied visit allows you to penetrate the unsuspected depths of this curious universe. The château is a site both of culture and of exchange, and, throughout the year, proposes a broad panel of exhibitions.

MUSEE ANTOINE BRUN > Place de l'Eglise – SAINT-CONSORCE ✆ **04 78 87 01 12.** Come and discover the very singular character who was Antoine Brun. This museum contains 130 limewood models, which were sculpted in the last century and portay some of the most beautiful monuments in the world.

MUSEE DU VIEUX L'ARBRESLE > 20, place Sapéon – L'ARBRESLE ✆ **04 74 01 48 87.** *Open from May to September, on Saturdays and Sundays from 15.00 to 18.00. From October to April on the 3rd Sunday of every month. Throughout the year, group visits by appointment.* This Museum of Local Heritage is largely devoted to the history and techniques of weaving. It covers a variety of professions and exhibits a number of models, some life-size and some miniature. Commentaries are given by Arbreslois weavers.

◆ROMANESQUE CHURCHES IN THE *LYONNAIS*

Churches open from Easter to All Saints' Day from 15.00 to 19.00 the 1st Sunday of every month. A circuit covers 9 sites in the *Coteaux* and the *Monts du Lyonnais* : Messimy, Montagny, Montrottier, Pollionnay, Saint-Laurent-d'Agny, Saint-Martin-de-Cornas, Saint-Martin-en-Haut, Taluyers, Yzeron.

EGLISE DE SAINT-SYMPHORIEN-SUR-COISE ✆ **04 78 44 37 57.** *By appointment for groups.* Here, you'll discover three pages of the *Eglise de Saint-Symphorien-sur-Coise's* local history. The old walls with barred windows remind you of the feudal château, which was built in the 10th and 11th centuries ; the base of the clock-tower dates from the first Romanesque church in the 13th century, and the top of the tower and the right side-door reveal part of the church as it was in the 15th century.

REGIONAL PRODUCE

Lyon, world capital of gastronomy, nourishes its reputation with local, Lyonnais produce. A varying landcape, with alternating valleys and slopes which reach an altitude of 800 metres above sea level, offer the palate a wide variety of produce. Over time, some have become regional specialities.

COTEAUX DU LYONNAIS WINES > Brignais ✆ **04 72 31 59 64.** The white and rosé "Coteaux du Lyonnais" AOC wines provide a balance betwwen the fruity and the full-bodied. Men of tradition, the winemakers in the Coteaux du Lyonnais open their cellar doors in order to demonstrate some of their knowledge to you. A free guidebook is available in all Tourist Offices.

CAVE DES VIGNERONS REUNIS > Route Nationale 89 – SAIN-BEL ✆ **04 74 01 11 33.** *Open from Monday to Friday from 08.30 to 12.00 and from 14.00 to 18.00. On Saturdays, open without interruption from 08.30 to 18.00.* The only cooperative cellar in the *Coteaux du Lyonnais*, 170 winemakers (producing wine on 18 000 hectares) bring their wine here. Created in 1956, this important Winemakers' Union selects and vinifies the famous *Coteaux du Lyonnais*, along with *Beaujolais* (of which they produce one-third of the annual production). The red and rosé wines are made with the *gamay* grape, whilst the whites are produced using the *chardonnay* and *aligoté cépages*. The wine can be tasted at the sales shop during the week, and in the cellars on Sundays and Public Holidays. You can take advantage of this 'oenological stop' (other French wines are also on sale) to fill your baskets with regional produce - *charcuteries*, cheese, nuts, fruit juice…

CAVEAU DU PERE VIRICEL > D34 – GREZIEU-LE-MARCHE ✆ **04 78 48 41 02.** *Open everyday of the week, on Saturdays and Sundays by appointment.* Discover the red and white *Coteaux du Lyonnais* wines in *Père Viricel*'s pleasant, vaulted cellar. Free tasting, accompanied by regional sausages and cheese.

◆THE COTEAUX DU LYONNAIS VINE PEACH

Introduced from the Near East, the *Coteaux du Lyonnais* vine peach has been a regional product for centuries. An 'end-of-the-season' fruit, it's harvested from August to October, and is appreciated for its fine and subtle taste and for its bloody, perfumed and juicy flesh.

◆THE LYONNAIS REGION'S RED FRUIT

Red cherries, red currants, red berries, red raspberries, red strawberries – the orchards of the Lyonnais region produce a host of different red fruit. Used for wine and in cooking, eaten at meals and at traditional festivals, Lyonnais red fruit adds its tastes and aromas to the joy of living, and gives pleasure to the eye and to the palate.

◆THE SALAISONS (SALT-CURED MEAT) OF THE *MONTS DU LYONNAIS*

The *Monts du Lyonnais* sausage is an integral part of Lyonnais gastronomy. It's famous in France and throughout the world. It has an 'authentic' taste, and is made with traditional recipes, so you should head to where it's produced and taste it.

◆REGIONAL SALES OUTLETS

The wealth and 'authenticity' of Lyonnais produce isn't limited to just a few products, and there are numerous regional sales outlets where you can buy and taste a multitude of savours – cheese, *charcuteries*, *foie gras*, honey, jams...

LA FERME LYONNAISE > Avenue E. Millaud *(Open from Tuesday to Sunday inclusive)* – CRAPONNE 04 78 44 63 36 • UN DIMANCHE A LA CAMPAGNE > Route de Rontalon – THURINS 04 78 81 72 36 *(Open on Saturdays and Sundays from 15.00 to 19.00)* • **UNIFERME > Le Pont Rompu – SAINT-ANDEOL-LE-CHATEAU 04 78 44 05 07** *(Open all week, on Mondays and Tuesdays from 15.00 to 19.00).*

RELAX WITH THE FAMILY

PARC LACROIX-LAVAL > Domaine de Lacroix-Laval – MARCY-L'ETOILE ✆ 04 78 87 87 00.
Park open everyday from 06.00 to 21.00 in summer and from 07.00 to 20.00 in winter. Over and above the 115 hectares of meadow and forest it offers sportsmen and Nature-lovers, the park has become the theatre for a series of 'events', including summer sports competitions and free concerts from 15th June to 15th September.

TRAIN TOURISTIQUE LE FURET > Domaine de Lacroix-Laval – MARCY-L'ETOILE ✆ 04 78 42 88 70.
A circuit with commentary, lasting 35 minutes. Departures and arrivals in front of the château (Museum entrance) and at the main entrance to the park (on the Sain-Bel Road).

PARC ANIMALIER DE COURZIEU > Parc de Courzieu – COURZIEU ✆ 04 74 70 96 10. *Park opens at 10.00. Shows with birds of prey in flight at 14.30 and 16.30. 'In search of the Wolves' at 15.30.* This park provides an unusual excursion in the Lyonnais region, "between the eagles and the wolves". Come and enjoy a great moment, with a show involving birds of prey and an outing in search of the wolves. The Courzieu Park also offers a rambling circuit and a Botanical Garden and Path.

WHERE TO SLEEP AND EAT

HOTEL MERCURE > 78bis, route de Paris – CHARBONNIERES-LES-BAINS ✆ 04 78 34 72 79.
HO345@accor-hotels.com. Rooms at 495 F. Lying in the Rhône-Alpes Regional Council Park, facing the *Monts du Lyonnais* and ideally situated in the immediate vicinity of the business and tourist city of Lyon, the hotel offers 60 air-conditioned and soundproofed rooms, a meeting area, and an elegantly designed restaurant with seating for 80 people. The hotel also has a car park for 50 cars.

HOTEL RESTAURANT BONNIER > 51, route de la Vallée du Garon – THURINS ✆ 04 78 48 92 06.
12 rooms, Logis de France, 2 restaurant-rooms, business- and 'rambler' meals. At the foot of the *Monts du Lyonnais*, in the heart of 'Raspberry Country' and in a family atmosphere, come and enjoy this restaurant's specialities : game in season, frogs with parsley, pike soufflé, *moules marinières* and, of course, raspberry dessert. A pleasant stop to enjoy the region.

JACQUES CŒUR > La Giraudière – Route Nationale 89 – BRUSSIEU ✆ 04 74 70 87 88. *Open everyday except on Tuesday evenings and all day on Wednesdays. Menus from 68 F to 170 F.* Situated on the N89, a few kilomètres from Saint-Laurent-de-Chamousset, the *Jacques Cœur* restaurant is to be found in the same building as the Tourist Office. Its menu varies with the seasons, but includes regional specialities, like fricassee of fresh frog's legs with nuts and regional pork produce. Don't miss the desserts, because the chef just loves desserts, and all the pastries are his own creations. Both inside (large dining room with chimney) and out (terrace), the smile's included in the menu.

LE RELAIS DU PETIT COISATAIRE > Le Bourg – COISE ✆ 04 78 44 49 90. *Open all year. Closed on Mondays. 5 rooms from 155 F to 195 F. Menus from 78 F to 125 F. Groups by reservation.* At the centre of this typical village, *Le Relais du Petit Coisataire* has been tastefully restored, and offers you a traditional cuisine and bright rooms. If you order them, the restaurant will prepare their frog's legs *à la forézienne*. On Sunday evenings, your Country Menu will consist of omelette, *charcuteries*…

RESTAURANT CAP OUEST > 78bis, route de Paris – CHARBONNIERES-LES-BAINS ✆ 04 78 34 72 79.
HO345@accor-hotels.com. Air-conditioned restaurant open from Monday to Friday. Weekends : reserve your special events, receptions, etc. You're sure to appreciate the original design of the restaurant and its West Terrace opening onto the park – not to mention the delicious cuisine.

RESTAURANT COMMARMOND > La Giraudière – COURZIEU ✆ 04 74 70 85 02. *Closed all day on Wednesdays. Menus from 70 F to 130 F.* A traditional cuisine (served in a warm décor) and unbeatable prices have contributed to the success of this restaurant. The restaurant has two partners who offer a series of activities throughout the day. These begin in town, with a visit to the Miniature Palace in Old Lyon. At midday, you'll eat at the restaurant in Courzieu. At 15.00, you'll leave for the Courzieu Park to see the birds of prey and the wolves. All for 175 F.

Dauphine *Isere*

VIENNE

At the intersection of several departments, Vienne is on the border between the departments of the Isère and the Rhône. However, just 20 kilometres to the south, you come to the Drôme, the Ardèche and the Loire and to the first slopes of the Pilat *Massif*. Lyon has traditionally been Vienne's rival and, several centuries after Vienne was annexed to the French Crown, won the race to become the largest city in the region. Was it Lyon's proximity which prevented Vienne from developing more ? It's quite probable because, over time, the two towns have grown further and further apart – so much so that Vienne is now no more than a large suburban town outside the city which is Lyon. If Vienne is jealous of Lyon's success, it need not envy the regional capital when it comes to the richness of its history.

Ruins and more ruins – all you have to do is dig. Vienne earned the title of Latin Colony in 50 B.C., thanks to its loyalty to Rome during the Gallic Wars. It subsequently became a fully-fledged Roman Colony under Augustus (towards 16 – 15 B.C.), so that its inhabitants enjoyed the same privileges and rights as Roman citizens. At that time, the town developed along both banks of the Rhône. Magnificent monuments sprang up within the town's 7 kilometres of ramparts, which also housed a population estimated at 30 000 (as many as today !), thereby making it one of the largest cities in Gaul (today, it's simply the largest town in the canton…). The end of Antiquity marked the end of its glory. Vienne, then, was a town in the Roman Empire, but it was also a town in an empire situated further to the north. When the Emperor of Germany inherited the Realm of Burgundy in the 11th century (the Burgundians had succeeded the Romans), for four centuries Vienne became the 4th largest town in the German Empire. The town was attached to France in 1450, and it was then that its slow economic decline began.

Today, there are a number of reasons for 'going down' to Vienne. Firstly, to visit the countless museums which trace human development in the region. Secondly, for the beauty of the place – yes, the view from the belvedere on *Mont Piper* is genuinely beautiful, especially when the sun's out and everything's green. You can admire the town and the vestiges of its past, the River Rhône which winds its way between the hills, the ruins of the *Château de la Bâtie* on *Mont Salomon* and, in the distance, the spurs of the Pilat *Massif* – Lastly, you want to come here to taste French gastronomy not far from the famous Pyramid, the impressive remnants of the stadium where Roman chariot races were held, or at the restaurant set up by the legendary Fernand Point. This great chef (1897-1955) bought the Guieu Restaurant, opposite the Pyramid, in 1923. Ten years later, he received his third Michelin star (only three restaurants had this distinction), and through his kitchen passed an entire generation of talented, young chefs, many of who were to become Stars in their own right in the Post-War years. You'll want to spend some time considering one of the region's greatest riches – the vineyard. Vine, vineyard. Côte-Rôtie and Condrieu are among the most prestigious of the *Côtes-du-Rhône* wines. Well before Jesus Christ, on this spot people were tasting the wild grapes which made a heady drink. Naturally, over the course of 20 centuries, the quality of the vines and the knowledge of winemakers have improved so much that, today, you can now buy in and around Vienne some of the best (and the most expensive !) bottles to be found anywhere.

◆THINGS TO DISCOVER

MUSEE DES BEAUX-ARTS ET D'ARCHEOLOGIE > Place de Miremont ✆ **04 74 85 50 42.** *Open everyday except on Mondays and on Public Holidays (January, 1st May, 1st and 11th November and 25th December). From 1st April to 31st October from 09.30 to 13.00 and from 14.00 to 18.00. From 2nd November to 31st March from 09.30 to 12.30 and from 14.00 to 17.00 (on Sundays from 14.00 to 18.00 only). Admission fee 11 F, reduced rate 8 F.* Situated on the 1st floor of the old Grain Market, this museum contains objects dating from prehistory, along with items from the Gallo-Roman period which were discovered during the first archeological digs carried out under the Old Regime by Pierre Schneyder. Apart from objects from everyday life and statuettes, the museum exhibits a silver treasure dating from the 3rd century. This was discovered in 1984, and is one of the largest collections of its kind. You'll also find an interesting collection of faience (18th and 19th centuries) and paintings by 19th century Dauphinois artists.

Things to discover **Dauphine-Isere**

MUSEE DE LA DRAPERIE > Espace Saint-Germain – The Pyramid Districte © 04 74 85 73 37. *From 1st April to 30th September. Open everyday except on Mondays from 14.30 to 18.30.* This museum, which we owe to the Heritage of Viennois Textiles, recounts the history of the textile industry which domintaed Viennois life from the 17th to 20th centuries (the last cloth mill closed its doors in 1987). With the help of some 30 machines (still in working order) and video screenings, you'll discover the entire process of clothmaking, from the preparation of the yarn to the finished material.

MUSEE ET SITE ARCHEOLOGIQUE DE SAINT-ROMAIN-EN-GAL/VIENNE   SAINT-ROMAIN-EN-GAL © 04 74 53 74 00. *Open everyday except on Mondays and on 1st May from 09.30 to 18.30. Admission fee 30 F. Half-rate 15 F. Free for the under-12's and for the unemployed.* On the right bank of the Rhône. This museum, with a very modern architecture, recounts the development and organization of Ancient Vienne between the 1st century B.C. and the 3rd century A.D. It contains rich collections of mosaics, mural paintings and ceramics, as well as beautiful models which allow you better to visualize the entire town as it was at that time. The archeological site, covering several hectares alongside the museum, enables you to dive into life in the Ancient City, with its shops, warehouses, workshops, houses, therms and road system. Indeed, the right bank of the Rhône was a major and prosperous craftwork centre in the town, and remnants can still be seen. The museum organizes regular conferences (admission is free !) at 19.00 in its auditorium on a variety of themes to do with Antiquity. On 18th May : "Living and Eating in Rome" (Catherine Virvoulet, Professor at the University of Aix-Marseille I) ; on 15th June : "The Roman House in the Western Provinces of the Empire" (Pierre Gros, Professor at the University of Provence). With all enquiries, contact Odile Larue on 04 74 53 74 08.

Ancient sites

LE JARDIN ARCHEOLOGIQUE DE CYBELE > Rue Victor Hugo. This ensemble of public and private Roman monuments was almost certainly destined for municipal use. Its name probably derives from a cult devoted to Cybele (Phrygian Goddess of Fertility). Nearby, you can see two impressive arcades which formed part of the Roman porticoes, one of which is believed to have been the entrance to the Forum. During excavations in the 1930's, many objects were found, and these are exhibited in the *Musée des Beaux Arts et d'Archéologie* (Museum of Fine Arts and Archeology).

LA PYRAMIDE > Boulevard Fernand Point. In the southern part of the town, the Pyramid is, infact, a sort of obelisk, supported by four pillars. It marks the centre of the ancient Circus arena (of which it's the only surviving remnant), where the Romans' favourite sports competitions were held. 15.5 metres high and 4 metres wide at the base, very few similar monuments dating from Gallo-Roman days survive anywhere.

LE TEMPLE D'AUGUSTE ET DE LIVIE > Place Charlesde Gaulle. Built around 10 B.C., this Temple, with fluted columns and Corinthian capitals, was devoted to the Cults of Rome, of Augustus and, later, of his wife, Livia. It was part of the Forum, of which it is, sadly, one of the few remnants, and the porticoes and therms which surrounded it have disappeared. At the beginning of the Middle Ages, it was converted into a church, then into a Temple of Reason during the Revolution. Just afterwards, it became a Commercial Court, before being turned into a museum last century. It recovered much of its original beauty (its columns had disappeared in the masonry erected when, at one point, it was decided entirely to enclose the structure), thanks to the work carried out by Prosper Mérimée (1833-34).

LE THEATRE ANTIQUE > Rue du Cirque © 04 74 85 39 23. *Open everyday from 1st April to 31st August from 09.30 to 13.00 and from 14.00 to 18.00. The rest of the year, open everyday except on Mondays and on Public Holidays (1st January, 1st May, 1st and 11th November and 25th December). From 1st September to 31st October from 09.30 to 13.00 and from 14.00 to 18.00. From 2nd January to 31st March and from 2nd November to 31st December from 09.30 to 12.30 and from 14.00 to 17.00 (on Sundays from 13.30 to 17.30 only). Admission fee 11 F, reduced rate 8 F.* Situated on the slopes of the *Colline Pipet* (Pipet Hill), and facing towards the Rhône and the Pilat *Massif,* Vienne's Ancient Theatre was built in Augustinian times (1st Century), and is one of the most important constructions of its type to have survived from the Roman world. With a diameter of 130 metres, it had room for up to 13 000 spectators on 46 tiered rows. Vaulted galleries allowed spectators to move around and to leave the theatre at the same level as the orchestra. Unfortunately, the 72 metre-long stage wall has disappeared, and all that's left of the original décor is a frieze, which can be seen in the *Musée Saint-Pierre.* Restored in 1938, this theatre is now used for its original purpose, because it's the venue for an annual Jazz Festival and other events.

Dauphine-Isere *Things to discover*

L'ODEON > Montée Saint-Marcel. On the Colline Sain-Just (Saint Just Hill), this smaller construction (of which little remains) is next to the theatre and underlines the importance of cultural life in the city in Antiquity. Indeed, as far as we know today, Vienne was, with Lyon, the only city in the Gallo-Roman world to possess both a theatre and an odeon. This second auditorium was smaller (room for 2 000 to 3 000 people) and was used for choral performances, recitals and public readings. Probably built under Hadrian (2nd century) on an earlier construction, this odeon was used for around four centuries.

Mediaeval and historical sites

L'EGLISE SAINT-PIERRE/MUSEE LAPIDAIRE > Place Saint-Pierre ✆ 04 74 85 20 35. *Open everyday except on Mondays and Public Holidays (1st January, 1st May, 1st and 11th November and 25th December). From 1st April to 31st October from 09.30 to 13.00 and from 14.00 to 18.00. From 2nd November to 31st March from 09.30 to 12.30 and from 14.00 to 17.00 (on Sundays from 14.00 to 18.only). Admission fee 11 F, reduced rate 8 F.* The original, 5th century building is one of the oldest Christian edifices in France. Modified and extended countless times, it still has its original basilical design and its timbered nave. The rectangular clock-porch dates from the 12th century. In its time, this church has been a popular workshop, a museum and a factory. Since last century, the church has housed the Lapidary Museum and contains a collection of mosaics and ancient sculptures, including the famous *Tutela* or *Fortuna*, the Goddess/Protector of the city, who is portrayed with her attributes (a Horn of Abundance and a Mural Crown, symbol of power). The museum also exhibits collections concerning inscriptions and funerary cults. Next to it, the remnants of the ancient *Eglise St-Georges* have been cleared, and you can now see a 6th century Oratory and the remains of some remarkable tombs.

L'EGLISE ET LE CLOITRE DE SAINT-ANDRE-LE-BAS > Place du Jeu de Paume ✆ 04 74 85 18 49. *Open everyday except on Mondays and on Public Holidays (1st January, 1st May, 1st and 11th November and 25th December). From 1st April to 31st October from 09.30 to 13.00 and from 14.00 to 18.00. From 2nd November to 31st March from 09.30 to 12.30 and from 14.00 to 18.00 (on Sundays from 14.00 to 18.00 only). Admission fee 11 F (with exhibition), reduced rate 8 F.* The church and its Romanesque cloister (12th century), decorated with small columns and sculpted capitals, formed part of a powerful Abbey Church, which was founded in the 6th century and stretched over a number of streets as far down as the Rhône. The church was built in the 9th century, with a single nave and a circular, half-domed apse. It was modified (and its level raised) three centuries later in a Romanesque Viennois style. Note the beautiful, embellished capitals. The Cloister Room houses exhibitions organized by Viennois museums.

LA PRIMATIALE SAINT-MAURICE > Place Saint-Maurice. From the end of the 4th century onwards, the site was used to build an Episcopal Quarter. At the beginning of the 8th century, a cult dedicated to the relics of St-Maurice developed, and a community of canons occupied the site. Finally, Archbishop Léger ordered the construction of a cathedral, which was built between the end of the 11th and the beginning of the 16th centuries. In 1119, Pope Calixte II, formerly Archbisop of Vienne, granted the Vienne Episcopal Seat primacy over the six other provinces in the South of France. The Primatial Church (dedicated definitively to Saint-Maurice in the 13th century with the benediction of Pope Innocent VI) is the largest construction in Dauphiné (and, indeed, in the entire south-east of France) to have a Romanesque foundation and a Gothic structure. It has a majestuous facade with three portals, spandrels and beautifully sculpted curves. Inside, Romanesque pillars hold up some sixty capitals, decorated with carvings of leaves or Biblical illustrations – all characteristic of the great Viennois school of the 12th century.

L'EGLISE DE SAINT-ANDRE-LE-HAUT > Place André Rivoire. *Cannot be visited.* An old chapel belonging to the College of Jesuits and dedicated to Saint-Louis, its facade (end of the 17th century – beginning of the 18th century) is built on two levels, with an ornamental front in the pure Jesuit style. A media library is being built into the old Benedictine abbey.

WRITE TO US
info@petitfute.com

◆WHERE TO SLEEP

HOSTELLERIE LE MARAIS SAINT-JEAN > Chemin du Marais - CHONAS-L'AMBALLAN ✆ **04 74 58 83 28.** *Httpp://www.domaine-de-clairefontaine. fr. Annual closing in December and January. 18 air-conditioned rooms at 600 F (from the month of June). Breakfast 50 F. Gastronomic restaurant (closed all day on Wednesdays and at midday on Thursdays and Saturdays). Accees for the disabled, parking, tennis court, garden. Animals allowed.* The Provençal style permeates this very classy establishment where, after a delicious meal, you can rest in one of the rooms, all of which are extremely comfortable and luxurious.

HOTELLERIE BEAU-RIVAGE > 2, rue du Beau-Rivage - CONDRIEU ✆ **04 74 56 82 82.** *Open all year. 25 air-conditioned rooms from 550 F to 850 F. Breakfast 80 F. Gastronomic restaurant (menus from 195 F to 620 F). Access for the disabled, parking, garden. Animals allowed.* This hotel is justly reputed for the quality of its delicious cuisine and for its comfortable rooms.

LA PYRAMIDE - FERNAND POINT > 14, boulevard Fernand Point ✆ **04 74 53 01 96.** *Http://www.pyramide@relaischâteaux. Annual closing in January and February. 20 air-conditioned rooms from 770 F to 1 380 F for a flat. Breakfast 90 F. Gastronomic restaurant (closed on Tuesdays and Wednesdays from 1st October to 30th April). Access for the disabled, garden, parking. Animals allowed.* An obligatory stop if you're doing a *Tour de France* of the best restaurants, *La Pyramide* invites you to enjoy a relaxing stay in one of its rooms or suites. The quality of the service and the friendly welcome are as fine as the cuisine.

LE BELLEVUE > Quai du Rhône - LES ROCHES-DE-CONDRIEU ✆ **04 74 56 41 42.** *Annual closing one week in February and November. 16 rooms from 200 F to 320 F. Breakfast 40 F. Restaurant (closed on Mondays). Access for the disabled, parking. Garage 30 F. Animals allowed.* Opposite Condrieu, on the left bank of the river, this hotel's perfectly situated beside the pleasure port. The rooms are simple but comfortable, and the reception is among the most friendly we've ever encountered. You should note that this quality hotel has an excellent restaurant, so we recommend it highly.

◆WHERE TO EAT

BEAU RIVAGE > 2, rue du Beau Rivage - CONDRIEU ✆ **04 74 56 82 82.** *Open everyday. Menus from 195 F to 620 F. A la carte 400 F.* This establishment, which has a direct view over the Rhône, enjoys an excellent reputation throughout the region. Of course, there's no beach on the horizon, but there's an ocean of pleasure in store for your tastebuds. In this old fisherman's house, Gérard Donnet prepares a classic cuisine with a pinch of originality and with a refinement which will delight the most discerning. The wine list is very extensive, and the quality of the reception's worthy of the very best establishments.

LA PYRAMIDE > 14, boulevard Fernand Point ✆ **04 74 53 01 96.** *Open everyday except on Tuesdays and Wednesdays. Count around 700 F per person (child around 110 F).* Along the Nationale 7, there exists a constellation of stars which may inspire you to set off on a culinary pilgrimage towards the South. From Paris, you want to stop at the Troisgros' restaurant. Then, after a stop in Lyon itself, you should come to La *Pyramide*, which was created by Fernand Point, one of the great characters in French gastronomy. Point is no longer alive, but certain things haven't changed. It might have seemed dangerous to follow in such footsteps, but Patrick Henrioux has succeeded in breathing modernity into a classic cuisine. At this level, the service is irreproachable, the wine cellar quite staggering (in all price ranges), and the souvenir, unforgettable. And since the chef is a true artist, we can still envy the people who were lucky enough to be invited to the Tsar's Dinner – a faithful reconstruction of a gargantuan, Russian feast. This Pyramid continues to illuminate French cuisine.

LE BEC FIN > 7, place Saint-Maurice ✆ **04 74 85 76 72.** *Closed on Sunday evenings and on Mondays. Menus 98 F (at midday during the week) and from 138 F to 280 F. A la carte around 230 F.* The talented chef, Roger Jolivet, has considerable culinary prowess. The cuisine's classic, and the dishes are either local or regional. Hence, you can taste dishes which are typically Lyonnais (beef-tripe à la lyonnaise, pig's trotter parcels) or more traditional (sole meunière, fillet of John Dory with chives, breast of duck with raspberry vinegar) and, sometimes, inventive : *mousse de saint-jacques aux oursins* (scallop mousse with sea urchins), *médaillon de lotte en bouillabaisse* (medallion of anglerfish in a *bouillabaisse*), *tournedos au jus de truffe...* Connoisseurs of fine food regularly return to this fine restaurant (with an intimate ambiance) to taste the chef's latest creations.

Dauphine-Isere *Where to eat*

LE CLOITRE > 2, rue des Cloîtres © **04 74 31 93 57.** *Closed on Sundays and Mondays. Menus from 100 F to 260 F. A la carte 200 F.* Jacques Caron toils in his kitchen to prepare gastronomic dishes for the pleasure of all - *raviolis de homards au fenouil et à la badiane* (raviolis of lobster with fennel and badian anise), *gratin d'écrevisses à la crème* (gratin of crayfish with cream), *suprême de pintadeau aux morilles* (fillet of guinea-fowl with morel mushrooms)... The setting has a lot of class, both inside, with a beautiful, vaulted dining room giving onto an interior garden, and outside, with a covered terrace on the *Rue Calixte II* and a view over the cathedral gardens. *Le Cloître* is built into a 16th century house, which has been listed by the *Beaux-Arts*. The service, like the cuisine, is refined.

LE MOLIERE > 11, rue Molière © **04 74 53 08 41.** *Closed on Sundays and at midday on Mondays. Menus at 100 F (at midday during the week) and from 105 F to 215 F. A la carte 210 F.* Decorated in wood and stone, this restaurant lacks neither charm nor intimacy for those who want to enjoy a delicious meal *en tête à tête*. Mr. and Mrs. Forez offer a cuisine from the South-West (thinly-sliced breast of duck) and the South-East, including the pan-fried king prawns with its Provençal savours or their famous *bouillabaisse* (by order). Dishes are nicely prepared and attractively presented. It's a good address in summer and winter alike, since you can either eat on the terrace or beside the log fire burning in the chimneypiece.

◆ REGIONAL PRODUCE

If everyone knows the general *Côtes du Rhône appellation*, the reason is that within this vast area, which stretches from the Lyon region to Provence, there are some inspiring names, like *Côte-Rôtie, Condrieu, Hermitage* and *Chateauneuf-du-Pape* ! This wine region is one of the most ancient, and well before Jesus Christ people in this area were tasting the wild grapes which produced a heady drink. Naturally, over the course of 20 centuries, both the quality of the vines and the experience of winemakers has increased so much that, here, you'll now find some of the best (and most expensive !) bottles to be found anywhere.

The Côte-Rôtie AOC

This is the most notherly of the vineyards in the *Côtes du Rhône* and is to be found on the right bank of the river, to the south of Vienne (in the communes of Ampuis, Saint-Cyr-sur-Rhône and Tupins-Semons). It's perched, almost in defiance of gravity, on the steep slopes of hills (exposed to the south-west where the grape can "*rôtir*" (roast) in the burning sun) which have been fashioned by Man over the centuries. An interesting anecdote : the wine from this vineyard is made with grapes which grow either on the *Côte Blonde* or on the *Côte Brune*. The distinction dates back to the days of the Lord of Maugiron, who split his land between his two daughters, one of whom was blonde and the other brunette (the wine from the *Côte Brune* is reputed to be stronger and the wine from the *Côte Blonde*, more delicate) ! Two *cépages* grow on these steep slopes : the syrah, which produces powerful wines which need to be laid-down, and the viognier, which brings a fruitier, more perfumed and almost exotic taste to a wine which might otherwise seem a bit austere. Successfully combining the strength of tannin with the taste of blackberries and a hint of apricots, *Côte Rôtie is* certainly one of France's best red wines.

Condrieu AOC

Condrieu is one of those towns which you have problems in finding on a map, but whose name immediately brings to mind fine wine. And what wine ! Opposite the Rhône and dominating the river, steep hills are home to an exceptional vineyard, which has been carefully conserved. Indeed, although, some years ago, there were fears that lucrative property development might lead to the disappearance of what is one of the most difficult vineyards to cultivate, *Condrieu*'s reputation saved the appellation. Unlike *Côte-Rôtie, Condrieu* is a white wine, but there are similarities between the two, because of the presence in each of the *viognier cépage*. At Condrieu, the *cépage* (variety of grape) grows on barely 60 hectares of vine (the full extent of this appellation). The environment's hostile and the *cépage* is difficult (the *viognier* grape's famous for catching all sorts of diseases and has a low yield), but this enhances the wine's 'rarity-value'. But, provided you can afford it, *Condrieu* offers a unique pleasure. You only have to drink it once in your life to recognize that it's a " great wine ". Both dry and heavy, rough and round, it's a wine which makes you lose your head.

Loire

ROANNE

Discovering Roanne is like courting a discreet beauty who hides her treasures the more completely to seduce you. You'll fall in love with her with a delicate love, not with an uncontrolled, impulsive passion. As he strolls through the prettily-restored streets and winding walks, or ventures to its distant hamlets, the invisible slowly reveals itself to the patient and faithful visitor. Roanne has existed for 2 200 years (this is confirmed by the Regional Archeology Service on the basis of recent archeological findings in the *Place du Château*). And if you're still doubtful, read Ptolemy, the great travelling historian of Antiquity. He already spoke of a certain R*odumna* in his works. A fortified, Gallo-Roman 'molehill', a mediaeval seigneurie, sub-prefecture of the Loire (40 000 inhabitants at the last population count), the town has remained faithful to its motto : *Crescam et lucebo,* Grow and Shine. A difficult task, but one that has been fulfilled. Stuck between its two, larger 'cousins', Lyon and St Etienne, which tend to overshadow it, Roanne has always refused to be a simple 'stop-over' town between the North, the Rhône Valley and Italy (its ochre- and pink-coloured facades doubtless come from the neighbouring country). In the 19th century, the modest river port really took flight. The municipality launched a series of major works (the construction of the bridge over the Loire, the Town Hall, the theatre, the Rouchin Dam, the opening of France's first railway track). Consequently, Roanne became a dynamic, industrial and commercial town. Today, mondialisation and competition have cruelly hit its textile and metal industries, but Roanne remains the uncontested champion of meshwork, with 430 companies in the textile trade producing more than 70% of French ready-to-wear, knitted goods. But, the First Lady of Knitting does more than dress people, she also feeds them. Taking advantage of their privileged position at the heart of the Charolais region, industrial companies, local producers and shopowners have modernised the local food industry (1700 jobs, of which 400 were created in 1998), have maintained a high-quality tradition of meat production and handling, and have made Roanne the reference in matters of gastronomy. The TROISGROS establishment, that internationally-known temple of French cuisine, the highly-publicised chocolate-maker, François PRALUS, Maître Pilati, Prince of *Pâtisserie*, the *Roanne Gastronomie Internationale* Company (whose major shareholder is Christophe Lambert) – these are the most frequently cited local names. The Roannais region has also attracted dozens of young chefs, artisans of an innovative and daring regional cuisine. Finally, with its 1600 university students, Roanne is counting on modern youth, and wants to be known as the town which cultivates Culture. Its theatre season includes 50 shows, it has an ultra-modern media library and cinema building and holds a Science Fiction Festival…Roanne celebrated the beginning of the year 2000 with an enormous laser and firework display on the *Place de l'Hôtel de Ville*. Combining tradition and modernity, Roanne is very well-placed to participate in the great adventure of the third millennium.

◆WHERE TO SLEEP AND EAT

TROISGROS HOTEL > Place Jean Troisgros © **04 77 71 66 97.** If your guest is a Showbiz Star or the producer of your next film, there's only one place to reserve him a room - Troisgros. 19 rooms, duplex flats, flats and suites from 800 F to 2100 F. It's listed by *Relais et Châteaux*, *Gault et Millau* and by *Michelin.* Parking. Animals admitted free. Satellite TV. Located near the station. In short, Troisgros is the 'must' in the Roannais hotel trade and, therefore, offers the additional advantage that your film-making guest may bang into someone he knows. "Julia ! How nice to see you ! Are you going to Cannes ?"

TROISGROS RESTAURANT > Place Jean Troisgros © **04 77 71 66 97.** *Closed on Tuesdays and Wednesdays. 3 macaroons in the Michelin Guide. 19/20 in the Gault et Millau Guide. Menus from 690 F to 830 F.* This gastronomic paradise is just opposite the station, but there's not much more original we can say about it. This establishment has as many stars as the largest constellation and, quite simply, attracts all the superlatives. A meal *Chez Troisgros* confounds the saying "You eat to live, you don't live to eat". Need we remind you that, for meals at the weekend or during Public Holidays, it's wise to reserve several months in advance ? To keep you happy while you wait, have a look at the establishment's website – it reveals just a few of its recipes. Ideal for a foretaste of what's awaiting you.

L'ASTREE > 17bis, cours de la République   ©   **04 77 72 74 22.** *Closed on Saturdays and Sundays. Menus from 99 F to 400 F. 2 dishes : 150 F. 3 dishes : 180 F. Business Menu 105 F except on Public Holidays.* If the idea of some Charolais beef and bone-marrow cooked in red wine doesn't set your mouth watering, or if a back of plain-sautéed lobster batheing in its juice leaves you stone-cold, then keep walking. You'll like it one day, as Beethoven said. In the meantime, one of the best and most popular restaurants in the region combines the 'Art of the Table' with a creative intuition which merits recognition by the most discerning of food-lovers. The setting, which is subtly Art Deco, with round tables covered in white table linen and with bouquets of fresh flowers, is tasteful and refined, and transports you to a world of fine food rather than of love. Having said that, nothing prevents Céladons among you from inviting your beautiful Astrée here, so as to combine the best of both worlds.

L'AVENTURE > 24, rue Pierre Dépierre   ©   **04 77 68 01 15.** *Closed on Sundays and Mondays. Menus : 95 F, 128 F, 168 F, 190 F and 290 F.* You can come to *L' Aventure* without fearing bad surprises or disappointment. For less than 100 F (Business Menu during the week), the food-lover will have a meal which satisfies his expectations, and also astonishes him with its originality. Jean-Luc Trambouze combines the qualities of a fine chef and those of an inspired creator. The two glasses of wine included in the Business Menu prevent the bill from taking off. An imaginative and daring décor, which is in no way lacking in taste, and a pleasant patio, which is open in summer, convince the diner that he is well and truly at *24, Rue Pierre Dépierre,* in one of those restaurants you recommend as if you were giving a present.

THE ROANNAIS REGION

Flirting, in the north, with the Saône-et-Loire and the Allier, caught, in the east, between the Beaujolais and the *Monts du Lyonnais*, and, to the west, between the Bourbonnais and Auvergne, the Roannais region is bounded, to the south, by the *Monts Forez* and by the A72, which runs (from north to south) along its border. This special geographical area includes some of the richest heritage to be found anywhere in the department. Here, you'll find abbeys and mediaeval villages, a host of different museums, a river, lakes and canals, the mountainous countryside around the *Bois Noirs* and the *Monts de la Madeleine*... In short, the Roannais region has every bit as much to offer as the Auvergne and the Beaujolais regions. In spite of the diversity of countryside within it, the region remains homogeneous, and all its parts are anchored in the strong traditions of a common history. If you stop and talk to its people, you'll find generosity without ostentation, along with an acute sense of hospitality. Artisans, winemakers, producers of farm products – all enjoy sharing a taste of fine things with the visitor. Cradle of the Charolais race of cattle, the Roannais offers a gastronomic paradise to those who've come in search of good restaurants, be they covered with stars or simply with the polished, waxy tablecloth of the country inn. For lovers of history, the region offers real treasures : Saint-Haon-le-Châtel, Pommiers, Le Crozet and other towns and villages which have lost none of their yesteryear charm, like Charlieu and Ambierle. Visitors who enjoy quietly drifting along a river know that the port of Briennon's just waiting for them, whilst those who love swimming will make a bee-line for the artificial beaches at Villerest. Traditionally divided into 7 distinct regions – the *Pays de la Pacaudière* in the north, the Loire Gorges in the centre, the *Côte Roannaise* in the west, the *Pays d'Urfé*, the *Pays des Vals d'Aix* and the *Pays d'Isable* in the south-west, the Montagnes du Matin and the area around the Loire and the Rhône in the south and the south-east, the *Pays de Charlieu* and the *Pays de Belmont* in the north-east - the Roannais region offers marvellous tourist circuits, many of which are splendidly-forgotten by the summer hordes.

THE *COTE ROANNAISE*

Between the *Monts de la Madeleine* and the Forez Plain, the *Côte Roannaise* is a walker's paradise, because of the diversity of its countryside, symbol of a generous Nature. Dark green in summer, red in autumn and undefiled during the winter season, this land of vineyards produces an *A.O.C Côte Roannaise* which has earned its Letters of Nobility. From west to east, the countryside begins with the mountains and valleys of the *Monts de la Madeleine* and includes the three frontier communes of Allier, Arcon and Les Noës et Saint-Rirand. **195**

Loire *The Roannais region*

Then, there's a zone of steep hills, including the communes of Ambierle, Saint-Haon-le-Vieux, Saint-Haon-le-Chatel, Renaison, Saint-André d'Apchon and Saint-Alban. Finally, you come to the plains in the east, which gently slope down towards the Loire. Altitude varies from 1152 metres above sea level at Arcon to 300 metres above sea level in the Roannais plains. The Renaison, the Oudan and the Teyssonne rivers wind their way between these slopes and form a river network which provides the entire region with drinking water, thanks, particularly, to the La Tâche and Le Rouchain Dams.

The *Côte Roannaise* doesn't just produce water, but also red and rosé wines which appeared on the first winelists in France, dating from the reign of Louis XIII. Astrée, in the work by Honoré d'Urfé, speaks of "the crop of hills enriched by vineyards". Soil which was originally volcanic in the east, the south and the south-east proved ideal for vines, and the wine region reached its apogee in the 14th century, when more than 15 000 hectares of land were planted with vines. Then came the phylloxera disaster. The work undertaken in the 1960's to reestablish the importance of winegrowing in the region was rewarded in 1994, when *Côtes Roannaises* wine was elevated to the dignity of an *AOC* wine. Finally, the visitor to the region will discover a prestigious architectural, religious and cultural heritage. This can easily be seen in the Ambierle Museum, and is demonstrated by the 23 châteaux which were built in the region between the 10th and 18th centuries. Covered by the large, black woodland of the *Monts de la Madeleine*, the *Côte Roannaise* contains no less than 250 kms of signposted rambling path for fans of rambling, walking and mountain-biking.

SYNDICAT D'INITIATIVE (TOURIST INFORMATION) > 50, route de Roanne - RENAISON
℡ 04 77 62 17 07

TOURIST INFORMATION > Musée Alice Taverne - AMBIERLE ℡ 04 77 65 60 99.

Tourisme Information Côte Roannais > St-Jean-St-Maurice - ST-HAON-LE-CHATEL
℡ 04 77 64 45 30

AMBIERLE

This magnificent village with 1 800 inhabitants is perched on a promontory at an altitude of 400 metres above sea level. The village is constructed in successive circles around old Benedictine buildings. This religious community arrived here in the Middle Ages (505) and was under the authority of the Abbey of Cluny until the 10th century. The village was called, at first, *Adamberta,* and then *Amberta*. It's believed that this is a distortion of the German patronymic, "*Andebert*". Its long facade, which is listed as an Historical Monument, was destroyed by fire and re-built in the 18th century. An ancient priory chapel, the church has a remarkable roof in polished tiles, which is Burgundian in style. The choir has an altarpiece by the 15th century Flemish School and stalls in sculpted oak from the same period. The glasswork in the apse and the four stained-glass windows facing the north depict life-size figures of Christ, the Virgin and 44 Saints. These are a fine example of the extraordinary abilities of master glassworkers in the 15th century. The Priory, which is next to the church, has been entirely restored. It houses the Town Hall and a number of associative meeting rooms.

MUSEE ALICE TAVERNE > Arts and Trditions of Forez ℡ 04 77 65 60 99. *Open from 1st February to 30th November everyday from 10.00 to 12.00 and from 14.00 to 18.00.* Nicely called "The House of the Old Days", this museum is certainly one of the most attaching in the region. A visit here provokes a curious mixture of nostalgia and of endless returns to the past, as if the compass of present happiness needs always to be reflected in the troubling and unclear mirror of a recent past, that of eternal childhood. What secret reasons pushed the little Alice, daughter of a local Ambierlois dignity, to collect documents and various objects in the 1930's ? It makes no difference, because she opened the first room of her museum in 1951 in this 17th century gentleman's residence. Since then, it has grown considerably and offers a faithful reconstruction of peasant life in the old days. Since Alice Taverne's death in 1969, the Friends of the Museum Association have been running and promoting the museum.

Where to sleep and eat

LE PRIEURE > Le bourg © **04 77 65 63 24.** *Closed on Tuesday and Sunday evenings and on Wednesdays. Menus : 88 F 120 F, 148 F, 190 F to 300 F.* For the last 16 years, this has been one of the most prized restaurants in the Roannais region, and the chef, Frédéric Menth, is also President of the Association of Roannais Chefs (currently 35 members). Here, the word 'gastronomy' is in no way compomised, and the food is worthy of a bill which seldom has less than three figures to it. The *lingot moelleux de fruits de mer vinaigrette de crustacés* (soft 'ingot' of seafood and shellfish in a vinaigrette), the *gigot d'agneau de pays farci aux anchois et sauce aux câpres* (leg of country lamb stuffed with anchovies and with a caper sauce) or the *brioche caramélisée aux fraises poêlées* (caramelized brioche with pan-fried strawberries) are quite delicious. If temptation exists, it's so that you can give way to it, don't you think ?

Shopping

If you want to discover and taste the Ambierle *sablé* (shortbread), which is a creation of the village pâtissier, Christian Benetière, don't hesitate to visit his little enterprise. Here, a video film traces the various steps in the production of the *sablé*. His shop is opposite the Post Office.

It's also worth noting that the baker on the *Place Lancelot*, Bernard Fouillat, makes absolutely delicious bread.

SAINT-HAON-LE-CHATEL

Ancient capital of the Counts of Forez in the 15th century, this sentinel-village guarded the Roanne Plain throughout the Middle Ages. It was built little by little around its château. The little ramparts date from 1175 and 1200, whilst the larger ones were constructed in the middle of the 14th century. They have four doors and are flanked by 17 towers. Until the end of the Old Regime, Saint-Haon-le-Chatel remained a dynamic little town with a military barracks, administrative buildings and craftwork shops. Today, it's the principal village in the canton, with 400 inhabitants, and continues to dominate the Roannais Plain from its fortified promontory. A veritable open-air 'Museum of the Middle Ages and of the Renaissance', Saint-Haon should be visited by foot, starting at the *Porte de l'Horloge* (Clock Doorway) which still has its original shutters. The narrow streets hide a number of beautiful timber-framed houses and Renaissance homes. The *Hôtel du Prévôt Jean Pelletier*, which is a fine example of late 15th century architecture, is now the Town Hall. The *Manoir de la Fleur de Lys*, the *Maison des Maret* and the *Maison du Cadran Colaire* (House of the Sundial) are buildings which have to be seen during your stroll. The church, which has a Romanesque bell-tower, used to be the château chapel and was enlargened in the 16th and 17th centuries. It's full of typically Forézian furniture.

Information Point in season and Cultural Information Poster at the entrance to the village.

SYNDICAT D'INITIATIVE DE LA COTE ROANNAISE © **04 77 66 82 48**
TOURIST INFORMATION © **04 77 64 45 30**
GUIDED VISITS © **04 77 64 21 90.** *By appointment.*

RENAISON

In the past, Renaison was the last stop before Roanne on the road from Vichy, and is still quite dynamic, both economically and in terms of tourism. Well-situated at the heart of the Côte Roannaise and at the foot of the *Monts de la Madeleine*, the valley around it still has a number of large industries. In the east of the commune, the *Château de Boisy* (15th and 16th centuries) used to be the property of the *Grand Argentier de la Cour de France* (Treasurer of the French Court), Jacques Cœur. In one of the old village streets, the stroller find old houses and a Renaissance turret. The *Manoir de Beaucresson* should also be seen. The La Tâche and Le Rouchain Dams are just 6 kms from the village. Surrounded by deep forests, the site offers a majestic view over a wild countryside, and a number of signposted paths make for very pleasant walks in summer. The Chartrain Dam, which was built in 1891, will give you vertigo, because it's 221 metres high. Like the Rouchain Dam, it offers an exceptional panorama of the *Vieux Pays de la Madeleine.*

Loire *The Roannais region*

Where to sleep and eat

AUBERGE DU BARRAGE > La Tâche Dam *©* **04 77 64 41 23.** *Closed on Monday evenings and on Tuesdays. Menus 75 F to 200 F. Open everyday during the two summer months.* At the foot of the La Tâche and Le Rouchain Dams, and surrounded by beautiful, green scenery, the inn will tempt you with its specialities of frogs and trout à la **Bourbonnaise**, which come fresh from the stream beside the restaurant. In summer, the shady terrace is very popular. The owners of the inn are imaginative when it comes to attracting visitors, and have reserved a large area for camping-cars in their car park.

HOTEL RESTAURANT JACQUES COEUR > 15, rue de Roanne *©* **04 77 64 25 34.** *Closed on Sunday evenings and on Mondays. Menus 90 F (during the week) and from 130 F to 350 F. A la carte around 250 F. 2 stars. 8 rooms from 190 F to 258 F in a double, TV and telephone in the rooms, private parking, animals allowed. Terrace and access for the disabled.* This has to be one of the best restaurants in the region. The food's exquisite, and Jacques Cœur's motto used to be "nothing's impossible for the bold". If the new, young chef had a motto, it might be "everything's permitted to the daring chef". He passionately loves his profession, and never hesitates to break with tradition in order to innovate – as you'll see from his highly original Dessert List. Traditional food-lovers will recognize the incomparable taste of a fresh, home-made *foie gras*, whilst innovators will be tempted by the *émincé de bœuf charolais à la lie-de-vin* (thinly-sliced Charolais beef with its wine sauce).

Shopping

SABOTERIE DANIEL DRIGEARD > Chazelles *©* **04 77 64 25 66.** The Drigeard family have been sculpting and working clogs for 8 generations. Their first clog shop, then in the middle of a large forest, dates back to 1734. Today, Daniel and his wife are at the controls of a small, craftwork enterprise which is known as far away as Japan ! Production has diversified, because they now offer their customers security clogs, anatomical sandals, Swedish leather (the uppers) clogs, shoes for the medical profession and sandals with cork and elastomer soles - not forgetting the traditional clogs, of course. "Dig your garden in clogs, you'll get fine vegetables and you'll find it fun", affirms the master-clogmaker, who uses essentially two types of wood – birch and beech. His annual production is 2 000 pairs of wooden clogs and 7 000 to 8 000 pairs of leather (the uppers) clogs. Renaison clogs export well and are known throughout the world. You can visit the workshop from May to September, provided you make an appointment beforehand. During the visit, which lasts about an hour, you'll see the clogmaking process from A to Z. A large choice of models is on sale in the display shop.

SAINT-ALBAN-LES-EAUX

Saint-Alban reached its apogee at the end of the Second Empire, when 'watering-towns' were really fashionable. Indeed, the area's full of springs. In the 14th century, this tiny little village was placed under the patronage of Saint-Alban, the Christian martyr who was put to death in *Verulamium* (now St. Alban's) in England during the reign of Diocletius. When he was led to his execution on a very hot day, Alban took pity on his executioners and beseeched God to refresh them. An abundant spring immediately appeared at his feet. In 1815, after Waterloo,

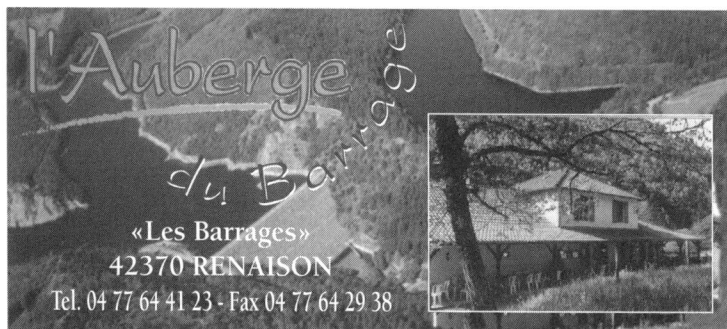

L'Auberge du Barrage

«Les Barrages»
42370 RENAISON
Tel. 04 77 64 41 23 · Fax 04 77 64 29 38

Maréchal Ney took refuge at Saint-Alban, but never had the time to enjoy the healing virtues of its waters. He was recognised and nearly lynched by a crowd which didn't go a bundle on the Imperial Regime. The Antonin Spring, which has been used for more than 2000 years, is rich in iron, bicarbonates, mineral salts and fluoride and, totally lacking in nitrates, is recommended for stomach and kidney infections. "At the same time as it cleans the internal organs, it also reduces hangover. Hence, it's doubly efficacious", says Elie Mouiller, in *"Le Vignoble de la Côte Roannaise"* (The Vineyard and the *Côte Roannaise*), cited by Jean Tibi and Robert Maréchal in their own work, *"La Loire et ses pays"* (The Loire and its Regions). De Borée Editions.

BOTTLED WATER

Two specialists in sugary drinks (the Dutchman, Winters and the Belgian, Sunco), have bought the Mineral Water Company of Saint-Alban and have built a bottling plant. In addition to the production of sparkling mineral water (25 million bottles), the company also produces soft drinks, including those for big names like *Pepsi-Cola, Liptonic, Seven Up, Tropico,* and *Choky.* The company has also taken on the old activity of Schweppes France. The new shareholders have restored the village inhabitants' ancient right to take free water from the well.

Where to sleep and eat

RESTAURANT LE PETIT PRINCE > Le Bourg   ©   **04 77 65 87 13.** *From May to September : closed on Mondays. From October to April : closed on Sunday evenings and on Mondays. Menus : 98 F,125 F, 160 F and 200 F. A la carte : 130 F.* On Charles Reure's initiative, this winemaking farm was converted in the 1930's into an hotel-restaurant. In 1988, Charles Rieure's two grandsons, Jean-François and Olivier, re-opened *Le Petit Prince*, firstly as a bar, and then, in 1992, as a restaurant. There are two tastefully-decorated dining rooms, with beams and suspended ceilings. In summer, the courtyard terrace is very much in demand, as you'd expect. Among the specialities on the menu, gourmets will choose between the fresh frogs and a terrine of mussels with nuts and leeks, some thinl-sliced breast of duck with red fruit or a seafood *pot-au-feu.* When dessert time finally arrives, the children, who have disappeared into the surrounding countryside, will suddenly and miraculously reappear, and will no longer complain that the seats are uncomfortable. The *croustillant aux fruits du moment* (the crispy fruits in season) and the chocolate and banana *terrine* are enough to bring regiments of Little Princes back from the moon.

Shopping

THE *COTE ROANNAISE* AND WINE : A LOVE STORY > The love story between the *Cote Roannaise* and wine doesn't date from yesterday. Written records of this idyll go back to the Middle Ages, when monks settled in the region. They left many documents testifying to the existence of a large vineyard and of an active wine trade. From the 13th century onwards, references to winemaking multiplied. The market quotation of local wines dates from 1439. In the 17th century, between 1620 and 1670, the surface area of local vineyards doubled. River navigation on the Loire allowed wine to be transported rapidly to the capital. At the end of the Old Regime, some 40 000 to 50 000 bottles of local wine were being sent to Paris every year. The extension of the winemaking area continued after the Revolution, but began to reduce as the continued conscription under the First Empire slowly emptied rural areas. The carnage of the Great War had precisely the same effect. But, like old mushrooms which cling to the best, sunny slopes, the Roannais winemaking soul lives on in the 14 communes of the *Côte Roannaise.* Today, its 160 hectares have earned their Letters of Nobility with a well-deserved *AOC appellation.* The Roannais Winemakers' Association, presided over by Albert Serol, groups 57 winemakers on some 20 estates, with an annual production of around 8 000 hectolitres. The arrival of the latest *Côte Roannaise* wine is celebrated every 15th December. The Wine Competition takes place on the first Saturday in February and is held in a different commune every year. The prizes are awarded by a very knowledgeable jury.

THE LOIRE – ITS 3 VINEYARDS AND 5 AOC'S

The solidarity and fraternity which exists between winemakers force us to announce a piece of good news : in the department of the Loire, the big event of the year was the recognition of *Côte du Forez* as an *Appellation d'Origine Contrôlée* wine! The decree was passed in February 2000, so that, from now on, there are 5 AOC wines produced in the region - *Côte du Roannais, Côte du Forez, Condrieu, Saint-Joseph, Château Grillet*. The Forez produces one-quarter of the white, Saint-Joseph appellation and 25% of the production of red, as well as 60% of *Condrieu* and a small quantity of *Côte Rôtie*. The Forézians asked for the *AOC* at the same time as the Roannais, five years ago. Their co-operative cellar at Trelins certainly saved the vineyard, but its monopoly prevented independent winemakers (guarantors of local winemaking tradition and knowledge) from developing. Dominique Chèze, the cellar's President, understood this, and encouraged private winemakers. Today, the new *AOC* honours 180 private co-operative members and 4 private winemakers whose produce is immediately identified with the region. The *appellation* covers 200 hectares, split over 17 communes between Boën-sur-Lignon and Montbrison. The *Côte du Forez* is a delicate but powerful wine, which is best drunk chilled.

THE *MONTAGNES DU MATIN*

Somewhere in Asia, around a bend of the Mekong or of the Yellow River, there has to be a "Land of the Morning Mountains". And if it doesn't feature on the maps, it lives in our exotic dreams. Perhaps there's no point in travelling that far to find it. The *Montagnes du Matin* well and truly exist between Lyon, Roanne and Saint Etienne, and derive this poetic name from their geographical situation in the extreme East of the Forez Plain. Here, our ancestors watched the sun rising on the crests. Through the flowery villages, the valley and hills, from *Mont Boussuivre* (Matagrin Tower), the highest point in the *Monts du Lyonnais* (1000m), to the banks of the Loire, the visitor discovers as soon as he reaches the *Montagnes du Matin* (on foot, horseback or mountain-bike) signposted pathways, little roads dotted with Romanesque chapels, beautiful views and fine restaurants.

THE *MONTAGNES DU MATIN* TOURIST OFFICE > 1, rue de la République - PANISSIERES
℃ **04 77 28 67 70.** *Open from Tuesday to Friday from 10.00 to 12.00 and from 13.30 to 17.30. On Saturdays, from 09.00 to 12.00.*

INFORMATION POINTS > Balbigny – Town Hall - RN82 ℃ **04 77 28 14 12.** *Open from Monday to Friday* • St Jodard - *Place du Village* - Enquiries at the Town Hall ℃ **04 77 63 42 42** • Violay – Town Hall - ℃ **04 74 63 90 92.** *Open all year. Self-service.*

BUSSIERES

In the extreme south-east of the Roannais region. A document dating from 984 proves that this village existed at that time. It has two faces – the one rural and the other industrial. It's true that the regional economy traditionally depends on agriculture, but, since time immemorial, weaving has played an important part in regional life, as can be seen from the name of the village of Chenevoux which, in the year 1000, was called *"cananerosus"*, then *"canabium"*, that is to say "land propitious for the growing of hemp". In the 19th century, during the period when the silk-weaving industry reached its apogee in the Lyonnais region, this activity reached Le Bussièrois and converted many peasants to silk-breeding and weaving. Today, the number of second houses in the area has risen dramatically, thereby demonstrating that the environment is a pleasant one. All of a sudden, the population has considerably increased, and craftwork and local trade is expanding enormously. The principal activity in Bussières remains weaving, and several companies produce Tergal fabric and silk.

*** MUSEE DU TISSAGE ET DE LA SOIRIE *** (THE SILK AND WEAVING MUSEUM) > Place Vaucanson. (Access for the disabled in the Impasse Branly) ℃ **04 77 27 33 95.** *Open from March to October from 15.00 to 19.00.* It was entirely logical that a Silk and Weaving Museum should see the light of day in Bussières. This museum was created in 1977 but was moved into an old weaving factory in 1998. It's a living museum, where local professionals come to share their knowledge with visitors by means of stories and anecdotes, and with the aid of numerous operational machines. From the silk thread to the finished article, you follow a history which begins long ago in China. In addition to learning about the different weaving professions, you can also admire a fine collection of Jacquard looms, spoolers, reels, warp beams, planters and entwiners, as well as a host of accessories and tools used in the weaving trade. The museum's the lifetime's work of Mr. Berchoux, who is in charge of the museum and is assisted by a number of Bussiérois who share his passion.

PANISSIERES

You could reproach Panissières for falling a few kilometres outside the Roannais region and for secretly flirting with the neighbouring department of the Rhône, but the 3 000 or so Panissièrois, like all good bordermen, cultivate a taste for independence and a love of freedom. Everything suggests that, as early as the 9th century, there was a town here which gradually developed around the St Loup Chapel. The ancient road from Feurs to Tarare (D60) crossed Panissières, and made it a favourite stopping-place of travellers. Today, the town controls movement along the major roads : the RD60 from Jas to Villechenève (Rhône), the RD103 from Montchal to the border with Essertines-en-Donzy and the RD27 from Cottance Chambost-Longessaigne (Rhône).

Destination *randonnée*

Autoroute A72, sortie FEURS ou BALBIGNY

MONTAGNES DU MATIN

Montagnes du matin
OFFICE DE TOURISME

CONSEIL GENERAL
LOIRE
EN RHÔNE-ALPES

Office de Tourisme des Montagnes du Matin
1 rue de la République — 42360 PANISSIÈRES
Tel. 04 77 28 67 70 — Fax 04 77 28 82 18

Loire *The Montagnes du Matin*

Property, here, was traditionally divided into small segments, a phenomenon which gave rise to a very particular, local economy, consisting of a large number of small farms, often completed by a "boutique". The rural countryside today still has this patchwork of dispersed houses and farms. In the old days, hemp, linen and, then, silk was weaved here. Cloth traders then sold the pieces of material at the markets in neighbouring communes. At the end of the Old Regime, a Cloth Commissioner was appointed, and it was his responsibility to collect various tithes and taxes. In 1704, regional records tell us that at the Panissières Market you could find 4 000 rolls of different cloths and cottons measuring 30 to 40 ells (1 ell = 1m188), 5 000 rolls of canvas or serge, 500 rolls of *couty* (wool thread and cotton) and 500 rolls of material for tablecloths and napkins measuring 20 ells. Production on this scale demonstrates extraordinary knowledge of weaving and the existence of a large, pre-industrial, textile infrastructure. The first factories producing table linen, fabric and muslin were built in the middle of the 19th century. The population at that time was almost 5000.

The *Montagnes du Matin* Tourist Office, in Panissières,(04 77 28 67 70) covers 27 communes in the cantons of Feurs and Néronde. Located in a converted and renovated shop, the Tourist Office also sells different, local textile products.

THE SEIGNE FARM > This old, 18th century farm, which is typical of the *Monts du Lyonnais*, is open to the public. It's been converted into a rural gîte. Visit by appointment on 04 77 28 67 70 or 04 77 28 69 68.

Where to sleep and eat

HOTEL DE LA POSTE > 15, rue J.B. Guerpillon ℂ **04 77 28 64 00.** *Open everyday. Restaurant closed at midday on saturdays. Menus from 65 F to 175 F. Two stars. 12 rooms from 220 F to 250 F for a double. TV and telephone in the rooms, private parking, pets welcome.* Mireille Collas welcomes the visitors, whilst Thierry Dié works at the oven and prepares them traditional little dishes with fresh produce. There's a large dining room and a smaller, younger 'sister' – both of them tastefully decorated. You'll enjoy your food in quiet.

THE COUNTRYSIDE BETWEEN THE LOIRE AND THE RHONE

Between the *Pays de Charlieu*, to the north, and the *Montagnes du Matin*, to the south, the *Pays de Saint-Symphorien-de-Lay* slopes gently upwards from the Loire Gorges as far as the *Col du Pin Bouchain* (885 m, in the *Monts du Beaujolais*). It's a country of traditions and of commercial exchange, located on the old Royal Road which became the Napoleon Road and, later, the RN7. The presence of the nearby Beaujolais region can be felt in the architecture of its farms and in the surrounding countryside. Along the country roads, you'll find 16 villages which are rich in a religious and historical heritage. Ramblers will particularly appreciate the signposted paths, which wind through picturesque sites and a rolling landscape.

TOURIST INFORMATION > Neulise Town Hall ℂ **04 77 64 61 13**
TOURIST OFFICE > Saint Symphorien de Lay ℂ **04 77 28 67 70**

CORDELLE

CAMPING MUNICIPAL DE MARS ℂ **04 77 64 94 42.** *Open from 3rd April to 30th September.* 3 star camping site. A real paradise for campers and bathers. 65 places. Swimming pool. Superb view of the Loire. Snackbar.

SAINT-SYMPORIEN-DE-LAY

This really is the countryside "between the Loire and the Rhône". To the east, the crags of the *Monts de Tarare* culminate at 900m in the area around Machézal, near the C*ol du Pin Bouchain.* To the north-west, the Pradines area is on the border of the Roanne Plain. In the middle, the *Seuil de Neulise*, where the altitude varies between 400 m and 500 m, offers a landscape of hills and plateaus. The west takes you to the Loire Gorges and to Saint-Priest-la Roche. Until the country was divided into departments during the Revolution, this area was on the borders of the provinces of Beaujolais and of Forez. The borderline between the two provinces ran through Neulise, Saint-Cyr-de-Favières and Saint-Just-la-Pendue. Cordelle and Saint-Piest-la-Roche belonged to Forez, whilst Régny was a Lyonnais enclave in Beaujolais.

The village of Lay (from the Latin "*latus*" : slope) was originally a Roman military post, which developed in successive circles around the ancient oppidum. The walk along the old ramparts is very plesant. Saint Symphorien-de-Lay, its neighbour, was better located on the Great Roman Road. In the Middle Ages, it was an important stopping-place on the road from Paris to Lyon (and going as far as Rome), which was successively called the Royal Road, the Imperial or Napoleon Road and, much later, the *Nationale 7.*

The area around Saint-Symphorien-de-Lay offers a variety of different countryside, depending on the commune you happen to be visiting. This fact was dictated by economic reasons. Principal economic activity in the Gand Basin was canvas weaving, whilst the Rhins Valley was devoted to cotton. On the other hand, around the Neulise Plateau, agriculture and cattle breeding predominated. Throughout the *Pays de Saint-Symphorien-de-Lay*, you'll find an extraordinary collection of historical, religious and architectural curiosities : the Cabin Oven at Saint-Victor-sur-Rhins is a craft oven for baking tiles ; between Lay and Neaux, there's the Roche sur Gand Viaduct as well as the *Etang de la Roche*, a fisherman's paradise ; Marchezal houses an intersting bust of Napoleon ; a 'religious heritage circuit' joins the Priory Church (12th and 13th centuries) in Saint-Symphorien-de-Lay to the ancient, fortified church in Chirassimont (10th century with porch); the *Chapelle Notre dame-de-Pitié*; the statues in painted wood and the miraculous Saint Fortunat's Fountain in Croizet -sur-Gand; the Pie VII's Cross in au Plat-Coupy. At Fourneaux, you'll find fine frescoes in the Church of Saint-Cyr-de-Favières ; the bell-tower in the church in Saint-Just-la-Pendue is also a water-tower. Also to be visited are the Cluniac Priory of Saint-Victor-sur-Rhins and the 18th century crystal chandelier in the church in Vendranges.

THE *TETE NOIRE* RELAY STATION > This is one of the oldest relay stations in France, and was named after a Moorish brigand who terrorized the region during the Hundred Years' War. On the Royal Road (also called the " Bourbonnais" Road) linking Paris to Rome via Lyon, the inn enjoys a privileged location. It was the last stop before the formidable *Montagne de Tarare*, which was feared both by horses and their riders, the first because of the slope, and the second because of the highwaymen who adored the area. From its construction under Louis XI to the Revolution, the relay station was visited by a host of VIP's : Joachim du Bellay, François 1st, Rabelais, Ronsard, Henri IV, Mazarin, Madame de Sévigné, Molière, J.J Rousseau, Napoleon and his mortal enemy, Pope Pius VII. The commune bought the *Relais de la Tête Noire* in 1992 and carried out a lot of restoration work. The discovery of a hidden, painted décor and of 16th and 17th century graffiti led to the inn's inclusion on the Additional List of Historic Monuments. It now houses the Tourist Office (04 77 62 77 77), its exhibition room and multi-media area. The exhibitions planned for the summer are : "*Odile Girardin, a Painting Exhibition*" ; "*The Loire, Land of Italy – Unusual Italy, a Photographic Exhibition*".

DISCOVER THE *PAYS ENTRE LOIRE ET RHÔNE*

TOURIST OFFICE FOR THE "PAYS entre LOIRE et RHÔNE"

rue de la Tête-Noire
42470 ST-SYMPHORIEN-DE-LAY
Tel. 04 77 62 77 77
Fax 04 77 62 77 78
e. mail :
OT-COPLER@monts-du-beaujolais

OPENING HOURS
Tuesday to Saturday : 09.00 to 12 .30 and 14.00 to 18 . 30.
Sundays and Public holydays :
09.30 to 12. 30
Infos : www.monts-du-beaujolais.org

Loire *The countryside between the Loire and the Rhone*

OFFICE DE TOURISME DU PAYS ENTRE LOIRE ET RHONE > 6, rue de la Tete Noire ℂ 04 77 62 77 77.
E-mail : OT-COPLER à monts-du-beaujolais.org site:www.monts-du-beaujolais.org

Where to sleep and eat

HOTEL RESTAURANT LA POSTE > 63, RN7   ℂ   04 77 64 75 35. *Closed on Tuesdays. Menus from 65 F to 135 F, Dish of the Day 40 F. 2 stars, Logis de France, 10 rooms from 190 F to 350 F in a double, TV and telephone in the rooms, private parking, pets welcome.* Located in the village centre. This well-known restaurant serves traditional dishes : chicken with crayfish, chicken liver salad, fillet of pike-perch and game (when in season).

FOURNEAUX

In the Middle Ages, the village was called *"Fornels"*, or 'ovens', thereby indicating that industrial activity was already well established. Later, muslin and satin-stitch was made here till the end of the 19th century, and the village was also active in embroidery-work. The textile industry has survived to the present day, and there's a silk factory here which is known throughout the world. Agriculture, on the other hand, has been reducing in scale from the 1960's although, in the last 12 months, there have been signs of a small recovery. Today, there are 528 inhabitants in the commune.

THE POPE'S CHASUBLE MADE IN FOURNEAUX

The Magat Weaving Company in Fourneaux dresses Arab emirs, English princesses, TV personalities and….the Pope. This family company, which has 72 employees and is run by Louis Magat, has been producing beautiful craftwork since 1930. At the entrance to the workshop, there are photos of celebrities, including King Hassan II and Miss France, as well as one of the Pope opening the Jubilee Doors. All are wearing clothes made with material which was weaved on 60 Jacquard looms in the Magat factory. A golden, silk cope, a chasuble with golden thread weaved in a complicated leaf design….the Holy Father's sacerdotal robes were just part of a huge order sent by the Vatican with extremely precise instructions. The clothes had to be light and supple, and had to dazzle at the slightest sunshine on the gold embroidery. The Church brought an old pontifical mitre to the factory, so that the weavers could reproduce the design on the current Pope's robes. In the factory archives, there's a collection of 500 volumes containing thousands of samples of materia made from 1835 to the present day – it's a silk encyclopaedia.

In the 12th century, the *Château de l'Aubépin* was, like many stronghouses, a simple, fortified farm, flanked by a simple, square tower. The château's appearance was modified between the 14th and the end of the 19th centuries, doubtless because of the civil wars which ravaged the realm during this period. Pillaged countless times by bands of German mercenaries under Protestant pay, the château was in a dilapidated condition just before the Great War. It was magnificently restored in the 1990's. The exterior of the château's beautiful, with a French garden-terrace and a fine, 15th century pavilion. The château's surrounded by dry moats, and there's a drawbridge at the entrance. It can be visited everyday except on Tuesdays, Wednesdays and Thursdays, from 11.00 to 18.00.

PRADINES

This commune runs parallel to the Roanne road (some 12 kms from it) and was called Pradines as long ago as 1293. The word derives from the Latin word *'pratum'*, or 'meadow', and the quickest glance at the village will tell you that it wasn't built yesterday.

Pradines is known primarily because of its Abbey, which is still occupied by nuns and is much-visited, especially at weekends. Of the château belonging to the Lords of Lestouf (built in the 17th century and located at the edge of the Rhins Valley, in the extreme south of the parish) little now remains of the original construction, which was flanked by two towers with loopholes. Under the Concordat, the Lyon Diocesis bought the château. Thérèse de Bavoz, a nun expelled from the Terraux Monastery in Lyon during the Terror, obtained permission in 1816 to continue her religious life (following the Order of Saint Benoît) in Pradines. Both Cardinal Fesch, Archbishop of Lyon and uncle of Napoléon 1st, and the Emperor's mother took refuge here after the rout of the Imperial armies. Under the Restoration, an Abbey Church was built in 1820.

Today, the 59 nuns pursuing a monastic life in the abbey lead a life of work and prayer. They live from the abbey's shop, workhouses (printing and binding) and liturgical ornaments. Since 1978, the abbey has been the responsibility of the abbess, Mother Superior Luc Congar. Although they have no direct contact with the outside world, the sisters take mail orders. The printing workshop produces wedding invitations, cards and writing paper, whilst the binding workshop binds reviews, memoirs, library books and collectors' items in both cloth and leather. It also restores and gilds ancient books and other documents. The abbey welcomes individuals or groups who want to follow a retreat, and guests can share the religious community's ecclesiastical life if they wish to. Enquiries to the Sister in charge of the hostel on 04 77 64 80 06. During your visit to the abbey, you can also watch a video film, which is screened on demand, and go to the abbey's craftwork shop which is open everyday from 10.00 to 12.00 and from 14.30 to 16.30 except on Tuesdays. The abbey also opens a pharmacy every morning from 10.00 to 12.00 (except on Mondays) and every afternoon from 14.45 to 19.00 (except on Sundays when it opens from 15.30 to 16.30).

MONTAGNY

FRANÇOIS DORIEUX'S ROSES ℂ **04 77 66 13 37.** The village looks like many others in the region. François Dorieux, however, is like nobody else. A talented rosegrower, he has won numerous national and international prizes, and has created several varieties of flower. This alchemist of a fragile but eternal beauty strives ceaselessly to create new varieties, which he impregnates with tiny brushes, or grafts onto climbing plants with deep-growing roots. This work requires both patience and passion before the miracle happens – the flowering. François Dorieux has also created some thirty varieties of rose, and, in the whole of France, there are just ten or so professional rosegrowers.

THE *PAYS DE CHARLIEU, DU SORNIN* AND DE BELMONT

In the north-east of the Roannais region, near the Rhône and the Saône-et-Loire, lies the *Pays de Charlieu*, itself consisting of the *Pays du Sornin* and the *Pays de Belmont*. The rivers Sornin and Loire meet at Pouilly, and fourteen communes have adopted this village as a logotype, showing, horizontally, the water in this region of the Roannais Plain bordered by rolling prairies. Vertically, a tower testifies to the history and of its surroundings. The *Pays de Belmont* is qualified with the additional words *"de la Loire"* so as to distinguish it from the 17 other Belmonts located in 14 departments. If it's called Belmont-de-la-Loire, it's also very nearly in the *Haut Beaujolais*. From La Grêle, in the south, to Saint-Germain-la-Montagne, in the north, the nine communes in the *Pays de Belmont* stretch over 30 kilometres, which look like a Loire peninsula forcing its way between the Rhône and the Saône-et-Loire departments. This longitudinal narrowness underlies the attaching relief which characterizes the *Pays de Belmont*. It's a region of little mountains, where altitudes vary between 400 m and 700 m. *Mont Pinay* culminates at a height of 883 m above sea level. The *Col des Echarmaux*, the canton's eastern gateway, is 720 metres above sea level. The valleys are irrigated by numerous rivers and streams – the Aaron and the Botoret (where trout are fished) feed the Rhins and the Sornin areas. Woodland covers 3 500 hectares, or 34.5% of the canton's surface area, and more than 70% of the woods are resinous.

A countryside which attracts 'green tourism', but which also offers cultural interest (with museums, abbeys and countless historic sites), the *Pays de Charlieu*, the *Pays du Sornin* and the *Pays de Belmont* have a great deal to offer history-lovers – the Silk Museum, the Hospital Museum, the Benedictine Abbey, the Cordeliers' Convent and the Abbey Church at La Bénisson-Dieu. The region's also full of traditional, rural homes. Finally, those who enjoy river tourism will love the canal leading to the Loire. At the port of Briennon, they'll be able to hire a boat, or go on a gastronomic cruise on a barge which has been converted to house a restaurant. Endless possibilities for lodging and the excellence of local restaurants make the *Pays de Charlieu* a little paradise for any visitor.

Loire *The pays de Charlieu, du Sornin and de Belmont*

THE PAYS DE CHARLIEU TOURIST > Place St Philibert ℭ **04 77 60 12 42.** *Open all year. From April to the end of September, everyday except on Mondays. From October to March, from Tuesday to Saturday.*

TOURIST INFORMATION FOR THE LA TEYSSONE VALLEY > Parvis Albéric - LA BÉNISSON-DIEU ℭ **04 77 66 64 65.**
INFORMATION POINTS > Briennon - Marins d'Eau Douce ℭ **04 77 69 92 92**

SAINT-ETIENNE

With 201 000 inhabitants and a surface area of 8 000 ha, Saint-Etienne is the second largest town in the Rhône-Alpes region and the 10th largest provincial town. Capital of the Forez, Prefecture of the department of the Loire, a town in which seven hills lead up from the major street (with its tramway), Saint-Etienne is situated where three valleys meet (the Ondaine, the Gier and the Furan Valleys). It's almost at the entrance to the Pilat Regional Park, and is just a few miles from the Loire Gorges. Hence, it enjoys a privileged location, and offers all sorts of leisure activities. In 1998, six World Cup matches were played at Saint-Etienne, and this provided the opportunity to improve the road network, to extend air links and to transform the town's hyper-centre. After months of works, the *Place Marengo* is now finished. From a shady garden, it's been turned into a vast esplanade which makes the best of the *Eglise Saint Charles*. A mining town in the old days, Saint-Etienne subsequently built a reputation in the field of metallurgy, of arms engraving, of passementerie and of bicycle production. It's a town which is geared for economic expansion and which is seeking to attract companies to the area. The Entreprise (Company) Magazine recently classed Saint-Etienne 7th in a list of French towns best-equipped to satisfy companies' business needs. Today, it's home to 18 000 companies, of which 4 000 are medium-sized companies, and 60 000 people are employed in the private sector. Companies with offices or production units in the town include some of the finest in the field of mechanical engineering, textiles, the bio-medical sector, the food industry, the water and the environmental fields. *Badoit, Casino, Bell, Excella, Floerger, Focal, Gibaud, Houlès, Obut, Thuasne, Verney Carron* and *Weiss* are just some of the major companies located here.

In spite of local industry, Saint-Etienne isn't a black town. Among the town's seven museums, the Museum of Modern Art (whose collection is one of the best to be found in the provinces) is one of the finest of its type. Major cultural events, including the Book Festival, 'Art in the Town', the International Design Biennial, the Massenet Festival, the 'Words and Music Festival', attract thousands of visitors. Built in 1947 by Jean Dasté as a conference centre and as a School of Dramatic Art, the *Centre Dramatique National de la Comédie* counts more than 150 000 spectators every year. In spite of a criminal fire which, in September 1998, ravaged the *Grand Théâtre*, the Esplanade is beginning to prove a success, and a number of musical, choreographic and theatrical productions are presented at the *Théâtre de l'Ephémère*. Many are the independent troupes and associations which testify to the town's creative dynamism. The Stéphanois heritage still boasts a multi-media library, a regional video library and two 'art and trial cinemas'. At the same time, many famous artists and personalities were born in Saint-Etienne : Bernard Lavilliers, Muriel Robin, Bruno Gaccio, Philippe Favier, Huguette Bouchardeau, Piem and Jean Guitton are just some of them...

Finally, the name of Saint-Etienne is inevitably linked to the world of football. After a grim period, the ASSE is back in Division 1, and Stéphanois are proud of the fact. Revived by the World Cup, the football flame sets alight the *Chaudron* (Cauldron), the nickname for the famous Geoffroy Guichard Stadium. *Les Verts* (The Greens) have found their old supporters - Saint-Etienne, too.

Where to sleep and eat

HOTEL ALBATROS > 67, rue Saint-Simon ℭ **04 77 41 41 00.** Opposite the Saint-Etienne Municipal Golf Course, this establishment offers a wide range of traditional menus, from 160 F to 300 F.

Ville de Saint-Etienne

Saint-Etienne !

There are places that no traveller can forget, even if their attachment is only a brief memory recalled years later.

Decidedly, Saint-Etienne is not just another city.

Because here, when you're from Saint-Etienne, be it by birth or adoption, you cannot help but take on this heritage as your own.

Here, one is inevitably stimulated by the force of the builders, inventors and creators that have provided France with arms for its defence, with steel for construction, with energy to live and with solidarity to surpass themselves.

Today, Saint-Etienne is facing the challenges of the third millenium with this same drive and courage. With the power of repeated success, with a passion for ambitious projects and the determination and confidence built on past achievements, Saint-Etienne is and will remain a reference for years to come.

Be sure its continued expansion will surprise no one.

185 000 inhabitants

10 parks (190 ha) + a 100 ha public golf course

1st place in french urban development, 1999

2nd city in the Rhône-Alpes region

14th city of France by population

2nd modern art collection in France

170 000 jobs

11 500 companies, including 4 000 in industrial firms

2 400 retail stores

20 000 students

www.mairie-st-etienne.fr

Loire *The Pilat region and the Gier Valley*

HOTEL MERCURE > Rue Wuppertal - Parc de l'Europe   ℰ   **04 77 42 81 84.** This 3-star hotel offers good quality and an excellent service. The hotel's various salons are regularly used for receptions, so you should reserve in advance. The menu prices (from 300 F upwards) reflect the quality and service on offer.

NOUVELLE > 30, rue Saint Jean   ℰ   **04 77 32 32 60.** *Menu of the Day 90 F, Business Menus at 98 F and 118 F. Menus at 150 F and 190 F (2 or 3 dishes). Composition Menus 210 F, 260 F and 310 F (2, 3 or 4 dishes). Grand 8 Menu by order 350 F. Closed on Mondays. Take away catering service.* Here, you'll find a very talented chef with hands made for cooking. The young Stéphane Laurier honours gastronomy with his three lobster dishes (295 F) and with his efforts to liven up Children's Menus. Food-lovers will love his **ombre chevalier poché au court-bouillon** (poached char in aromatic stock) and *tombée d'épinards frais avec crème brûlée à l'ail et fleurette au fenouil bronze* (fresh spinach with garlic and bronze-coloured fennel fleurette). He's studied under Orsi and the Troisgros brothers (amongst others) and confesses to looking through old recipes and adapting them, using the freshest of produce. The menu varies with the seasons, and the wine list contains a huge variety of wines from everywhere. The glass of wine (20 F) proposed to you is a ticket for the Spanish vineyards. The atmosphere's intimate, and the tables are made more beautiful with a little touch signed by *Fleur Bleue* (see the heading " Presents "). Sugar turns to honey around the *tarte fine de fourme de Montbrison et poire de pays* (thin tart of Montbrison fourme cheese and country pears), and the Dessert of the Day's topped with crisp caramel. You'll love it.

THE PILAT REGION AND THE GIER VALLEY

A green and slightly mountainous area not far from Saint-Etienne, the Pilat's characterized by a diversity of landscape : beech and pine forests high up on the crags dominating the Rhône Valley, grazing land dotted with beautiful granite farms on the high plateaux and vines and fruit trees in the area called Rhodanian Pilat (the Rhône part of the Pilat region).

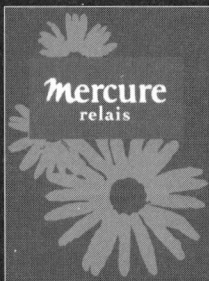

Set up in 1974, the Pilat Regional Natural Park covers 47 communes in 2 departments, the Loire and the Rhône. Its purpose is to promote and protect natural wealth in the region.

The Pilat offers the visitor a multitude of different activities : strolling through the narrow streets of typical villages, like Sainte-Croix-en-Jarez or Malleval ; discovering local heritage and knowledge at the *Maison de la Béate* in Marlhes, the *Maison de la Passementerie* in Jonzieux or the *Maison des Tresses et Lacets* in Terrasse-sur-Dorlay ; excursions (on foot, horseback or mountain-bike) or cross-country skiing along the clearly-signposted country paths and tracks which wind through the region ; local wine- and food tasting... Each visitor will prepare his itinerary according to his tastes, but any visit should include an outing to the top of the mountains – for example, to the *Crêt de la Perdrix*, the region's highest summit at an altitude of 1 432 metres above sea level, or to the *Crêt de l'Œillon*, at 1 370 m, from both of which you have a splendid view over the entire south-east of France.

THE RIGHT BANK OF FOREZ, THE *PAYS DE COISE ET LYONNAIS*

Running along the banks of the Loire at the extreme eastern point of the department, this area includes picturesque sites and a rich historical heritage : the *Château de Montrond*, old Saint-Galmier, the Hat Museum in Chazelles-sur-Lyon, the Assier Museum in Feurs, etc. It's also a region for relaxation and leisure activities : the thermal resort at Montrond-les-Bains, the racecourse in Saint-Galmier, the casinos in Montrond and Saint-Galmier and, of course for gastronomy – at Montrond, you'll find the famous restaurant, *La Poularde*.

CHAZELLES-SUR-LYON

The little town of Chazelles-sur-Lyon owes its fame to the felt hat industry. If, in the old days, there were as many as 30 hat-making factories, today, only one is still in existence.

THE HAT MUSEUM > 16, route de Saint-Galmier ✆ **04 77 94 23 29.** *Open everyday except on Tuesdays from 14.00 to 18.00 (everyday in July and August). Demonstrations on the 1st, 2nd and 3rd Sundays of each month, everyday during the week. Boutique. Entrance fee 26 F.* Built into an old factory, the museum traces nearly four centuries of hatmaking tradition. During the guided visit, you'll learn (by admiring reconstructed workshops and operational machines) about the history of rabbit hair turned into hats. There are also reconstructions of fashion, blocker- and straw hat-making workshops. In a fashion gallery, you'll see 300 hats from the end of the 18th century to the present day, as well as hairstyles worn by famous men and women.

SAINT-GALMIER

TOURIST OFFICE > Boulevard du Sud ✆ **04 77 54 06 08.** At an altitude of 400 m above sea level, and situated on a promontory, the town of Saint-Galmier domintaes the Forez Plain. It's listed as a climatic and hydro-mineral resort, a 'green' holiday resort and a 'flower town'. Whatever your age, you can practise a host of sports, including the craziest, like parachuting, for example. The less daring will also find activities to their taste. There's a pretty, municipal park, a swimming pool, a *'boulodrome'*, a racetrack, a casino…

Throughout the year, there are a lot of different events in Saint-Galmier : on the first Sunday in July, there's the Painters' Festival ; the "Cinema under the Stars" Festival is held at the beginning of July ; on the last weekend in August, there's the Antiques Fair, whilst, on 25th November, there's the Saint Catherine's Fair… etc.

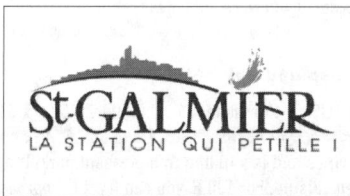

St-GALMIER
LA STATION QUI PÉTILLE !

OFFICE DU TOURISME
42330 St GALMIER
Tel. 04 77 54 06 08 - Fax 04 77 54 06 07
www.ot-stgalmier.fr

Loire *The Right Bank of Forez*

Old Saint-Galmier

Saint-Galmier owes its name to one of its children - Baldomérus. This is why its inhabitants are known as Baldomerians. An ancient Gallo-Roman town, at the top of the village you'll find the 15th century Gothic church, which was built on the site of the ancient château. From the keep to the top of the bell-tower, 146 steps lead you to a superb viewpoint over the Forez Plain and the *Monts du Lyonnais*. As you stroll through the streets, you'll discover the *Porte de la Devise*, the *Maison Renaissance*, the *Chapelle Notre-Dame* and the *Cloître de l'Hôpital.* Guided visits are organized on Sundays from May to September. Enquiries to the Tourist Office.

Other visits

LA MAISON MAGIQUE 📞 **04 77 54 12 96.** At the heart of the old town, and assisted by an invisible genie, the magician, POL, leads you through six tableaux, which are historically and voluntarily crazy.

L'ATELIER DU SOUFFLEUR DE VERRE **(THE GLASSBLOWING WORKSHOP)** 📞 **04 77 52 50 36.** Under the vaults of a red brick ceiling, Pierre Marion will present glasswork to you. The glass is brought to a temperature of 1 200° C in an oven which is never extinguished. Shaped, coloured, gilded in silver and gold, these crystal objects are blown in front of you and are turned into unique items.

THE *BADOIT* SPRING, PRIDE OF SAINT-GALMIER

Who's never heard of "light and sparkling" *Badoit*, the water which helps you to digest easily ?

Badoit is France's most-sold sparkling water, with a market share of 30%. Almost a million bottles are produced everyday, 340 million a year.

The *Badoit* Spring was known as far back as the 16th century, when it bubbled up at the foot of Saint-Galmier Hill, having filtered upwards from a depth of roughly 300 metres, deep in the sedimentary rock below the Forez Plain.

With an average mineral content (180 mg of sodium per litre), *Badoit* water has a number of properties. Its bicarbonates (1700 mg per litre) help the digestive function ; the fluoride (1.4 mg per litre) helps take care of the teeth, and the magnesium (102 mg per litre) helps ward off fatigue. At the same time, the joint action of its calcium (272 mg per litre) and fluoride assists childgrowth.

Free, guided visits to the bottling plant are possible. Enquiries to the Tourist Office.

It's also worth knowing that, at the kiosk (as you come from Saint-Etienne and enter Saint-Galmier, turn left before the bridge) you can get two, free 1.5 litre bottles of Badoit. However, don't think that you can fill up a jerrycan or two – the kiosk's watched over by a security guard (a very pleasant man, in fact !)

Where to sleep and eat

LE BOUGAINVILLIER > Pré Château 📞 **04 77 54 03 31.** *Closed on Sunday evenings and on Mondays. Menus at 130 F, 185 F, 225 F and 305 F. A la carte : 255 F.* This beautiful house is covered with vines and is situated in a pleasant park. It has two dining rooms, where you can enjoy a refined cuisine. For 130 F, you can try the *'Approach' Menu* consisting of a *feuillantine de poissons aux herbes fraîches* (fish and fresh herbs in puff pastry), a *lieu jaune cuit à la vapeur de citron* (pollack cooked in lemon steam) or a *coquelet confit dans un jus de tomate au vinaigre de cidre* (preserved cockerel in a juice made with tomatoes in cider vinegar). The chef also prepares (amongst other mouth-watering dishes) a ***jarret de veau farci aux pistaches avec crème de cèpes*** (knuckle of veal stuffed with pistachio nuts and served with a cep cream), a *poêlée d'escargots sous un sablé au lard fumé et au thym* (pan-fried snails under a sablé of smoked bacon and thyme) or a *rouelle de cuisse de canard fondue de choux et manchons confits* (round slice of leg of duck with melted cabbage). Interestingly, the wine list contains a selection of bottles at low prices. Also to note : the restaurant prepares take away dishes.

LE FOREZ > 6, rue Didier Guetton ℭ **04 77 54 00 23.** *Menu at 98 F. A la carte : 165 F.* Adjoining the hotel of the same name, the retaurant has a terrace in an interior courtyard which is very pleasant in summer. Alain Renaudier, who used to be a rally car driver, has decorated the bar room with rally car number plates and cups he has won. The cuisine here is prepared with market produce, and the menus vary with the seasons. To give you an idea of the dishes, the day we dropped by there was *tartare de saumon et blé tendre aux poivrons de Provence* (tartare of salmon with tender wheat and Provençal sweet red peppers) and baked tuna or beef with garlic in its skin. The beautiful vaulted rooms in the basement have been done up, and, very shortly, a restaurant room will be opened here with room for 50 to 120 people. This will allow Theme Evenings and banquets to be organized. There's also a tasting cellar and a boutique selling regional wines and produce.

Shopping

DELICES FOREZIENS > Les Sermages - SAINT-CYR-LES-VIGNES ℭ **04 77 94 62 04.** But, what are these Forezian delicacies ? Well, they're ice-creams and sorbets – 30 different flavours of them. Since 1991, this shop has been buying its fruit from regional producers and now delivers 15 000 litres of ice-cream, sorbets, baked Alaskas etc. every year. These are sent to restaurateurs throughout the Loire and in neighbouring departments. *Les Délices Foréziens* exhibit their products at a number of fairs to promote regional produce, but you can also taste the products at the shop. You're given very good advice.

Going out

CASINO LE LION BLANC > Boulevard du Docteur Cousin ℭ **04 77 54 01 99.** *Open 7/7 days, from 10.00 to 04.00.* Jackpot ! I've won the Jackpot ! The three crowns are in line ! Whether you're an occasional or an inveterate gambler, you'll find all sorts here. In a delightful setting, the *Casino Le Lion Blanc* in Saint-Galmier has just offered itself a face-lift. In fact, they've even pushed the walls a bit, and the casino now has an extra 1 200 m2 to play with. Hence, the Georgia Salon, in addition to having two Roulette and one Blackjack tables, also houses a charming and intimate food area, called the *Scarlett Room*. *Le Tara* is now the salon-restaurant. It's set out in a semi-circle, with large bay windows and a superb, monumental chandelier, and has room for 500 diners, so that shows can now be organized. It's also the ideal place for wedding receptions, and cocktail parties can be thrown beside the swimming pool. There's also a little restaurant, called *La Paillote*, which is right next to the garden, beside the swimming pool, and very popular.

HIPPODROME > The Cuzieu Road ℭ **04 77 54 04 68.** You left the casino with a bit of money in your pocket ? Then, all you have to do is come to the race course. It offers a show which you can enjoy even at night. Indeed, the Saint-Galmier hippodrome is the only one in the Rhône-Alpes region to have night races on Fridays and Saturdays. In addition to having a 1 225-metre pozzolana and a 1 325-metre grass track, the hippodrome also has a number of polyvalent rooms and a restaurant. A new building's currently under construction. The racing calendar can be obtained at the Tourist Office.

MONTROND-LES-BAINS

TOURIST INFORMATION ℭ **04 77 94 64 74.** A 'treatment' town, a gambling town, an historic town, a gastronomical town, Montrond, on the banks of the Loire, offers a variety of things to visitors.

THE CHATEAU > Built in the 11th century by the Counts of Forez to protect and defend the ford on the Loire between Lyon and Montbrison, the *Château de Montrond* owes its name to the volcanic hill it's built on, called the *Mont Rond.* During the Renaissance, this fortress, which had played a military rôle in the Middle Ages, became a rich, private residence. Pillaged at the end of the 16th century, the château was set alight in 1793 by Revolutionary hordes, under the command of the Sieur Javogues. It remained abandoned for many years. In 1969, the Friends of the Château Association succeeded in partially restoring it. Since 1984, when it was bought by the municipality, the château can be visited in summer and holds various exhibitions, concerts and other festivities. **211**

Loire *The Right Bank of Forez*

Where to sleep and eat

HOSTELLERIE LA POULARDE ℘ **04 77 54 40 06.** *3 stars. Relais & Châteaux. Swimming pool. Salons for seminars. Access for the disabled. Air-conditioning. 13 rooms from 340 to 580 F for a double.*

Thermalism

ETABLISSEMENT THERMAL ℘ **04 77 94 67 61.** The thermal water in the Geyser IV and Geyser Detente resorts is drilled from a depth of 500 metres, and is typical of warm (37°), carbon- and sodium-rich water. It's used for the treatment of digestive ailments (stomach, liver, intestines) and nutrition-related illnesses (obesity, type II sugar diabetese). Treatment is given here by means of drink cures, water treatment (immersion, jet showers, baths, swimming pool, underwater massage, etc.) and nutritional cures. Several services/formulae are on offer: an 18 day cure paid for by the National Health or similar organization, the *Détente* (Relaxation) Card with 10 treatments of your choice, different fitness courses, and anti-cellulite treatment, aqua-gym, gym… The establishment also has a beauty section, which carries out body re-modelling, facial care, pedicures, manicures, hair removal and make-up.

Going out

LAS VEGAS LES BAINS ℘ **04 77 54 41 13.** The Casino is particularly well-equipped in machines of all sorts. It's kept clean by an army of carefully-chosen staff and, curiously enough, there have never been any problems with… money. You start by looking around. Are you going to go for a one-armed bandit?... *"Faites vos jeux, rien ne va plus"*. A final little tour before selecting that machine, there (the one that's free, because it's always crowded on Saturdays). Throughout the year there are different events, shows and tombolas either in front of the casino or in the discothèque, Le Saxo. And don't forget the restaurant, Le Dauphin, to spend your well-deserved winnings or to drown your sorrows enjoyably.

THE LEFT BANK OF THE FOREZ REGION, THE MOUNTAINS

The Forez region offers two types of countryside : the plain and its *étangs* (pans/basins) where the Loire flows, and the mountainous highlands. Between the *Puy-de-Dôme* and the Loire, the *Monts du Forez* form a natural barrier. At Pierre-sur-Haute, they culminate at an altitude of 1 640 metres above sea level.

The *Route des Balcons* (Balcony Road) invites you to discover the wild and secret beauty of the Forez *Massif*, its heather-covered plateaus, its meadows, its high summits with beech and pine forests, its streams and its torrents.

Marked out by volcanic hills, remnants of the tertiary era, the *Route Basalte* winds through the Forez Plain, which is dotted with *étangs* in a mosaic of colours which change with the seasons : sunflowers, colza, maize, corn, grazing land, conifers and, on the hill slopes, the vines of the *Côtes du Forez* vineyards.

As for Montbrison, the ancient capital of the County of Forez, it has kept much of its old charm, with narrow streets and canals lined with curious, overhanging houses.

Useful address

SOUTH FOREZ TOURIST OFFICE > 7, place de la Paix - SAINT-JUST-SAINT-RAMBERT ℘ **04 77 52 05 14.** *Open on Mondays from 14.30 to 17.30, from Tuesday to Friday from 09.00 to 12.00 and from 14.30 to 18.15, on Saturdays from 09.00 to 12.00 and from 14.30 to 17.30.* The South Forez Tourist office will provide you with all practical and tourist information about the communes in South Forez (lodging, restaurants, sites, museums, festivals, leisure activities, etc.). It also organizes guided visits for groups to Herirage Sites.

FIND US ON THE NET
www.petitfute.com

USSON-EN-FOREZ

TOURIST INFORMATION ℂ **04 77 50 66 15.** Having crossed the wild plateaux and valleys, along a road which winds between forests and meadows and which, here and there, goes over rivers and streams, you'll come to Usson. Its water-basin offers a multitude of possibilities for relaxation : walks, picnics, fishing…

The *Monts du Forez* **Ecomuseum**, a rural museum, gives you a picture of everyday life at the beginning of the century in the Haut-Forez : the production of harvesting baskets, the work of the blacksmith and the cartwright, long-forgotten agricultural activities and professions, the oral heritage, etc. (Enquiries on : 04 77 50 67 97).

SAINT-BONNET-LE-CHATEAU

Sometimes called "the Forez Pearl", Saint-Bonnet-le-Château is built on a promontory. For centuries, the town was an important craftwork and judicial centre. Its Mediaeval Quarter is remarkable. As you climb up the narrow streets, you'll see numerous Renaissance houses, including the *Maison de la Châtelaine* and the *Maison de Mandrin* (the famous brigand who honoured the town by ransomming its leading citizens in 1754).

THE COLLEGIATE CHURCH > Its birth certificate is carved into the crypt : 8th May 1400. In this Gothic church's sacristy, you'll find find religious ornaments and some early printed books. It's surrounded by eight chapels.

LE CAVEAU DES MOMIES > A burial place for priests and local dignities, this church has some 20 vaults. One of them was the site of a sinister discovery, made when works were carried out on the church in 1837 – 40 perfectly conserved bodifies, which had mummified naturally in the positions they had died in. The muffication process was due to alum and arsenic deposits in the soil. The massacre which took place here is said to have been carried out by the Baron of Les Adrets who kidnapped some of the Montbrison family in 1562, using the Wars of Religion as a pretext.

MUSEE INTERNATIONAL DE LA PETANQUE ET DES BOULES > **Esplanade de la Boule** ℂ **04 77 50 15 33.** At the instigation of its Managing Director, the Obut company created a 'Temple of Marbles and *Boules*' in Saint-Bonnet-le-Château, which was already the capital of *pétanque*. You can see a collection of studded *boules* from the second half of the 19th and the beginning of 20th centuries.

LE PLAN D'EAU (THE WATER BASIN) > Near the camping site, there's a large beach, surrounded by trees and a number of paths winding through greenery. Perfect for relaxation and fishing.
Montbrison

Loire *The Left Bank of the Forez region*

TOURIST OFFICE > Cloître des Cordeliers - Hôtel de Ville ℂ **04 77 96 08 69.** A town rich in history and with monuments which testify to its prestigious past, Montbrison was for several centuries the capital of the Counts of Forez, before becoming, in the 19th century, the department of the Loire's prefecture. At the heart of the Forez region, Montbrison's now the sub-prefecture, and is a charming town to visit. Here and there, the River Vizézy crosses ancient little streets, lined with houses with fine architecture. From the Calvaire Ramparts, you have an exceptional view over the town. Old, 17th and 18th century town houses and a few Renaissance homes dot the town, which is bounded by large boulevards on the site of the ancient town moats. On Saturday mornings, you'll find a market which brings together a large number of regional producers.

THE NOTRE-DAME-D'ESPÉRANCE COLLEGIATE CHURCH > The architecture and cathedral-like size of this Gothic church, which dates from the 11th and 13th centuries, make it one of the most beautiful in the region. Its 42-metre high bell-tower offers a fine view over Old Montbrison.

La Diana, the meeting room of the 13th century Estates of Forez, has a fine, vaulted wooden ceiling, decorated with coats of arms. It's one of Montbrison's most famous monuments, which isn't surprising, bearing in mind that, for a room of this type, it's unique in France. Its archeological museum contains remnants from the principal archeological sites in Forez, as well as a library containing more than 20 000 works. (Enquiries to 04 77 96 01 10)

***LE MUSEE D'ALLARD* > 13, boulevard de la Préfecture** ℂ **04 77 58 33 07.** *Open everyday except on Tuesdays from 14.30 to 18.00. Admission fee 16 F.* Originally, in the 19th century, this was quite simply the private Natural History library belonging to Jean-Baptiste d'Allard. Now, however, it's a museum with a collection of 500 minerals, and houses the Henri Chaperon Collection of more than 400 bedside stoups, an aviary with birds from all over the world, and an exhibition of 200 toy trains from 1900 to the present day.

THE DOLL MUESEUM > On the first floor of the Allard Museum, 600 exhibits recount the history of the doll. The dolls are in wax or porcelain, and they're exotic, folkloric, or 'industrial' (like the GéGé dolls made in Montbrison until 1980). This universal toy will bring back childhood memories.

VERRIERES-EN-FOREZ

AUBERGE DE CONOL > Conol ℂ **04 77 76 23 08.** *Open 7/7 days. Menus at 58 F and 75 F.* As soon as you approach the inn, its facade tempts you to come in, and if you do, you won't regret it. This hotel-restaurant also has guest rooms, a camping site, and rooms for wedding receptions, banquets and seminars. In the large dining room, you'll find excellent country specialities : *charcuterie*, roast meat and coq au vin. At the weekend, when it's strongly advised to reserve, the menus are more elaborate. In season, you can eat game. If a walk should take you by Conol, don't hesitate to stop at the inn for a snack.

Index *of Lyon*

Index of Lyon